Read, **Reason**, Write

AN ARGUMENT TEXT AND READER

ELEVENTH EDITION

Dorothy U. Seyler

ENG 102: Read, Reason, Write
UNIVERSITY OF NEVADA LAS VEGAS

Mc
Graw
Hill
Education

3 4 5 6 7 8 9 0 CCI CCI 17 16 15

ISBN-13: 978-1-259-33203-6
ISBN-10: 1-259-33203-9

Learning Solutions Consultant: Adam Poston
Project Manager: Vanessa Arnold
Cover Photo Credits: Jupiterimages, Jupiterimages Corporation, Fancy Photography/Veer, BananaStock/Jupiterimages

Brief Contents

Contents

New to the Eleventh Edition

This new edition continues the key features of previous editions while adding new material that will make it even more helpful to both students and instructors. Significant changes include the following.

- **New essays.** Both the student essay in MLA style and the student essay in APA are new. The first is longer and focuses on the interesting topic of genetically modified foods; the second, written for a sociology course, is presented in full.
- **New coverage.** There is **new material on paraphrasing** in Chapter 1 and **new material on preparing an annotated bibliography** in Chapter 12.
- **More visuals.** There are more visuals throughout the text, consistent with the increased use of visuals in all our media today.
- **Streamlined content.** The new edition is more streamlined, without any loss of significant coverage or readings.
- **New readings.** With thirty readings in the instructional chapters and forty-six readings in the anthology chapters, this edition has a total of seventy-six readings. In addition there are now nine student essays and the literature in the Appendix. Fifty-one of the readings are new, and some readings from the tenth edition are in new places, paired with new readings, providing a fresh perspective.
- **Enhanced coverage of documentation**. Two of the new readings are rather lengthy studies, complete with documentation, offering students further examples of documentation, supporting the four student essays that contain documentation.
- **Focus on current issues that are relevant to students**. Of the eight chapters in the anthology section, all have new readings, and most have a new focus. For example, the chapter on education in this edition concentrates entirely on issues relating to colleges, issues of cost and value to students as well as the purpose of higher education. The sports chapter examines the Penn State scandal and doping in sports, especially in cycling. The final chapter is still about America, this time looking to the future through the prism of past and present problems and successes.

Features of Read, Reason, Write

These are among the features that have made *Read, Reason, Write* a best-selling text for so many editions.

- An emphasis on good reading skills for effective arguing and writing.
- Instruction, models, and practice in understanding reading context and analyzing elements of style.
- Instruction, models, and practice in writing clear, accurate summaries.
- Focus on argument as contextual: written (or spoken) to a specific audience with the expectation of counterarguments.
- Explanations and models of various types of arguments that bridge the gap between an understanding of logical structures and the ways we actually write arguments.
- Presentation of Aristotelian, Toulmin, and Rogerian models of argument as useful guides to analyzing the arguments of others and organizing one's own arguments.
- In-depth coverage of induction, deduction, analogy, and logical fallacies.
- Guidelines and revision boxes throughout the text that provide an easy reference for students.
- Instruction, models, and practice in finding and evaluating sources and in composing and documenting researched papers.
- A rich collection of readings, both timely and classic, that provides examples of the varied uses of language and strategies for argument.
- A brief but comprehensive introduction to reading and analyzing literature, found in the Appendix.

Let Connect Composition Help Your Students Achieve Their Goals

McGraw-Hill's solutions are proven to improve student performance. Powered by a four-year student subscription to Connect Composition Plus Essentials 3.0, *Read, Reason, Write* offers **LearnSmart Achieve**, a groundbreaking adaptive learning resource that individualizes writing instruction and helps improve student writing.

LearnSmart Achieve combines a continuously adaptive learning plan with learning resources that focus students on building proficiency in the language and critical processes of composition. Learning resources include contextualized grammar and writing lessons, videos, animations, and interactive exercises. Students are also provided with immediate feedback on their work and progress. A built-in time-management tool keeps students on track to ensure they achieve their course goals.

LearnSmart Achieve represents the goals of individual instructors and writing programs and provides valuable reports related to progress, achievement, and students who may be at risk. With LearnSmart Achieve, instructors can have the confidence of knowing—and the data that demonstrates—that their students, however diverse, are moving toward their highest course expectations: better prepared, confident thinkers and writers with transferable skills. See the next page for more details on what you will find in LearnSmart Achieve.

McGraw-Hill's **Digital Success Academy** offers a wealth of online training resources and course creation tips to help get you started. Go to connectsuccessacademy.com.

LearnSmart Achieve provides instruction and practice for your students in the following areas.

UNIT	TOPIC	
THE WRITING PROCESS	The Writing Process Generating Ideas Planning and Organizing	Writing a Rough Draft Revising Proofreading, Formatting, and Producing Texts
CRITICAL READING	Reading to Understand Literal Meaning Evaluating Truth and Accuracy in a Text	Evaluating the Effectiveness and Appropriateness of a Text

THE RESEARCH PROCESS	Developing and Implementing a
	    Research Plan
	Evaluating Information and Sources
		Integrating Source Material into
		    a Text
		Using Information Ethically
		    and Legally

REASONING AND ARGUMENT	Developing an Effective Thesis or Claim
	Using Evidence and Reasoning to
	    Support a Thesis or Claim
		Using Ethos (Ethics) to Persuade
		    Readers
		Using Pathos (Emotion) to Persuade
		    Readers
		Using Logos (Logic) to Persuade
		    Readers

MULTILINGUAL WRITERS	Helping Verbs, Gerunds and Infinitives, and Phrasal Verbs Nouns, Verbs, and Objects Articles	Count and Noncount Nouns Sentence Structure and Word Order Subject-Verb Agreement Participles and Adverb Placement
GRAMMAR AND COMMON SENTENCE PROBLEMS	Parts of Speech Phrases and Clauses Sentence Types Fused (Run-on) Sentences Comma Splices Sentence Fragments Pronouns	Pronoun-Antecedent Agreement Pronoun Reference Subject-Verb Agreement Verbs and Verbals Adjectives and Adverbs Dangling and Misplaced Modifiers Mixed Constructions Verb Tense and Voice Shifts
PUNCTUATION AND MECHANICS	Commas Semicolons Colons End Punctuation Apostrophes Quotation Marks Dashes	Parentheses Hyphens Abbreviations Capitalization Italics Numbers Spelling
STYLE AND WORD CHOICE	Wordiness Eliminating Redundancies Sentence Variety Coordination and Subordination	Faulty Comparisons Word Choice Clichés, Slang, and Jargon Parallelism

LearnSmart Achieve can be assigned by units and/or topics.

Let the Customizable Resources of Create Help You to Achieve Your Course's Goals

Your courses evolve over time—shouldn't your course material evolve as well? With McGraw-Hill CREATE, you can easily arrange and customize material from a variety of sources, including your own. You can choose your format (print or electronic) and what you want from:

- Chapters of *Read, Reason, Write*—choose only those chapters that you cover.
- A range of additional selections from other McGraw-Hill collections such as *The Ideal Reader* (800 readings by author, genre, mode, theme, and discipline) and many more.
- Your own resources, such as syllabi, institutional information, study guides, assignments, diagrams, artwork, student writing, art, photos, and more.

Go to www.mcgrawhillcreate.com and register today.

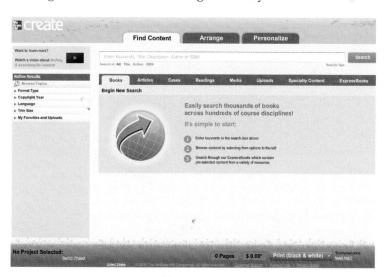

From the Author

I have written in previous prefaces to *Read, Reason, Write* that being asked to prepare a new edition is much like being asked back to a friend's home. Although you count on it, you are still delighted when the invitation comes. I am happy that the tenth edition kept old friends and made new ones as well and that once again I am writing a preface, this time to the eleventh edition. *Read, Reason, Write* is now almost 30 years old! Over all of these years, the text has grown in size—most books have—but also in stature within the teaching community and in its value to students. Of course, even though I have retired from full-time teaching, like fine wine neither this text nor I am getting older—only better.

Although some important new material strengthens the eleventh edition, the essential character of *Read, Reason, Write* remains the same. This text still unites instruction in critical reading and analysis, argument, and research strategies with a rich collection of readings that provide both practice for these skills and new ideas and insights for readers. A key purpose of *Read, Reason, Write* remains the same: to help students develop into better writers of the kinds of papers they are most often required to write, both in college and in the workplace, that is, summaries, analyses, reports, arguments, and documented essays. To fulfill this key purpose, the text must do more than offer instruction and opportunities for practice; it must also show students how these skills connect in important ways. Through all of its years, this text has been committed to showing students how reading, analytic, argumentative, and research skills are interrelated and how these skills combine to develop each student's critical thinking ability.

About the Author

Dorothy Seyler is Professor Emerita of English at Northern Virginia Community College. A Phi Beta Kappa graduate of the College of William and Mary, Dr. Seyler holds advanced degrees from Columbia University and the State University of New York at Albany. She taught at Ohio State University, the University of Kentucky, and Nassau Community College before moving with her family to Northern Virginia.

She is the author of *Introduction to Literature* (second edition), *Doing Research* (second edition), *The Reading Context* and *Steps to College Reading* (both in their third editions), and *Patterns of Reflection* (seventh edition). In 2007 Dr. Seyler was elected to membership in the Cosmos Club in Washington, DC for "excellence in education."

Professor Seyler has published articles in professional journals and popular magazines. She is currently working on a narrative nonfiction book about early-nineteenth-century explorer William John Bankes. She enjoys tennis and golf, traveling, and writing about both sports and travel.

Acknowledgments

No book of value is written alone. I am pleased to acknowledge the contributions of others in shaping this text. My thanks are due—as always—to the library staff at the Annandale Campus of Northern Virginia Community College who over the years helped me find needed information. I would also like to thank all of the students whose essays grace this text. They should be proud of the skill and effort they put into their writing. And I am indebted to Erik Neilson of the University of Richmond and Michael Hughes of Virginia Tech University for providing me with the student essays from their colleges, giving me a nice "stack" from which to choose the new essays for this edition. I appreciate the input of many reviewers over the years.

My former editor Steve Pensinger needs to be remembered for steering me through four editions. I am also grateful to Tim Julet and Alexis Walker for guidance through the fifth edition and to Chris Narozny, developmental editor of the sixth edition. My hat's off to Lisa Moore, executive editor for the sixth and seventh editions; to Christopher Bennem, sponsoring editor for the eighth, ninth, and tenth editions. Last, but not least, my thanks go to past developmental editors Joshua Feldman, Phil Butcher, Janice Wiggins-Clarke, and to my current developmental editor Susan Messer. I have been blessed with a chorus of voices enriching this text through my wonderful journey with this book: May you all live long and prosper!

I'll close by once again dedicating *Read, Reason, Write* to my daughter Ruth who, in spite of her own career and interests, continues to give generously of her time, reading possible essays for each new edition and listening patiently to my endless debates about changes. And for all students who use my text: May you understand that it is the liberal education that makes continued growth of the human spirit both possible and pleasurable.

Dorothy U. Seyler

Professor Emerita

Northern Virginia Community College

Critical Reading and Analysis

Writers and Their Sources

READ: What is the situation in the photo? Who are the two figures, where are they, and how do they differ?

REASON: What ideas are suggested by the photo?

REFLECT/WRITE: Why might this visual have been chosen for Chapter 1?

"Are you happy with your new car?" Oscar asks.

"Oh, yes, I love my new car," Rachel responds.

"Why?" queries Oscar.

"Oh, it's just great—and dad paid for most of it," Rachel exclaims.

"So you like it because it was cheap," Oscar says. "But, wasn't your father going to pay for whatever car you chose?"

"Well, yes—within reason."

"Then why did you choose the Corolla? Why is it so great?"

Rachel ponders a moment and then replies: "It's small enough for me to feel comfortable driving it, but not so small that I would be frightened by trucks. It gets good mileage, and Toyota cars have a good reputation."

"Hmm. Maybe I should think about a Corolla. Then again, I wouldn't part with my Miata!" Oscar proclaims.

A simple conversation, right? In fact, this dialogue represents an **argument**. You may not recognize it as a "typical" argument. After all, there is no real dispute between Oscar and Rachel—no yelling, no hurt feelings. But in its most basic form, an argument is a *claim* (Rachel's car is great) supported by *reasons* (the car's size, mileage, and brand). Similar arguments could be made in favor of this car in other contexts. For instance, Rachel might have seen (and been persuaded by) a television or online Toyota advertisement, or she might have read an article making similar claims in a magazine such as *Consumer Reports*. In turn, she might decide to develop her argument into an essay or speech for one of her courses.

READING, WRITING, AND THE CONTEXTS OF ARGUMENT

Arguments, it seems, are everywhere. Well, what about this textbook, you counter. Its purpose is to inform, not to present an argument. True—to a degree. But textbook authors also make choices about what is important to include and how students should learn the material. Even writing primarily designed to inform says to readers: Do it my way! Well, what about novels, you "argue." Surely they are not arguments. A good point—to a degree. The ideas about human life and experience we find in novels are more subtle, more indirect, than the points we meet head-on in many arguments. Still, expressive writing presents ideas, ways of seeing the world. It seems that arguments can be simple or profound, clearly stated or implied. And we can find them in much—if not most—of our uses of language.

You can accept this larger scope of argument and still expect that in your course on argument and critical thinking you probably will not be asked to write a textbook or a novel. You might, though, be asked to write a summary or a style analysis, so you should think about how those tasks might connect to the world of argument. Count on this: You will be asked to write! Why work on your writing skills? Here are good answers to this question:

- Communication skills are the single most important skill sought by employers.
- The better writer you become, the better reader you will be.

- The more confident a writer you become, the more efficiently you will handle written assignments in all your courses.
- The more you write, the more you learn about who you are and what really matters to you.

You are about to face a variety of writing assignments. Always think about what role each assignment asks of you. Are you a student demonstrating knowledge? A citizen arguing for tougher drunk-driving laws? A scholar presenting the results of research? A friend having a conversation about a new car? Any writer—including you—will take on different roles, writing for different audiences, using different strategies to reach each audience. There are many kinds of argument and many ways to be successful—or unsuccessful—in preparing them. Your argument course will be challenging. This text will help you meet that challenge.

RESPONDING TO SOURCES

If this is a text about *writing* arguments, why does it contain so many readings? (You noticed!) There are good reasons for the readings you find here:

- College and the workplace demand that you learn complex information through reading. This text will give you lots of practice.
- You need to read to develop your critical thinking skills.
- Your reading will often serve as a basis for writing. In a course on argument, the focus of attention shifts from you to your subject, a subject others have debated before you. You will need to understand the issue, think carefully about the views of others, and only then join in the conversation.

To understand how critical thinkers may respond to sources, let's examine "The Gettysburg Address," Abraham Lincoln's famous speech dedicating the Gettysburg Civil War battlefield. We can use this document to see the various ways writers respond—in writing—to the writing of others.

THE GETTYSBURG ADDRESS | ABRAHAM LINCOLN

Fourscore and seven years ago our fathers brought forth on this continent a new nation, conceived in liberty and dedicated to the proposition that all men are created equal. Now we are engaged in a great civil war, testing whether that nation, or any nation so conceived and so dedicated, can long endure. We are met on a great battlefield of that war. We have come to dedicate a portion of that field as a final resting place for those who here gave their lives that that nation might live. It is altogether fitting and proper that we should do this. But, in a larger sense, we cannot dedicate—we cannot consecrate—we cannot hallow—this ground. The brave men, living and dead, who struggled here have consecrated it far above our poor power to add or to detract.

The world will little note nor long remember what we say here, but it can never forget what they did here. It is for us, the living, rather to be dedicated here to the unfinished work which they who fought here have thus far so nobly advanced. It is rather for us to be here dedicated to the great task remaining before us—that from these honored dead we take increased devotion to that cause for which they gave the last full measure of devotion; that we here highly resolve that these dead shall not have died in vain; that this nation, under God, shall have a new birth of freedom; and that government of the people, by the people, for the people shall not perish from the earth.

What Does It Say?   THE RESPONSE TO CONTENT

Instructors often ask students to *summarize* their reading of a complex chapter, a supplementary text, or a series of journal articles on library reserve. Frequently, book report assignments specify that summary and evaluation be combined. Your purpose in writing a summary is to show your understanding of the work's main ideas and of the relationships among those ideas. If you can put what you have read into your own words and focus on the text's chief points, then you have command of that material. Here is a sample restatement of Lincoln's "Address":

> Our nation was initially built on a belief in liberty and equality, but its future is now being tested by civil war. It is appropriate for us to dedicate this battlefield, but those who fought here have dedicated it better than we. We should dedicate ourselves to continue the fight to maintain this nation and its principles of government.

Sometimes it is easier to recite or quote famous or difficult works than to state, more simply and in your own words, what has been written. The ability to summarize reflects strong writing skills. For more coverage of writing summaries, see pages 10–13. (For coverage of paraphrasing, a task similar to summary, see pp. 18–20.)

How Is It Written?
How Does It Compare
with Another Work?   THE ANALYTIC RESPONSE

Summary requirements are often combined with analysis or evaluation, as in a book report. Most of the time you will be expected to *do something* with what you have read, and to summarize will be insufficient. Frequently you will be asked to analyze a work—that is, to explain the writer's choice of style (or the work's larger rhetorical context). This means examining sentence patterns, organization, metaphors, and other techniques selected by the writer to convey attitude and give force to ideas. Developing your skills in analysis will make you both a better reader and a better writer.

Many writers have examined Lincoln's word choice, sentence structure, and choice of metaphors to make clear the sources of power in this speech.* Analyzing Lincoln's style, you might examine, among other elements, his effective use of *tricolon:* the threefold repetition of a grammatical structure, with the three points placed in ascending order of significance.

> Lincoln uses two effective tricolons in his brief address. The first focuses on the occasion for his speech, the dedication of the battlefield: "we cannot dedicate—we cannot consecrate—we cannot hallow. . . ." The best that the living can do is formally dedicate; only those who died there for the principle of liberty are capable of making the battlefield "hallow." The second tricolon presents Lincoln's concept of democratic government, a government "of the people, by the people, for the people." The purpose of government—"for the people"—resides in the position of greatest significance.

A second type of analysis, a comparison of styles of two writers, is a frequent variation of the analytic assignment. By focusing on similarities and differences in writing styles, you can see more clearly the role of choice in writing and may also examine the issue of the degree to which differences in purpose affect style. One student, for example, produced a thoughtful and interesting study of Lincoln's style in contrast to that of Martin Luther King Jr.:

> Although Lincoln's sentence structure is tighter than King's and King likes the rhythms created by repetition, both men reflect their familiarity with the King James Bible in their use of its cadences and expressions. Instead of saying eighty-seven years ago, Lincoln, seeking solemnity, selects the biblical expression "Fourscore and seven years ago." Similarly, King borrows from the Bible and echoes Lincoln when he writes "Five score years ago."

Is It Logical?
Is It Adequately Developed?
Does It Achieve Its Purpose?   THE EVALUATION RESPONSE

Even when the stated purpose of an essay is "pure" analysis, the analysis implies a judgment. We analyze Lincoln's style because we recognize that "The Gettysburg Address" is a great piece of writing and we want to see how it achieves its power. On other occasions, evaluation is the stated purpose for close reading and analysis. The columnist who challenges a previously published editorial has analyzed the editorial and found it flawed. The columnist may fault the editor's logic or lack of adequate or relevant support for the editorial's main idea. In each case the columnist makes a negative evaluation of the editorial, but that judgment is an informed one based on the columnist's knowledge of language and the principles of good argument.

Part of the ability to judge wisely lies in recognizing each writer's (or speaker's) purpose, audience, and occasion. It would be inappropriate to assert

---

* See, for example, Gilbert Highet's essay, "The Gettysburg Address," in *The Clerk of Oxenford: Essays on Literature and Life* (New York: Oxford UP, 1954), to which I am indebted in the following analysis.

that Lincoln's address is weakened by its lack of facts about the battle. The historian's purpose is to record the number killed or to analyze the generals' military tactics. Lincoln's purpose was different.

> As Lincoln reflected upon this young country's being torn apart by civil strife, he saw the dedication of the Gettysburg battlefield as an opportunity to challenge the country to fight for its survival and the principles upon which it was founded. The result was a brief but moving speech that appropriately examines the connection between the life and death of soldiers and the birth and survival of a nation.

These sentences begin an analysis of Lincoln's train of thought and use of metaphors. The writer shows an understanding of Lincoln's purpose and the context in which he spoke.

How Does It Help Me to Understand Other Works, Ideas, Events?   THE RESEARCH RESPONSE

Frequently you will read not to analyze or evaluate but rather to use the source as part of learning about a particular subject. Lincoln's address is significant for the Civil War historian both as an event of that war and as an influence on our thinking about that war. "The Gettysburg Address" is also vital to the biographer's study of Lincoln's life or to the literary critic's study either of famous speeches or of the Bible's influence on English writing styles. Thus Lincoln's brief speech is a valuable source for students in a variety of disciplines. It becomes part of their research process. Able researchers study it carefully, analyze it thoroughly, place it in its proper historical, literary, and personal contexts, and use it to develop their own arguments.

To practice reading and responding to sources, study the following article by Deborah Tannen. The exercises that follow will check your reading skills and your understanding of the various responses to reading just discussed. Use the prereading questions to become engaged with Tannen's essay.

WHO DOES THE TALKING HERE? | DEBORAH TANNEN

Professor of linguistics at Georgetown University, Deborah Tannen writes popular books on the uses of language by "ordinary" people. Among her many books are *Talking from 9 to 5* (1994) and *I Only Say This Because I Love You* (2004). Here she responds to the debate over who talks more, men or women.

PREREADING QUESTIONS What is the occasion for Tannen's article—what is she responding to? Who does most of the talking in your family—and are you okay with the answer?

It's no surprise that a one-page article published this month in the journal 1
Science inspired innumerable newspaper columns and articles. The study, by Matthias Mehl and four colleagues, claims to lay to rest, once and for all, the

stereotype that women talk more than men, by proving—scientifically—that women and men talk equally.

2   The notion that women talk more was reinforced last year when Louann Brizendine's "The Female Brain" cited the finding that women utter, on average, 20,000 words a day, men 7,000. (Brizendine later disavowed the statistic, as there was no study to back it up.) Mehl and his colleagues outfitted 396 college students with devices that recorded their speech. The female subjects spoke an average of 16,215 words a day, the men 15,669. The difference is insignificant. Case closed.

3   Or is it? Can we learn who talks more by counting words? No, according to a forthcoming article surveying 70 studies of gender differences in talkativeness. (Imagine—70 studies published in scientific journals, and we're still asking the question.) In their survey, Campbell Leaper and Melanie Ayres found that counting words yielded no consistent differences, though number of words per speaking turn did. (Men, on average, used more.)

4   This doesn't surprise me. In my own research on gender and language, I quickly surmised that to understand who talks more, you have to ask: What's the situation? What are the speakers using words for?

5   The following experience conveys the importance of situation. I was addressing a small group in a suburban Virginia living room. One man stood out because he talked a lot, while his wife, who was sitting beside him, said nothing at all. I described to the group a complaint common among women about men they live with: At the end of a day she tells him what happened, what she thought and how she felt about it. Then she asks, "How was your day?"—and is disappointed when he replies, "Fine," "Nothing much" or "Same old rat race."

6   The loquacious man spoke up. "You're right," he said. Pointing to his wife, he added, "She's the talker in our family." Everyone laughed. But he explained, "It's true. When we come home, she does all the talking. If she didn't, we'd spend the evening in silence."

7   The "how was your day?" conversation typifies the kind of talk women tend to do more

Who is the most passive figure in this group?

of: spoken to intimates and focusing on personal experience, your own or others'. I call this "rapport-talk." It contrasts with "report-talk"—giving or exchanging information about impersonal topics, which men tend to do more.

Studies that find men talking more are usually carried out in formal experi- 8 ments or public contexts such as meetings. For example, Marjorie Swacker observed an academic conference where women presented 40 percent of the papers and were 42 percent of the audience but asked only 27 percent of the questions; their questions were, on average, also shorter by half than the men's questions. And David and Myra Sadker showed that boys talk more in mixed-sex classrooms—a context common among college students, a factor skewing the results of Mehl's new study.

Many men's comfort with "public talking" explains why a man who tells his 9 wife he has nothing to report about his day might later find a funny story to tell at dinner with two other couples (leaving his wife wondering, "Why didn't he tell me first?").

In addition to situation, you have to consider what speakers are doing with 10 words. Campbell and Ayres note that many studies find women doing more "affiliative speech" such as showing support, agreeing or acknowledging others' comments. Drawing on studies of children at play as well as my own research of adults talking, I often put it this way: For women and girls, talk is the glue that holds a relationship together. Their best friend is the one they tell everything to. Spending an evening at home with a spouse is when this kind of talk comes into its own. Since this situation is uncommon among college students, it's another factor skewing the new study's results.

Women's rapport-talk probably explains why many people think women 11 talk more. A man wants to read the paper, his wife wants to talk; his girlfriend or sister spends hours on the phone with her friend or her mother. He concludes: Women talk more.

Yet Leaper and Ayres observed an overall pattern of men speaking more. 12 That's a conclusion women often come to when men hold forth at meetings, in social groups or when delivering one-on-one lectures. All of us—women and men—tend to notice others talking more in situations where we talk less.

Counting may be a start—or a stop along the way—to understanding gen- 13 der differences. But it's understanding when we tend to talk and what we're doing with words that yields insights we can count on.

Source: *Washington Post*, July 15, 2007, copyright Deborah Tannen. Reprinted by permission.

QUESTIONS FOR READING AND REASONING

1. What was the conclusion of the researchers who presented their study in *Science*?

2. Why are their results not telling the whole story, according to Tannen? Instead of counting words, what should we study?

3. What two kinds of talk does Tannen label? Which gender does the most of each type of talking?

4. What is Tannen's main idea or thesis?

QUESTIONS FOR REFLECTION AND WRITING

5. How do the details—and the style—in the opening and concluding paragraphs contribute to the author's point? Write a paragraph answer to this question. Then consider: Which one of the different responses to reading does your paragraph illustrate?

6. Do you agree with Tannen that understanding how words are used must be part of any study of men and women talking? If so, why? If not, how would you respond to her argument?

7. "The Gettysburg Address" is a valuable document for several kinds of research projects. For what kinds of research would Tannen's essay be useful? List several possibilities and be prepared to discuss your list with classmates.

WRITING SUMMARIES

Preparing a good summary is not easy. *A summary briefly restates, in your own words, the main points of a work in a way that does not misrepresent or distort the original.* A good summary shows your grasp of main ideas and your ability to express them clearly. You need to condense the original while giving all key ideas appropriate attention. As a student you may be assigned a summary to

- show that you have read and understood assigned works;
- complete a test question;
- have a record of what you have read for future study or to prepare for class discussion; or
- explain the main ideas in a work that you will also examine in some other way, such as in a book review.

When assigned a summary, pay careful attention to word choice. Avoid judgment words, such as "Brown then proceeds to develop the *silly* idea that. . . ." Follow these guidelines for writing good summaries.

GUIDELINES for Writing Summaries

1. **Write in a direct, objective style, using your own words.** Use few, if any, direct quotations, probably none in a one-paragraph summary.

2. **Begin with a reference to the writer (full name) and the title of the work, and then state the writer's thesis.** (You may also want to include where and when the work was published.)

3. **Complete the summary by providing other key ideas.** Show the reader how the main ideas connect and relate to one another.

4. **Do not include specific examples, illustrations, or background sections.**

5. **Combine main ideas into fewer sentences than were used in the original.**

6. **Keep the parts of your summary in the same balance as you find in the original.** If the author devotes about 30 percent of the essay to one idea, that idea should get about 30 percent of the space in your summary.

7. **Select precise, accurate verbs to show the author's relationship to ideas.** Write Jones *argues*, Jones *asserts*, Jones *believes*. Do not use vague verbs that provide only a list of disconnected ideas. Do *not* write Jones *talks about*, Jones *goes on to say*.

8. **Do not make any judgments about the writer's style or ideas.** Do *not* include your personal reaction to the work.

EXERCISE: Summary

With these guidelines in mind, read the following two summaries of Deborah Tannen's "Who Does the Talking Here?" (see pp. 8–9). Then answer the question: What is flawed or weak about each summary? To aid your analysis, (1) underline or highlight all words or phrases that are inappropriate in each summary, and (2) put the number of the guideline next to any passage that does not adhere to that guideline.

SUMMARY 1

I really thought that Deborah Tannen's essay contained some interesting ideas about how men and women talk. Tannen mentioned a study in which men and women used almost the same number of words. She goes on to talk about a man who talked a lot at a meeting in Virginia. Tannen also says that women talk more to make others feel good. I'm a man, and I don't like to make small talk.

SUMMARY 2

In Deborah Tannen's "Who Does the Talking Here?" (published July 15, 2007), she talks about studies to test who talks more—men or women. Some people think the case is closed—they both talk about the same number of words. Tannen goes on to say that she thinks people use words differently. Men talk a lot at events; they use "report-talk." Women use "rapport-talk" to strengthen relationships; their language is a glue to maintain relationships. So just counting words does not work. You have to know why someone is speaking.

Although we can agree that the writers of these summaries have read Tannen's essay, we can also find weaknesses in each summary. Certainly the second summary is more helpful than the first, but it can be strengthened by eliminating some details, combining some ideas, and putting more focus on Tannen's main idea. Here is a much-improved version:

REVISED SUMMARY

In Deborah Tannen's essay "Who Does the Talking Here?" (published July 15, 2007), Tannen asserts that recent studies to determine if men or women do the most talking are not helpful in answering that question. These studies focus on just counting the words that men and women use. Tannen argues that the only useful study of this issue is one that examines how each gender uses words and in which situations each gender does the most talking. She explains that men tend to use "report-talk" whereas women tend to use "rapport-talk." That is, men will do much of the talking in meetings when they have something to report. Women, on the other hand, will do more of the talking when they are seeking to connect in a relationship, to make people feel good. So, if we want to really understand the differences, we need to stop counting words and listen to what each gender is actually doing with the words that are spoken.

At times you may need to write a summary of a page or two rather than one paragraph. Frequently, long reports are preceded by a one-page summary. A longer summary may become part of an article-length review of an important book. Or instructors may want a longer summary of a lengthy or complicated article or text chapter. The following is an example of a summary of a lengthy article on cardiovascular health.

SAMPLE LONGER SUMMARY

In her article "The Good Heart," Anne Underwood (*Newsweek*, October 3, 2005) explores recent studies regarding heart disease that, in various ways, reveal the important role that one's attitudes have on physical health, especially the health of the heart. She begins with the results of a study published in the *New England Journal of Medicine* that examined the dramatic increase in cardiovascular deaths after an earthquake in Los Angeles in 1994. People who were not hurt by the quake died as a result of the fear and stress brought on by the event. As Underwood explains in detail, however, studies continue to show that psychological and social factors affect coronaries even more than sudden shocks such as earthquakes. For example, according to Dr. Michael Frenneaux, depression "at least doubles an otherwise healthy person's heart-attack risk." A Duke University study showed that high levels of hostility also raised the risk of death by heart disease. Another study showed that childhood traumas can increase heart disease risks by 30 to 70 percent. Adults currently living under work and family stress also increase their risks significantly.

How do attitudes make a difference? A number of studies demonstrate that negative attitudes, anger, and hostile feelings directly affect the chemistry of the body in ways that damage blood vessels. They also can raise blood pressure. Less directly, people with these attitudes and under stress often eat more, exercise less, and are more likely to smoke. These behaviors add to one's risk. Some physicians are seeking to use this information to increase the longevity of heart patients. They are advising weight loss and exercise, yoga and therapy, recognizing, as Underwood concludes, that "the heart does not beat in isolation, nor does the mind brood alone."

Observe the differences between the longer summary of Anne Underwood's article and the paragraph summary of Deborah Tannen's essay:

- Some key ideas or terms may be presented in direct quotation.
- Results of studies may be given in some detail.
- Appropriate transitional and connecting words are used to show how the parts of the summary connect.
- The author's name is often repeated to keep the reader's attention on the article summarized, not on the author of the summary.

ACTIVE READING: USE YOUR MIND!

Reading is not about looking at black marks on a page—or turning the pages as quickly as we can. Reading means constructing meaning, getting a message. We read with our brains, not our eyes and hands! This concept is often underscored by the term *active reading*. To help you always achieve active reading, not passive page turning, follow these guidelines.

GUIDELINES for Active Reading

1. **Understand your purpose in reading.** Do not just start turning pages to complete an assignment. Think first about your purpose. Are you reading for knowledge on which you will be tested? Focus on your purpose as you read, asking yourself, "What do I need to learn from this work?"

2. **Reflect on the title before reading further.** Titles are the first words writers give us. Take time to look for clues in a title that may reveal the work's subject and perhaps the writer's approach or attitude as well. Henry Fairlie's title "The Idiocy of Urban Life," for example, tells you both Fairlie's subject (urban or city living) and his position (urban living is idiotic).

3. **Become part of the writer's audience.** Not all writers have you and me in mind when they write. As an active reader, you need to "join" a writer's audience by learning about the writer, about the time in which the piece was written, and about the writer's expected audience. For readings in this text you are aided by introductory notes; study them.

4. **Predict what is coming.** Look for a writer's main idea or purpose statement. Study the work's organization. Then use this information to anticipate what

is coming. When you read "There are three good reasons for requiring a dress code in schools," you know the writer will list *three* reasons.

5. **Concentrate.** Slow down and give your full attention to reading. Watch for transition and connecting words that show you how the parts of a text connect. Read an entire article or chapter at one time—or you will need to start over to make sense of the piece.

6. **Annotate as you read.** The more senses you use, the more active your involvement. That means marking the text as you read (or taking notes if the material is not yours). Underline key sentences, such as the writer's thesis. Then, in the margin, indicate that it is the thesis. With a series of examples (or reasons), label them and number them. When you look up a word's definition, write the definition in the margin next to the word. Draw diagrams to illustrate concepts; draw arrows to connect example to idea. Studies have shown that students who annotate their texts get higher grades. Do what successful students do.

7. **Keep a reading journal.** In addition to annotating what you read, you may want to develop the habit of writing regularly in a journal. A reading journal gives you a place to note impressions and reflections on your reading, your initial reactions to assignments, and ideas you may use in your next writing.

EXERCISE: Active Reading

Read the following essay, studying the annotations that are started for you. As you read, add your own notes. Then test your active reading by responding to the questions that follow the essay.

THE RISE OF THE NEW GROUPTHINK | SUSAN CAIN

A graduate of Princeton and Harvard Law and former corporate attorney, Susan Cain thought about her preference for reading and small groups over public speaking and decided to write on the subject. Her book *Quiet: The Power of Introverts in a World That Can't Stop Talking* (2012) is the result. The following article, drawn from ideas for her book, appeared January 15, 2012.

Topic.

1   Solitude is out of fashion. Our companies, our schools and our culture are in thrall to an idea I call the New Groupthink, which holds that creativity and achievement come from an oddly gregarious place. Most of us now work in teams, in offices without walls, for managers who prize people skills above all else. Lone geniuses are out. Collaboration is in.

Author seems to disagree?

2   But there's a problem with this view. Research strongly suggests that people are more creative when they enjoy privacy and freedom from interruption. And the most spectacularly creative people in many fields are often introverted, according to studies by the psychologists Mihaly Csikszentmihalyi and Gregory Feist. They're extroverted enough to exchange and advance ideas, but see themselves as independent and individualistic. They're not joiners by nature.

One explanation for these findings is that introverts are comfortable working alone—and solitude is a catalyst to innovation. As the influential psychologist Hans Eysenck observed, introversion fosters creativity by "concentrating the mind on the tasks in hand, and preventing the dissipation of energy on social and sexual matters unrelated to work." In other words, a person sitting quietly under a tree in the backyard, while everyone else is clinking glasses on the patio, is more likely to have an apple land on his head. (Newton was one of the world's great introverts: William Wordsworth described him as "A mind for ever/ Voyaging through strange seas of Thought, alone.")

Solitude has long been associated with creativity and transcendence. "Without great solitude, no serious work is possible," Picasso said. A central narrative of many religions is the seeker—Moses, Jesus, Buddha—who goes off by himself and brings profound insights back to the community.

Culturally, we're often so dazzled by charisma that we overlook the quiet part of the creative process. Consider Apple. In the wake of Steve Jobs's death, we've seen a profusion of myths about the company's success. Most focus on Mr. Jobs's supernatural magnetism and tend to ignore the other crucial figure in Apple's creation: a kindly, introverted engineering wizard, Steve Wozniak, who toiled alone on a beloved invention, the personal computer.

Rewind to March 1975: Mr. Wozniak believes the world would be a better place if everyone had a user-friendly computer. This seems a distant dream—most computers are still the size of minivans, and many times as pricey. But Mr. Wozniak meets a simpatico band of engineers that call themselves the Homebrew Computer Club. The Homebrewers are excited about a primitive new machine called the Altair 8800. Mr. Wozniak is inspired, and immediately begins work on his own magical version of a computer. Three months later, he unveils his amazing creation for his friend, Steve Jobs. Mr. Wozniak wants to give his invention away free, but Mr. Jobs persuades him to co-found Apple Computer.

The story of Apple's origin speaks to the power of collaboration. Mr. Wozniak wouldn't have been catalyzed by the Altair but for the kindred spirits of Homebrew. And he'd never have started Apple without Mr. Jobs.

But it's also a story of solo spirit. If you look at how Mr. Wozniak got the work done—the sheer hard work of creating something from nothing—he did it alone. Late at night, all by himself.

Intentionally so. In his memoir, Mr. Wozniak offers this guidance to aspiring inventors:

"Most inventors and engineers I've met are like me . . . they live in their heads. They're almost like artists. In fact, the very best of them are artists. And artists work best alone. . . . I'm going to give you some advice that might be hard to take. That advice is: Work alone . . . Not on a committee. Not on a team."

11   And yet The New Groupthink has overtaken our workplaces, our schools and our religious institutions. Anyone who has ever needed noise-canceling headphones in her own office or marked an online calendar with a fake meeting in order to escape yet another real one knows what I'm talking about. Virtually all American workers now spend time on teams and some 70 percent inhabit open-plan offices, in which no one has "a room of one's own." During the last decades, the average amount of space allotted to each employee shrank 300 square feet, from 500 square feet in the 1970s to 200 square feet in 2010.

12   Our schools have also been transformed by the New Groupthink. Today, elementary school classrooms are commonly arranged in pods of desks, the better to foster group learning. Even subjects like math and creative writing are often taught as committee projects. In one fourth-grade classroom I visited in New York City, students engaged in group work were forbidden to ask a question unless every member of the group had the very same question.

13   The New Groupthink also shapes some of our most influential religious institutions. Many mega-churches feature extracurricular groups organized around every conceivable activity, from parenting to skateboarding to real estate, and expect worshipers to join in. They also emphasize a theatrical style of worship—loving Jesus out loud, for all the congregation to see. "Often the role of a pastor seems closer to that of church cruise director than to the traditional roles of spiritual friend and counselor," said Adam McHugh, an evangelical pastor and author of "Introverts in the Church."

14   Some teamwork is fine and offers a fun, stimulating, useful way to exchange ideas, manage information and build trust.

15   But it's one thing to associate with a group in which each member works autonomously on his piece of the puzzle; it's another to be corralled into endless meetings or conference calls conducted in offices that afford no respite from the noise and gaze of co-workers. Studies show that open-plan offices make workers hostile, insecure and distracted. They're also more likely to suffer from high blood pressure, stress, the flu and exhaustion. And people whose work is interrupted make 50 percent more mistakes and take twice as long to finish it.

16   Many introverts seem to know this instinctively, and resist being herded together. Backbone Entertainment, a video game development company in Emeryville, Calif., initially used an open-plan office, but found that its game developers, many of whom were introverts, were unhappy. "It was one big warehouse space, with just tables, no walls, and everyone could see each other," recalled Mike Mika, the former creative director. "We switched over to cubicles and were worried about it—you'd think in a creative environment that people would hate that. But it turns out they prefer having nooks and crannies they can hide away in and just be away from everybody."

17   Privacy also makes us productive. In a fascinating study known as the Coding War Games, consultants Tom DeMarco and Timothy Lister compared the work of more than 600 computer programmers at 92 companies. They found that people from the same companies performed at roughly the same level—but that there was an enormous performance gap between organizations. What

distinguished programmers at the top-performing companies wasn't greater experience or better pay. It was how much privacy, personal workspace and freedom from interruption they enjoyed. Sixty-two percent of the best performers said their workspace was sufficiently private compared with only 19 percent of the worst performers. Seventy-six percent of the worst programmers but only 38 percent of the best said that they were often interrupted needlessly.

Solitude can even help us learn. According to research on expert perfor- 18 mance by the psychologist Anders Ericsson, the best way to master a field is to work on the task that's most demanding for you personally. And often the best way to do this is alone. Only then, Mr. Ericsson told me, can you "go directly to the part that's challenging to you. If you want to improve, you have to be the one who generates the move. Imagine a group class—you're the one generating the move only a small percentage of the time."

Conversely, brainstorming sessions are one of the worst possible ways to 19 stimulate creativity. The brainchild of a charismatic advertising executive named Alex Osborn who believed that groups produced better ideas than individuals, workplace brainstorming sessions came into vogue in the 1950s. "The quantitative results of group brainstorming are beyond question," Mr. Osborn wrote. "One group produced 45 suggestions for a home appliance promotion, 56 ideas for a money-raising campaign, 124 ideas on how to sell more blankets."

But decades of research show that individuals almost always perform better 20 than groups in both quality and quantity, and group performance gets worse as group size increases. The "evidence from science suggests that business people must be insane to use brainstorming groups," wrote the organizational psychologist Adrian Furnham. "If you have talented and motivated people, they should be encouraged to work alone when creativity or efficiency is the highest priority."

The reasons brainstorming fails are instructive for other forms of group 21 work, too. People in groups tend to sit back and let others do the work; they instinctively mimic others' opinions and lose sight of their own; and, often succumb to peer pressure. The Emory University neuroscientist Gregory Berns found that when we take a stance different from the group's, we activate the amygdala, a small organ in the brain associated with the fear of rejection. Professor Berns calls this "the pain of independence."

The one important exception to this dismal record is electronic brain- 22 storming, where large groups outperform individuals; and the larger the group the better. The protection of the screen mitigates many problems of group work. This is why the Internet has yielded such wondrous collective creations. Marcel Proust called reading a "miracle of communication in the midst of solitude," and that's what the Internet is, too. It's a place where we can be alone together—and this is precisely what gives it power.

MY point is not that man is an island. Life is meaningless without love, 23 trust and friendship.

And I'm not suggesting that we abolish teamwork. Indeed, recent studies 24 suggest that influential academic work is increasingly conducted by teams rather than by individuals. (Although teams whose members collaborate remotely, from separate universities, appear to be the most influential of all.) The problems we face in science, economics and many other fields are more complex than ever before, and we'll need to stand on one another's shoulders if we can possibly hope to solve them.

25   But even if the problems are different, human nature remains the same. And most humans have two contradictory impulses: we love and need one another, yet we crave privacy and autonomy.

26   To harness the energy that fuels both these drives, we need to move beyond the New Groupthink and embrace a more nuanced approach to creativity and learning. Our offices should encourage casual, cafe-style interactions, but allow people to disappear into personalized, private spaces when they want to be alone. Our schools should teach children to work with others, but also to work on their own for sustained periods of time. And we must recognize that introverts like Steve Wozniak need extra quiet and privacy to do their best work.

27   Before Mr. Wozniak started Apple, he designed calculators at Hewlett-Packard, a job he loved partly because HP made it easy to chat with his colleagues. Every day at 10 a.m. and 2 p.m., management wheeled in doughnuts and coffee, and people could socialize and swap ideas. What distinguished these interactions was how low-key they were. For Mr. Wozniak, collaboration meant the ability to share a doughnut and a brainwave with his laid-back, poorly dressed colleagues—who minded not a whit when he disappeared into his cubicle to get the real work done.

QUESTIONS FOR READING AND REASONING

1. What does Cain mean by the "new groupthink"? Where do we find this phenomenon and how do we recognize it?

2. According to research, what kinds of people are most creative? What environment is most conducive to productivity and creativity?

3. What is Cain's thesis—the claim of her argument?

4. How does she support her claim? List specific details of her support.

QUESTIONS FOR REFLECTION AND WRITING

5. How does Cain qualify her claim in the final five paragraphs? What makes this an effective conclusion to her essay?

6. What is the most interesting piece of information or concept, for you, in Cain's argument? Why? Write a journal entry—four or five sentences at least—in response to this question.

USING PARAPHRASE

Paraphrasing's goal is the same as summary's: An accurate presentation of the information and ideas of someone else. Unlike summary, we paraphrase an entire short work. This can be a poem (see p. 539 for a paraphrase of a poem) or a complex section of prose that needs a simpler (but often longer than the original) restatement so that we are clear about its meaning. We paraphrase short but complex pieces; we summarize an entire essay or chapter or book.

Writers also use paraphrasing to restate *some* of the information or ideas from a source as part of developing their own work. They do this extensively in a researched essay, but they may also paraphrase parts of a source to add support to their discussion—or to be clear about another writer's ideas that they will evaluate or challenge in some way.

Think, for a moment, about the writing process. Writers use many kinds of experiences to develop their work. Formal researched essays contain precise documentation and may use summary, paraphrase, and direct quotations, but they rarely include personal references. Today, however, writers may blend styles and strategies—in personal essays and researched essays, for example—rather than keeping them distinct. And some scholars today also write books for nonspecialists. In these books—or articles—documentation is placed only at the back, a more informal style is used, and personal experiences may be included to engage readers. Journalists, too, often blend personal experience and informal styles while drawing on one or more sources to develop and support their ideas. Among the readings in this text you will find a few personal essays and scholarly essays as well as works demonstrating a blending of styles and strategies. This blending can be confusing for college students. Make sure that you always understand what kind of work you are expected to produce in each class, for every assignment.

Now, to illustrate paraphrase, suppose you don't want to summarize Lincoln's entire speech, but you do want to use his opening point as a lead-in to commenting on our own times. You might write:

> Lincoln's famous speech at the dedication of the Gettysburg battlefield begins with the observation that our nation was initially built on a belief in liberty and equality, but the country's future had come to a point of being tested. We are not actually facing a civil war today, but we are facing a culture war, a war of opposing values and beliefs, that seems to be tearing our country apart.

Paraphrasing—putting Lincoln's idea into your own words—is a much more effective opening than quoting Lincoln's first two sentences. It's his idea that you want to use, not his language. Observe three key points:

1. The idea is Lincoln's but the word choice is entirely different. Resist the urge to borrow any of Lincoln's phrases—that would be quoting and would require quotation marks—and that does not serve your purpose.
2. You still give credit to Lincoln for the idea.
3. Summary, paraphrasing, and quoting all share this one characteristic: You let readers know that you are using someone else's information or ideas.

EXERCISE: Paraphrase

1. Find several examples of paraphrasing in Cain's essay.
2. Assume that you are writing an essay on the disadvantages of brainstorming. Paraphrase the ideas in Cain's paragraph 20 to use in this assumed essay.

3. For an essay on the value of solitude in our too-bustling world, evaluate the following two paragraphs that use some of the material from Cain's paragraphs 3 and 4.

PARAPHRASE 1

Introverts have no trouble with solitude. Most adults are socialized to want close friends and family connections, but introverts are also content to have time alone to read, think, and create. What extroverts must learn is that no serious work is possible without solitude. Newton and other insightful people use their solitude as a catalyst for innovation, even, as Susan Cain notes, for transcendence.

PARAPHRASE 2

Introverts have no trouble with solitude. Most adults are socialized to want close friends and family connections, but introverts are also content to have time alone to read, think, and create. In her essay "The Rise of the New Groupthink," Susan Cain worries that today's emphasis on group projects fostered in open office spaces will not provide the solitude that can lead to new ideas. Yet, as Cain observes, it is often those who are given opportunities to think and work by themselves who provide us with new insights and new inventions.

ACKNOWLEDGING SOURCES INFORMALLY

As you have seen in the summaries and paraphrases above, even when you are not writing a formally documented paper, you must identify each source by author. What follows are some of the conventions of writing to use when writing about sources.

Referring to People and Sources

Readers in academic, professional, and business contexts expect writers to follow specific conventions of style when referring to authors and to various kinds of sources. Study the following guidelines and examples and then mark the next few pages for easy reference—perhaps by turning down a corner of the first and last pages.

References to People

- In a first reference, give the person's full name (both the given name and the surname): *Ellen Goodman, Robert J. Samuelson.* In second and subsequent references, use only the last name (surname): *Goodman, Samuelson.*
- Do not use Mr., Mrs., or Ms. Special titles such as President, Chief Justice, or Doctor may be used in the first reference with the person's full name.
- Never refer to an author by her or his first name. Write *Tannen*, not *Deborah*; *Lincoln*, not *Abraham*.

References to Titles of Works

Titles of works must *always* be written as titles. Titles are indicated by capitalization and by either quotation marks or italics.

Guidelines for Capitalizing Titles

- The first and last words are capitalized.
- The first word of a subtitle is capitalized.
- All other words in titles are capitalized except
  — Articles (*a, an, the*).
  — Coordinating conjunctions (*and, or, but, for, nor, yet, so*).
  — Prepositions (*in, for, about*).

Titles Requiring Quotation Marks

Titles of works published within other works—within a book, magazine, or newspaper—are indicated by quotation marks.

ESSAYS	"Who Does the Talking Here?"
SHORT STORIES	"The Story of an Hour"
POEMS	"To Daffodils"
ARTICLES	"Choose Your Utopia"
CHAPTERS	"Writers and Their Sources"
LECTURES	"Crazy Mixed-Up Families"
TV EPISODES	"Pride and Prejudice" (one drama on the television show *Masterpiece Theatre*)

Titles Requiring Italics

Titles of works that are separate publications and, by extension, titles of items such as works of art and websites are in italics.

PLAYS	*A Raisin in the Sun*
NOVELS	*War and Peace*
NONFICTION BOOKS	*Read, Reason, Write*
BOOK-LENGTH POEMS	*The Odyssey*
MAGAZINES AND JOURNALS	*Wired*
NEWSPAPERS	*Wall Street Journal*
FILMS	*The Wizard of Oz*
PAINTINGS	*The Birth of Venus*
TELEVISION PROGRAMS	*Star Trek*
WEBSITES	*worldwildlife.org*
DATABASES	*ProQuest*

Read the following article and respond by answering the questions that follow. Observe, as you read, how the author refers to the various sources he uses to develop his article and how he presents material from those sources. We will use this article as a guide to handling quotations.

THE FUTURE IS NOW: IT'S HEADING RIGHT AT US, BUT WE NEVER SEE IT COMING

JOEL ACHENBACH

A former humor columnist and currently a staff writer for the *Washington Post,* Joel Achenbach also has a regular blog on *washingtonpost.com.* His books include anthologies of his columns and *Captured by Aliens: The Search for Life and Truth in a Very Large Universe* (2003). The following article was published April 13, 2008.

PREREADING QUESTIONS What is nanotechnology? What do you think will be the next big change—and what field will it come from?

1   The most important things happening in the world today won't make tomorrow's front page. They won't get mentioned by presidential candidates or Chris Matthews[1] or Bill O'Reilly[2] or any of the other folks yammering and snorting on cable television.

2   They'll be happening in laboratories—out of sight, inscrutable and unhyped until the very moment when they change life as we know it.

3   Science and technology form a two-headed, unstoppable change agent. Problem is, most of us are mystified and intimidated by such things as biotechnology, or nanotechnology, or the various other -ologies that seem to be threatening to merge into a single unspeakable and incomprehensible thing called biotechnonanogenomicology. We vaguely understand that this stuff is changing our lives, but we feel as though it's all out of our control. We're just hanging on tight, like Kirk and Spock when the Enterprise starts vibrating at Warp 8.

4   What's unnerving is the velocity at which the future sometimes arrives. Consider the Internet. This powerful but highly disruptive technology crept out of the lab (a Pentagon think tank, actually) and all but devoured modern civilization—with almost no advance warning. The first use of the word "internet" to refer to a computer network seems to have appeared in this newspaper on Sept. 26, 1988, in the Financial section, on page F30—about as deep into the paper as you can go without hitting the bedrock of the classified ads.

5   The entire reference: "SMS Data Products Group Inc. in McLean won a $1,005,048 contract from the Air Force to supply a defense data network internet protocol router." Perhaps the unmellifluous compound noun "data network internet protocol router" is one reason more of us didn't pay attention. A couple of months later, "Internet"—still lacking the "the" before its name—finally elbowed its way to the front page when a virus shut down thousands of computers. The story referred to "a research network called Internet," which "links as many as 50,000 computers, allowing users to send a variety of information to each other." The scientists knew that computer networks could

---

[1] Political talk-show host on MSNBC.—Ed.
[2] Radio and television talk-show host on the FOX News Channel.—Ed.

SPEED BUMP. By permission of Dave Coverly and Creators Syndicate, Inc.

be powerful. But how many knew that this Internet thing would change the way we communicate, publish, sell, shop, conduct research, find old friends, do homework, plan trips and on and on?

Joe Lykken, a theoretical physicist at the Fermilab research center in   6
Illinois, tells a story about something that happened in 1990. A Fermilab visitor, an English fellow by the name of Tim Berners-Lee, had a new trick he wanted to demonstrate to the physicists. He typed some code into a little blank box on the computer screen. Up popped a page of data.

Lykken's reaction: *Eh.*   7

He could already see someone else's data on a computer. He could have   8
the colleague e-mail it to him and open it as a document. Why view it on a separate page on some computer network?

But of course, this unimpressive piece of software was the precursor to   9
what is known today as the World Wide Web. "We had no idea that we were seeing not only a revolution, but a trillion-dollar idea," Lykken says.

Now let us pause to reflect upon the fact that Joe Lykken is a very smart 10
guy—you don't get to be a theoretical physicist unless you have the kind of brain that can practically bend silverware at a distance—and even he, with that giant cerebral cortex and the billions of neurons flashing and winking, saw the proto-Web and harrumphed. It's not just us mortals, even scientists don't always grasp the significance of innovations. Tomorrow's revolutionary technology may be in plain sight, but everyone's eyes, clouded by conventional thinking, just can't detect it. "Even smart people are really pretty incapable of envisioning a situation that's substantially different from what they're in," says Christine Peterson, vice president of Foresight Nanotech Institute in Menlo Park, Calif.

So where does that leave the rest of us?   11

In technological Palookaville.   12

Science is becoming ever more specialized; technology is increasingly a   13
series of black boxes, impenetrable to but a few. Americans' poor science literacy means that science and technology exist in a walled garden, a geek ghetto. We are a technocracy in which most of us don't really understand

what's happening around us. We stagger through a world of technological and medical miracles. We're zombified by progress.

14   Peterson has one recommendation: Read science fiction, especially "hard science fiction" that sticks rigorously to the scientifically possible. "If you look out into the long-term future and what you see looks like science fiction, it might be wrong," she says. "But if it doesn't look like science fiction, it's definitely wrong."

15   That's exciting—and a little scary. We want the blessings of science (say, cheaper energy sources) but not the terrors (monsters spawned by atomic radiation that destroy entire cities with their fiery breath).

16   Eric Horvitz, one of the sharpest minds at Microsoft, spends a lot of time thinking about the Next Big Thing. Among his other duties, he's president of the Association for the Advancement of Artificial Intelligence. He thinks that, sometime in the decades ahead, artificial systems will be modeled on living things. In the Horvitz view, life is marked by robustness, flexibility, adaptability. That's where computers need to go. Life, he says, shows scientists "what we can do as engineers—better, potentially."

17   Our ability to monkey around with life itself is a reminder that ethics, religion and old-fashioned common sense will be needed in abundance in decades to come. . . . How smart and flexible and rambunctious do we want our computers to be? Let's not mess around with that Matrix business.

18   Every forward-thinking person almost ritually brings up the mortality issue. What'll happen to society if one day people can stop the aging process? Or if only rich people can stop getting old?

19   It's interesting that politicians rarely address such matters. The future in general is something of a suspect topic . . . a little goofy. Right now we're all focused on the next primary, the summer conventions, the Olympics and their political implications, the fall election. The political cycle enforces an emphasis on the immediate rather than the important.

20   And in fact, any prediction of what the world will be like more than, say, a year from now is a matter of hubris. The professional visionaries don't even talk about predictions or forecasts but prefer the word "scenarios." When Sen. John McCain, for example, declares that radical Islam is the transcendent challenge of the 21st century, he's being sincere, but he's also being a bit of a soothsayer. Environmental problems and resource scarcity could easily be the dominant global dilemma. Or a virus with which we've yet to make our acquaintance. Or some other "wild card."

21   Says Lykken, "Our ability to predict is incredibly poor. What we all thought when I was a kid was that by now we'd all be flying around in anti-gravity cars on Mars."

22   Futurists didn't completely miss on space travel—it's just that the things flying around Mars are robotic and take neat pictures and sometimes land and sniff the soil.

23   Some predictions are bang-on, such as sci-fi writer Arthur C. Clarke's declaration in 1945 that there would someday be communications satellites orbiting the Earth. But Clarke's satellites had to be occupied by repairmen who would maintain the huge computers required for space communications. Even

in the late 1960s, when Clarke collaborated with Stanley Kubrick on the screen-play to *2001: A Space Odyssey,* he assumed that computers would, over time, get bigger. "The HAL 9000 computer fills half the spaceship," Lykken notes.

Says science-fiction writer Ben Bova, "We have built into us an idea that tomorrow is going to be pretty much like today, which is very wrong." 24

The future is often viewed as an endless resource of innovation that will make problems go away—even though, if the past is any judge, innovations create their own set of new problems. Climate change is at least in part a con-sequence of the invention of the steam engine in the early 1700s and all the industrial advances that followed. 25

Look again at the Internet. It's a fantastic tool, but it also threatens to dis-perse information we'd rather keep under wraps, such as our personal medical data, or even the instructions for making a fission bomb. 26

We need to keep our eyes open. The future is going to be here sooner than we think. It'll surprise us. We'll try to figure out why we missed so many clues. And we'll go back and search the archives, and see that thing we should have noticed on page F30. 27

QUESTIONS FOR READING AND REASONING

1. What is Achenbach's subject? What is his thesis? Where does he state it?
2. What two agents together are likely to produce the next big change?
3. Summarize the evidence Achenbach provides to support the idea that we don't recognize the next big change until it is here.
4. If we want to try to anticipate the next big change, what should we do?
5. What prediction did Arthur C. Clarke get right? In what way was his imagina-tion incorrect? What can readers infer from this example?
6. Are big changes always good? Explain.
7. How does Achenbach identify most of his sources? He does not identify Chris Matthews or Bill O'Reilly in paragraph 1. What does this tell you about his expected audience?

PRESENTING DIRECT QUOTATIONS: A GUIDE TO FORM AND STYLE

Although most of your papers will be written in your own words and style, you will sometimes use direct quotations. Just as there is a correct form for ref-erences to people and to works, there is a correct form for presenting borrowed material in direct quotations. Study the guidelines and examples and then mark these pages, as you did the others, for easy reference.

Reasons for Using Quotation Marks

We use quotation marks in four ways:

- To indicate dialogue in works of fiction and drama
- To indicate the titles of some kinds of works
- To indicate the words that others have spoken or written
- To separate ourselves from or call into question particular uses of words

The following guidelines apply to all four uses of quotation marks, but the focus will be on the third use.

A Brief Guide to Quoting

1. *Quote accurately.* Do not misrepresent what someone else has written. Take time to compare what you have written with the original.
2. *Put all words taken from a source within quotation marks.* (To take words from a source without using quotation marks is to plagiarize, a form of stealing punished in academic and professional communities.)
3. *Never change any of the words within your quotation marks.* Indicate any deleted words with ellipses [spaced periods (. . .)]. If you need to add words to make the meaning clear, place the added words in [square brackets], not (parentheses).
4. *Always make the source of the quoted words clear.* If you do not provide the author of the quoted material, readers will have to assume that you are calling those words into question—the fourth reason for quoting. Observe that Achenbach introduces Joe Lykken in paragraph 6 and then uses his last name or "he" through the next three paragraphs so that readers always know to whom he is referring and quoting.
5. *When quoting an author who is quoted by the author of the source you are using, you must make clear that you are getting that author's words from your source, not directly from that author.*
   For example:

ORIGINAL:	"We had no idea that we were seeing not only a revolution, but a trillion-dollar idea."
INCORRECT:	Referring to his first experience with the World Wide Web, Lykken observed: "We had no idea that we were seeing . . . a revolution."
CORRECT:	To make his point about our failure to recognize big changes when they first appear, Achenbach quotes theoretical physicist Joe Lykken's response to first seeing the World Wide Web: "We had no idea that we were seeing . . . a revolution."

6. *Place commas and periods inside the closing quotation mark—even when only one word is quoted:* Unable to anticipate big changes coming from modern science, we are, Achenbach observes, in "technological Palookaville."

7. *Place colons and semicolons outside the closing quotation mark:* Achenbach jokingly explains our reaction to the complexities of modern technologies in his essay "The Future Is Now": "We're zombified by progress."

8. *Do not quote unnecessary punctuation.* When you place quoted material at the end of a sentence you have written, use only the punctuation needed to complete your sentence.

ORIGINAL:	The next big change will be "happening in laboratories—out of sight, inscrutable, and unhyped."
INCORRECT:	Achenbach explains that we will be surprised by the next big change because it will, initially, be hidden, "happening in laboratories—."
CORRECT:	Achenbach explains that we will be surprised by the next big change because it will, initially, be hidden, "happening in laboratories."

9. *When the words you quote are only a part of your sentence, do not capitalize the first quoted word, even if it was capitalized in the source.* **Exception:** You introduce the quoted material with a colon.

INCORRECT:	Achenbach observes that "The future is often viewed as an endless resource of innovation."
CORRECT:	Achenbach observes that "the future is often viewed as an endless resource of innovation."
ALSO CORRECT:	Achenbach argues that we count too much on modern science to solve problems: "The future is often viewed as an endless resource of innovation."

10. *Use single quotation marks (the apostrophe key on your keyboard) to identify quoted material within quoted material:* Achenbach explains that futurists "prefer the word 'scenarios.'"

11. *Depending on the structure of your sentence, use a colon, a comma, or no punctuation before a quoted passage.* A colon provides a formal introduction to a quoted passage. (See the example in item 9.) Use a comma only when your sentence requires it. Quoted words presented in a "that" clause are not preceded by a comma.

ORIGINAL:	"What's unnerving is the velocity at which the future sometimes arrives."
CORRECT:	"What's unnerving," Achenbach notes, "is the velocity at which the future sometimes arrives."
ALSO CORRECT:	Achenbach observes that we are often unnerved by "the velocity at which the future sometimes arrives."

12. *To keep quotations brief, omit irrelevant portions. Indicate missing words with ellipses.* For example: Achenbach explains that "we want the blessings of science . . . but not the terrors." Some instructors want the ellipses placed

in square brackets—[. . .]—to show that you have added them to the original. Modern Language Association (MLA) style does not require the square brackets unless you are quoting a passage that already has ellipses as part of that passage. The better choice would be not to quote that passage.

13. *Consider the poor reader.*
   - Always give enough context to make the quoted material clear.
   - Do not put so many bits and pieces of quoted passages into one sentence that your reader struggles to follow the ideas.
   - Make sure that your sentences are complete and correctly constructed. Quoting is never an excuse for a sentence fragment or distorted construction.

> **NOTE:** All examples of quoting given above are in the present tense. We write that "Achenbach notes," "Achenbach believes," "Achenbach asserts." Even though his article was written in the past, we use the present tense to describe his ongoing ideas.

FOR READING AND ANALYSIS

As you read the following article, practice active reading, including annotating each essay. Concentrate first on what the author has to say, but also observe the organization of the essay and the author's use of quotations and references to other authors and works.

FIVE LEADERSHIP LESSONS FROM JAMES T. KIRK
ALEX KNAPP

Currently Social Media editor at *Forbes* magazine and popular blogger, Alex Knapp has been a freelance writer and editor for many years. He holds a law degree from the University of Kansas and focuses, in his writing, on the future of technology and culture.

PREREADING QUESTIONS What lessons might Captain Kirk have to offer to businesspeople who read *Forbes* magazine? How might these lessons have value to you as a college student?

1   Captain James T. Kirk is one of the most famous Captains in the history of Starfleet. There's a good reason for that. He saved the planet Earth several times, stopped the Doomsday Machine, helped negotiate peace with the Klingon Empire, kept the balance of power between the Federation and the Romulan Empire, and even managed to fight Nazis. On his five-year mission commanding the U.S.S. Enterprise, as well as subsequent commands,

James T. Kirk was a quint-essential leader, who led his crew into the unknown and continued to succeed time and time again.

Kirk's success was no 2 fluke, either. His style of command demonstrates a keen understanding of leadership and how to maintain a team that succeeds time and time again, regardless of the dangers faced. Here are five of the key leadership lessons that you can take away from Captain Kirk as you pilot your own organization into unknown futures.

1. NEVER STOP LEARNING

"You know the greatest danger facing us is ourselves, an irrational fear of 3 *the unknown. But there's no such thing as the unknown— only things temporarily hidden, temporarily not understood."*

Captain Kirk may have a reputation as a suave ladies man, but don't let 4 that exterior cool fool you. Kirk's reputation at the Academy was that of a "walking stack of books," in the words of his former first officer, Gary Mitchell. And a passion for learning helped him through several missions. Perhaps the best demonstration of this is in the episode "Arena," where Kirk is forced to fight a Gorn Captain in single combat by advanced beings. Using his own knowledge and materials at hand, Kirk is able to build a rudimentary shotgun, which he uses to defeat the Gorn.

If you think about it, there's no need for a 23rd Century Starship Captain 5 to know how to mix and prepare gunpowder if the occasion called for it. After all, Starfleet officers fight with phasers and photon torpedoes. To them, gunpowder is obsolete. But the same drive for knowledge that drove Kirk to the stars also caused him to learn that bit of information, and it paid off several years later.

In the same way, no matter what your organization does, it helps to never 6 stop learning. The more knowledge you have, the more creative you can be. The more you're able to do, the more solutions you have for problems at your disposal. Sure, you might never have to face down a reptilian alien on a desert planet, but you never know what the future holds. Knowledge is your best key to overcoming whatever obstacles are in your way.

2. HAVE ADVISORS WITH DIFFERENT WORLDVIEWS

"One of the advantages of being a captain, Doctor, is being able to ask for 7 *advice without necessarily having to take it."*

Kirk's closest two advisors are Commander Spock, a Vulcan committed to 8 a philosophy of logic, and Dr. Leonard McCoy, a human driven by compassion and scientific curiosity. Both Spock and McCoy are frequently at odds with each other, recommend different courses of action and bringing very different types of arguments to bear in defense of those points of view. Kirk sometimes goes with one, or the other, or sometimes takes their advice as a springboard to developing an entirely different course of action.

9   However, the very fact that Kirk has advisors who have a different world-view not only from each other, but also from himself, is a clear demonstration of Kirk's confidence in himself as a leader. Weak leaders surround themselves with yes men who are afraid to argue with them. That fosters an organizational culture that stifles creativity and innovation, and leaves members of the organization afraid to speak up. That can leave the organization unable to solve problems or change course. Historically, this has led to some serious disasters, such as *Star Wars Episode I: The Phantom Menace.*

10   Organizations that allow for differences of opinion are better at developing innovation, better at solving problems, and better at avoiding groupthink. We all need a McCoy and a Spock in our lives and organizations.

3. BE PART OF THE AWAY TEAM

11   *"Risk is our business. That's what this starship is all about. That's why we're aboard her."*

12   Whenever an interesting or challenging mission came up, Kirk was always willing to put himself in harm's way by joining the Away Team. With his boots on the ground, he was always able to make quick assessments of the situation, leading to superior results. At least, superior for everyone with a name and not wearing a red shirt. Kirk was very much a hands-on leader, leading the vanguard of his crew as they explored interesting and dangerous situations.

13   When you're in a leadership role, it's sometimes easy to let yourself get away from leading Away Team missions. After all, with leadership comes perks, right? You get the nice office on the higher floor. You finally get an assistant to help you with day to day activities, and your days are filled with meetings and decisions to be made, and many of these things are absolutely necessary. But it's sometimes easy to trap yourself in the corner office and forget what life is like on the front lines. When you lose that perspective, it's that much harder to understand what your team is doing, and the best way to get out of the problem. What's more, when you're not involved with your team, it's easy to lose their trust and have them gripe about how you don't understand what the job is like.

14   This is a lesson that was actually imprinted on me in one of my first jobs, making pizzas for a franchise that doesn't exist anymore. Our general manager spent a lot of time in his office, focused on the paperwork and making sure that we could stay afloat on the razor-thin margins we were running. But one thing he made sure to do, every day, was to come out during peak times and help make pizza. He didn't have to do that, but he did. The fact that he did so made me like him a lot more. It also meant that I trusted his decisions a lot more. In much the same way, I'm sure, as Kirk's crew trusted his decisions, because he knew the risks of command personally.

4. PLAY POKER, NOT CHESS

"Not chess, Mr. Spock. Poker. Do you know the game?"   15

In one of my all-time favorite *Star Trek* episodes, Kirk and his crew face 16 down an unknown vessel from a group calling themselves the "First Federation." Threats from the vessel escalate until it seems that the destruction of the *Enterprise* is imminent. Kirk asks Spock for options, who replies that the *Enterprise* has been playing a game of chess, and now there are no winning moves left. Kirk counters that they shouldn't play chess they should play poker. He then bluffs the ship by telling them that the *Enterprise* has a substance in its hull called "corbomite" which will reflect the energy of any weapon back against an attacker. This begins a series of actions that enables the *Enterprise* crew to establish peaceful relations with the First Federation.

I love chess as much as the next geek, but chess is often taken too seri- 17 ously as a metaphor for leadership strategy. For all of its intricacies, chess is a game of defined rules that can be mathematically determined. It's ultimately a game of boxes and limitations. A far better analogy to strategy is poker, not chess. Life is a game of probabilities, not defined rules. And often understanding your opponents is a much greater advantage than the cards you have in your hand. It was knowledge of his opponent that allowed Kirk to defeat Khan in *Star Trek II by* exploiting Khan's two-dimensional thinking. Bluffs, tells, and bets are all a big part of real-life strategy. Playing that strategy with an eye to the psychology of our competitors, not just the rules and circumstances of the game, can often lead to better outcomes than following the rigid lines of chess.

5. BLOW UP THE ENTERPRISE

"'All I ask is a tall ship and a star to steer her by.' You could feel the wind 18 *at your back in those days. The sounds of the sea beneath you, and even if you take away the wind and the water it's still the same. The ship is yours. You can feel her. And the stars are still there, Bones."*

One recurring theme in the original *Star Trek* series is that Kirk's first love is 19 the *Enterprise*. That love kept him from succumbing to the mind-controlling spores in "This Side of Paradise," and it's hinted that his love for the ship kept him from forming any real relationships or starting a family. Despite that love, though, there came a point in *Star Trek III: The Search For Spock,* where Captain Kirk made a decision that must have pained him enormously—in order to defeat the Klingons attacking him and save his crew, James Kirk destroyed the *Enterprise*. The occasion, in the film, was treated with the solemnity of a funeral, which no doubt matched Kirk's mood. The film ends with the crew returning to Vulcan on a stolen Klingon vessel, rather than the *Enterprise*. But they returned victorious.

We are often, in our roles as leaders, driven by a passion. It might be a 20 product or service, it might be a way of doing things. But no matter how much that passion burns within us, the reality is that times change. Different products are created. Different ways of doing things are developed. And there will come times in your life when that passion isn't viable anymore. A time when it no longer makes sense to pursue your passion. When that happens, no matter how painful it is, you need to blow up the *Enterprise*. That is, change what isn't working and embark on a new path, even if that means having to live in a Klingon ship for awhile.

FINAL TAKEAWAY:

21   In his many years of service to the Federation, James Kirk embodied several leadership lessons that we can use in our own lives. We need to keep exploring and learning. We need to ensure that we encourage creativity and innovation by listening to the advice of people with vastly different opinions. We need to occasionally get down in the trenches with the members of our teams so we understand their needs and earn their trust and loyalty. We need to understand the psychology of our competitors and also learn to radically change course when circumstances dictate. By following these lessons, we can lead our organizations into places where none have gone before.

QUESTIONS FOR READING

1. What is Knapp's subject?
2. What does the first point—never stop learning—reveal about Kirk's academy behavior?
3. What does having advisors with differing views reveal about a leader?
4. Explain what the author means by destroying the *Enterprise* as a leadership strategy.

QUESTIONS FOR REASONING AND ANALYSIS

5. Knapp appears to use just a simple list as his structure. What other structure does the author use?
6. Knapp clearly loved the *Star Trek* TV series. How does he guide readers who may not have grown up watching Captain Kirk?
7. The author argues that leaders should play poker, not chess. Explain his view of life and the point of his game analogy.

QUESTIONS FOR REFLECTION AND WRITING

8. The *Star Trek* series has been one of the most popular and long running. If you have not watched this series, has Knapp's essay piqued your interest in Captain Kirk and encouraged you to seek out the reruns? Why or why not?
9. Which of the five lessons seems most easily applied to college students? Why? Explain your choice.
10. Which of the five lessons seems least applicable to college students? Why? Now, you are one of Captain Kirk's advisors. What good advice can you find in the lesson that has been put at the bottom of the list?

SUGGESTIONS FOR DISCUSSION AND WRITING

1. Write a one-paragraph summary of Alex Knapp's essay. Be sure that your summary clearly states the author's main idea, the claim of his argument. Take your time and polish your word choice.

2. Read actively and then prepare a one-and-a-half-page summary of Patricia B. Strait's "When Societies Collide," (pp. 500–11). Your readers want an accurate and balanced but much shorter version of the original because they will not be reading the original article. Explain not only what the writer's main ideas are but also how the writer develops her essay. That is, what kind of research supports the article's thesis? Pay close attention to your word choice.

3. A number of years ago, before the first Kindle, Bill Gates argued that e-books will replace paper books. What are the advantages of e-books? What are the advantages of paper books? Are there any disadvantages to either type of book? Which do you prefer? How would you argue for your preference?

GOING ONLINE

Select one futuristic idea that interests you—robots in the home, cars that don't need drivers, artificial intelligence, a moon colony, or whatever else captures your imagination—and see what you can learn about it online. Be prepared to share your information in a class discussion, or consider exploring your topic in an essay.

Responding Critically to Sources

READ: What is the situation? Who is hiding under the bed?

REASON: Whom do we expect to be under the bed? What strategy has been used?

REFLECT/WRITE: What makes this cartoon clever?

In some contexts, the word *critical* carries the idea of harsh judgment: "The manager was critical of her secretary's long phone conversations." In other contexts, the term means to evaluate carefully. When we speak of the critical reader or critical thinker, we have in mind someone who reads actively, who thinks about issues, and who makes informed judgments. Here is a profile of the critical reader or thinker:

TRAITS OF THE CRITICAL READER/THINKER

- **Focused on the facts.**
  Give me the facts and show me that they are relevant to the issue.
- **Analytic.**
  What strategies has the writer/speaker used to develop the argument?
- **Open-minded.**
  Prepared to listen to different points of view, to learn from others.
- **Questioning/skeptical.**
  What other conclusions could be supported by the evidence presented?
  How thorough has the writer/speaker been?
  What persuasive strategies are used?
- **Creative.**
  What are some entirely different ways of looking at the issue or problem?
- **Intellectually active, not passive.**
  Willing to analyze logic and evidence.
  Willing to consider many possibilities.
  Willing, after careful evaluation, to reach a judgment, to take a stand on issues.

EXAMINING THE RHETORICAL CONTEXT OF A SOURCE

Reading critically requires preparation. Instead of "jumping into reading," begin by asking questions about the work's rhetorical context. Rhetoric is about the *art of writing* (or *speaking*). Someone has chosen to shape a text in a particular way at this time for an imagined audience to accomplish a specific goal. The better you understand all of the decisions shaping a particular text, the better you will understand that work. And, then, the better you will be able to judge the significance of that work. So, try to answer the following five questions before reading. Then complete your answers while you read—or by doing research and thinking critically after you finish reading.

Who Is the Author?

Key questions to answer include:

- *Does the author have a reputation for honesty, thoroughness, and fairness?* Read the biographical note, if there is one. Ask your instructor about the author or learn about the author in a biographical dictionary or online. Try *Book Review Digest* (in your library or online) for reviews of the author's books.
- *Is the author writing within his or her area of expertise?* People can voice opinions on any subject, but they cannot transfer expertise from one subject area to another. A football player endorsing a political candidate is a citizen with an opinion, not an expert on politics.
- *Is the author identified with a particular group or set of beliefs? Does the biography place the writer or speaker in a particular institution or organization?* For example, a member of a Republican administration may be expected to favor a Republican president's policies. A Roman Catholic priest may be expected to take a stand against abortion. These kinds of details provide hints, but you should not decide, absolutely, what a writer's position is until you have read the work with care. Be alert to reasonable expectations but avoid stereotyping.

What Type—or Genre—of Source Is It?

Are you reading a researched and documented essay by a specialist—or the text of a speech delivered the previous week to a specific audience? Is the work an editorial—or a letter to the editor? Does the syndicated columnist (such as Dave Barry, who appears later in this chapter) write humorous columns? Is the cartoon a comic strip or a political cartoon from the editorial page of a newspaper? (You will see both kinds of cartoons in this text.) Know what kind of text you are reading before you start. That's the only way to give yourself the context you need to be a good critical reader.

What Kind of Audience Does the Author Anticipate?

Understanding the intended audience helps you answer questions about the depth and sophistication of the work and a possible bias or slant.

- *Does the author expect a popular audience, a general but educated audience, or a specialist audience of shared expertise? Does the author anticipate an audience that shares cultural, political, or religious values?* Often you can judge the expected audience by noting the kind of publication in which the article appears, the publisher of the book, or the venue for the speech. For example, *Reader's Digest* is written for a mass audience, and *Psychology Today* for a general but more knowledgeable reader. By contrast, articles in the *Journal of the American Medical Association* are written by physicians and research scientists for a specialized reader. (It would be inappropriate, then, for a general reader to complain that an article in *JAMA* is not well written because it is too difficult.)

- *Does the author expect an audience favorable to his or her views? Or with a "wait and see" attitude? Or even hostile?* Some newspapers and television news organizations are consistently liberal whereas others are noticeably conservative. (Do you know the political leanings of your local paper? Of the TV news that you watch? Of the blogs you choose?) Remember: All arguments are "slanted" or "biased"—that is, they take a stand. That's as it should be. Just be sure to read or listen with an awareness of the author's particular background, interests, and possible stands on issues.

What Is the Author's Primary Purpose?

Is the work primarily informative or persuasive in intent? Designed to entertain or be inspiring? Think about the title. Read a book's preface to learn of the author's goals. Pay attention to tone as you read.

What Are the Author's Sources of Information?

Much of our judgment of an author and a work is based on the quality of the author's choice of sources. So always ask yourself: Where was the information obtained? Are sources clearly identified? Be suspicious of those who want us to believe that their unnamed "sources" are "reliable." Pay close attention to dates. A biography of King George III published in 1940 may still be the best source. An article urging more development based on county population statistics from the 1990s is no longer reliable.

> **NOTE:** None of the readings in this textbook were written for publication in this textbook. They have all come from some other context. To read them with understanding you must identify the original context and think about how that should guide your reading.

EXERCISES: Examining the Context

1. For each of the following works, comment on what you might expect to find. Consider author, occasion, audience, and reliability.
    a. An article on the Republican administration, written by a former campaign worker for a Democratic presidential candidate.
    b. A discussion, published in the Boston *Globe,* of the New England Patriots' hope for the next Super Bowl.
    c. A letter to the editor about conservation, written by a member of the Sierra Club. (What is the Sierra Club? Check out its website.)
    d. A column in *Newsweek* on economics. (Look at the business section of this magazine. Your library has it.)
    e. A 1988 article in *Nutrition Today* on the best diets.

    f. A biography of Benjamin Franklin published by Oxford University Press.

    g. A *Family Circle* article about a special vegetarian diet written by a physician. (Who is the audience for this magazine? Where is it sold?)

    h. A *New York Times* editorial written after the Supreme Court's striking down of Washington, DC's handgun restrictions.

    i. A speech on new handgun technology delivered at a convention of the National Rifle Association.

    j. An editorial in your local newspaper titled "Stop the Highway Killing."

2. Analyze an issue of your favorite magazine. Look first at the editorial pages and the articles written by staff, then at articles contributed by other writers. Answer these questions for both staff writers and contributors:

    a. Who is the audience?

    b. What is the purpose of the articles and of the entire magazine?

    c. What type of article dominates the issue?

3. Select one environmental website and study what is offered. The EnviroLink Network (www.envirolink.org) will lead you to many sites. Write down the name of the site you chose and its address (URL). Then answer these questions:

    a. Who is the intended audience?

    b. What seems to be the primary purpose or goal of the site?

    c. What type of material dominates the site?

    d. For what kinds of writing assignments might you use material from the site?

ANALYZING THE STYLE OF A SOURCE

Critical readers read for implication and are alert to tone or nuance. When you read, think not only about *what* is said but also about *how* it is said. Consider the following passage:

> Bush's stupid "war"—so much for the Congress declaring war—drags on, costing unhappy taxpayers billions, while the "greatest army in the world" cannot find the real villain hiding somewhere in a cave.

This passage observes that the Iraq War continues, costing much money, while the United States still has not found the perpetrator of 9/11. But, it actually says more than that, doesn't it? Note the writer's attitude toward Bush, the war, and the U.S. military.

How can we rewrite this passage to make it more favorable? Here is one version produced by students in a group exercise:

> President Bush continues to defend the war in Iraq—which Congress never declared but continues to fund—in spite of the considerable cost to stabilize that country and the region. Meanwhile more troops will be needed to finally capture bin Laden and bring him to justice.

The writers have not changed their view that the Iraq War is costing a lot and that so far we have failed to capture bin Laden. But, in this version neither Bush nor the military is ridiculed. What is the difference in the two passages? Only the word choice.

Denotative and Connotative Word Choice

The students' ability to rewrite the passage on the war in Iraq to give it a positive attitude tells us that, although some words may have similar meanings, they cannot always be substituted for one another without changing the message. Words with similar meanings have similar *denotations*. Often, though, words with similar denotations do not have the same connotations. A word's *connotation* is what the word suggests, what we associate the word with. The words *house* and *home*, for example, both refer to a building in which people live, but the word *home* suggests ideas—and feelings—of family and security. Thus the word *home* has a strong positive connotation. *House* by contrast brings to mind a picture of a physical structure only because the word doesn't carry any "emotional baggage."

We learn the connotations of words the same way we learn their denotations—in context. Most of us, living in the same culture, share the same connotative associations of words. At times, the context in which a word is used will affect the word's connotation. For example, the word *buddy* usually has positive connotations. We may think of an old or trusted friend. But when an unfriendly person who thinks a man may have pushed in front of him says, "Better watch it, *buddy*," the word has a negative connotation. Social, physical, and language contexts control the connotative significance of words. Become more alert to the connotative power of words by asking what words the writers could have used instead.

> **NOTE:** Writers make choices; their choices reflect and convey their attitudes. *Studying the context in which a writer uses emotionally charged words is the only way to be sure that we understand the writer's attitude.*

EXERCISES: Connotation

1. For each of the following words or phrases, list at least two synonyms that have a more negative connotation than the given word.
   a. child
   b. persistent
   c. thin
   d. a large group
   e. scholarly
   f. trusting
   g. underachiever
   h. quiet

2. For each of the following words, list at least two synonyms that have a more positive connotation than the given word.
   a. notorious
   b. fat
   c. politician
   d. old (people)
   e. fanatic
   f. reckless
   g. drunkard
   h. cheap

3. Read the following paragraph and decide how the writer feels about the activity described. Note the choice of details and the connotative language that make you aware of the writer's attitude.

> Needing to complete a missed assignment for my physical education class, I dragged myself down to the tennis courts on a gloomy afternoon. My task was to serve five balls in a row into the service box. Although I thought I had learned the correct service movements, I couldn't seem to translate that knowledge into a decent serve. I tossed up the first ball, jerked back my racket, swung up on the ball—clunk—I hit the ball on the frame. I threw up the second ball, brought back my racket, swung up on the ball—ping—I made contact with the strings, but the ball dribbled down on my side of the net. I trudged around the court, collecting my tennis balls; I had only two of them.

4. Write a paragraph describing an activity that you liked or disliked without saying how you felt. From your choice of details and use of connotative language, convey your attitude toward the activity. (The paragraph in exercise 3 is your model.)

5. Select one of the words listed below and explain, in a paragraph, what the word connotes to you personally. Be precise; illustrate your thoughts with details and examples.

   a. nature   d. geek
   b. mother   e. playboy
   c. romantic   f. artist

COLLABORATIVE EXERCISES: On Connotation

1. List all of the words you know for *human female* and for *human male.* Then classify them by connotation (positive, negative, neutral) and by level of usage (formal, informal, slang). Is there any connection between type of connotation and level of usage? Why are some words more appropriate in some social contexts than in others? Can you easily list more negative words used for one sex than for the other? Why?

2. Some words can be given a different connotation in different contexts. First, for each of the following words, label its connotation as positive, negative, or neutral. Then, for each word with a positive connotation, write a sentence in which the word would convey a more negative connotation. For each word with a negative connotation, write a sentence in which the word would suggest a more positive connotation.

   a. natural   d. free
   b. old   e. chemical
   c. committed   f. lazy

3. Each of the following groups of words might appear together in a thesaurus, but the words actually vary in connotation. After looking up any words whose connotation you are unsure of, write a sentence in which each word is used

correctly. Briefly explain why one of the other words in the group should not be substituted.

a. brittle, hard, fragile
b. quiet, withdrawn, glum
c. shrewd, clever, cunning
d. strange, remarkable, bizarre
e. thrifty, miserly, economical

Tone

We can describe a writer's attitude toward the subject as positive, negative, or (rarely) neutral. Attitude is the writer's position on, or feelings about, his or her subject. The way that attitude is expressed—the voice we hear and the feelings conveyed through that voice—is the writer's *tone*. Writers can choose to express attitude through a wide variety of tones. We may reinforce a negative attitude through an angry, somber, sad, mocking, peevish, sarcastic, or scornful tone. A positive attitude may be revealed through an enthusiastic, serious, sympathetic, jovial, light, or admiring tone. We cannot be sure that just because a writer selects a light tone, for example, the attitude must be positive. Humor columnists such as Dave Barry often choose a light tone to examine serious social and political issues. Given their subjects, we recognize that the light and amusing tone actually conveys a negative attitude toward the topic.

COLLABORATIVE EXERCISES: On Tone

With your class partner or in small groups, examine the following three paragraphs, which are different responses to the same event. First, decide on each writer's attitude. Then describe, as precisely as possible, the tone of each paragraph.

1. It is tragically inexcusable that this young athlete was not examined fully before he was allowed to join the varsity team. The physical examinations given were unbelievably sloppy. What were the coach and trainer thinking of not to insist that each youngster be examined while undergoing physical stress? Apparently they were not thinking about our boys at all. We can no longer trust our sons and our daughters to this inhuman system so bent on victory that it ignores the health—indeed the very lives—of our children.
2. It was learned last night, following the death of varsity fullback Jim Bresnick, that none of the players was given a stress test as part of his physical examination. The oversight was attributed to laxness by the coach and trainer, who are described today as being "distraught." It is the judgment of many that the entire physical education program must be reexamined with an eye to the safety and health of all students.
3. How can I express the loss I feel over the death of my son? I want to blame someone, but who is to blame? The coaches, for not administering more rigorous physical checkups? Why should they have done more than other coaches have done before or than other coaches are doing at other schools? My son, for not telling me that he felt funny after practice? His teammates, for not telling the coaches that my son said he did not feel well? Myself, for not knowing that

something was wrong with my only child? Who is to blame? All of us and none of us. But placing blame will not return my son to me; I can only pray that other parents will not have to suffer so. Jimmy, we loved you.

■ ■

Level of Diction

In addition to responding to a writer's choice of connotative language, observe the *level of diction* used. Are the writer's words primarily typical of conversational language or of a more formal style? Does the writer use slang words or technical words? Is the word choice concrete and vivid or abstract and intellectual? These differences help to shape tone and affect our response to what we read. Lincoln's word choice in "The Gettysburg Address" (see pp. 4–5) is formal and abstract. Lincoln writes "on this continent" rather than "in this land," "we take increased devotion" rather than "we become more committed." Another style, the technical, will be found in some articles in this text. The social scientist may write that "the child . . . is subjected to extremely punitive discipline," whereas a nonspecialist, more informally, might write that "the child is controlled by beatings or other forms of punishment."

One way to create an informal style is to choose simple words: *land* instead of *continent*. To create greater informality, a writer can use contractions: *we'll* for *we will*. There are no contractions in "The Gettysburg Address."

> **NOTE:** In your academic and professional writing, you should aim for a style informal enough to be inviting to readers but one that, in most cases, avoids contractions or slang words.

Sentence Structure

Attitude is conveyed and tone created primarily through word choice, but sentence structure and other rhetorical strategies are also important. Studying a writer's sentence patterns will reveal how they affect style and tone. When analyzing these features, consider the following questions:

1. *Are the sentences generally long or short, or varied in length?*
Are the structures primarily:

- *Simple* (one independent clause)
  In 1900 empires dotted the world.
- *Compound* (two or more independent clauses)
  Women make up only 37 percent of television characters, yet women make up more than half of the population.
- *Complex* (at least one independent and one dependent clause)
  As nations grew wealthier, traditional freedom wasn't enough.

Sentences that are both long and complex create a more formal style. Compound sentences joined by *and* do not increase formality much because such sentences are really only two or more short, simple patterns hooked together.

On the other hand, a long "simple" sentence with many modifiers will create a more formal style. The following example, from an essay on leadership by Michael Korda, is more complicated than the sample compound sentence above:

- *Expanded simple sentence*
  [A] leader is like a mirror, reflecting back to us our own sense of purpose, putting into words our own dreams and hopes, transforming our needs and fears into coherent policies and programs.

In "The Gettysburg Address" three sentences range from 10 to 16 words, six sentences from 21 to 29 words, and the final sentence is an incredible 82 words. All but two of Lincoln's sentences are either complex or compound-complex sentences. By contrast, in "The Future Is Now," Joel Achenbach includes a paragraph with five sentences. These sentences are composed of 7, 11, 3, 11, and 19 words each. All five are simple sentences.

2.   Does the writer use sentence fragments (incomplete sentences)?

Although many instructors struggle to rid student writing of fragments, professional writers know that the occasional fragment can be used effectively for emphasis. Science fiction writer Bruce Sterling, thinking about the "melancholic beauty" of a gadget no longer serving any purpose, writes:

- Like Duchamp's bottle-rack, it becomes a found objet d'art. A metallic fossil of some lost human desire. A kind of involuntary poem.

The second and third sentences are, technically, fragments, but because they build on the structure of the first sentence, readers can add the missing words *It becomes* to complete each sentence. The brevity, repetition of structure, and involvement of the reader to "complete" the fragments all contribute to a strong conclusion to Sterling's paragraph.

3.   Does the writer seem to be using an overly simplistic style? If so, why?

Overly simplistic sentence patterns, just like an overly simplistic choice of words, can be used to show that the writer thinks the subject is silly or childish or insulting. In one of her columns, Ellen Goodman objects to society's over-simplifying of addictions and its need to believe in quick and lasting cures. She makes her point with reference to two well-known examples—but notice her technique:

- Hi, my name is Jane and I was once bulimic but now I am an exercise guru . . .
- Hi, my name is Oprah and I was a food addict but now I am a size 10.

4.   Does the writer use parallelism (coordination) or antithesis (contrast)?

When two phrases or clauses are parallel in structure, the message is that they are equally important. Look back at Korda's expanded simple sentence. He coordinates three phrases, asserting that a leader is like a mirror in these three ways:

- Reflects back our purpose
- Puts into words our dreams
- Transforms our needs and fears

Antithesis creates tension. A sentence using this structure says "not this" but "that." Lincoln uses both parallelism and antithesis in one striking sentence:

- The world will little note nor long remember
        <u>what</u> we say here,
    but it [the world] can never forget
        <u>what</u> they did here.

Metaphors

When Korda writes that a leader is like a mirror, he is using a *simile.* When Lincoln writes that the world will not remember, he is using a *metaphor*—actually *personification.* Metaphors, whatever their form, all make a comparison between two items that are not really alike. The writer is making a *figurative comparison,* not a literal one. The writer wants us to think about some ways in which the items are similar. Metaphors state directly or imply the comparison; similes express the comparison using a connecting word; personification always compares a nonhuman item to humans. The exact label for a metaphor is not as important as

- recognizing the use of a figure of speech,
- identifying the two items being compared,
- understanding the point of the comparison, and
- grasping the emotional impact of the figurative comparison.

> **REMEMBER:** Pay attention to each writer's choice of metaphors. Metaphors reveal much about feelings and perceptions of life. And, like connotative words, they affect us emotionally even if we are not aware of their use. Become aware. Be able to "open up"—explain—metaphors you find in your reading.

EXERCISE: Opening Up Metaphors

During World War II, E. B. White, the essayist and writer of children's books, defined the word *democracy* in one of his *New Yorker* columns. His definition contains a series of metaphors. One is: Democracy "is the hole in the stuffed shirt through which the sawdust slowly trickles." We can open up or explain the metaphor this way:

> Just as one can punch a hole in a scarecrow's shirt and discover that there is only sawdust inside, nothing to be impressed by, so the idea of equality in a democracy "punches" a hole in the notion of an aristocratic ruling class and reveals that aristocrats, underneath, are ordinary people, just like you and me.

Here are two more of White's metaphors on democracy. Open up each one in a few sentences.

> Democracy is "the dent in the high hat."
> Democracy is "the score at the beginning of the ninth."

Organization and Examples

Two other elements of writing, organization and choice of examples, also reveal attitude and help to shape the reader's response. When you study a work's organization, ask yourself questions about both placement and volume. Where are these ideas placed? At the beginning or end—the places of greatest emphasis—or in the middle, suggesting that they are less important? With regard to volume, ask yourself, "What parts of the discussion are developed at length? What points are treated only briefly?" *Note:* Sometimes simply counting the number of paragraphs devoted to the different parts of the writer's subject will give you a good understanding of the writer's main idea and purpose in writing.

Repetition

Well-written, unified essays will contain some repetition of key words and phrases. Some writers go beyond this basic strategy and use repetition to produce an effective cadence, like a drum beating in the background, keeping time to the speaker's fist pounding the lectern. In his repetition of the now-famous phrase "I have a dream," Martin Luther King Jr. gives emphasis to his vision of an ideal America. In the following paragraph, a student tried her hand at repetition to give emphasis to her definition of liberty:

> Liberty is having the right to vote and not having other laws which restrict that right; it is having the right to apply to the university of your choice without being rejected because of race. Liberty exists when a gay man has the right to a teaching position and is not released from the position when the news of his orientation is disclosed. Liberty exists when a woman who has been offered a job does not have to decline for lack of access to day care for her children, or when a 16-year-old boy from a ghetto can get an education and is not instead compelled to go to work to support his needy family.

These examples suggest that repetition generally gives weight and seriousness to writing and thus is appropriate when serious issues are being discussed in a forceful style.

Hyperbole, Understatement, and Irony

These three strategies create some form of tension to gain emphasis. Hyperbole overstates:

- "I will love you through all eternity!"

Understatement says less than is meant:

- Coming in soaking wet, you say, "It's a bit damp outside."

Irony creates tension by stating the opposite of what is meant:

- To a teen dressed in torn jeans and a baggy sweatshirt, the parent says, "Dressed for dinner, I see."

Quotation Marks, Italics, and Capital Letters

Several visual techniques can also be used to give special attention to certain words. A writer can place a word or phrase within quotation marks to question its validity or meaning in that context. Ellen Goodman writes, for example:

- I wonder about this when I hear the word "family" added to some politician's speech.

Goodman does not agree with the politician's meaning of the word *family*. The expression *so-called* has the same effect:

- There have been restrictions on the Tibetans' so-called liberty.

Italicizing a key word or phrase or using all caps also gives additional emphasis. Dave Barry, in an essay satirizing "smart" technology, uses all caps for emphasis:

- Do you want appliances that are smarter than you? Of course not. Your appliances should be DUMBER than you, just like your furniture, your pets and your representatives in Congress.

Capitalizing words not normally capitalized has the same effect of giving emphasis. As with exclamation points, writers need to use these strategies sparingly, or the emphasis sought will be lost.

EXERCISES: Recognizing Elements of Style

1. Name the technique or techniques used in each of the following passages. Then briefly explain the idea of each passage.
   a. We are becoming the tools of our tools. (Henry David Thoreau)
   b. The bias and therefore the business of television is to *move* information, not collect it. (Neil Postman)
   c. If guns are outlawed, only the government will have guns. Only the police, the secret police, the military. The hired servants of our rulers. Only the government—and a few outlaws. (Edward Abbey)
   d. Having read all the advice on how to live 900 years, what I think is that eating a tasty meal once again will surely doom me long before I reach 900 while not eating that same meal could very well kill me. It's enough to make you reach for a cigarette! (Russell Baker)
   e. If you are desperate for a quick fix, either legalize drugs or repress the user. If you want a civilized approach, mount a propaganda campaign against drugs. (Charles Krauthammer)
   f. Oddly enough, the greatest scoffers at the traditions of American etiquette, who scorn the rituals of their own society as stupid and stultifying, voice respect for the customs and folklore of Native Americans, less industrialized people, and other societies they find more "authentic" than their own. (Judith Martin)

g. Text is story. Text is event, performance, special effect. Subtext is ideas. It's motive, suggestions, visual implications, subtle comparisons. (Stephen Hunter)

h. This flashy vehicle [the school bus] was as punctual as death: seeing us waiting at the cold curb, it would sweep to a halt, open its mouth, suck the boy in, and spring away with an angry growl. (E. B. White)

2. Read the following essay by Dave Barry. Use the questions that precede and follow the essay to help you determine Barry's attitude toward his subject and to characterize his style.

■ ■

NOW THAT IT'S ALL OVER, LET'S EAT! | DAVE BARRY

A humor columnist for the *Miami Herald* for many years, Dave Barry is syndicated in more than 150 newspapers. He is a Pulitzer Prize winner for his humor columns and is the author of a number of books, including *Dave Barry's Complete Guide to Guys* (2000), a laugh-out-loud look at what guys are thinking, and not thinking, and, with Ridley Pearson, a series of illustrated books for young readers 10 and up. The following column appeared September 6, 2012.

PREREADING QUESTIONS What is Barry's purpose in writing? What does he want to accomplish—besides being funny?

After many standing ovations and much shouting of "whoo," the ¹ Democrats have wrapped up their convention and are heading home, except for Bill Clinton, who is expected to conclude his remarks sometime around Halloween.

So now both major political parties have presented their visions for ² America's future, which can be summarized as follows:

THE DEMOCRATIC VISION: If we elect Mitt Romney and Paul Ryan, the ³ nation is going straight down the toilet.

THE REPUBLICAN VISION: If we reelect Barack Obama and Joe Biden, ⁴ the nation is going straight down the toilet.

And now, at last, the time has come for us, the American people—having ⁵ been presented with these two starkly contrasting philosophies of government at a critical time in our nation's history—to watch football. But first let's take a few minutes to look back on the two conventions, and see what observations we can make.

OBSERVATION ONE: The atmosphere sometimes produces weather. ⁶

You'd think that two political parties teeming with highly informed ⁷ geniuses eager to run the country would already be aware of this fact, but apparently they are not, since the Republicans scheduled their convention in Florida during hurricane season, and the Democrats scheduled their big night for an outdoor stadium in North Carolina in the summer. I am not suggesting here that these geniuses are stupid.

No, wait, I am suggesting that. ⁸

9   OBSERVATION TWO: Street protests are ineffective, by which I mean stupid.

10   For two weeks now, I have watched protesters shouting. They never talk; they always shout, often through bullhorns—at the police, at the media, at each other, at civilian passersby, and sometimes at nothing. I do not believe any of these protesters changed anybody's mind about anything, because—follow me closely—normal people do not like to be shouted at.

11   Normal people also are not inclined to listen receptively to arguments presented by anybody dressed as a giant vagina, or a giant anything else. One night in Tampa, as I was walking to my rental car, a convertible pulled up, and in the back seat, riding parade style, were two people wearing full-body furry pink pig costumes. They told me that they were riding around Tampa at night dressed as pigs to persuade people to stop eating meat. As they explained their views, my reaction was not to think, "They're right! I shall become a vegetarian"! My reaction was a combination of, "These people are insane," and "I could go for some barbecue."

12   OBSERVATION THREE: Political conventions are not as much fun as they used to be.

13   By "fun," I mean, yet again, stupid, but this time in a good way. I'm talking about the days when almost all the delegates wore giant ridiculous hats, and people got off-message, and unscripted things happened, including the occasional fistfight, and the schedule got so screwed up that the presidential nominee had to deliver his acceptance speech at 3:30 a.m. in a haze of cigarette smoke and tear gas.

14   I'm talking about the days when every convention featured "favorite son" candidates—politicians who had absolutely no chance to win, but their state delegations nominated them anyway, purely so they could have big pointless fun celebrations on the convention floor. I still vividly remember watching, on TV, the 1968 Republican convention, during which the Hawaii delegation nominated Sen. Hiram Fong, thereby setting off a wondrously entertaining 20-minute demonstration—a joyful conga line of people weaving around the floor wearing leis and waving signs that said "HI HI Hiram!"

15   That could never happen today. For one thing, Hiram is dead. (Although I would still vote for him.) But the main reason is that nothing remotely frivolous or spontaneous is allowed to happen at conventions anymore. This means that almost all the "excitement" comes from judging how well or poorly a given speaker executed a given speech. Inside the convention bubble, everybody gets very worked up about this; much of what passes for journalism consists of journalists declaring, with journalistic certainty, how a given speaker made them feel.

16   Anyway, the conventions are over. We won't go through this again for another four years. And we have no way of knowing where the nation will be then.

17   No, wait, we do: the toilet.

18   I don't know about you, but I'm ready for some football.

Source: *Miami Herald*, September 6, 2012. Reprinted by permission of Tribune Media Services.

QUESTIONS FOR READING AND REASONING

1. Humor is not a subject; it may be a purpose or a strategy. What is Barry's subject?
2. What is his claim—that is, what point does he want to make about his subject?
3. How would you describe the essay's tone? Does a nonserious tone exclude the possibility of a degree of serious purpose? Explain your answer.

QUESTIONS FOR REFLECTION AND WRITING

4. What passage in Barry's column do you find the funniest? Why?
5. What specific strategies does Barry use to create tone and convey attitude? List, with examples, as many as you can.

WRITING ABOUT STYLE

What does it mean to "do a style analysis"? A style analysis answers the question "How is it written?" Let's think through the steps in preparing a study of a writer's choice and arrangement of language.

Understanding Purpose and Audience

A style analysis is not the place for challenging the ideas of the writer. A style analysis requires the discipline to see how a work has been put together *even if you disagree with the writer's views.* You do not have to agree with a writer to appreciate his or her skill in writing.

If you think about audience in the context of your purpose, you should conclude that a summary of content does not belong in a style analysis. Why? Because we write style analyses for people who have already read the work. Remember, though, that your reader may not know the work in detail, so give examples to illustrate the points of your analysis.

Planning the Essay

First, organize your analysis according to elements of style, not according to the organization of the work. Scrap any thoughts of "hacking" your way through the essay, commenting on the work paragraph by paragraph. This approach invites summary and means that you have not selected an organization that supports your purpose in writing. Think of an essay as like the pie in Figure 2.1. We could divide the pie according to key ideas—if we were summarizing. But we can also carve the pie according to elements of style, the techniques we have discussed in this chapter. This is the general plan you want to follow for your essay.

Choose those techniques you think are most important in creating the writer's attitude and discuss them one at a time. Do not try to include the entire pie; instead, select three or four elements to examine in detail. If you were asked to write an analysis of the Dave Barry column, for example, you might select his

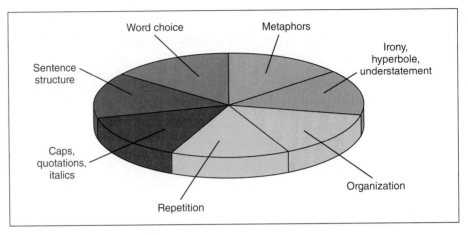

FIGURE 2.1 Analyzing Style

use of quotation marks, hyperbole, and irony. These are three techniques that stand out in Barry's writing.

Drafting the Style Analysis

If you were to select three elements of style, as in the Dave Barry example above, your essay might look something like this:

Paragraph 1: Introduction	1. Attention-getter 2. Author, title, publication information of article/book 3. Brief explanation of author's subject 4. Your thesis—that you will be looking at style
Paragraph 2: First body paragraph	Analysis of quotation marks. (See below for more details on body paragraphs.)
Paragraph 3: Second body paragraph	1. Topic sentence that introduces analysis of hyperbole 2. Three or more examples of hyperbole 3. Explanation of how each example connects to the author's thesis—that is, how the example of hyperbole works to convey attitude. This is your analysis; don't forget it!

Paragraph 4: Third body paragraph	Analysis of irony—with same three parts as listed above.

Paragraph 5: Conclusion	Restate your thesis: We can understand Barry's point through a study of these three elements of his style.

A CHECKLIST FOR REVISION

When revising and polishing your draft, use these questions to complete your essay.

☐ Have I handled all titles correctly?

☐ Have I correctly referred to the author?

☐ Have I used quotation marks correctly when presenting examples of style? (Use the guidelines in Chapter 1 for these first three questions.)

☐ Do I have an accurate, clear presentation of the author's subject and thesis?

☐ Do I have enough examples of each element of style to show my readers that these elements are important?

☐ Have I connected examples to the author's thesis? That is, have I shown my readers how these techniques work to develop the author's attitude?

To reinforce your understanding of style analysis, read the following essay by Ellen Goodman, answer the questions that follow, and then study the student essay that analyzes Goodman's style.

IN PRAISE OF A SNAIL'S PACE | ELLEN GOODMAN

Author of *Close to Home* (1979), *At Large* (1981), and *Keeping Touch* (1985), collections of her essays, Ellen Goodman began as a feature writer for the Boston *Globe* in 1967 and was a syndicated columnist from 1976 until her retirement in 2009. The following column was published August 13, 2005.

PREREADING QUESTIONS Why might someone write in praise of snail mail? What does Goodman mean by "hyperactive technology"?

CASCO BAY, Maine—I arrive at the island post office carrying an artifact 1
from another age. It's a square envelope, handwritten, with a return address that can be found on a map. Inside is a condolence note, a few words of memory and sympathy to a wife who has become a widow. I could have sent these words far more efficiently through e-mail than through this "snail mail." But I am among those who still believe that sympathy is diluted by two-thirds when it arrives over the Internet transom.

2   I would no more send an e-condolence than an e-thank you or an e-wedding invitation. There are rituals you cannot speed up without destroying them. It would be like serving Thanksgiving dinner at a fast-food restaurant.

3   My note goes into the old blue mailbox and I walk home wondering if slowness isn't the only way we pay attention now in a world of hyperactive technology.

4   Weeks ago, a friend lamented the trouble she had communicating with her grown son. It wasn't that her son was out of touch. Hardly. They were connected across miles through e-mail and cell phone, instant-messaging and text-messaging. But she had something serious to say and feared that an e-mail would elicit a reply that said: I M GR8. Was there no way to get undivided attention in the full in-box of his life? She finally chose a letter, a pen on paper, a stamp on envelope.

5   How do you describe the times we live in, so connected and yet fractured? Linda Stone, a former Microsoft techie, characterizes ours as an era of "continuous partial attention." At the extreme end are teenagers instant-messaging while they are talking on the cell phone, downloading music and doing homework. But adults too live with all systems go, interrupted and distracted, scanning everything, multi-technological-tasking everywhere.

Are we having fun yet?

We suffer from the illusion, Stone says, that we can expand our personal 6 bandwidth, connecting to more and more. Instead, we end up overstimulated, overwhelmed and, she adds, unfulfilled. Continuous partial attention inevitably feels like a lack of full attention.

But there are signs of people searching for ways to slow down and listen 7 up. We are told that experienced e-mail users are taking longer to answer, freeing themselves from the tyranny of the reply button. Caller ID is used to find out who we don't have to talk to. And the next "killer ap," they say, will be e-mail software that can triage the important from the trivial.

Meanwhile, at companies where technology interrupts creativity and 8 online contact prevents face-to-face contact, there are no e-mail-free Fridays. At others, there are bosses who require that you check your BlackBerry at the meeting door.

If a ringing cell phone once signaled your importance to a client, now that 9 client is impressed when you turn off the cell phone. People who stayed connected 10 ways, 24-7, now pride themselves on "going dark."

"People hunger for more attention," says Stone, whose message has been 10 welcomed even at a conference of bloggers. "Full attention will be the aphrodisiac of the future."

Indeed, at the height of our romance with e-mail, "You've Got Mail" was 11 the cinematic love story. Now e-mail brings less thrill—"who will be there?" And more dread—"how many are out there?" Today's romantics are couples who leave their laptops behind on the honeymoon.

As for text-message flirtation, a young woman ended hers with a man who 12 wrote, "C U L8R." He didn't have enough time to spell out Y-O-U?

Slowness guru Carl Honore began "In Praise of Slowness" after he found 13 himself seduced by a book of condensed classic fairy tales to read to his son. One-minute bedtime stories? We are relearning that paying attention briefly is as impossible as painting a landscape from a speeding car.

It is not just my trip to the mailbox that has brought this to mind. I come 14 here each summer to stop hurrying. My island is no Brigadoon: WiFi is on the way, and some people roam the island with their cell phones, looking for a hot spot. But I exchange the Internet for the country road.

Georgia O'Keeffe once said that it takes a long time to see a flower. No 15 technology can rush the growth of the leeks in the garden. All the speed in the Internet cannot hurry the healing of a friend's loss. Paying attention is the coin of this realm.

Sometimes, a letter becomes the icon of an old-fashioned new fashion. 16 And sometimes, in this technological whirlwind, it takes a piece of snail mail to carry the stamp of authenticity.

1. What has Goodman just done? How does this action serve the author as a lead-in to her subject?
2. What is Goodman's main idea or thesis?
3. What examples illustrate the problem the author sees in our times? What evidence does Goodman present to suggest that people want to change the times?
4. What general solutions does Goodman suggest?

5. How do the details at the beginning and end of the essay contribute to Goodman's point? Write a paragraph answer to this question. Then consider: Which one of the different responses to reading does your paragraph illustrate?
6. The author describes our time as one of "continuous partial attention." Does this phrase sum up our era? Why or why not? If you agree, do you think this is a problem? Why or why not?
7. For what kinds of research projects would this essay be useful? List several possibilities to discuss with classmates.

STUDENT ESSAY

A Convincing Style

James Goode

Ellen Goodman's essay, "In Praise of a Snail's Pace," is not, of course, about snails. It is about a way of communicating that our society has largely lost or ignored: the capability to pay full attention in communications and relationships. Her prime example of this is the "snail mail" letter, used for cards, invitations, and condolences. Anything really worth saying, she argues, must be written fully and sent by mail to make us pay attention. Goodman's easy, winning style of word choice and metaphor persuades us to agree with her point, a point also backed up by the logic of her examples.

"In Praise of a Snail's Pace" starts innocently. The author is merely taking a walk to the post office with a letter, surely nothing unusual. But as Goodman describes her letter, she reveals her belief that "snail mail" is a much more authentic way of sharing serious tidings than a message that "arrives over the

Internet transom." The letter, with its "square" envelope and "handwritten" address, immediately sounds more personal than the ultramodern electronic message. The words have guided the reader's thinking. Goodman also describes our times as "connected yet fractured" and us as living in a world of "continuous partial attention." "Being connected" becomes synonymous by the end of the essay with "not paying attention." Word choice is crucial here. The author creates in the reader's mind a dichotomy: be fast and false, or slow down and mean it.

Goodman's metaphors make a point, too. "A picture is worth a thousand words" and the pictures created by the words here further the fast/slow debate. The idea that sending an e-condolence would be "like serving Thanksgiving dinner at a fast-food restaurant" gives an instant image of the worthlessness of an e-mail condolence note. The mother trying to get attention in the "full in-box" of her son's life shows us that a divided and distracted brain answering five hundred e-mails cannot be expected to concentrate on any of them. Again, trying to pay attention briefly is just as impossible as "painting a landscape from a speeding car." The "tyranny" of the reply button must be overcome by our "going dark." Getting away from our electronic world, Goodman reasons, helps us restore meaning to what we do.

But while the reader listens to clever words and paints memorable mind pictures, any resistance is worn away with a steady stream of examples. From the author mailing an envelope to Georgia O'Keeffe's remark that it takes a long time to see a flower, example after example supports her view. The mother wishing for the total attention of her son and the office workers' turning off cell phones and computers have already been mentioned. Linda Stone, a former Microsoft techie and a credible authority on modern communications and their effects on users, is quoted several times. Goodman notes with excellent effect that Stone's message has been received even at a conference of bloggers—if the most connected group out there supports this, why shouldn't everyone else? The author herself comes to an island every year to escape the mad hurry of the business world by wandering country roads. These examples build until the reader is convinced that snail mail is the mark of authenticity and connectedness.

"In Praise of a Snail's Pace" is a thoughtful essay that takes aim at the notion that one person can do it all and still find meaning. The "connected" person is in so much of a hurry that he or she must not be really interested in much of anything. By showing "interrupted and distracted" readers that "no technology can rush the growth of the leeks in the garden," the author makes a convincing case for the real effectiveness of written mail. Whether through word choice, metaphor, or example, Ellen Goodman's message comes through: Slow down and send some "snail mail" and be really connected for once.

ANALYZING TWO OR MORE SOURCES

Scientists examining the same set of facts do not always draw the same conclusions; neither do historians and biographers agree on the significance of the same documents. How do we recognize and cope with these disparities? As critical readers we analyze what we read, pose questions, and refuse to believe everything we find in print or online. To develop these skills in recognizing differences, instructors frequently ask students to contrast the views of two or more writers. In psychology class, for example, you may be asked to contrast the views of Sigmund Freud and John B. Watson on child development. In a communications course, you may be asked to contrast the moderator styles of two talk-show hosts. We can examine differences in content or presentation, or both. Here are guidelines for preparing a contrast of sources.

GUIDELINES for Preparing a Contrast Essay

- **Work with sources that have something in common.** Think about the context for each, that is, each source's subject and purpose. (There is little sense in contrasting a textbook chapter, for example, with a TV talk show because their contexts are so different.)
- **Read actively to understand the content of the two sources.** Tape films, radio, or TV shows so that you can listen/view them several times, just as you would read a written source more than once.

- **Analyze for differences, focusing on your purpose in contrasting.** If you are contrasting the ideas of two writers, for example, then your analysis will focus on ideas, not on writing style. To explore differences in two news accounts, you may want to consider all of the following: the impact of placement in the newspaper/magazine, accompanying photographs or graphics, length of each article, what is covered in each article, and writing styles. Prepare a list of specific differences.
- **Organize your contrast.** It is usually best to organize by points of difference. If you write first about one source and then about the other, the ways that the sources differ may not be clear for readers. Take the time to plan an organization that clearly reveals your contrast purpose in writing. To illustrate, a paper contrasting the writing styles of two authors can be organized according to the following pattern:

Introduction: Introduce your topic and establish your purpose to contrast styles of writer A and writer B.

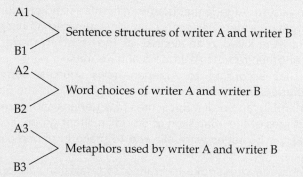

Conclusion: Explain the effect of the differences in style of the writers.

- **Illustrate and discuss each of the points of difference for each of the sources.** Provide examples and explain the impact of the differences.
- **Always write for an audience who may be familiar with your general topic but not with the specific sources you are discussing.** Be sure to provide adequate context (names, titles of works, etc.).

EXERCISE: Analyzing Two Sources

Whenever two people choose to write on the same topic, there are bound to be differences in choice of specifics and emphasis—as well as differences in political, social, or philosophical perspective. So, we need to read widely and not settle for only one source for our information. When reading newspapers, journals of opinion, and blogs, we need to become aware of the "leaning" or "slant" of each source.

Read the following two articles on the taking of hostages at an Algerian oil field by jihadists and the death of some hostages and some kidnappers when Algerian armed forces sought to free the hostages, an event that was covered by all news outlets as the story unfolded. Analyze each article for possible differences on the following points: impact of any visuals, length of treatment, differences in key points about the story, differences in how the issue is framed—in the context provided—and differences in style and tone.

Bring detailed notes to class for discussion, or write an analysis that contrasts the two articles on several key points of difference.

ALGERIAN HOSTAGE CRISIS HEIGHTENS AS SCORES ARE REPORTED DEAD

ARTHUR BRIGHT

This article was posted January 17, 2013, by the *Christian Science Monitor* at CSMonitor.com.

1   Dozens of hostages, both Algerian and foreign, have reportedly escaped the natural gas field in eastern Algeria that Islamic militants seized on Monday, but as the hostage situation enters its second day, an estimated 35 hostages and 15 hostage-takers were killed in an airstrike as they tried to move from one plant location to another, reports Al Jazeera and Reuters.

2   Reuters reports that according to Algerian news sources, some 30 Algerians and 15 foreigners have escaped the natural gas field in the Sahara Desert near the Algerian-Libyan border. But scores of Algerians and dozens of foreigners remain hostages of the "Battalion of Blood" militant group, according to statements that the hostages were allowed to make in phone calls to news outlets.

3   An unidentified hostage who spoke to France 24 television said prisoners were being forced to wear explosive belts. Their captors were heavily armed and had threatened to blow up the plant if the Algerian army tried to storm it.

4   Two hostages, identified as British and Irish, spoke to Al Jazeera television and called on the Algerian army to withdraw from the area to avoid casualties.

5   "We are receiving care and good treatment from the kidnappers. The (Algerian) army did not withdraw and they are firing at the camp," the British man said. "There are around 150 Algerian hostages. We say to everybody that negotiations is a sign of strength and will spare many any loss of life."

6   Reuters adds that US, French, and British officials did not confirm the numbers of their respective citizens who were being held by the terrorist group.

7   Although the raid on the field comes just days after the start of France's intervention in Mali, it is unlikely the attack was a spur-of-the-moment response to events in Mali. Helima Croft, a Barclays Capital senior geopolitical strategist, told the *New York Times* that "this type of attack had to have advanced planning. It's not an easy target of opportunity."

HOSTAGES REPORTEDLY DEAD IN ALGERIAN OIL FIELD SIEGE | JAMIE DETTMER

The kidnapping of oil workers—including several Americans—on Algerian soil by jihadists has apparently ended in tragedy.

This article also appeared on January 17, 2013, posted at *The Daily Beast*.

1 At least half-a-dozen Western oil workers including Americans held hostage since Wednesday by heavily armed al-Qaeda-linked Islamists at a natural gas complex in eastern Algeria died today when Algerian government forces mounted an attack to free them, say the militants holding them.

2 Amid confusing reports, the casualties at the sprawling Amenas gas complex 800 miles southeast of Algiers are being put at anything from six hostages to 34, including Algerian workers. Several captors, including the kidnappers' ground leader, Abou El Baraa, are said to have died, too, in the mission mounted by Algerian security forces that involved low-flying helicopter assaults.

A private security source working for oil companies in Algeria told *The Daily Beast* the operation to retake the facility was "messy." He added: "The Algerian soldiers were firing pretty indiscriminately. This wasn't a surgical operation."

3 A spokesman for the British Foreign Office confirmed an "ongoing military operation" against the hostage takers but couldn't verify whether there'd been casualties. Nor would he comment on reports that about 15 foreign hostages had escaped earlier from the gas field near the Libyan border that's run by BP, the Norwegian company Statoil, and Algeria's state oil agency.

4 The Algerian operation mounted to break the Sahara Desert siege came as security experts started to pin down the motives behind the seizing of the gas field by militants loyal to the notorious one-eyed Jihadist warlord, Mokhtar Belmokhtar, who is nicknamed variously "The Uncatchable"—he has been reported killed several times—or "Mr. Marlboro" for his involvement in cigarette smuggling that has helped to finance his operations.

5 Militants seized the facility on Wednesday, saying the attack was in response to France's military intervention in neighboring Mali, where French Foreign legionnaires have joined Malian government troops in halting advances by Islamists who have taken over much of northern Mali.

6 But terrorism analysts say Belmokhtar had more than one objective in mind when he ordered his fighters in a well-planned operation to seize the facility and secure Western hostages, including boosting his own standing among jihadists after he was recently passed over for promotion within al-Qaeda.

7 An Algerian native with a storied two-decade history of armed militancy, Belmokhtar was one of the leading figures of al-Qaeda in the Islamic Maghreb (AQIM) and commanded a highly effective cell of fighters in north Mali until October, when Yahya Abou El Hamame was appointed over him as AQIM's "Emir of the Sahel."

8 "He has a reputation as an autonomous operator," says Stephen Ellis of the African Studies Center at the University of Leiden in The Netherlands. "He is well known as going his own way both when it comes to his criminal and smuggling activities and his militancy. In the Sahel the various jihadist groups are very fissiparous. They split and re-form regularly only to split again."

Mokhtar Belmokhtar

9   Some of the differences that cause division are not only connected to disputes over terrorism strategy or ideology. Leaders clash over the spoils that
can be made—from ransoms paid for the release of Western hostages to the
distribution of profits from smuggling guns, drugs, and tobacco.

10   Following his being passed over for promotion, Belmokhtar left the
al-Qaeda franchise to set up his own jihadi outfit, naming it Khaled Abu-al-
Abbas Brigaed or al-Muwaqqu'un bil-Dima (Those Who Sign in Blood).

. . .

11   One of his associates, Oumar Ould Hamaha, told the Associated Press in
the autumn that they were leaving al-Qaeda "so that we can better operate in
the field. . . . We want to enlarge our zone of operation throughout the entire
Sahara, going from Niger through to Chad and Burkina Faso."

12   Born in Ghardaia, Algeria, in 1972, Belmokhtar traveled to Afghanistan as a
19-year-old to join training camps run by jihadists, returning in 1992 to his homeland,
joining first Algeria's Islamic Armed Group (GIA) then helping to set up the Salafist
Group for Preaching and combat (GSPC) that subsequently merged with al-Qaeda.

13   Belmokhtar is reported to be in alliance now with another former AQIM
fighter Hamadou Ould Khairou, a Mauritanian that U.S. security sources say is
involved in the drug trade.

. . .

14   "In my opinion, even if Belmokhtar uses the slogan of the French attack in
Mali, this is not his real intention," said Ely Karmon, a Senior Research Scholar
at the Institute for Counter-Terrorism at the Interdisciplinary Center in Herzliya,
Israel. "It is motivated by money."

15   Last month, the Signed-in-Blood brigade warned against the West trying
to halt the Islamist takeover of northern Mali. "We will respond forcefully; we
promise we will follow you to your homes and you will feel pain and we will
attack your interests," warned the group.

FOR READING AND ANALYSIS

THE "F WORD" | FIROOZEH DUMAS

Born in Iran, Firoozeh Dumas moved to California when she was seven, returned to Iran with her family for two years, and then came back to California. She attended the University of California at Berkeley, married, and has three children. Initially she started to write stories for her children. These were developed into *Funny in Farsi: A Memoir of Growing Up Iranian in America* (2003), from which the following excerpt is taken. *Laughing Without an Accent* was followed in 2008.

PREREADING QUESTIONS Based on her title, what did you first think this work would be about? How does the information above help you to adjust your thinking?

My cousin's name, Farbod, means "Greatness."   1

When he moved to America, all the kids called him "Farthead." My brother   2
Farshid ("He Who Enlightens") became "Fartshit." The name of my friend
Neggar means "Beloved," although it can be more accurately translated as
"She Whose Name Almost Incites Riots." Her brother Arash ("Giver") initially
couldn't understand why every time he'd say his name, people would laugh
and ask him if it itched.

All of us immigrants knew that moving to America would be fraught with   3
challenges, but none of us thought that our names would be such an obstacle.
How could our parents have ever imagined that someday we would end up in a
country where monosyllabic names reign supreme, a land where "William" is
shortened to "Bill," where "Susan" becomes "Sue," and "Richard" somehow
evolves into "Dick"? America is a great country, but nobody without a mask and
a cape has a z in his name. And have Americans ever realized the great scope of
the guttural sounds they're missing? Okay, so it has to do with linguistic roots,
but I do believe this would be a richer country if all Americans could do a little
tongue aerobics and learn to pronounce "kh," a sound more commonly associated in this culture with phlegm, or "gh," the sound usually made by actors in the
final moments of a choking scene. It's like adding a few new spices to the kitchen
pantry. Move over, cinnamon and nutmeg, make way for cardamom and sumac.

Exotic analogies aside, having a foreign name in this land of Joes and Marys   4
is a pain in the spice cabinet. When I was twelve, I decided to simplify my life by
adding an American middle name. This decision serves as proof that sometimes simplifying one's life in the short run only complicates it in the long run.

My name, Firoozeh, chosen by my mother, means "Turquoise" in Persian.   5
In America, it means "Unpronounceable" or "I'm Not Going to Talk to You
Because I Cannot Possibly Learn Your Name and I Just Don't Want to Have to
Ask You Again and Again Because You'll Think I'm Dumb or You Might Get
Upset or Something." My father, incidentally, had wanted to name me Sara. I
do wish he had won that argument.

To strengthen my decision to add an American name, I had just finished   6
fifth grade in Whittier, where all the kids incessantly called me "Ferocious."
That summer, my family moved to Newport Beach, where I looked forward to

starting a new life. I wanted to be a kid with a name that didn't draw so much attention, a name that didn't come with a built-in inquisition as to when and why I had moved to America and how was it that I spoke English without an accent and was I planning on going back and what did I think of America?

7   My last name didn't help any. I can't mention my maiden name, because:

8   "Dad, I'm writing a memoir."

9   "Great! Just don't mention our name."

10   Suffice it to say that, with eight letters, including a *z*, and four syllables, my last name is as difficult and foreign as my first. My first and last name together generally served the same purpose as a high brick wall. There was one exception to this rule. In Berkeley, and only in Berkeley, my name drew people like flies to baklava. These were usually people named Amaryllis or Chrysanthemum, types who vacationed in Costa Rica and to whom lentils described a type of burger. These folks were probably not the pride of Poughkeepsie, but they were refreshingly nonjudgmental.

11   When I announced to my family that I wanted to add an American name, they reacted with their usual laughter. Never one to let mockery or good judgment stand in my way, I proceeded to ask for suggestions. My father suggested "Fifi." Had I had a special affinity for French poodles or been considering a career in prostitution, I would've gone with that one. My mom suggested "Farah," a name easier than "Firoozeh" yet still Iranian. Her reasoning made sense, except that Farrah Fawcett was at the height of her popularity and I didn't want to be associated with somebody whose poster hung in every postpubescent boy's bedroom. We couldn't think of any American names beginning with *F*, so we moved on to *J*, the first letter of our last name. I don't know why we limited ourselves to names beginning with my initials, but it made sense at that moment, perhaps by the logic employed moments before bungee jumping. I finally chose the name "Julie" mainly for its simplicity. My brothers, Farid and Farshid, thought that adding an American name was totally stupid. They later became Fred and Sean.

12   That same afternoon, our doorbell rang. It was our new next-door neighbor, a friendly girl my age named Julie. She asked me my name and after a moment of hesitation, I introduced myself as Julie. "What a coincidence!" she said. I didn't mention that I had been Julie for only half an hour.

13   Thus I started sixth grade with my new, easy name and life became infinitely simpler. People actually remembered my name, which was an entirely refreshing new sensation. All was well until the Iranian Revolution, when I found myself with a new set of problems. Because I spoke English without an accent and was known as Julie, people assumed I was American. This meant that I was often privy to their real feelings about those "damn I-raynians." It was like having those X-ray glasses that let you see people naked, except that what I was seeing was far uglier than people's underwear. It dawned on me that these people would have probably never invited me to their house had they known me as Firoozeh. I felt like a fake.

14   When I went to college, I eventually went back to using my real name. All was well until I graduated and started looking for a job. Even though I had graduated with honors from UC–Berkeley, I couldn't get a single interview. I was guilty of being a humanities major, but I began to suspect that there was more to

my problems. After three months of rejections, I added "Julie" to my résumé. Call it coincidence, but the job offers started coming in. Perhaps it's the same kind of coincidence that keeps African Americans from getting cabs in New York.

Once I got married, my name became Julie Dumas. I went from having an 15 identifiably "ethnic" name to having ancestors who wore clogs. My family and non-American friends continued calling me Firoozeh, while my coworkers and American friends called me Julie. My life became one big knot, especially when friends who knew me as Julie met friends who knew me as Firoozeh. I felt like those characters in soap operas who have an evil twin. The two, of course, can never be in the same room, since they're played by the same person, a struggling actress who wears a wig to play one of the twins and dreams of moving on to bigger and better roles. I couldn't blame my mess on a screen writer; it was my own doing.

I decided to untangle the knot once and for all by going back to my real 16 name. By then, I was a stay-at-home mom, so I really didn't care whether people remembered my name or gave me job interviews. Besides, most of the people I dealt with were in diapers and were in no position to judge. I was also living in Silicon Valley, an area filled with people named Rajeev, Avishai, and Insook.

Every once in a while, though, somebody comes up with a new permutation 17 and I am once again reminded that I am an immigrant with a foreign name. I recently went to have blood drawn for a physical exam. The waiting room for blood work at our local medical clinic is in the basement of the building, and no matter how early one arrives for an appointment, forty coughing, wheezing people have gotten there first. Apart from reading *Golf Digest* and *Popular Mechanics,* there isn't much to do except guess the number of contagious diseases represented in the windowless room. Every ten minutes, a name is called and everyone looks to see which cough matches that name. As I waited patiently, the receptionist called out, "Fritzy, Fritzy!" Everyone looked around, but no one stood up. Usually, if I'm waiting to be called by someone who doesn't know me, I will respond to just about any name starting with an *F.* Having been called Froozy, Frizzy, Fiorucci, and Frooz and just plain "Uhhhh . . . ," I am highly accommodating. I did not, however, respond to "Fritzy" because there is, as far as I know, no *t* in my name. The receptionist tried again, "Fritzy, Fritzy DumbAss." As I stood up to this most linguistically original version of my name, I could feel all eyes upon me. The room was momentarily silent as all of these sick people sat united in a moment of gratitude for their own names.

Despite a few exceptions, I have found that Americans are now far more 18 willing to learn new names, just as they're far more willing to try new ethnic foods. Of course, some people just don't like to learn. One mom at my children's school adamantly refused to learn my "impossible" name and instead settled on calling me "F Word." She was recently transferred to New York where, from what I've heard, she might meet an immigrant or two and, who knows, she just might have to make some room in her spice cabinet.

QUESTIONS FOR READING

1. What happened when the author changed her name to Julie?
2. What happened when she sought a job after college, using her original name?
3. When did she decide to use only her original name?
4. When Dumas is called at the medical clinic, what does she think the other patients are feeling?

QUESTIONS FOR REASONING AND ANALYSIS

5. Although this essay may not have the "feel" of an argument, it nonetheless makes a point. What is Dumas's claim?
6. What has changed in America since her arrival as a young girl? Is the change complete? What would she like to see Americans learn to do?
7. What writing strategies are noteworthy in creating her style? Illustrate with examples.

QUESTIONS FOR REFLECTION AND WRITING

8. How much effort do you make to pronounce names correctly? Why is it important to get a person's name right?
9. Have you had the experience of Americans impatient with the pronunciation of your name—or just refusing to get it right? If so, what has been your response?
10. What might be some of the reasons Americans have trouble with the pronunciation of ethnic names—whether the names belong to foreign nationals or to ethnic Americans? Reflect on possible causes.
11. What are the advantages of facing the world with humor?

LOVE TO READ, KIDS? YOUR TIME IS ALMOST UP | ALEXANDRA PETRI

A graduate of Harvard University, Alexandra Petri writes the ComPost blog, a "lighter take" on current issues, and is an op-ed columnist for the *Washington Post*. She wrote for the *Harvard Crimson* while at college and has appeared on Boston's Comedy Studio and Comedy Connection. The following column was published December 8, 2012.

PREREADING QUESTIONS Does the author's title make you curious about her subject? What do you expect her to be writing about?

1   Forget *The Catcher in the Rye.*

2   New Common Core standards (which affect 46 states and the District) will require that, by 2014, 70 percent of high school seniors' reading assignments be nonfiction. Some suggested texts include "FedViews" by the Federal Reserve Bank of San Francisco, the EPA's "Recommended Levels of Insulation" and "Invasive Plant Inventory" by California's Invasive Plant Council.

Forget *Huckleberry Finn* and *Moby Dick*. Bring out the woodchipping 3
manuals!

I like reading. I love reading. I always have. I read recreationally still. I read 4
on buses, in planes, while crossing streets. My entire apartment is covered in
books. And now, through some strange concatenation of circumstances, I
write for a living.

And it's all because, as a child, my parents took the time to read me 4
"Recommended Levels of Insulation."

Oh. "Recommended Levels of Insulation." That was always my favorite, 6
although "Invasive Plant Inventory" was a close second. (What phrases in literature or life will ever top the rich resonance of its opening line? "The
Inventory categorizes plants as High, Moderate, or Limited, reflecting the level
of each species' negative ecological impact in California. Other factors, such
as economic impact or difficulty of management, are not included in this
assessment." "Call me Ishmael" has nothing on it!)

"It is important to note that even Limited species are invasive and should 7
be of concern to land managers," I frequently tell myself in moments of crisis.
"Although the impact of each plant varies regionally, its rating represents
cumulative impacts statewide." How true that is, even today.

My dog-eared copy of "Recommended Levels of Insulation" still sits on 8
my desk. That was where I first learned the magic of literature.

"Insulation levels are specified by R-Value. R-Value is a measure of insula- 9
tion's ability to resist heat traveling through it." What authority in that
sentence!

And then came the table of insulation values. I shudder every time that 10
table appears. It is one of the great villains in the history of the English language. Uriah Heep and Captain Ahab can't hold a candle to it. In fact, I do not
know who these people are. I have never read about them.

I do remember curling up with "Recommended Levels of Insulation" and 11
reading it over and over again. It was this that drove me to pursue writing as a
career—the hope one day of crafting a sentence that sang the way "Drill holes
in the sheathing and blow insulation into the empty wall cavity before install-
ing the new siding" sings.

Look, I was an English major, so I may be biased. But life is full of enough 12
instruction manuals.

The best way to understand what words can do is to see them in their 13
natural habitat, not constrained in the dull straitjackets of legalese and regula-
tionish and manualect. It's like saying the proper way of encountering puppies
is in puppy mills. Words in regulations and manuals have been mangled and
tortured and bent into unnatural positions, and the later you have to discover
such cruelty, the better.

The people behind the core have sought to defend it, saying that this 14
change is not meant to supplant literature. This increased emphasis on nonfiction would not be a concern if the core worked the way it was supposed to,
with teachers in other disciplines like math and science assigning the hard
technical texts that went along with their subjects.

15   But teachers worry that this will not happen. Principals seem to be having trouble comprehending the requirement themselves. Besides, the other teachers are too busy, well, teaching their subjects, to inflict technical manuals on their students, and they may expect the English department to pick up the slack. Hence the feared great Purge of Literature.

16   The core has good intentions, but it will be vital to make sure the execution is as good, or we will head down the road usually paved with good intentions. There, in the ninth circle, students who would otherwise have been tearing through Milton and Shakespeare with great excitement are forced to come home hugging manuals of Exotic Plants.

17   All in all, this is a great way to make the kids who like reading hate reading.

QUESTIONS FOR READING

1. What event has prompted Petri to write?
2. How does the author describe the language of manuals?
3. How do the Core creators defend the new requirements?
4. What does Petri think will happen?

QUESTIONS FOR REASONING AND ANALYSIS

5. What is Petri's thesis—that is, the claim of her argument?
6. How would you describe the essay's tone? Is it appropriate to say that there is more than one? Explain.
7. Analyze the author's style: What strategies does she use? Are they effective? Why or why not?

QUESTIONS FOR REFLECTING AND WRITING

8. What is your reaction to the new Core standards? Is it important for students to know how to read nonfiction? Are manuals a good choice to develop this skill? Explain your views.
9. Should students read great works of literature throughout middle and high school? If yes, why? If no, why not?

SUGGESTIONS FOR DISCUSSION AND WRITING

1. Analyze the style of one of the essays from Section 5 of this text. Do not comment on every element of style; select several elements that seem to characterize the writer's style and examine them in detail. Remember that style analyses are written for an audience familiar with the work, so summary is not necessary.

2. Many of the authors included in this text have written books that you will find in your library. Select one that interests you, read it, and prepare a review of it that synthesizes summary, analysis, and evaluation. Prepare a review of about 300 words; assume that the book has just been published.

3. Choose two newspaper and/or magazine articles that differ in their discussion of the same person, event, or product. You may select two different articles on a person in the news, two different accounts of a news event, an advertisement and a *Consumer Reports* analysis of the same product, or two reviews of a book or movie. Analyze differences in both content and presentation and then consider why the two accounts differ. Organize by points of difference and write to an audience not necessarily familiar with the articles.

4. Choose a recently scheduled public event (the Super Bowl, the Olympics, a presidential election, the Academy Award presentations, the premiere of a new television series) and find several articles written before and several after the event. First compare articles written after the event to see if they agree factually. If not, decide which article appears to be more accurate and why. Then examine the earlier material and decide which was the most and which the least accurate. Write an essay in which you explain the differences in speculation before the event and why you think these differences exist. Your audience will be aware of the event but not necessarily aware of the articles you are studying.

The World of Argument

CHAPTER 3

Understanding the Basics of Argument

CUL DE SAC   **BY RICHARD THOMPSON**

READ: What is the situation? What is the reaction of the younger children? What does the older boy try to do?

REASON: Why is the older boy frustrated?

REFLECT/WRITE: What can happen to those who lack scientific knowledge?

In this section we will explore the processes of thinking logically and analyzing issues to reach informed judgments. Remember: Mature people do not need to agree on all issues to respect one another's good sense, but they do have little patience with uninformed or illogical statements masquerading as argument.

CHARACTERISTICS OF ARGUMENT

Argument Is Conversation with a Goal

When you enter into an argument (as speaker, writer, or reader), you become a participant in an ongoing debate about an issue. Since you are probably not the first to address the issue, you need to be aware of the ways that the issue has been debated by others and then seek to advance the conversation, just as you would if you were having a more casual conversation with friends. If the time of the movie is set, the discussion now turns to whose car to take or where to meet. If you were to just repeat the time of the movie, you would add nothing useful to the conversation. Also, if you were to change the subject to a movie you saw last week, you would annoy your friends by not offering useful information or showing that you valued the current conversation. Just as with your conversation about the movie, you want your argument to stay focused on the issue, to respect what others have already contributed, and to make a useful addition to our understanding of the topic.

Argument Takes a Stand on an Arguable Issue

A meaningful argument focuses on a debatable issue. We usually do not argue about facts. "Professor Jones's American literature class meets at 10:00 on Mondays" is not arguable. It is either true or false. We can check the schedule of classes to find out. (Sometimes the facts change; new facts replace old ones.) We also do not debate personal preferences for the simple reason that they are just that—personal. If the debate is about the appropriateness of boxing as a sport, for you to declare that you would rather play tennis is to fail to advance the conversation. You have expressed a personal preference, interesting perhaps, but not relevant to the debate.

Argument Uses Reasons and Evidence

Some arguments merely "look right." That is, conclusions are drawn from facts, but the facts are not those that actually support the assertion, or the conclusion is not the only or best explanation of those facts. To shape convincing arguments, we need more than an array of facts. We need to think critically, to analyze the issue, to see relationships, to weigh evidence. We need to avoid the temptation to "argue" from emotion only, or to believe that just stating our opinion is the same thing as building a sound argument.

Argument Incorporates Values

Arguments are based not just on reason and evidence but also on the beliefs and values we hold and think that our audience may hold as well. In a reasoned debate, you want to make clear the values that you consider relevant to the argument. In an editorial defending the sport of boxing, one editor wrote that boxing "is a sport because the world has not yet become a place in which the qualities that go into excellence in boxing [endurance, agility, courage] have no value" (*Washington Post,* February 5, 1983). But James J. Kilpatrick also appeals to values when he argues, in an editorial critical of boxing, that we should not want to live in a society "in which deliberate brutality is legally authorized and publicly applauded" (*Washington Post,* December 7, 1982). Observe, however, the high level of seriousness in the appeal to values. Neither writer settles for a simplistic personal preference: "Boxing is exciting," or "Boxing is too violent."

Argument Recognizes the Topic's Complexity

Much false reasoning (the logical fallacies discussed in Chapter 6) results from a writer's oversimplifying an issue. A sound argument begins with an understanding that most issues are terribly complicated. The wise person approaches such ethical concerns as abortion or euthanasia or such public policy issues as tax cuts or trade agreements with the understanding that there are many philosophical, moral, and political issues that complicate discussions of these topics. Recognizing an argument's complexity may also lead us to an understanding that there can be more than one "right" position. The thoughtful arguer respects the views of others, seeks common ground when possible, and often chooses a conciliatory approach.

THE SHAPE OF ARGUMENT: WHAT WE CAN LEARN FROM ARISTOTLE

Still one of the best ways to understand the basics of argument is to reflect on what the Greek philosopher Aristotle describes as the three "players" in any argument: the *writer* (or *speaker*), the *argument itself,* and the *reader* (or *audience*). Aristotle also reminds us that the occasion or "situation" (*kairos*) is important in understanding and evaluating an argument. Let's examine each part of this model of argument.

Ethos (about the Writer/Speaker)

It seems logical to begin with *ethos* because without this player we have no argument. We could, though, end with the writer because Aristotle asserts that this player in any argument is the most important. No argument, no matter how logical, no matter how appealing to one's audience, can succeed if the audience rejects the arguer's credibility, his or her *ethical* qualities.

Think how often in political contests those running attack their opponent's character rather than the candidate's programs. Remember the smear campaign against Obama—he is (or was) a Muslim and therefore unfit to be president, the first point an error of fact, the second point an emotional appeal to voters' fears. Candidates try these smear tactics, even without evidence, because they understand that every voter they can convince of an opponent's failure of *ethos* is a citizen who will vote for them.

Many American voters want to be assured that a candidate is patriotic, religious (but of course not fanatic!), a loyal spouse, and a loving parent. At times, we even lose sight of important differences in positions as we focus on the person instead. But, this tells us how much an audience values their sense of the arguer's credibility. During his campaign for reelection, after the Watergate break-in, Nixon was attacked with the line "Would you buy a used car from this guy?" (In defense of used-car salespeople, not all are untrustworthy!)

Logos (about the Logic of the Argument)

Logos refers to the argument itself—to the assertion and the support for it. Aristotle maintains that part of an arguer's appeal to his or her audience lies in the logic of the argument and the quality of the support provided. Even the most credible of writers will not move thoughtful audiences with inadequate evidence or sloppy reasoning. Yes, "arguments" that appeal to emotions, to our needs and fantasies, will work for some audiences—look at the success of advertising, for example. But, if you want to present a serious claim to critical readers, then you must pay attention to your argument. Paying attention means not only having good reasons but also organizing them clearly. Your audience needs to see *how* your evidence supports your point. Consider the following argument in opposition to the war on Iraq.

> War can be justified only as a form of self-defense. To initiate a war, we need to be able to show that our first strike was necessary as a form of self-defense. The Bush administration argued that Iraq had weapons of mass destruction and intended to use them against us. Responding to someone's "intent" to do harm is always a difficult judgment call. But, in this case, there were no weapons of mass destruction so there could not have been any intent to harm the United States, or at least none that was obvious and immediate. Thus we must conclude that this war was not the right course of action for the United States.

You may disagree (many will) with this argument's assertion, but you can respect the writer's logic, the clear connecting of one reason to the next. One good way to strengthen your credibility is to get respect for clear reasoning.

Pathos (about Appeals to the Audience)

Argument implies an audience, those whose views we want to influence in some way. Aristotle labels this player *pathos*, the Greek word for both passion and suffering (hence *pathology*, the study of disease). Arguers need to be aware of their audience's feelings on the issue, the attitudes and values that will affect their response to the argument. There are really two questions arguers must answer: "How can I engage my audience's interest?" and "How can I engage their sympathy for my position?"

Some educators and health experts believe that childhood obesity is a major problem in the United States. Other Americans are much more focused on the economy—or their own careers. Al Gore is passionately concerned about the harmful effects of global warming; others, though increasingly fewer, think he lacks sufficient evidence of environmental degradation. How does a physician raise reader interest in childhood obesity? How does Gore convince doubters that we need to reduce carbon emissions? To prepare an effective argument, we need always to plan our approach with a clear vision of how best to connect to a specific audience—one which may or may not agree with our interests or our position.

Kairos (about the Occasion or Situation)

While *ethos, logos,* and *pathos* create the traditional three-part communication model, Aristotle adds another term to enhance our understanding of any argument "moment." The term *kairos* refers to the occasion for the argument, the situation that we are in. What does this moment call for from us? Is the lunch table the appropriate time and place for an argument with your coworker over her failure to meet a deadline that is part of a joint project? You have just received a 65 on your history test; is this the best time to e-mail your professor to protest

Personal confrontation at a business meeting: Not cool.

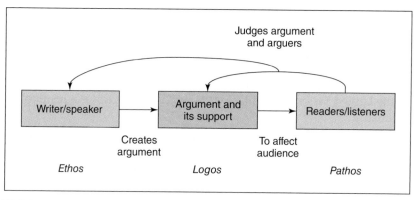

FIGURE 3.1 **Aristotelian Structure of Argument**

the grade? Would the professor's office be the better place for your discussion than an e-mail sent from your BlackBerry minutes after you have left class?

The concept of *kairos* asks us to consider what is most appropriate for the occasion, to think through the best time, place, and genre (type of argument) to make a successful argument. This concept has special meaning for students in a writing class who sometimes have difficulty thinking about audience at all. When practicing writing for the academic community, you may need to modify the language or tone that you use in other situations.

We argue in a specific context of three interrelated parts, as illustrated in Figure 3.1.

We present support for an assertion to a specific audience whose expectations and character we have given thought to when shaping our argument. And we present ourselves as informed, competent, and reliable so that our audience will give us their attention.

THE LANGUAGE OF ARGUMENT

We could title this section the *languages* of argument because arguments come in visual language as well as in words. But visual arguments—cartoons, photos, ads—are almost always accompanied by some words: figures speaking in bubbles, a caption, a slogan (Nike's "Just Do It!"). So we need to think about the kinds of statements that make up arguments, whether those arguments are legal briefs or cartoons, casual conversations or scholarly essays. To build an argument we need some statements that support other statements that present the main idea or claim of the argument.

- Claims: usually either inferences or judgments, for these are debatable assertions.
- Support: facts, opinions based on facts (inferences), or opinions based on values, beliefs, or ideas (judgments) or some combination of the three.

Let's consider what kinds of statements each of these terms describes.

Facts

Facts are statements that are verifiable. Factual statements refer to what can be counted or measured or confirmed by reasonable observers or trusted experts.

> There are twenty-six desks in Room 110.
>
> In the United States about 400,000 people die each year as a result of smoking.

These are factual statements. We can verify the first by observation—by counting. The second fact comes from medical records. We rely on trusted record-keeping sources and medical experts for verification. By definition, we do not argue about the facts. Usually. Sometimes "facts" change, as we learn more about our world. For example, only in the last thirty years has convincing evidence been gathered to demonstrate the relationship between smoking and various illnesses of the heart and lungs. And sometimes "facts" are false facts. These are statements that sound like facts but are incorrect. For example: Nadel has won more Wimbledon titles than Federer. Not so.

Inferences

Inferences are opinions based on facts. Inferences are the conclusions we draw from an analysis of facts.

> There will not be enough desks in Room 110 for upcoming fall-semester classes.
>
> Smoking is a serious health hazard.

Predictions of an increase in student enrollment for the coming fall semester lead to the inference that most English classes scheduled in Room 110 will run with several more students per class than last year. The dean should order new desks. Similarly, we infer from the number of deaths that smoking is a health problem; statistics show more people dying from tobacco than from AIDS, or murder, or car accidents, causes of death that get media coverage but do not produce nearly as many deaths.

Inferences vary in their closeness to the facts supporting them. That the sun will "rise" tomorrow is an inference, but we count on its happening, acting as if it is a fact. However, the first inference stated above is based not just on the fact of twenty-six desks but on another inference—a projected increase in student enrollment—and two assumptions. The argument looks like this:

FACT:	There are twenty-six desks in Room 110.
INFERENCE:	There will be more first-year students next year.
ASSUMPTIONS:	1. English will remain a required course.
	2. No additional classrooms are available for English classes.
CLAIM:	There will not be enough desks in Room 110 for upcoming fall-semester classes.

This inference could be challenged by a different analysis of the facts supporting enrollment projections. Or, if additional rooms can be found, the dean will not need to order new desks. Inferences can be part of the support of an argument, or they can be the claim of an argument.

Judgments

Judgments are opinions based on values, beliefs, or philosophical concepts. (Judgments also include opinions based on personal preferences, but we have already excluded these from argument.) Judgments concern right and wrong, good and bad, better or worse, should and should not:

> No more than twenty-six students should be enrolled in any English class.
>
> Cigarette advertising should be eliminated, and the federal government should develop an antismoking campaign.

> **NOTE:** Placing such qualifiers as "I believe," "I think," or "I feel" in an assertion does not free you from the need to support that claim. The statement "I believe that President Bush was a great president" calls for an argument based on evidence and reasons.

To support the first judgment, we need to explain what constitutes overcrowding, or what constitutes the best class size for effective teaching. If we can support our views on effective teaching, we may be able to convince the college president that ordering more desks for Room 110 is not the best solution to an increasing enrollment in English classes. The second judgment also offers a solution to a problem, in this case a national health problem. To reduce the number of deaths, we need to reduce the number of smokers, either by encouraging smokers to quit or nonsmokers not to start. The underlying assumption: Advertising does affect behavior.

EXERCISE: Facts, Inferences, and Judgments

Compile a list of three statements of fact, three inferences, and three judgments. Try to organize them into three related sets, as illustrated here:

- Smoking is prohibited in some restaurants.
- Secondhand smoke is a health hazard.
- Smoking should be prohibited in all restaurants.

We can classify judgments to see better what kind of assertion we are making and, therefore, what kind of support we need to argue effectively.

FUNCTIONAL JUDGMENTS (guidelines for judging how something or someone works or could work)

Tiger Woods is the best golfer to play the game.

Antismoking advertising will reduce the number of smokers.

AESTHETIC JUDGMENTS (guidelines for judging art, literature, music, or natural scenes)

The sunrise was beautiful.

The Great Gatsby's structure, characters, and symbols are perfectly wedded to create the novel's vision of the American dream.

ETHICAL JUDGMENTS (guidelines for group or social behavior)

Lawyers should not advertise.

It is discourteous to talk during a film or lecture.

MORAL JUDGMENTS (guidelines of right and wrong for judging individuals and for establishing legal principles)

Taking another person's life is wrong.

Equal rights under the law should not be denied on the basis of race or gender.

Functional and aesthetic judgments generally require defining key terms and establishing criteria for the judging or ranking made by the assertion. How, for example, do we compare golfers? On the amount of money won? The number of tournaments won? Or the consistency of winning throughout one's career? What about the golfer's quality and range of shots? Ethical and moral judgments may be more difficult to support because they depend not just on how terms are defined and criteria established but on values and beliefs as well. If taking another person's life is wrong, why isn't it wrong in war? Or is it? These are difficult questions that require thoughtful debate.

EXERCISES: Understanding Assumptions, Facts, False Facts, Inferences, and Judgments

1. Categorize the judgments you wrote for the previous exercise (p. 77) as either aesthetic, moral, ethical, or functional. Alternatively, compile a list of three judgments that you then categorize.

2. For each judgment listed for exercise 1, generate one statement of support, either a fact or an inference or another judgment. Then state any underlying assumptions that are part of each argument.

3. Read the following article and then complete the exercise that follows. This exercise tests both careful reading and your understanding of the differences among facts, inferences, and judgments.

YOUR BRAIN LIES TO YOU | SAM WANG and SANDRA AAMODT

Dr. Samuel S. H. Wang is a professor of molecular biology and neuroscience at Princeton, where he manages a research lab. Dr. Sandra Aamodt, former editor of *Nature Neuroscience*, is a freelance science writer. Drs. Wang and Aamodt are the authors of *Welcome to Your Brain: Why You Lose Your Car Keys but Never Forget How to Drive and Other Puzzles of Everyday Life* (2008). The following article appeared on June 27, 2008, in the *New York Times*.

False beliefs are everywhere. Eighteen percent of Americans think the sun 1 revolves around the earth, one poll has found. Thus it seems slightly less egregious that, according to another poll, 10 percent of us think that Senator Barack Obama, a Christian, is instead a Muslim. The Obama campaign has created a Web site to dispel misinformation. But this effort may be more difficult than it seems, thanks to the quirky way in which our brains store memories—and mislead us along the way.

The brain does not simply gather and stockpile information as a comput- 2 er's hard drive does. Current research suggests that facts may be stored first in the hippocampus, a structure deep in the brain about the size and shape of a fat man's curled pinkie finger. But the information does not rest there. Every time we recall it, our brain writes it down again, and during this re-storage, it is also reprocessed. In time, the fact is gradually transferred to the cerebral cortex and is separated from the context in which it was originally learned. For example, you know that the capital of California is Sacramento, but you probably don't remember how you learned it.

This phenomenon, known as source amnesia, can also lead people to for- 3 get whether a statement is true. Even when a lie is presented with a disclaimer, people often later remember it as true.

With time, this misremembering only gets worse. A false statement from a 4 non-credible source that is at first not believed can gain credibility during the months it takes to reprocess memories from short-term hippocampal storage to longer-term cortical storage. As the source is forgotten, the message and its implications gain strength. This could explain why, during the 2004 presidential campaign, it took some weeks for the Swift Boat Veterans for Truth campaign against Senator John Kerry to have an effect on his standing in the polls.

Even if they do not understand the neuroscience behind source amnesia, 5 campaign strategists can exploit it to spread misinformation. They know that if their message is initially memorable, its impression will persist long after it is debunked. In repeating a falsehood, someone may back it up with an opening line like "I think I read somewhere" or even with a reference to a specific source.

In one study, a group of Stanford students was exposed repeatedly to an 6 unsubstantiated claim taken from a Web site that Coca-Cola is an effective paint thinner. Students who read the statement five times were nearly one-third more likely than those who read it only twice to attribute it to *Consumer Reports* (rather than *The National Enquirer*, their other choice), giving it a gloss of credibility.

7   Adding to this innate tendency to mold information we recall is the way our brains fit facts into established mental frameworks. We tend to remember news that accords with our worldview, and discount statements that contradict it.

8   In another Stanford study, 48 students, half of whom said they favored capital punishment and half of whom said they opposed it, were presented with two pieces of evidence, one supporting and one contradicting the claim that capital punishment deters crime. Both groups were more convinced by the evidence that supported their initial position.

9   Psychologists have suggested that legends propagate by striking an emotional chord. In the same way, ideas can spread by emotional selection, rather than by their factual merits, encouraging the persistence of falsehoods about Coke—or about a presidential candidate.

10   Journalists and campaign workers may think they are acting to counter misinformation by pointing out that it is not true. But by repeating a false rumor, they may inadvertently make it stronger. In its concerted effort to "stop the smears," the Obama campaign may want to keep this in mind. Rather than emphasize that Mr. Obama is not a Muslim, for instance, it may be more effective to stress that he embraced Christianity as a young man.

11   Consumers of news, for their part, are prone to selectively accept and remember statements that reinforce beliefs they already hold. In a replication of the study of students' impressions of evidence about the death penalty, researchers found that even when subjects were given a specific instruction to be objective, they were still inclined to reject evidence that disagreed with their beliefs.

12   In the same study, however, when subjects were asked to imagine their reaction if the evidence had pointed to the opposite conclusion, they were more open-minded to information that contradicted their beliefs. Apparently, it pays for consumers of controversial news to take a moment and consider that the opposite interpretation may be true.

13   In 1919, Justice Oliver Wendell Holmes of the Supreme Court wrote that "the best test of truth is the power of the thought to get itself accepted in the competition of the market." Holmes erroneously assumed that ideas are more likely to spread if they are honest. Our brains do not naturally obey this admirable dictum, but by better understanding the mechanisms of memory perhaps we can move closer to Holmes's ideal.

Source: Originally appeared in the *New York Times*, June 27, 2008. Reprinted by permission of the authors.

Label each of the following sentences as F (fact), FF (false fact), I (inference), or J (judgment).

_____ 1. Campaigns have trouble getting rid of misinformation about their candidate.

_____ 2. When we reprocess information we may get the information wrong, but we always remember the source.

_____ 3. The Obama campaign should stress that he became a Christian as a young man.

_____ 4. Most of us remember information that matches our view of the world.

_____ 5. When students were told to be objective in evaluating evidence, they continued to reject evidence they disagreed with.

_____ 6. Coke is an effective paint thinner.

_____ 7. True statements should be accepted and false statements rejected.

_____ 8. Justice Holmes was wrong about the power of truth to spread more widely than falsehood.

_____ 9. The more we understand about the way the world works, the better our chances of separating truth from falsehood.

_____ 10. Americans do not seem to understand basic science.

■ ■

THE SHAPE OF ARGUMENT: WHAT WE CAN LEARN FROM TOULMIN

British philosopher Stephen Toulmin adds to what we have learned from Aristotle by focusing our attention on the basics of the argument itself. First, consider this definition of argument: _An argument consists of evidence and/or reasons presented in support of an assertion or claim that is either stated or implied._ For example:

CLAIM:	We should not go skiing today
GROUNDS:	because it is too cold.
GROUNDS:	Because some laws are unjust,
CLAIM:	civil disobedience is sometimes justified.
GROUNDS:	It's only fair and right for academic institutions to
CLAIM:	accept students only on academic merit.

The parts of an argument, Toulmin asserts, are actually a bit more complex than these examples suggest. Each argument has a third part that is not stated in the preceding examples. This third part is the "glue" that connects the support—the evidence and reasons—to the argument's claim and thus fulfills the logic of the argument. Toulmin calls this glue an argument's _warrants_. These are the principles or assumptions that allow us to assert that our evidence or reasons—what Toulmin calls the _grounds_—do indeed support our claim. (Figure 3.2 illustrates these basics of the Toulmin model of argument.)

CLAIM:	Academic institutions should accept students only on academic merit.
GROUNDS:	It is only fair and right.
WARRANT:	(1) Fair and right are important values. (2) Academic institutions are only about academics.

FIGURE 3.2 The Toulmin Structure of Argument

Look again at the sample arguments to see what warrants must be accepted to make each argument work:

CLAIM:	We should not go skiing today.
GROUNDS:	It is too cold.
WARRANTS:	When it is too cold, skiing is not fun; the activity is not sufficient to keep one from becoming uncomfortable. AND: Too cold is what is too cold for me.
CLAIM:	Civil disobedience is sometimes justified.
EVIDENCE:	Some laws are unjust.
WARRANTS:	To get unjust laws changed, people need to be made aware of the injustice. Acts of civil disobedience will get people's attention and make them aware that the laws need changing.
CLAIM:	Academic institutions should accept students only on academic merit.
EVIDENCE:	It is fair and right.
WARRANTS:	Fair and right are important values. AND: Academic institutions are only about academics.

Warrants play an important role in any argument, so we need to be sure to understand what they are. Note, for instance, the second warrant operating in the first argument: The temperature considered uncomfortable for the speaker will also be uncomfortable for her companions—an uncertain assumption. In the second argument, the warrant is less debatable, for acts of civil disobedience usually get media coverage and thus dramatize the issue. The underlying assumptions in the third example stress the need to know one's warrants. Both warrants will need to be defended in the debate over selection by academic merit only.

COLLABORATIVE EXERCISE: Building Arguments

With your class partner or in small groups, examine each of the following claims. Select two, think of one statement that could serve as evidence for each claim, and then think of the underlying assumption(s) that complete each of the arguments.

1. Professor X is not a good instructor.
2. Americans need to reduce the fat in their diets.
3. Tiger Woods is a great golfer.
4. Military women should be allowed to serve in combat zones.
5. College newspapers should be free of supervision by faculty or administrators.

Toulmin was particularly interested in the great range or strength or probability of various arguments. Some kinds of arguments are stronger than others because of the language or logic they use. Other arguments must, necessarily, be heavily qualified for the claim to be supportable. Toulmin developed his language to provide a strategy for analyzing the degree of probability in a given argument and to remind us of the need to qualify some kinds of claims. You have already seen how the idea of warrants, or assumptions, helps us think about the "glue" that presumably makes a given argument work. Taken together, Toulmin terms and concepts help us analyze the arguments of others and prepare more convincing arguments of our own.

Claims

A claim is what the argument asserts or seeks to prove. It answers the question "What is your point?" In an argumentative speech or essay, the claim is the speaker's or writer's main idea or thesis. Although an argument's claim "follows" from reasons and evidence, we often present an argument—whether written or spoken—with the claim stated near the beginning of the presentation. We can better understand an argument's claim by recognizing that we can have claims of fact, claims of value, and claims of policy.

Claims of Fact

Although facts usually support claims, we do argue over some facts. Historians and biographers may argue over what happened in the past, although they are more likely to argue over the significance of what happened. Scientists also argue over the facts, over how to classify an unearthed fossil, or whether the fossil indicates that the animal had feathers. For example:

CLAIM: The small, predatory dinosaur *Deinonychus* hunted its prey in packs.

This claim is supported by the discovery of several fossils of *Deinonychus* close together and with the fossil bones of a much larger dinosaur. Their teeth have also been found in or near the bones of dinosaurs that have died in a struggle.

Assertions about what will happen are sometimes classified as claims of fact, but they can also be labeled as inferences supported by facts. Predictions about a future event may be classified as claims of fact:

CLAIM: The United States will win the most gold medals at the 2012 Olympics.

CLAIM: I will get an A on tomorrow's psychology test.

What evidence would you use to support each of these claims? (And, did the first one turn out to be correct?)

Claims of Value

These include moral, ethical, and aesthetic judgments. Assertions that use such words as *good* or *bad, better* or *worse,* and *right* or *wrong* will be claims of value. The following are all claims of value:

CLAIM: Roger Federer is a better tennis player than Andy Roddick.

CLAIM: *Adventures of Huckleberry Finn* is one of the most significant American novels.

CLAIM: Cheating hurts others and the cheater too.

CLAIM: Abortion is wrong.

Arguments in support of judgments demand relevant evidence, careful reasoning, and an awareness of the assumptions one is making. Support for claims of value often include other value statements. For example, to support the claim that censorship is bad, arguers often assert that the free exchange of ideas is good and necessary in a democracy. The support is itself a value statement.

Claims of Policy

Finally, claims of policy are assertions about what should or should not happen, what the government ought or ought not to do, how to best solve social problems. Claims of policy debate, for example, college rules, state gun laws, or federal aid to Africans suffering from AIDS. The following are claims of policy:

CLAIM: College newspapers should not be controlled in any way by
                    college authorities.

CLAIM: States should not have laws allowing people to carry concealed
                    weapons.

CLAIM: The United States must provide more aid to African countries
                    where 25 percent or more of the citizens have tested positive
                    for HIV.

Claims of policy are often closely tied to judgments of morality or political philosophy, but they also need to be grounded in feasibility. That is, your claim needs to be doable, to be based on a thoughtful consideration of the real world and the complexities of public policy issues.

Grounds (or Data or Evidence)

The term *grounds* refers to the reasons and evidence provided in support of a claim. Although the words *data* and *evidence* can also be used, note that *grounds* is the most general term because it includes reasons or logic as well as examples or statistics. We determine the grounds of an argument by asking the question "Why do you think that?" or "How do you know that?" When writing your own arguments, you can ask yourself these questions and answer by using a *because* clause:

CLAIM: Smoking should be banned in restaurants because

GROUNDS: secondhand smoke is a serious health hazard.

CLAIM: Federer is a better tennis player than Roddick
                    because

GROUNDS:	1. he was ranked number one longer,
	2. he won more tournaments than Roddick, and
	3. he won more major tournaments than Roddick.

Warrants

Why should we believe that your grounds do indeed support your claim? Your argument's warrants answer this question. They explain why your evidence really is evidence. Sometimes warrants reside in language itself, in the meanings of the words we are using. If I am *younger* than my brother, then my brother must be *older* than I am. In a court case attempting to prove that Jones murdered Smith, the relation of evidence to claim is less assured. If the police investigation has been properly managed and the physical evidence is substantial, then Smith may be Jones's murderer. The prosecution has—presumably beyond a reasonable doubt—established motive, means, and opportunity for Smith to commit the murder. In many arguments based on statistical data, the argument's warrant rests on complex analyses of the statistics—and on the conviction that the statistics have been developed without error.

Still, without taking courses in statistics and logic, you can develop an alertness to the "good sense" of some arguments and the "dubious sense" of others. You know, for example, that good SAT scores are a predictor of success in college. Can you argue that you will do well in college because you have good SATs? No. We can determine only a statistical probability. We cannot turn probabilities about a group of people into a warrant about one person in the group. (In addition, SAT scores are only one predictor. Another key variable is motivation.)

What is the warrant for the Federer claim?

CLAIM:	Federer is a better tennis player than Roddick.
GROUNDS:	The three facts listed above.
WARRANT:	It is appropriate to judge and rank tennis players on these kinds of statistics. That is, the better player is one who has held the number-one ranking for the longest time, has won the most tournaments, and also has won the most major tournaments.

Backing

Standing behind an argument's warrant may be additional *backing*. Backing answers the question "How do we know that your evidence is good evidence?" You may answer this question by providing authoritative sources for the data used (for example, the Census Bureau or the U.S. Tennis Association). Or, you may explain in detail the methodology of the experiments performed or the surveys taken. When scientists and social scientists present the results of their research, they anticipate the question of backing and automatically provide a detailed explanation of the process by which they acquired their evidence. In criminal trials, defense attorneys challenge the backing of the prosecution's argument. They question the handling of blood samples sent to labs for DNA testing, for instance. The defense attorneys want jury members to doubt the *quality* of the evidence.

This discussion of backing returns us to the point that one part of any argument is the audience. To create an effective argument, ask yourself: Will my warrants and backing be accepted? Is my audience likely to share my values, religious beliefs, or scientific approach? If you are speaking to a group at your church, then backing based on the religious beliefs of that church may be effective. If you are preparing an argument for a general audience, then using specific religious assertions as warrants or backing probably will not result in an effective argument.

Qualifiers

Some arguments are absolute; they can be stated without qualification. *If I am younger than my brother, then he must be older than I am.* Most arguments need some qualification; many need precise limitations. If, when playing bridge, I am dealt eight spades, then my opponents and partner together must have five spade cards—because there are thirteen cards of each suit in a deck. My partner *probably* has one spade but *could* be void of spades. My partner *possibly* has two or more spades, but I would be foolish to count on it. When bidding my hand, I must be controlled by the laws of probability. Look again at the smoking-ban claim. Observe the absolute nature of both the claim and its support. If secondhand smoke is indeed a health hazard, it will be that in *all* restaurants, not just in some. With each argument ask what qualification is needed for a successful argument.

Sweeping generalizations often come to us in the heat of a debate or when we first start to think about an issue. For example: *Gun control is wrong because it restricts individual rights.* But on reflection surely you would not want to argue against all forms of gun control. (Remember: An unqualified assertion is understood by your audience to be absolute.) Would you sell guns to felons in jail or to children on the way to school? Obviously not. So, let's try the claim again, this time with two important qualifiers:

QUALIFIED	Adults without a criminal record should not be restricted in the
CLAIM:	purchase of guns.

Others may want this claim further qualified to eliminate particular types of guns or to control the number purchased or the process for purchasing. The gun-control debate is not about absolutes; it is all about which qualified claim is best.

Rebuttals

Arguments can be challenged. Smart debaters assume that there are people who will disagree with them. They anticipate the ways that opponents can challenge their arguments. When you are planning an argument, you need to think about how you can counter or rebut the challenges you anticipate. Think of yourself as an attorney in a court case preparing your argument *and* a defense of the other attorney's challenges to your argument. If you ignore the important role of rebuttals, you may not win the jury to your side.

USING TOULMIN'S TERMS TO ANALYZE ARGUMENTS

Terms are never an end in themselves; we learn them when we recognize that they help us to organize our thinking about a subject. Toulmin's terms can aid your reading of the arguments of others. You can "see what's going on" in an argument if you analyze it, applying Toulmin's language to its parts. Not all terms will be useful for every analysis because, for example, some arguments will not have qualifiers or rebuttals. But to recognize that an argument is *without qualifiers* is to learn something important about that argument.

First, here is a simple argument broken down into its parts using Toulmin's terms:

GROUNDS:	Because Dr. Bradshaw has an attendance policy,
CLAIM:	students who miss more than seven classes will
QUALIFIER:	most likely (last year, Dr. Bradshaw did allow one student, in unusual circumstances, to continue in the class) be dropped from the course.
WARRANT:	Dr. Bradshaw's syllabus explains her attendance policy, a
BACKING:	policy consistent with the concept of a discussion class that depends on student participation and consistent with the attendance policies of most of her colleagues.
REBUTTAL:	Although some students complain about an attendance policy of any kind, Dr. Bradshaw does explain her policy and her reasons for it the first day of class. She then reminds students that the syllabus is a contract between them; if they choose to stay, they agree to abide by the guidelines explained on the syllabus.

This argument is brief and fairly simple. Let's see how Toulmin's terms can help us analyze a longer, more complex argument. Read actively and annotate the following essay while noting the existing annotations using Toulmin's terms. Then answer the questions that follow the article.

THE THREAT TO FREE
SPEECH AT UNIVERSITIES   GREG LUKIANOFF

An attorney, Greg Lukianoff holds degrees from American University and Stanford Law School. He is the president of the Foundation for Individual Rights in Education (FIRE), a regular columnist at *Huffington Post,* and the author of *Unlearning Liberty: Campus Censorship and the End of the American Debate* (2012). The following argument was published January 6, 2012.

PREREADING QUESTIONS Are there good reasons to have campus speech codes? Are there problems with speech codes?

Toulmin's Terms   1   Activists embarked on a campaign in the 1980s to eradicate hurtful, big-oted and politically incorrect speech by enacting speech codes at universities across the country. Although the movement presented itself as a forward-thinking way to make campuses welcoming, the initiative stood in stark contrast to the celebrated "free speech movement" of the 1960s, whose proponents understood that vague exceptions to free speech were inevitably used by those in power to punish opinions they dislike or disagree with. And unfortunately the effort gained momentum as prestigious institutions passed speech codes.

Rebutted—universities wrongly motivated

Claim implied in word choice   2   The legal fig leaf upon which the speech-codes movement relied was the concept of "hostile work environment" harassment. Because civil rights laws, chief among them Title IX, banned sexual discrimination on campuses, harass-ment jurisprudence—sometimes combined with other tenuous rationales—became the primary legal tool universities used to formulate speech codes.

Grounds   3   Courts, however, understood that merely naming a restriction a "harass-ment" code did not inoculate it from First Amendment scrutiny. In nearly a dozen courtroom losses between 1989 and 2010, harassment-based speech codes have been defeated at campuses from the University of Michigan to Stanford. Amazingly, these defeats have not slowed the spread of these codes. The Foundation for Individual Rights in Education (FIRE), of which I am presi-dent, conducts an extensive annual study of campus speech codes; our 2012 report found that 65 percent of nearly 400 top colleges maintain codes that prohibit substantial amounts of clearly protected speech.

4   Overly broad harassment codes remain the weapon of choice on campus to punish speech that administrators dislike. In a decade fighting campus cen-sorship, I have seen harassment defined as expressions as mild as "inappropri-ately directed laughter" and used to police students for references to a student government candidate as a "jerk and a fool" (at the University of Central Florida in 2006) and a factually verifiable if unflattering piece on Islamic extremism in a conservative student magazine (at Tufts University in 2007). Other examples abound. Worryingly, such broad codes and heavy-handed

Warrant   enforcement are teaching a generation of students that it may be safer to keep their mouths shut when important or controversial issues arise. Such illib-eral lessons on how to live in a free society are poison to freewheeling debate and thought experimentation and, therefore, to the innovative thinking that both higher education and our democracy need.

The Education Department's Office for Civil Rights (OCR), which enforces Title IX on college campuses, tried in 2003 to put a stop to the "government made me do it" excuse for speech codes. It issued a letter to every college receiving federal funds—so, virtually all—making clear that harassment requires a serious pattern of discriminatory behavior, not just mere offense. Since then, the number of campus speech codes has slowly begun to decline.

Grounds [5]

But last year the OCR backpedaled. The agency issued a 19-page letter in April dictating to colleges the procedures they must follow in sexual harassment and assault cases. Among its many troubling points, including a requirement that sexual harassment cases be adjudicated using the lowest possible standard of evidence allowable in court, is the fact that the letter makes no mention of the First Amendment or free speech. This ignores the role that vague and broad definitions of harassment have played in justifying campus speech codes and censorship over the past few decades. By mandating so many procedural steps colleges must take to respond to allegations of sexual harassment while simultaneously failing to mandate a consistent, limited and constitutional definition of harassment, the OCR encourages those on campus who are already inclined to use such codes to punish speech they simply dislike.

Rebuttal [6]

Rather than proffer shifting rules, the OCR should end the threat of harassment-based campus speech codes once and for all. The Supreme Court offered its only guidance on the thorny issue of student-on-student harassment in the 1999 case *Davis v. Monroe County Board of Education*. The justices recognized the necessity of carefully defining what constitutes "harassment" in the educational context, lest everyday interactions be rendered a federal offense. The court defined harassment as discriminatory conduct, directed at an individual, that is "so severe, pervasive, and objectively offensive" that "victim-students are effectively denied equal access to an institution's resources and opportunities."

Backing, with claim in paragraph 8 [7]

This definition, if applied fairly, poses little threat to free speech and effectively prohibits real harassment

[8]

This week, FIRE and a broad coalition of organizations (the Tully Center for Free Speech at Syracuse University, National Coalition Against Censorship, the Heartland Institute, National Association of Scholars, Alliance Defense Fund Center for Academic Freedom, Feminists for Free Expression, Woodhull Sexual Freedom Alliance, American Booksellers Foundation for Free Expression, Accuracy in Academia, and the American Council of Trustees and Alumni) are writing to the OCR to request that it publicly affirm the *Davis* standard as the controlling definition for harassment on campus.

Backing-support for claim [9]

By simply following the Supreme Courts guidance, the OCR would assure that serious harassment is punished on campus while free speech is robustly protected. In one move, OCR could rid campuses of a substantial portion of all speech codes while protecting institutions from losing still more First Amendment lawsuits. Most important, by recognizing the *Davis* standard, the OCR would send a message that free speech and free minds are essential to—not incompatible with—the development of creative, critical and innovative thinkers on our nations campuses.

Claim restated [10]

Warrant

Source: *Washington Post*, January 6, 2012. Reprinted by permission of the author.

QUESTIONS FOR READING

1. What is Lukianoff's subject? (Free speech is not sufficiently precise as an answer.)
2. What is the legal basis for colleges' speech codes? How has this law been challenged in the past?
3. Explain the shifting positions of the Office of Civil Rights; what does the author want this office to do now?

QUESTIONS FOR REASONING AND ANALYSIS

4. What is Lukianoff's claim?
5. What is his primary support? (Add a "because" clause to his claim to find his grounds.)
6. Review the author's comments about college authorities—those he holds responsible for speech codes. What, in Lukianoff's view, is their reason for wanting speech codes? Does the author provide evidence for this warrant? Is support needed?

QUESTIONS FOR REFLECTION AND WRITING

7. Reflect on the author's position that codes let colleges punish views they don't like. Is this the only reason for speech codes? Do you agree that it is the primary motivation of college officials?
8. Lukianoff asserts that it is possible to punish "serious harassment" on campus without restricting free speech. How should colleges do this? (One student's free speech is often another's perceived insult.) What suggestions do you have for writing clear guidelines for students that will define the author's desired balance?
9. How can colleges create a sense of community with mutual respect while still embracing the free exchange of ideas?

Toulmin's terms can help you to see what writers are actually "doing" in their arguments. Just remember that writers do not usually follow the terms in precise order. Indeed, you can find both grounds and backing in the same sentence, or claim and qualifiers in the same paragraph, and so on. Still, the terms can help you to sort out your thinking about a claim you want to support. Now use your knowledge of argument as you read and analyze the following arguments.

FOR ANALYSIS AND DEBATE

CHEERING FREE SPEECH | JEFFREY MATEER AND ERIN LEU

Jeff Mateer is General Counsel of Liberty Institute, overseeing the legal team in the organization's commitment to the support of religious liberty. His law degree is from Southern Methodist University, and he is admitted to the bar in Texas. Erin Leu, a graduate of Harvard Law School, was an attorney at Liberty and represented the Kountze cheerleaders. She is now an associate with a law firm in the Dallas area. Their article was published November 5, 2012.

PREREADING QUESTIONS Once you read the opening sentence, can you appreciate the title's clever play with words? What do you expect the essay to be about?

Cheerleaders in Kountze, Tex., recently learned an invaluable lesson about the Constitution and the importance of individual expression without government censorship. Ironically, it's a lesson they had to watch a court teach their school district.

Controversy arose this fall when the cheerleaders at Kountze High School decided to model good sportsmanship by replacing the often-violent messages on their banners, such as "Scalp the Indians," with encouraging religious messages. The only complaints came from an antireligion advocacy group more than 1,000 miles away. In response, the Kountze superintendent issued an unlawful directive banning all such religious speech.

The cheerleaders sued their school district to preserve their rights to free speech and religious expression. Their cause gained international support, from tens of thousands of individuals across six continents. Texas Gov. Rick Perry and state Attorney General Greg Abbott spoke out, applauding the students for standing up for their rights and denouncing government hostility toward religion.

Two weeks ago a Texas court issued a temporary injunction allowing the cheerleaders to display their banners for at least the remainder of the season. Free speech prevailed, reminding us of the well-established principle that students do not shed their constitutional rights to freedom of speech or expression at the schoolhouse gate.

People from all political persuasions should be celebrating this decision. Many are mistakenly arguing, however, that the outcome is incorrect because the Supreme Court struck down school-sponsored prayer at football games in the 2000 case *Santa Fe v. Doe*. But *Santa Fe* recognized that "there is a crucial difference between *government* speech endorsing religion, which the Establishment Clause forbids, and *private* speech endorsing religion, which the Free Speech and Free Exercise Clauses protect."

In *Santa Fe*, the court held that a school policy that created a majoritarian election on religion and explicitly encouraged prayer created government speech. Conversely, in this case, both Texas law and the school's policies affirm that when students speak at school events, including football games, they are engaging in private speech and their views do not reflect the position of the school. Indeed, the policies at issue in *Kountze* create a forum for student speech and require the school district to remain neutral toward all viewpoints. *Santa Fe* involved government speech; *Kountze* involves private student speech.

The Kountze cheerleaders alone decide what message to place on their banners. The team is student-run, with school officials present only to monitor safety. Each week two cheerleaders take turns leading the team, including choosing whether to create banners and, if so, what messages they should bear. The supplies to create the banners are paid for with private funds, as are the cheerleaders' uniforms, further demonstrating the private nature of their speech.

In *Santa Fe*, the court stated that: "By no means do [the Religion Clauses] impose a prohibition on all religious activity in our public schools. . . . Indeed, the common purpose of the Religion Clauses is to secure religious liberty." When football players or cheerleaders are on the field in uniform, they do not become agents of the state. No one would argue that high school football players are prohibited from praying together. In the same manner, just because cheerleaders wear uniforms and are on school property does not mean that they become instruments of the school or that they must surrender their right to free speech.

9   High school students' rights to free speech should be robustly protected. These students are nearly adults; they are about to enter college, military service or the workforce. Schools should be teaching students about the First Amendment and the free marketplace of ideas, including that other individuals may advocate for messages with which they disagree, instead of censoring speech that some might find offensive. As the Supreme Court has stated: "The vigilant protection of constitutional freedoms is nowhere more vital than in the community of American schools."

10   This is because "[t]he Nation's future depends upon leaders trained through wide exposure to that robust exchange of ideas which discovers truth out of a multitude of tongues, [rather] than through any kind of authoritative selection."

11   We better serve our students by educating them about our country's commitment to free expression rather than shutting out certain views. Otherwise, our schools do a great disservice to students and fail to prepare them to be citizens of our free society.

12   Nonetheless, the character of the Kountze cheerleaders should give us hope for the future. With young adults like these ready to respectfully stand for our Constitution, our freedoms are more secure.

Source: *Washington Post*, November 5, 2012. Reprinted by permission of the authors.

QUESTIONS FOR READING

1. What is the situation that led to this essay? What did the cheerleaders do?
2. What was the court's ruling? The authors write that Texas law has supported the cheerleaders, but is this case closed?

QUESTIONS FOR REASONING AND ANALYSIS

3. What is the authors' claim? What grounds (reasons/evidence) do they provide?
4. Mateer and Leu agree with the court's ruling that football players can pray on the field. They argue that the cheerleaders' religious signs are not the same. How do they defend the similarity?
5. Study the final four paragraphs; what makes them an effective conclusion? How are the authors "defining" the issue in these paragraphs?

QUESTIONS FOR REFLECTION AND WRITING

6. The core of this argument is that the cheerleaders' signs are private speech because they do not represent the school. Do you agree with their position? If you agree, how would you add to their discussion? If you disagree, how would you challenge it?
7. If you were the judge making the final ruling on this case, how would you rule? Why?

HOW CAN WE BAN INSULTS
AGAINST JEWS BUT NOT MUSLIMS? | WILLIAM SALETAN

A graduate of Swarthmore College, William Saletan writes about science, technology, and politics for the online magazine *Slate*. He has published several books, including *Bearing Right: How Conservatives Won the Abortion War* (2004). The following article was posted September 28, 2012.

PREREADING QUESTIONS Does your college have rules against hate speech? Are such rules consistent with First Amendment rights?

How can we ban hate speech against Jews while defending mockery of 1 Muslims? Jews have too much influence over U.S. foreign policy. Gay men are too promiscuous. Muslims commit too much terrorism. Blacks commit too much crime.

Each of those claims is poorly stated. Each, in its clumsy way, addresses a 2 real problem or concern. And each violates laws against hate speech. In much of what we call the free world, for writing that paragraph, I could be jailed.

Libertarians, cultural conservatives, and racists have complained about 3 these laws for years. But now the problem has turned global. Islamic governments, angered by an anti-Muslim video that provoked protests and riots in their countries, are demanding to know why insulting the Prophet Mohammed is free speech but vilifying Jews and denying the Holocaust isn't. And we don't have a good answer.

If we're going to preach freedom of expression around the world, we have 4 to practice it. We have to scrap our hate-speech laws.

Muslim leaders want us to extend these laws. At this week's meeting of the 5 U.N. General Assembly, they lobbied for tighter censorship. Egypt's president said freedom of expression shouldn't include speech that is "used to incite hatred" or "directed towards one specific religion." Pakistan's president urged the "international community" to "criminalize" acts that "endanger world security by misusing freedom of expression." Yemen's president called for "international legislation" to suppress speech that "blasphemes the beliefs of nations and defames their figures." The Arab League's secretary-general proposed a binding "international legal framework" to "criminalize psychological and spiritual harm" caused by expressions that "insult the beliefs, culture and civilization of others."

President Obama, while condemning the video, met these proposals with 6 a stout defense of free speech. Switzerland's president agreed: "Freedom of opinion and of expression are core values guaranteed universally which must be protected." And when a French magazine published cartoons poking fun at Mohammed, the country's prime minister insisted that French laws protecting free speech extend to caricatures.

This debate between East and West, between respect and pluralism, isn't 7 a crisis. It's a stage of global progress. The Arab spring has freed hundreds of millions of Muslims from the political retardation of dictatorship. They're taking responsibility for governing themselves and their relations with other countries. They're debating one another and challenging us. And they should, because we're hypocrites.

Pakistani activists of the hard line Sunni party Jamaat-e-Islami (JI) burn a U.S. flag during a protest against an anti-Islam movie in Peshawar on September 18, 2012. Police used tear gas to disperse a crowd of more than 2,000 protesters trying to reach the US consulate in northwest Pakistan as fresh demonstrations erupted against an anti-Islam film.

8   From Pakistan to Iran to Saudi Arabia to Egypt to Nigeria to the United Kingdom, Muslims scoff at our rhetoric about free speech. They point to European laws against questioning the Holocaust. Monday on CNN, Iranian President Mahmoud Ahmedinejad needled British interviewer Piers Morgan: "Why in Europe has it been forbidden for anyone to conduct any research about this event? Why are researchers in prison? . . . Do you believe in the freedom of thought and ideas, or no?" On Tuesday, Pakistan's U.N. ambassador, speaking for the Organization of Islamic Cooperation, told the U.N. Human Rights Council:

9   We are all aware of the fact that laws exist in Europe and other countries which impose curbs, for instance, on anti-Semitic speech, Holocaust denial, or racial slurs. We need to acknowledge, once and for all, that Islamophobia in particular and discrimination on the basis of religion and belief are contemporary forms of racism and must be dealt with as such. Not to do so would be a clear example of double standards. Islamophobia has to be treated in law and practice equal to the treatment given to anti-Semitism.

10   He's right. Laws throughout Europe forbid any expression that "minimizes," "trivializes," "belittles," "plays down," "contests," or "puts in doubt" Nazi crimes. Hungary, Poland, and the Czech Republic extend this prohibition to communist atrocities. These laws carry jail sentences of up to five years. Germany adds two years for anyone who "disparages the memory of a deceased person."

Hate speech laws go further. Germany punishes anyone found guilty of 11 "insulting" or "defaming segments of the population." The Netherlands bans anything that "verbally or in writing or image, deliberately offends a group of people because of their race, their religion or beliefs, their hetero- or homo-sexual orientation or their physical, psychological or mental handicap." It's ille-gal to "insult" such a group in France, to "defame" them in Portugal, to "degrade" them in Denmark, or to "expresses contempt" for them in Sweden. In Switzerland, it's illegal to "demean" them even with a "gesture." Canada punishes anyone who "willfully promotes hatred." The United Kingdom out-laws "insulting words or behavior" that arouse "racial hatred." Romania for-bids the possession of xenophobic "symbols."

What have these laws produced? Look at the convictions upheld or accepted 12 by the European Court of Human Rights. Four Swedes who distributed leaflets that called homosexuality "deviant" and "morally destructive" and blamed it for AIDS. An Englishman who displayed in his window a 9/11 poster proclaiming, "Islam out of Britain." A Turk who published two letters from readers angry at the government's treatment of Kurds. A Frenchman who wrote an article disput-ing the plausibility of poison gas technology at a Nazi concentration camp.

Look at the defendants rescued by the court. A Dane "convicted of aiding 13 and abetting the dissemination of racist remarks" for making a documentary in which three people "made abusive and derogatory remarks about immigrants and ethnic groups." A man "convicted of openly inciting the population to hatred" in Turkey by "criticizing secular and democratic principles and openly calling for the introduction of Sharia law." Another Turkish resident "convicted of disseminat-ing propaganda" after he "criticized the United States' intervention in Iraq and the solitary confinement of the leader of a terrorist organization." Two Frenchmen who wrote a newspaper article that "portrayed Marshal Pétain in a favorable light, drawing a veil over his policy of collaboration with the Nazi regime."

Beyond the court's docket, you'll find more prosecutions of dissent. A 14 Swedish pastor convicted of violating hate-speech laws by preaching against homosexuality. A Serb convicted of discrimination for saying, "We are against every gathering where homosexuals are demonstrating in the streets of Belgrade and want to show something, which is a disease, like it is normal." An Australian columnist convicted of violating the Racial Discrimination Act by sug-gesting that "there are fair-skinned people in Australia with essentially European ancestry . . . who, motivated by career opportunities available to Aboriginal people or by political activism, have chosen to falsely identify as Aboriginal."

My favorite case involves a Frenchman who sought free-speech protection 15 under Article 10 of the European Convention on Human Rights:

Denis Leroy is a cartoonist. One of his drawings representing the attack on 16 the World Trade Centre was published in a Basque weekly newspaper . . . with a caption which read: "We have all dreamt of it . . . Hamas did it." Having been sentenced to payment of a fine for "condoning terrorism," Mr Leroy argued that his freedom of expression had been infringed.

The Court considered that, through his work, the applicant had glorified the 17 violent destruction of American imperialism, expressed moral support for the perpetrators of the attacks of 11 September, commented approvingly on the violence perpetrated against thousands of civilians and diminished the dignity of the victims. Despite the newspaper's limited circulation, the Court observed that the drawing's publication had provoked a certain public reaction, capable of stirring up violence and of having a demonstrable impact on public order in the Basque Country. The Court held that there had been no violation of Article 10.

18   How can you justify prosecuting cases like these while defending cartoonists and video makers who ridicule Mohammed? You can't. Either you censor both, or you censor neither. Given the choice, I'll stand with Obama. "Efforts to restrict speech," he warned the U. N., "can quickly become a tool to silence critics and oppress minorities."

19   That principle, borne out by the wretched record of hate-speech prosecutions, is worth defending. But first, we have to live up to it.

QUESTIONS FOR READING

1. What event has led to Saletan's article?
2. Which groups/countries want to extend hate speech laws? Which countries have defended free speech?
3. What is the Muslim world's view of the West's "commitment" to free speech?

QUESTIONS FOR REASONING AND ANALYSIS

4. What is Saletan's claim? (Be precise; he isn't just taking a position on hate speech laws.)
5. What evidence does the author provide? What is especially significant about the ruling on the cartoonist Leroy?
6. Examine Saletan's opening paragraphs; what makes his opening effective?

QUESTIONS FOR REFLECTION AND WRITING

7. Were you aware of the extent of hate speech laws in the West? Are you surprised? Should you be more surprised by the inconsistency in rulings? Reflect on these questions.
8. Has Saletan convinced you that we do not practice what we preach? Why or why not? If you disagree, how would you refute Saletan?
9. Is it possible to understand hate speech restrictions in Western Europe relative to the Holocaust? Is it possible to understand and still oppose prosecution of someone who wants to argue that there was no Holocaust? Is it possible to legislate against ignorance or stupidity? Reflect on these questions.

1. Compare the style and tone of Mateer/Leu's and Saletan's essays. Has each one written in a way that works for the author's approach to this issue? Be prepared to explain your views or develop them into a comparative analysis of style.

2. Reread and study the essay "Your Brain Lies to You" (pp. 79–80) and then analyze the argument's parts, using Toulmin's terms.

GOING ONLINE

Another issue on college campuses is student drinking. Should colleges find ways to crack down on underage student alcohol use and binge drinking? You may be able to offer some answers to this question based on your knowledge and experience. You may also want to go online for some statistics about college drinking and health and safety risks. Drawing on both experience and data, what claim can you support?

CHAPTER 4

Writing Effective Arguments

READ: Who are the figures in the painting? What are they doing?

REASON: What details in the painting help to date the scene?

REFLECT/WRITE: What is significant about the moment captured in this painting?

The basics of good writing remain much the same for works as seemingly different as the personal essay, the argument, and the researched essay. Good writing is focused, organized, and concrete. Effective essays are written in a style and tone that are suited to both the audience and the writer's purpose. These are sound principles, all well known to you. But how, exactly, do you achieve them when writing argument? This chapter will help you answer that question.

KNOW YOUR AUDIENCE

Too often students plunge into writing without thinking much about audience, for, after all, their "audience" is only the instructor who has given the assignment, and their purpose is to complete the assignment and get a grade. These views of audience and purpose are likely to lead to badly written arguments. First, if you are not thinking about readers who may disagree with you, you may not develop the best defense of your claim. Second, you may ignore your essay's needed introductory material on the assumption that the instructor, knowing the assignment, has a context for understanding your writing. To avoid these pitfalls, use the following questions to sharpen your understanding of audience.

Who Is My Audience?

If you are writing an essay for the student newspaper, your audience consists—primarily—of students, but do not forget that faculty and administrators also read the student newspaper. If you are preparing a letter-to-the-editor refutation of a recent column in your town's newspaper, your audience will be the readers of that newspaper—that is, adults in your town. Some instructors give assignments that create an audience such as those just described so that you will practice writing with a specific audience in mind.

If you are not assigned a specific audience, imagine your classmates, as well as your instructor, as part of your audience. In other words, you are writing to readers in the academic community. These readers are intelligent and thoughtful, expecting sound reasoning and convincing evidence. From diverse cultures and experiences, these readers also represent varied values and beliefs. Do not confuse the shared expectations of writing conventions with shared beliefs.

What Will My Audience Know about My Topic?

What can you expect a diverse group of readers to know? Whether you are writing on a current issue or a centuries-old debate, you must expect most readers to have some knowledge of the issues. Their knowledge does not free you from the responsibility of developing your support fully, though. In fact, their knowledge creates further demands. For example, most readers know the main arguments on both sides of the abortion issue. For you to write as if they do not—and thus to ignore the arguments of the opposition—is to produce an argument that probably adds little to the debate on the subject.

On the other hand, what some readers "know" may be little more than an overview of the issues from TV news—or the emotional outbursts of a family member. Some readers may be misinformed or prejudiced, but they embrace their views enthusiastically nonetheless. So, as you think about the ways to develop and support your argument, you will have to assess your readers' knowledge and sophistication. This assessment will help you decide how much background information to provide or what false facts need to be revealed and dismissed.

Where Does My Audience Stand on the Issue?

Expect readers to hold a range of views, even if you are writing to students on your campus or to an organization of which you are a member. It is not true, for instance, that all students want coed dorms or pass/fail grading. And, if everyone already agrees with you, you have no reason to write. An argument needs to be about a topic that is open to debate. So:

- Assume that some of your audience will probably never agree with you but may offer you grudging respect if you compose an effective argument.
- Assume that some readers do not hold strong views on your topic and may be open to convincing, if you present a good case.
- Assume that those who share your views will still be looking for a strong argument in support of their position.
- Assume that if you hold an unpopular position your best strategy will be a conciliatory approach. (See p. 103 for a discussion of the conciliatory argument.)

How Should I Speak to My Audience?

Your audience will form an opinion of you based on how you write and how you reason. The image of argument—and the arguer—that we have been creating in this text's discussion is of thoughtful claims defended with logic and evidence. However, the heated debate at yesterday's lunch does not resemble this image of argument. Sometimes the word *persuasion* is used to separate the emotionally charged debate from the calm, intellectual tone of the academic argument. Unfortunately, this neat division between argument and persuasion does not describe the real world of debate. The thoughtful arguer also wants to be persuasive, and highly emotional presentations can contain relevant facts in support of a sound idea. Instead of thinking of two separate categories— argument and persuasion—think instead of a continuum from the most rigorous logic to extreme flights of fantasy. Figure 4.1 suggests this continuum with some kinds of arguments placed along it.

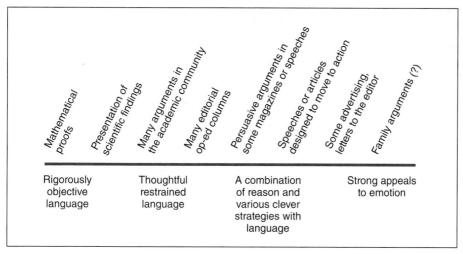

FIGURE 4.1 A Continuum of Argumentative Language

Where should you place yourself along this continuum of language? You will have to answer this question with each specific writing context. Much of the time you will choose "thoughtful, restrained language" as expected by the academic community, but there may be times that you will use various persuasive strategies. Probably you will not select "strong appeals to emotion" for your college or workplace writing. Remember that you have different roles in your life, and you use different *voices* as appropriate to each role. Most of the time, you will want to use the serious voice you normally select for serious conversations with other adults. This is the voice that will help you establish your credibility, your *ethos.*

As you learned in Chapter 2, irony is a useful rhetorical strategy for giving one's words greater emphasis by actually writing the opposite of what you mean. Many writers use irony effectively. Irony catches our attention, makes us think, and engages us with the text. Sarcasm is not quite the same as irony. Irony can cleverly focus on life's complexities. Sarcasm is more often vicious than insightful, relying on harsh, negative word choice. Probably in most of your academic work, you will want to avoid sarcasm and think carefully about using any strongly worded appeal to your readers' emotions. Better to persuade your audience with the force of your reasons and evidence than to lose them because of the static of nasty language. But the key, always, is to know your audience and understand how best to present a convincing argument to that specific group.

UNDERSTAND YOUR WRITING PURPOSE

There are many types or genres of argument and different reasons for writing—beyond wanting to write convincingly in defense of your views. Different types of arguments require different approaches, or different kinds of evidence. It helps to be able to recognize the kind of argument you are contemplating.

What Type (Genre) of Argument Am I Preparing?

Here are some useful ways to classify arguments and think about their support.

- **Investigative paper similar to those in the social sciences.** If you are asked to collect evidence in an organized way to support a claim about advertising strategies or violence in children's TV programming, then you will be writing an investigative essay. You will present evidence that you have gathered and analyzed to support your claim.

- **Evaluation.** If your assignment is to explain why others should read a particular book or take a particular professor's class, then you will be preparing an evaluation argument. Be sure to think about your criteria: What makes a book or a professor good? Why do you dislike Lady Gaga? Is it her music—or her lifestyle?

- **Definition.** If you are asked to explain the meaning of a general or controversial term, you will be writing a definition argument. What do we mean by *wisdom*? What are the characteristics of *cool*? A definition argument usually requires both specific details to illustrate the term and general ideas to express its meaning.

- **Claim of values.** If you are given the assignment to argue for your position on euthanasia, trying juveniles as adults, or the use of national identification cards, recognize that your assignment calls for a position paper, a claim based heavily on values. Pay close attention to your warrants or assumptions in any philosophical debate.

- **Claim of policy.** If you are given a broad topic: "What should we do about _____?" and you have to fill in the blank, your task is to offer solutions to a current problem. What should we do about childhood obesity? About home foreclosures? These kinds of questions are less philosophical and more practical. Your solutions must be workable.

- **Refutation or rebuttal.** If you are given the assignment to find a letter to the editor, a newspaper editorial, or an essay in this text with which you disagree, your job is to write a refutation essay, a specific challenge to a specific argument. You know, then, that you will repeatedly refer to the work you are rebutting, so you will need to know it thoroughly.

What Is My Goal?

It is also helpful to consider your goal in writing. Does your topic call for a strong statement of views (i.e., "These are the steps we must take to reduce childhood obesity")? Or, is your goal an exploratory one, a thinking through of possible answers to a more philosophical question ("Why is it often difficult to separate performance from personality when we evaluate a star?")? Thinking about your goal as well as the argument's genre will help to decide on the kinds of evidence needed and on the approach to take and tone to select.

Will the Rogerian or Conciliatory Approach Work for Me?

Psychologist Carl Rogers asserts that the most successful arguments take a conciliatory approach. The characteristics of this approach include

- showing respect for the opposition in the language and tone of the argument,
- seeking common ground by indicating specific facts and values that both sides share, and
- qualifying the claim to bring opposing sides more closely together.

In their essay "Euthanasia—A Critique," authors Peter A. Singer and Mark Siegler provide a good example of a conciliatory approach. They begin their essay by explaining and then rebutting the two main arguments in favor of euthanasia. After stating the two arguments in clear and neutral language, they write this in response to the first argument:

> We agree that the relief of pain and suffering is a crucial goal of medicine. We question, however, whether the care of dying patients cannot be improved without resorting to the drastic measure of euthanasia. Most physical pain can be relieved with the appropriate use of analgesic agents. Unfortunately, despite widespread agreement that dying patients must be provided with necessary analgesia, physicians continue to underuse analgesia in the care of dying patients because of the concern about depressing respiratory drive or creating addiction. Such situations demand better management of pain, not euthanasia.

In this paragraph the authors accept the value of pain management for dying patients. They go even further and offer a solution to the problem of suffering among the terminally ill—better pain management by doctors. They remain thoughtful in their approach and tone throughout, while sticking to their position that legalizing euthanasia is not the solution.

Consider how you can use the conciliatory approach to write more effective arguments. It will help you avoid "overheated" language and maintain your focus on what is doable in a world of differing points of view. There is the expression that "you can catch more flies with honey than with vinegar." Using "honey" instead of "vinegar" might also make you feel better about yourself.

MOVE FROM TOPIC TO CLAIM TO POSSIBLE SUPPORT

When you write a letter to the editor of a newspaper, you have chosen to respond to someone else's argument that has bothered you. In this writing context, you already know your topic and, probably, your claim as well. You also know that your purpose will be to refute the article you have read. In composition classes, the context is not always so clearly established, but you will usually be given some guidelines with which to get started.

Selecting a Topic

Suppose that you are asked to write an argument that is in some way connected to First Amendment rights. Your instructor has limited and focused your topic choice and purpose. Start thinking about possible topics that relate to freedom of speech and censorship issues. To aid your topic search and selection, use one or more invention strategies:

- Brainstorm (make a list).
- Freewrite (write without stopping for ten minutes).
- Map or cluster (connect ideas to the general topic in various spokes, a kind of visual brainstorming).
- Read through this text for ideas.

Your invention strategies lead, let us suppose, to the following list of possible topics:

Administrative restrictions on the college newspaper
Hate speech restrictions or codes
Deleting certain books from high school reading lists
Controls and limits on alcohol and cigarette advertising
Restrictions on violent TV programming
Dress codes/uniforms

Looking over your list, you realize that the last item, dress codes/uniforms, may be about freedom but not freedom of speech, so you drop it from consideration. All of the other topics have promise. Which one do you select? Two considerations should guide you: interest and knowledge. First, your argument is likely to be more thoughtful and lively if you choose an issue that matters to you. But, unless you have time for study, you are wise to choose a topic about which you already have some information and ideas. Suppose that you decide to write about television violence because you are concerned about violence in American society and have given this issue some thought. It is time to phrase your topic as a tentative thesis or claim.

Drafting a Claim

Good claim statements will keep you focused in your writing—in addition to establishing your main idea for readers. Give thought both to your position on the issue and to the wording of your claim. *Claim statements to avoid:*

- Claims using vague words such as *good* or *bad*.

    VAGUE: TV violence is bad for us.

    BETTER: We need more restrictions on violent TV programming.

- Claims in loosely worded "two-part" sentences.

    UNFOCUSED: Campus rape is a serious problem, and we need to do something about it.

| BETTER: | College administrators and students need to work together to reduce both the number of campus rapes and the fear of rape. |

- Claims that are not appropriately qualified.

| OVERSTATED: | Violence on television is making us a violent society. |
| BETTER: | TV violence is contributing to viewers' increased fear of violence and insensitivity to violence. |

- Claims that do not help you focus on your purpose in writing.

| UNCLEAR PURPOSE: | Not everyone agrees on what is meant by violent TV programming. |

(Perhaps this is true, but more important, this claim suggests that you will define violent programming. Such an approach would not keep you focused on a First Amendment issue.)

| BETTER: | Restrictions on violent TV programs can be justified. |

(Now your claim directs you to the debate over restrictions of content.)

Listing Possible Grounds

As you learned in Chapter 3, you can generate grounds to support a claim by adding a "because" clause after a claim statement. We can start a list of grounds for the topic on violent TV programming in this way:

We need more restrictions on violent television programming *because*

- Many people, including children and teens, watch many hours of TV (get stats).
- People are affected by the dominant activities/experiences in their lives.
- There is a connection between violent programming and desensitizing and fear of violence and possibly more aggressive behavior in heavy viewers (get detail of studies).
- Society needs to protect young people.

You have four good points to work on, a combination of reasons and inferences drawn from evidence.

Listing Grounds for the Other Side or Another Perspective

Remember that arguments generate counterarguments. Continue your exploration of this topic by considering possible rebuttals to your proposed grounds. How might someone who does not want to see restrictions placed on television programming respond to each of your points? Let's think about them one at a time:

We need more restrictions on violent television programming because

1. *Many people, including children and teens, watch many hours of TV.*

Your opposition cannot really challenge your first point on the facts, only its relevance to restricting programming. The opposition might argue that if parents think their children are watching too much TV, they should turn it off. The restriction needs to be a family decision.

2.   *People are affected by the dominant activities/experiences in their lives.*

It seems common sense to expect people to be influenced by dominant forces in their lives. Your opposition might argue, though, that many people have the TV on for many hours but often are not watching it intently for all of that time. The more dominant forces in our lives are parents and teachers and peers, not the TV. The opposition might also argue that people seem to be influenced to such different degrees by television that it is not fair or logical to restrict everyone when perhaps only a few are truly influenced by their TV viewing to a harmful degree.

3.   *There is a connection between violent programming and desensitizing and fear of violence and possibly more aggressive behavior in heavy viewers.*

Some people are entirely convinced by studies showing these negative effects of violent TV programming, but others point to the less convincing studies or make the argument that if violence on TV were really so powerful an influence, most people would be violent or fearful or desensitized.

4.   *Society needs to protect young people.*

Your opposition might choose to agree with you in theory on this point—and then turn again to the argument that parents should be doing the protecting. Government controls on programming restrict adults, as well as children, whereas it may only be some children who should watch fewer hours of TV and not watch adult "cop" shows at all.

Working through this process of considering opposing views can help you see

- where you may want to do some research for facts to provide backing for your grounds,
- how you can best develop your reasons to take account of typical counter-arguments, and
- if you should qualify your claim in some ways.

Planning Your Approach

Now that you have thought about arguments on the other side, you decide that you want to argue for a qualified claim that is also more precise:

> To protect young viewers, we need restrictions on violence in children's programs and ratings for prime-time adult shows that clearly establish the degree of violence in those shows.

This qualified claim responds to two points of the rebuttals. Our student hasn't given in to the other side but has chosen to narrow the argument to emphasize the protection of children, an area of common ground.

Next, it's time to check some of the articles in this text or go online to get some data to develop points 1 and 3. You need to know that 99 percent of homes

have at least one TV; you need to know that by the time young people graduate from high school, they have spent more time in front of the TV than in the
classroom. Also, you can find the average number of violent acts by hour of TV
in children's programs. Then, too, there are the various studies of fearfulness
and aggressive behavior that will give you some statistics to use to develop the
third point. Be sure to select reliable sources and then cite the sources you use.
*Citing sources is not only required and right; it is also part of the process of establishing
your credibility and thus strengthening your argument.*

Finally, how are you going to answer the point about parents controlling their children? You might counter that in theory this is the way it should
be—but in fact not all parents are at home watching what their children are
watching, and not all parents care enough to pay attention. However, all of us
suffer from the consequences of those children who are influenced by their TV
watching to become more aggressive or fearful or desensitized. These children
grow up to become the adults the rest of us have to interact with, so the problem becomes one for the society as a whole to solve. If you had not disciplined
yourself to go through the process of listing possible rebuttals, you may not
have thought through this part of the debate.

DRAFT YOUR ARGUMENT

Many of us can benefit from a step-by-step process of invention—such as we
have been exploring in the last few pages. In addition, the more notes you have
from working through the Toulmin structure, the easier it will be to get started
on your draft. Students report that they can control their writing anxiety
when they generate detailed notes. A page of notes that also suggests
an organizational strategy can remove that awful feeling of staring at a blank
computer screen.

In the following chapters on argument, you will find specific suggestions
for organizing the various kinds of arguments. But you can always rely on one
of these two basic organizations, regardless of the specific genre:

PLAN 1: ORGANIZING AN ARGUMENT

Attention-getting opening (why the issue is important, or current, etc.)

Claim statement

Reasons and evidence in order from least important to most important

Challenge to potential rebuttals or counterarguments

Conclusion that reemphasizes claim

PLAN 2: ORGANIZING AN ARGUMENT

Attention-getting opening

Claim statement (or possibly leave to the conclusion)

Order by arguments of opposing position, with your challenge to each

Conclusion that reemphasizes (or states for the first time) your claim

GUIDELINES for Drafting

- **Try to get a complete draft in one sitting so that you can "see" the whole piece.**
- **If you can't think of a clever opening, state your claim and move on to the body of your essay.** After you draft your reasons and evidence, a good opening may occur to you.
- **If you find that you need something more in some parts of your essay, leave space there as a reminder that you will need to return to that paragraph later.**
- **Try to avoid using either a dictionary or thesaurus while drafting.** Your goal is to get the ideas down. You will polish later.
- **Learn to draft at your computer.** Revising is so much easier that you will be more willing to make significant changes if you work at your PC. If you are handwriting your draft, leave plenty of margin space for additions or for directions to shift parts around.

REVISE YOUR DRAFT

If you have drafted at the computer, begin revising by printing a copy of your draft. Most of us cannot do an adequate job of revision by looking at a computer screen. Then remind yourself that revision is a three-step process: rewriting, editing, and proofreading.

Rewriting

You are not ready to polish the writing until you are satisfied with the argument. Look first at the total piece. Do you have all the necessary parts: a claim, support, some response to possible counterarguments? Examine the order of your reasons and evidence. Do some of your points belong, logically, in a different place? Does the order make the most powerful defense of your claim? Be willing to move whole paragraphs around to test the best organization. Also reflect on the argument itself. Have you avoided logical fallacies? Have you qualified statements when appropriate? Do you have enough support? The best support?

Consider development: Is your essay long enough to meet assignment requirements? Are points fully developed to satisfy the demands of readers? One key to development is the length of your paragraphs. If most of your paragraphs are only two or three sentences, you have not developed the point of each paragraph satisfactorily. It is possible that some paragraphs need to be combined because they are really on the same topic. More typically, short paragraphs need further explanation of ideas or examples to illustrate ideas. Compare the following paragraphs for effectiveness:

First Draft of a Paragraph from an Essay on Gun Control

One popular argument used against the regulation of gun ownership is the need of citizens, especially in urban areas where the crime rate is higher, to possess a handgun for personal protection, either carried or kept in the home. Some citizens may not be aware of the dangers to themselves or their families when they purchase a gun. Others, more aware, may embrace the myth that "bad things only happen to other people."

Revised Version of the Paragraph with Statistics Added

One popular argument used against the regulation of gun ownership is the need of citizens, especially in urban areas where the crime rate is higher, to possess a handgun for personal protection, whether it is carried or kept in the home. Although some citizens may not be aware of the dangers to themselves or their families when they purchase a gun, they should be. According to the Center to Prevent Handgun Violence, from their web page "Firearm Facts," "guns that are kept in the home for self-protection are 22 times more likely to kill a family member or friend than to kill in self-defense." The Center also reports that guns in the home make homicide three times more likely and suicide five times more likely. We are not thinking straight if we believe that these dangers apply only to others.

A quick trip to the Internet has provided this student with some facts to support his argument. Observe how he has referred informally but fully to the source of his information. (If your instructor requires formal MLA documentation in all essays, then you will need to add a Works Cited page and give a full reference to the website. See pp. 318–329.)

Editing

Make your changes, print another copy, and begin the second phase of revision: editing. As you read through this time, pay close attention to unity and coherence, to sentence patterns, and to word choice. Read each paragraph as a separate unit to be certain that everything is on the same subtopic. Then look at your use of transition and connecting words, both within and between paragraphs. Ask yourself: Have you guided the reader through the argument using appropriate connectors such as *therefore, in addition, as a consequence, also,* and so forth?

Read again, focusing on each sentence, checking to see that you have varied sentence patterns and length. Read sentences aloud to let your ear help you find awkward constructions or unfinished thoughts. Strive as well for word choice that is concrete and specific, avoiding wordiness, clichés, trite expressions, or incorrect use of specialized terms. Observe how Samantha edited one paragraph in her essay "Balancing Work and Family":

Draft Version of Paragraph   ?   agr

Women have come a long way in equalizing themselves, but inequality within marriages do exist. One reason for this can be found in the media. Just last week America turned on their televisions to watch a grotesque dramatization of skewed priorities. On *Who Wants to Marry a Millionaire,* a panel of

Vague reference.

Wordy.

Short sentences.

women vied for the affections of a millionaire who would choose one of them to be his wife. This show said that women can be purchased. Also that men must provide and that money is worth the sacrifice of one's individuality. The show also suggests that physical attraction is more important than the building of a complete relationship. Finally, the show says that women's true

Vague reference.

value lies in their appearance. This is a dangerous message to send to both men and women viewers.

Edited Version of Paragraph

Although women have come a long way toward equality in the workplace, inequality within marriages can still be found. The media may be partly to blame for this continued inequality. Just last week Americans watched a grotesque dramatization of skewed priorities. On *Who Wants to Marry a Millionaire*, a panel of women vied for the affections of a millionaire who would choose one of them to be his wife. Such displays teach us that women can be purchased, that men must be the providers, that the desire for money is worth the sacrifice of one's individuality, that physical attraction is more important than a complete relationship, and that women's true value lies in their appearance. These messages discourage marriages based on equality and mutual support.

Samantha's editing has eliminated wordiness and vague references and has combined ideas into one forceful sentence. Support your good argument by taking the time to polish your writing.

A Few Words about Words and Tone

You have just been advised to check your word choice to eliminate wordiness, vagueness, clichés, and so on. Here is a specific checklist of problems often found in student papers with some ways to fix the problems:

- *Eliminate clichés.* Do not write about "the fast-paced world we live in today" or the "rat race." First, do you know for sure that the pace of life for someone who has a demanding job is any faster than it was in the past? Using time effectively has always mattered. Also, clichés suggest that you are too lazy to find your own words.
- *Avoid jargon.* In the negative sense of this word, *jargon* refers to nonspecialists who fill their writing with "heavy-sounding terms" to give the appearance of significance. Watch for any overuse of "scientific" terms such as *factor* or *aspect*, or other vague, awkward language.
- *Avoid language that is too informal for most of your writing contexts.* What do you mean when you write: "*Kids* today watch too much TV"? Alternatives include *children, teens, adolescents.* These words are less slangy and more precise.
- *Avoid nasty attacks on the opposition.* Change "those jerks who are foolish enough to believe that TV violence has no impact on children" to language that explains your counterargument without attacking those who

may disagree with you. After all, you want to change the thinking of your audience, not make them resent you for name-calling.

- *Avoid all discriminatory language.* In the academic community and the adult workplace, most people are bothered by language that belittles any one group. This includes language that is racist or sexist or reflects negatively on older or disabled persons or those who do not share your sexual orientation or religious beliefs. Just don't do it!

Proofreading

You also do not want to lose the respect of readers because you submit a paper filled with "little" errors—errors in punctuation, mechanics, and incorrect word choice. Most readers will forgive one or two little errors but will become annoyed if they begin to pile up. So, after you are finished rewriting and editing, print a copy of your paper and read it slowly, looking specifically at punctuation, at the handling of quotations and references to writers and to titles, and at those pesky words that come in two or more "versions": *to, too,* and *two; here* and *hear; their, there,* and *they're;* and so forth. If instructors have found any of these kinds of errors in your papers over the years, then focus your attention on the kinds of errors you have been known to make.

Refer to Chapter 1 for handling references to authors and titles and for handling direct quotations. Use a glossary of usage in a handbook for homonyms (words that sound alike but have different meanings), and check a handbook for punctuation rules. Take pride in your work and present a paper that will be treated with respect. What follows is a checklist of the key points for writing good arguments that we have just examined.

A CHECKLIST FOR REVISION ▪▫▪▫▪▫▪▫▪▫▪▫▪▫▪▫▪▫▪▫▪▫▪▫▪▫▪▫

- ☐ Have I selected an issue and purpose consistent with assignment guidelines?
- ☐ Have I stated a claim that is focused, appropriately qualified, and precise?
- ☐ Have I developed sound reasons and evidence in support of my claim?
- ☐ Have I used Toulmin's terms to help me study the parts of my argument, including rebuttals to counterarguments?
- ☐ Have I taken advantage of a conciliatory approach and emphasized common ground with opponents?
- ☐ Have I found a clear and effective organization for presenting my argument?
- ☐ Have I edited my draft thoughtfully, concentrating on producing unified and coherent paragraphs and polished sentences?
- ☐ Have I eliminated wordiness, clichés, jargon?
- ☐ Have I selected an appropriate tone for my purpose and audience?
- ☐ Have I used my word processor's spell-check and proofread a printed copy with great care? ▪▫▪▫▪▫▪▫▪▫▪▫▪▫▪▫▪▫▪▫▪▫▪▫▪▫▪▫▪▫

FOR ANALYSIS AND DEBATE

FIVE MYTHS ABOUT TORTURE AND TRUTH | DARIUS REJALI

A professor of political science at Reed College, Iranian-born Darius Rejali is a recognized expert on the causes and meaning of violence, especially on torture, in our world. His book *Torture and Democracy* (2007) has won acclaim and resulted in frequent interview sessions for Rejali. His latest book is *Spirituality and the Ethics of Torture* (2009). The following essay appeared on December 16, 2007, in the *Washington Post*.

PREREADING QUESTIONS Can you think of five myths about torture? What do you expect Rejali to cover in this essay?

1   *So the CIA did indeed torture Abu Zubaida, the first al-Qaeda terrorist suspect to have been waterboarded. So says John Kiriakou, the first former CIA employee directly involved in the questioning of "high-value" al-Qaeda detainees to speak out publicly. He minced no words last week in calling the CIA's "enhanced interrogation techniques" what they are.*

2   *But did they work? Torture's defenders, including the wannabe tough guys who write Fox's "24," insist that the rough stuff gets results. "It was like flipping a switch," said Kiriakou about Abu Zubaida's response to being waterboarded. But the al-Qaeda operative's confessions—descriptions of fantastic plots from a man who intelligence analysts were convinced was mentally ill—probably didn't give the CIA any actionable intelligence. Of course, we may never know the whole truth, since the CIA destroyed the videotapes of Abu Zubaida's interrogation. But here are some other myths that are bound to come up as the debate over torture rages on.*

3   **1. Torture worked for the Gestapo.** Actually, no. Even Hitler's notorious secret police got most of their information from public tips, informers and interagency cooperation. That was still more than enough to let the Gestapo decimate anti-Nazi resistance in Austria, Czechoslovakia, Poland, Denmark, Norway, France, Russia and the concentration camps.

4   Yes, the Gestapo did torture people for intelligence, especially in later years. But this reflected not torture's efficacy but the loss of many seasoned professionals to World War II, increasingly desperate competition for intelligence among Gestapo units and an influx of less disciplined younger members. (Why do serious, tedious police work when you have a uniform and a whip?) It's surprising how unsuccessful the Gestapo's brutal efforts were. They failed to break senior leaders of the French, Danish, Polish and German resistance. I've spent more than a decade collecting all the cases of Gestapo torture "successes" in multiple languages; the number is small and the results pathetic, especially compared with the devastating effects of public cooperation and informers.

5   **2. Everyone talks sooner or later under torture.** Truth is, it's surprisingly hard to get anything under torture, true or false. For example, between 1500

and 1750, French prosecutors tried to torture confessions out of 785 individuals. Torture was legal back then, and the records document such practices as the bone-crushing use of splints, pumping stomachs with water until they swelled and pouring boiling oil on the feet. But the number of prisoners who said anything was low, from 3 percent in Paris to 14 percent in Toulouse (an exceptional high). Most of the time, the torturers were unable to get any statement whatsoever.

And such examples could be multiplied. The Japanese fascists, no strangers to torture, said it best in their field manual, which was found in Burma during World War II: They described torture as the clumsiest possible method of gathering intelligence. Like most sensible torturers, they preferred to use torture for intimidation, not information.   6

3. People will say anything under torture. Well, no, although this is a favorite chestnut of torture's foes. Think about it: Sure, someone would lie under torture, but wouldn't they also lie if they were being interrogated without coercion?   7

In fact, the problem of torture does not stem from the prisoner who *has* information; it stems from the prisoner who doesn't. Such a person is also likely to lie, to say anything, often convincingly. The torture of the informed may generate no more lies than normal interrogation, but the torture of the ignorant and innocent overwhelms investigators with misleading information. In these cases, nothing is indeed preferable to anything. Anything needs to be verified, and the CIA's own 1963 interrogation manual explains that "a time-consuming delay results"—hardly useful when every moment matters.   8

Intelligence gathering is especially vulnerable to this problem. When police officers torture, they know what the crime is, and all they want is the confession. When intelligence officers torture, they must gather information about what they don't know.   9

4. Most people can tell when someone is lying under torture. Not so—and we know quite a bit about this. For about 40 years, psychologists have been testing police officers as well as normal people to see whether they can spot lies, and the results aren't encouraging. Ordinary folk have an accuracy rate of about 57 percent, which is pretty poor considering that 50 percent is the flip of a coin. Likewise, the cops' accuracy rates fall between 45 percent and 65 percent—that is, sometimes less accurate than a coin toss.   10

Why does this matter? Because even if torturers break a person, they have to recognize it, and most of the time they can't. Torturers assume too much and reject what doesn't fit their assumptions. For instance, Sheila Cassidy, a British physician, cracked under electric-shock torture by the Chilean secret service in the 1970s and identified priests who had helped the country's socialist opposition. But her devout interrogators couldn't believe that priests would ever help the socialists, so they tortured her for another week until they finally became convinced. By that time, she was so damaged that she couldn't remember the location of the safe house.   11

12   In fact, most torturers are nowhere near as well trained for interrogation as police are. Torturers are usually chosen because they've endured hardship and pain, fought with courage, kept secrets, held the right beliefs and earned a reputation as trustworthy and loyal. They often rely on folklore about what lying behavior looks like—shifty eyes, sweaty palms and so on. And, not surprisingly, they make a lot of mistakes.

13   **5. You can train people to resist torture.** Supposedly, this is why we can't know what the CIA's "enhanced interrogation techniques" are: If Washington admits that it waterboards suspected terrorists, al-Qaeda will set up "waterboarding-resistance camps" across the world. Be that as it may, the truth is that no training will help the bad guys.

14   Simply put, nothing predicts the outcome of one's resistance to pain better than one's own personality. Against some personalities, nothing works; against others, practically anything does. Studies of hundreds of detainees who broke under Soviet and Chinese torture, including Army-funded studies of U.S. prisoners of war, conclude that during, before and after torture, each prisoner displayed strengths and weaknesses dependent on his or her own character. The CIA's own "Human Resources Exploitation Manual" from 1983 and its so-called Kubark manual from 1963 agree. In all matters relating to pain, says Kubark, the "individual remains the determinant."

15   The thing that's most clear from torture-victim studies is that you can't train for the ordeal. There is no secret knowledge out there about how to resist torture. Yes, there are manuals, such as the IRA's "Green Book," the anti-Soviet "Manual for Psychiatry for Dissidents" and "Torture and the Interrogation Experience," an Iranian guerrilla manual from the 1970s. But none of these volumes contains specific techniques of resistance, just general encouragement to hang tough. Even al-Qaeda's vaunted terrorist-training manual offers no tips on how to resist torture, and al-Qaeda was no stranger to the brutal methods of the Saudi police.

16   And yet these myths persist. "The larger problem here, I think," one active CIA officer observed in 2005, "is that this kind of stuff just makes people feel better, even if it doesn't work."

Source: *Washington Post*, June 28, 2008. Reprinted by permission of the author.

QUESTIONS FOR READING

1. What context for his discussion does the author provide in the opening two paragraphs?
2. What worked better than torture for the Gestapo? What led to an increase in torture in the Gestapo?
3. What do the data show about getting people to speak by torturing them?
4. Who are the people most likely to lie under torture?
5. Why are interrogators not very good at recognizing when the tortured are lying?

QUESTIONS FOR REASONING AND ANALYSIS

6. What structure does the author use? What kind of argument is this?
7. What is Rejali's position on torture, the claim of his argument?
8. What grounds does he present in support of his claim?
9. Describe Rejali's style; how does his style of writing help his argument?

QUESTIONS FOR REFLECTION AND WRITING

10. Which of the five discussions has surprised you the most? Why?
11. Has the author convinced you that all five myths lack substance? Why or why not? If you disagree, how would you refute Rejali?
12. Why do intelligence and military personnel continue to use harsh interrogation strategies even though the evidence suggests that what, if anything, they learn will not be useful? Ponder this question.

TORTURE IS WRONG—BUT IT MIGHT WORK | M. GREGG BLOCHE

A law professor at Georgetown University, Gregg Bloche is also a physician. His MD and JD degrees are both from Yale University. Bloche specializes in medical ethics, health care law, and human rights law. Widely published, he is the author of *The Hippocratic Myth* (2011). His essay on torture appeared on May 29, 2011.

PREREADING QUESTIONS Has Bloche intrigued you with his title? What do you expect his position to be?

Torture, liberals like me often insist, isn't just immoral, it's ineffective. We like this proposition because it portrays us as protectors of the nation, not wusses willing to risk American lives to protect terrorists. And we love to quote seasoned interrogators' assurances that building rapport with the bad guys will get them to talk. 1

But the killing of Osama bin Laden four weeks ago has revived the old debate about whether torture works. Could it be that "enhanced interrogation techniques" employed during the George W. Bush administration helped find bin Laden's now-famous courier and track him to the terrorist in chief's now-infamous lair? 2

Sen. John McCain (R-Ariz.) and current administration officials say no. Former attorney general Michael Mukasey and former vice president Dick Cheney say yes. 3

The idea that waterboarding and other abuses may have been effective in getting information from detainees is repellant to many, including me. It's 4 contrary to the meme many have embraced: that torture doesn't work because people being abused to the breaking point will say anything to get the brutality to stop—anything they think their accusers want to hear.

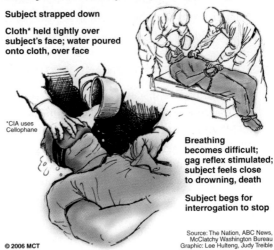

What is water-boarding?

Water-boarding is a harsh interrogation method that simulates drowning and near death; origins traced to the Spanish Inquisition.

Subject strapped down

Cloth* held tightly over subject's face; water poured onto cloth, over face

*CIA uses Cellophane

Breathing becomes difficult; gag reflex stimulated; subject feels close to drowning, death

Subject begs for interrogation to stop

Source: The Nation, ABC News, McClatchy Washington Bureau
Graphic: Lee Hulteng, Judy Treible

© 2006 MCT

5   But this position is at odds with some behavioral science, I've learned. The architects of enhanced interrogation are doctors who built on a still-classified, research-based model that suggests how abuse can indeed work.

6   I've examined the science, studied the available paper trail and interviewed key actors, including several who helped develop the enhanced interrogation program and who haven't spoken publicly before. This inquiry has made it possible to piece together the model that under-girds enhanced interrogation.

7   This model holds that harsh methods can't, by themselves, force terrorists to tell the truth. Brute force, it suggests, stiffens resistance. Rather, the role of abuse is to induce hopelessness and despair. That's what sleep deprivation, stress positions and prolonged isolation were designed to do. Small gestures of contempt—facial slaps and frequent insults—drive home the message of futility. Even the rough stuff, such as "walling" and waterboarding, is meant to dispirit, not to coerce.

8   Once a sense of hopelessness is instilled, the model holds, interrogators can shape behavior through small rewards. Bathroom breaks, reprieves from foul-tasting food and even the occasional kind word can coax broken men to comply with their abusers' expectations.

9   Certainly, interrogators using this approach have obtained false confessions. Chinese interrogators did so intentionally, for propaganda purposes, with American prisoners during the Korean War. McCain and other critics of "torture-lite" cite this precedent to argue that it can't yield reliable information. But the same psychological sequence—induction of hopelessness, followed by rewards to shape compliance—can be used to get terrorism suspects to tell the truth, or so the architects of enhanced interrogation hypothesize.

10   Critical to this model is the ability to assess suspects' truthfulness in real time. To this end, CIA interrogators stressed speedy integration of intelligence from all sources. The idea was to frame questions to detect falsehoods; interrogators could then reward honesty and punish deceit.

It's been widely reported that the program was conceived by a former Air 11 Force psychologist, James Mitchell, who had helped oversee the Pentagon's program for training soldiers and airmen to resist torture if captured. That Mitchell became the CIA's maestro of enhanced interrogation and personally water-boarded several prisoners was confirmed in 2009 through the release of previously classified documents. But how Mitchell got involved and why the agency embraced his methods remained a mystery.

The key player was a clinical psychologist turned CIA official, Kirk Hubbard, 12 I learned through interviews with him and others. On the day 19 hijackers bent on mass murder made their place in history, Hubbard's responsibilities at the agency included tracking developments in the behavioral sciences with an eye toward their tactical use. He and Mitchell knew each other through the network of psychologists who do national security work. Just retired from the Air Force, Mitchell figured he could translate what he knew about teaching resistance into a methodology for breaking it. He convinced Hubbard, who introduced him to CIA leaders and coached him through the agency's bureaucratic rivalries.

Journalistic accounts have cast Mitchell as a rogue who won a CIA con- 13 tract by dint of charisma. What's gone unappreciated is his reliance on a research base. He had studied the medical and psychological literature on how Chinese interrogators extracted false confessions. And he was an admirer of Martin Seligman, the University of Pennsylvania psychologist who had developed the concept of "learned helplessness" and invoked it to explain depression.

Mitchell, it appears, saw connections and seized upon them. The despair 14 that Chinese interrogators tried to instill was akin to learned helplessness. Seligman's induction of learned helplessness in laboratory animals, therefore, could point the way to prison regimens capable of inducing it in people. And—this was Mitchell's biggest conceptual jump—the Chinese way of shaping behavior in prisoners who were reduced to learned helplessness held a broader lesson.

To motivate a captive to comply, a Chinese interrogator established an 15 aura of omnipotence. For weeks or months, the interrogator was his prisoner's sole human connection, with monopoly power to praise, punish and reward. Rapport with the interrogator offered the only escape from despair. This opened possibilities for the sculpting of behavior and belief. For propaganda purposes, the Chinese sought sham confessions. But Mitchell saw that behavioral shaping could be used to pursue other goals, including the extraction of truth.

Did the methods Mitchell devised help end the hunt for bin Laden? Have 16 they prevented terrorist attacks? We'll never know. Not only are counterterrorism operations shrouded in secrecy, but it's impossible to prove or disprove claims that enhanced interrogation works better than other methods when prisoners are intent on saying nothing.

Scientific study of this question would require random sorting of suspects 17 into groups that receive either torture-lite or conventional forms of interrogation. To frame this inquiry is to show why it can't be carried out: It would violate international law and research ethics. The CIA, Hubbard told me, conducted no such study for this reason.

18   So we're left with the unsavory possibility that torture-lite works—and that it may have helped find bin Laden. It does no good to point out, as some human rights advocates have, that the detainees who yielded information about his courier did so after the abuse stopped. The model on which enhanced interrogation is based can account for this. The detainees' cooperation could have ensued from hopelessness and despair, followed by interrogators' adroit use of their power to punish and reward.

19   This possibility poses the question of torture in a more unsettling fashion, by denying us the easy out that torture is both ineffective and wrong. We must choose between its repugnance to our values and its potential efficacy. To me, the choice is almost always obvious: Contempt for the law of nations would put us on a path toward a more brutish world. Conservatives are fond of saying, on behalf of martial sacrifice, that freedom isn't free. Neither is basic decency.

Source: *Washington Post*, May 29, 2011. Reprinted by permission of the author.

QUESTIONS FOR READING

1. What argument is embraced by those who are opposed to the use of torture?
2. What did Bloche learn about the purpose of "enhanced interrogation"? How is it used as part of a process for getting information?
3. What must interrogators assess for this model to work? How do they try to do this?
4. Why can we not know for certain if torture works?

QUESTIONS FOR REASONING AND ANALYSIS

5. What is Bloche's claim? (Be careful; it is not a simple statement.)
6. What grounds does he present in support of his claim?
7. Study the author's introduction; what does he gain by announcing his position on torture in his opening paragraph?
8. Study Bloche's conclusion: Why is deciding on one's position more difficult now? What does Bloche mean by his final sentence?

QUESTIONS FOR REFLECTION AND WRITING

9. Has Bloche convinced you that the issue of using enhanced interrogation has become more complex? Why or why not? If you disagree with the author, how would you refute him?
10. Both Bloche and Rejali discuss the issue of interrogators needing to assess what, if any, good information they may be getting from interrogation. What does this tell you about the task of intelligence gathering? Ponder this issue for class discussion or writing.

1. Do Rejali and Bloche hold opposing viewpoints on the use of torture—or are their differences more that of approach and focus? Read each author again and then write an analysis of their differences in style, approach to the issue, and position on the issue.

2. Reflect on what you have learned about torture from Rejali and Bloche and then consider: What may be the greatest "unknown" part of the equation in the use of interrogation as a strategy for finding people who have broken the law? Or, put another way, what do you see as the biggest problem to assuring success from questioning people under pressure to get intelligence from them?

3. Should the debate over enhanced interrogation procedures be about effectiveness or ethics? And, if it should be about effectiveness, then how much evidence is needed to defend torture on the grounds that it works? Ponder these questions.

GOING ONLINE

The debate over the use of enhanced interrogation techniques and of hidden sites abroad continues. Bloche mentions several studies in his discussion. Go online and see what more you can learn about this debate. Ponder this question: Why do some continue these strategies when studies fail to confirm that they work?

CHAPTER 5

Reading, Analyzing, and Using Visuals and Statistics in Argument

READ: This photo is of Princess Cottage, built in 1855 on Union Beach, NJ, as it looked after Hurricane Sandy (Fall 2012). The cottage has since been torn down.

REASON: What is your initial reaction to this photo? How does it make you feel? What does it make you think about?

REFLECT/WRITE: There are many images of the hurricane's destruction; why would someone select this image for publication?

We live in a visual age. Many of us go to movies to appreciate and judge the film's visual effects. The Internet is awash in pictures and colorful icons. Perhaps the best symbol of our visual age is *USA Today*, a paper filled with color photos and many tables and other graphics as a primary way of presenting information. *USA Today* has forced the more traditional papers to add color to compete. We also live in a numerical age. We refer to the events of September 11, 2001, as 9/11—without any disrespect. This chapter brings together these markers of our times as they are used in argument—and as argument. Finding statistics and visuals used as part of argument, we also need to remember that cartoons and advertisements are arguments in and of themselves.

RESPONDING TO VISUAL ARGUMENTS

Many arguments bombard us today in visual forms. These include photos, political cartoons, and advertising. Most major newspapers have a political cartoonist whose drawings appear regularly on the editorial page. (Some comic strips are also political in nature, at least some of the time.) These cartoons are designed to make a political point in a visually clever and amusing way. (That is why they are both "cartoons" and "political" at the same time.) Their uses of irony and caricatures of known politicians make them among the most emotionally powerful, indeed stinging, of arguments.

Photographs accompany many newspaper and magazine articles, and they often tell a story. Indeed some photographers are famous for their ability to capture a personality or a newsworthy moment. So accustomed to these visuals today, we sometimes forget to study photographs. Be sure to examine each photo, remembering that authors and editors have selected each one for a reason.

Advertisements are among the most creative and powerful forms of argument today. Remember that ads are designed to take your time (for shopping) and your money. Their messages need to be powerful to motivate you to action. With some products (what most of us consider necessities), ads are designed to influence product choice, to get us to buy brand A instead of brand B. With other products, ones we really do not need or which may actually be harmful to us, ads need to be especially clever. Some ads do provide information (car X gets better gas mileage than car Y). Other ads (perfume ads, for example) take us into a fantasy land so that we will spend $50 on a small but pretty bottle. Another type of ad is the "image advertisement," an ad that assures us that a particular company is top-notch. If we admire the company, we will buy its goods or services.

Here are guidelines for reading visual arguments. You can practice these steps with the exercises that follow.

GUIDELINES for Reading Photographs

- **Is a scene or situation depicted?** If so, study the details to identify the situation.
- **Identify each figure in the photo.**
- **What details of scene or person(s) carry significance?**
- **How does the photograph make you feel?**

GUIDELINES for Reading Political Cartoons

- **What scene is depicted?** Identify the situation.
- **Identify each of the figures in the cartoon.** Are they current politicians, figures from history or literature, the "person in the street," or symbolic representations?
- **Who speaks the lines in the cartoon?**
- **What is the cartoon's general subject?** What is the point of the cartoon, the claim of the cartoonist?

GUIDELINES for Reading Advertisements

- **What product or service is being advertised?**
- **Who seems to be the targeted audience?**
- **What is the ad's primary strategy?** To provide information? To reinforce the product's or company's image? To appeal to particular needs or desires? For example, if an ad shows a group of young people having fun and drinking a particular beer, to what needs/desires is the ad appealing?
- **Does the ad use specific rhetorical strategies such as humor, understatement, or irony?**
- **What is the relation between the visual part of the ad (photo, drawing, typeface, etc.) and the print part (the text, or copy)?** Does the ad use a slogan or catchy phrase? Is there a company logo? Is the slogan or logo clever? Is it well known as a marker of the company? What may be the effect of these strategies on readers?
- **What is the ad's overall visual impression?** Consider both images and colors used.

EXERCISES: Analyzing Photos, Cartoons, and Ads

1. Analyze the photo on page 123, using the guidelines previously listed.
2. Review the photos that open Chapters 1, 4, 5, 8, 10, 19, and 22. Select the one you find most effective. Analyze it in detail to show why you think it is the best.

3. Analyze the cartoon below using the guidelines listed previously. You may want to jot down your answers to the questions to be well prepared for class discussion.
4. Review the cartoons that open Chapters 2, 3, 6, 7, 9, 15, 16, 17, 20, and 21. Select the one you find most effective. Analyze it in detail to show why you think it is the cleverest.
5. Analyze the ads on pages 124–26, again using the guidelines listed above. After answering the guideline questions, consider these as well: Will each ad appeal effectively to its intended audience? If so, why? If not, why not?

the river of life

Retracing a historic journey to help fight malaria.

In 1858, Scottish missionary David Livingstone embarked on a historic journey along the Zambezi River in southern Africa. On that trip, malaria claimed the life of Livingstone's wife, Mary Livingstone himself also later died from the disease.

Today, 150 years later, malaria remains a threat. Over one million people, mostly children and pregnant women, die from malaria each year. About 40 percent of the global population is vulnerable to the disease.

But an unprecedented global action—by governments and corporations, NGOs and health organizations—has been mobilized against malaria. And this combined effort is yielding results:

- Across Africa, people are receiving anti-malarial medications, as well as bed nets and insecticides that protect against the mosquitoes that transmit the disease.

Photo by Helge Bendl

- In Rwanda, malaria cases are down by 64 percent, and deaths by 66 percent. Similar results are seen in Ethiopia and Zambia. And in Mozambique, where 9 out of 10 children had been infected, that number is now 2 in 10.

- Scientists are expanding the pipeline of affordable, effective anti-malarial medicines, while also making progress on discovering a vaccine.

April 25 is World Malaria Day. As part of that event, a team of medical experts will retrace Livingstone's journey along the Zambezi, the "River of Life." As part of the Roll Back Malaria Zambezi Expedition, they will travel 1,500 miles in inflatable boats through Angola, Namibia, Botswana, Zambia, Zimbabwe and Mozambique.

By exposing the difficulties of delivering supplies to remote areas, the expedition will demonstrate that only a coordinated, cross-border action can beat back the disease, and turn the lifeline of southern Africa into a "River of Life" for those threatened by malaria.

ExxonMobil is the largest non-pharmaceutical private-sector contributor to the fight against malaria. But our support is more than financial. We are actively partnering with governments and agencies in affected countries, enabling them to combat malaria with the same disciplined, results-based business practices that ExxonMobil employs in its global operations.

Livingstone once said, "I am prepared to go anywhere, provided it be forward." The communities burdened by this disease cannot move forward until malaria is controlled and, someday, eradicated. We urge everyone to join in this global effort.

For more information, visit www.zambezi-expedition.org and www.rollbackmalaria.org.

Your business side. Your creative side.
Inspire both. Introducing Avid's new editing lineup.

Quality, performance and value. A new way of thinking. A new way of doing business.
Take a closer look at **Avid.com/NewThinkingScript.**

READING GRAPHICS

Graphics—photographs, diagrams, tables, charts, and graphs—present a good bit of information in a condensed but also visually engaging format. Graphics are everywhere: in textbooks, magazines, newspapers, and the Internet. It's a rare training session or board meeting that is conducted without the use of graphics to display information. So, you want to be able to read graphics and create them, when appropriate, in your own writing. First, study the chart below that illustrates the different uses of various visuals. General guidelines for reading graphics follow. The guidelines will use Figure 5.1 to illustrate points. Study the figure repeatedly as you read through the guidelines.

Understanding How Graphics Differ

Each type of visual serves specific purposes. You can't use a pie chart, for example, to explain a process; you need a diagram or a flowchart. So, when reading graphics, understand what each type can show you. When preparing your own visuals, select the graphic that will most clearly and effectively present the particular information you want to display.

TYPE	PURPOSE	EXAMPLE
Diagram	show details demonstrate process	drawing of knee tendons photosynthesis
Table	list numerical information	income of U.S. households
Bar chart	comparative amounts of related numbers	differences in suicide rates by age and race
Pie chart	relative portions of a whole	percentages of Americans by educational level
Flowchart	steps in a process	purification of water
Graph	relationship of two items	income increases over time
Map	information relative to a geographical area	locations of world's rain forests

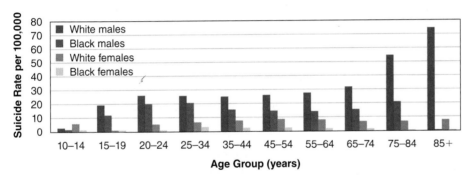

FIGURE 5.1 Differences in Suicide Rate According to Race, Gender, and Age
(Source: Data from the U.S. Bureau of the Census, 1994)

GUIDELINES for Reading Graphics

1. **Locate the particular graphic referred to in the text and study it at that point in your reading.** Graphics may not always be placed on the same page as the text reference. Stop your reading to find and study the graphic; that's what the writer wants you to do. Find Figure 5.1 on the previous page.

2. **Read the title or heading of the graphic.** Every graphic is given a title. What is the subject of the graphic? What kind of information is provided? Figure 5.1 shows differences in suicide rates by race, gender, and age.

3. **Read any notes, description, and the source information at the bottom of the graphic.** Figure 5.1 came from the U.S. Bureau of the Census for 1994. Critical questions: What is this figure showing me? Is the information coming from a reliable source? Is it current enough to still be meaningful?

4. **Study the labels—and other words—that appear as part of the graphic.** You cannot draw useful conclusions unless you understand exactly what is being shown. Observe in Figure 5.1 that the four bars for each age group (shown along the horizontal axis) represent white males, black males, white females, and black females, in that order, for each age category.

5. **Study the information, making certain that you understand what the numbers represent.** Are the numerals whole numbers, numbers in hundreds or thousands, or percentages? In Figure 5.1 we are looking at suicide *rates per 100,000 people* for four identified groups of people at different ages. So, to know exactly how many white males between 15 and 19 commit suicide, we need to know how many white males between 15 and 19 there are (or were in 1994) in the United States population. The chart does not give us this information. It gives us *comparative rates* per 100,000 people in each category and tells us that almost 20 in every 100,000 white males between 15 and 19 commit suicide.

6. **Draw conclusions.** Think about the information in different ways. Critical questions: What does the author want to accomplish by including these figures? How are they significant? What conclusions can you draw from Figure 5.1? Answer these questions to guide your thinking:

   a. Which of the four compared groups faces the greatest risk from suicide over his or her lifetime? Would you have guessed this group? Why or why not? What might be some of the causes for the greatest risk to this group?

   b. What is the greatest risk factor for increased suicide rate—race, gender, age, or a combination? Does this surprise you? Would you have guessed a different factor? Why?

   c. Which group, as young teens, is at greatest risk? Are you surprised? Why or why not? What might be some of the causes for this?

Graphics provide information, raise questions, explain processes, engage us emotionally, make us think. Study the various graphics in the exercises that follow to become more expert in reading and responding critically to visuals.

EXERCISES: Reading and Analyzing Graphics

1. Study the pie charts in Figure 5.2 and then answer the following questions.
   a. What is the subject of the charts?
   b. In addition to the information within the pie charts, what other information is provided?
   c. Which group increases by the greatest relative amount? How would you account for that increase?
   d. Which figure surprises you the most? Why?
2. Study the line graph in Figure 5.3 and then answer the following questions.
   a. What two subjects are treated by the graph?
   b. In 2000 what percentage of men's income did women earn?
   c. During which five-year period did men's incomes increase by the greatest amount?
   d. Does the author's prediction for the year 2005 suggest that income equality for women will have taken place?
   e. Are you bothered by the facts on this graph? Why or why not?
3. Study the table in Figure 5.4 and then answer the following questions.
   a. What is being presented and compared in this table?
   b. What, exactly, do the numerals in the second line represent? What, exactly, do the numerals in the third line represent? (Be sure that you understand what these numbers mean.)
   c. For the information given in lines 2, 3, 4, and 5, in which category have women made the greatest gains on men?
   d. See if you can complete the missing information in the last line. Where will you look to find out how many men and women were single parents in 2000? (In 2010?)
   e. Which figure surprises you the most? Why?
4. Maps can be used to show all kinds of information, not just the locations of cities, rivers, or mountains. Study the map in Figure 5.5 and then answer the questions that follow.
   a. What, exactly, does the map show? Why does it not "look right"?
   b. How many electoral votes did each candidate win?
   c. How are the winning states for each candidate clustered? What conclusions can you draw from observing this clustering?
   d. What advice would you give to each party to ensure that party's presidential win in 2016?
   e. How would the map look if it were drawn to show population by state? Would the red states look bigger or smaller?

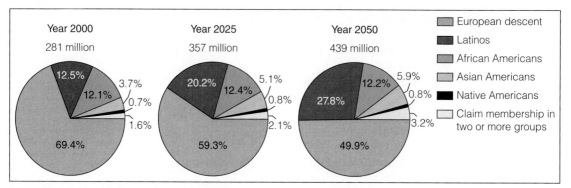

FIGURE 5.2 The Shifting of U.S. Racial-Ethnic Mix (Source: James M. Henslin, *Essentials of Sociology: A Down-to-Earth Approach*, 9th Edition, Figure 9.11 (p. 241), © 2011. Reprinted by permission of Pearson Education, Inc., Upper Saddle River, NJ.)

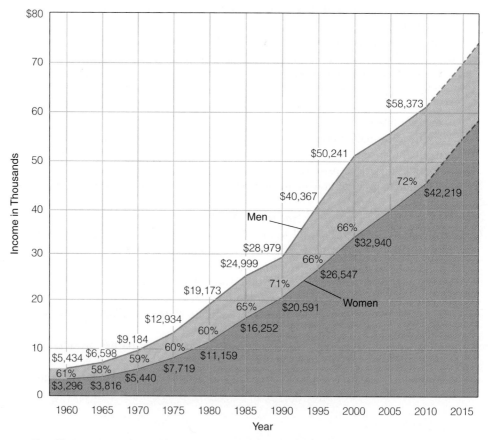

Note: The income jump from 1990 to 1995 is probably due to a statistical procedure. The 1995 source (for 1990 income) uses "median income," while the 1997 source (for 1995 income) merely says "average earnings." How the "average" is computed is not stated. Broken lines indicate the author's estimates.

FIGURE 5.3 The Gender Gap Over Time: What Percentage of Men's Income Do Women Earn? (Source: James M. Henslin, *Essentials of Sociology: A Down-to-Earth Approach*, 9th Edition, Figure 10.8 (p. 264), © 2011. Reprinted by permission of Pearson Education, Inc., Upper Saddle River, NJ.)

	1970		2000	
	MEN	**WOMEN**	**MEN**	**WOMEN**
Estimated life expectancy	67.1	74.1	74.24	79.9
% high school graduates	53	52	87	88
% of BAs awarded	57	43	45	55
% of MAs awarded	60	40	45	55
% of PhDs awarded	87	13	61	39
% in legal profession	95	5	70	30
Median earnings	$26,760	$14,232	$35,345	$25,862
Single parents	1.2 million	5.6 million	n/a	n/a

FIGURE 5.4 Men and Women in a Changing Society (Sources: for 1970: *1996 Statistical Abstract,* U.S. Dept. of Commerce, Economics and Statistics Administration, Bureau of the Census. 2000 data: National Center for Education Statistics http://nces.ed.gov/fastfacts)

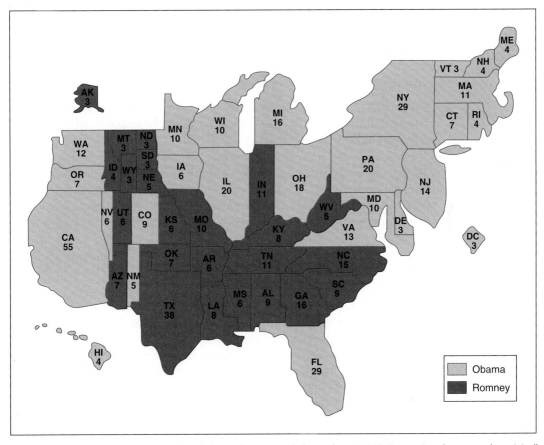

Note: **States drawn in proportion to number of electoral votes. Total electoral votes: 538** (Source: Based on a map that originally appeared in *New York Times,* November 5, 2002. Reprinted by permission of NYT Graphics. From O'Connor and Sabato, *American Government* © 2002; published by Allyn and Bacon, Boston, MA Copyright © 2002 by Pearson Education. Updated for the 2012 election by the author.)

FIGURE 5.5 Electoral Votes per State for the 2012 Presidential Election

THE USES OF AUTHORITY AND STATISTICS

Most of the visuals you have just studied provide a way of presenting statistics—data that many today consider essential to defending a claim. One reason you check the source information accompanying graphics is that you need to know—and evaluate—the authority of that source. When a graphic's numbers have come from the Census Bureau, you know you have a reliable source. When the author writes that "studies have shown . . . ," you want to become suspicious of the authority of the data. All elements of the arguments we read—and write—affect a writer's credibility.

Judging Authorities

We know that movie stars and sports figures are not authorities on soft drinks and watches. But what about *real* authorities? When writers present the opinions or research findings of authorities as support for a claim, they are saying to readers that the authority is trustworthy and the opinions valuable. But what they are asserting is actually an assumption or warrant, part of the glue connecting evidence to claim. Remember: Warrants can be challenged. If the "authority" can be shown to lack authority, then the logic of the argument is destroyed. Use this checklist of questions to evaluate authorities:

- ☐ *Is the authority actually an authority on the topic under discussion?* When a famous scientist supports a candidate for office, he or she speaks as a citizen, not as an authority.

- ☐ *Is the work of the authority still current?* Times change; expertise does not always endure. Galileo would be lost in the universe of today's astrophysicists. Be particularly alert to the dates of information in the sciences in general, in genetics and the entire biomedical field, in health and nutrition. It is almost impossible to keep up with the latest findings in these areas of research.

- ☐ *Does the authority actually have legitimate credentials?* Are the person's publications in respected journals? Is he or she respected by others in the same field? *Just because it's in print does not mean it's a reliable source!*

- ☐ *Do experts in the field generally agree on the issue?* If there is widespread disagreement, then referring to one authority does not do much to support a claim. This is why you need to understand the many sides of a controversial topic before you write on it, and you need to bring knowledge of controversies and critical thinking skills to your reading of argument. This is also why writers often provide a source's credentials, not just a name, unless the authority is quite famous.

- ☐ *Is the authority's evidence reliable, so far as you can judge, but the interpretation of that evidence seems odd, or seems to be used to support strongly held beliefs?* Does the evidence actually connect to the claim? A respected authority's work can be stretched or manipulated in an attempt to defend a claim that the authority's work simply does not support.

EXERCISES: Judging Authorities

1. Jane Goodall has received worldwide fame for her studies of chimpanzees in Gombe and for her books on those field studies. Goodall is a vegetarian. Should she be used as an authority in support of a claim for a vegetarian diet? Why or why not? Consider:
   a. Why might Goodall have chosen to become a vegetarian?
   b. For what arguments might Goodall be used as an authority?
   c. For what arguments might she be used effectively for emotional appeal?

2. Suppose a respected zoologist prepares a five-year study of U.S. zoos, compiling a complete list of all animals at each zoo. He then updates the list for each of the five years, adding births and deaths. When he examines his data, he finds that deaths are one and one-half times the number of births. He considers this loss alarming and writes a paper arguing for the abolishing of zoos on the grounds that too many animals are dying. Because of his reputation, his article is published in a popular science magazine. How would you evaluate his authority and his study?
   a. Should you trust the data? Why or why not?
   b. Should you accept his conclusions? Why or why not?
   c. Consider: What might be possible explanations for the birth/death ratio?

Understanding and Evaluating Statistics

There are two useful clichés to keep in mind: "Statistics don't lie, but people lie with statistics" and "There are lies, damned lies, and statistics." The second cliché is perhaps a bit cynical. We don't want to be naïve in our faith in numbers, but neither do we want to become so cynical that we refuse to believe any statistical evidence. What we do need to keep in mind is that when statistics are presented in an argument they are being used by someone interested in winning that argument.

Some writers use numbers without being aware that the numbers are incomplete or not representative. Some present only part of the relevant information. Some may not mean to distort, but they do choose to present the information in language that helps their cause. There are many ways, some more innocent than others, to distort reality with statistics. Use the following guidelines to evaluate the presentation of statistical information.

GUIDELINES for Evaluating Statistics

- **Is the information current and therefore still relevant?** Crime rates in your city based on 2000 census data probably are no longer relevant, certainly not current enough to support an argument for increased (or decreased) police department spending.

- **If a sample was used, was it randomly selected and large enough to be significant?** Sometimes in medical research, the results of a small study are publicized to guide researchers to important new areas of study. When these results are reported in the press or on TV, however, the small size of the study is not always made clear. Thus one week we learn that coffee is bad for us, the next week that it is okay.
- **What information, exactly, has been provided?** When you read "Two out of three chose the Merit combination of low tar and good taste," you must ask yourself "Two-thirds of how many altogether?"
- **How have the numbers been presented?** And what is the effect of that presentation? Numbers can be presented as fractions, whole numbers, or percentages. Writers who want to emphasize budget increases will use whole numbers—billions of dollars. Writers who want to de-emphasize those increases select percentages. Writers who want their readers to respond to the numbers in a specific way add words to direct their thinking: "a *mere* 3 percent increase" or "the *enormous* $5 billion increase."

EXERCISES: Reading Tables and Charts and Using Statistics

1. Figure 5.6, a table from the Census Bureau, shows U.S. family income data from 1980 to 2009. Percentages and median income are given for all families and then, in turn, for white, black, Asian, and Hispanic families. Study the data and then complete the exercises that follow.
   a. In a paper assessing the advantages of a growing economy, you want to include a paragraph on family income growth to show that a booming economy helps everyone, that "a rising tide lifts all boats." Select data from the table that best support your claim. Write a paragraph beginning with a topic sentence and including your data as support. Think about how to present the numbers in the most persuasive form.
   b. Write a second paragraph with the topic sentence "Not all Americans have benefited from the boom years" or "A rising tide does not lift all boats." Select data from the table that best support this topic sentence and present the numbers in the most persuasive form.
   c. Exchange paragraphs with a classmate and evaluate each other's selection and presentation of evidence.
2. Go back to Figure 5.1 (p. 127) and reflect again on the information that it depicts. Then consider what conclusions can be drawn from the evidence and what the implications of those conclusions are. Working in small groups or with a class partner, decide how you want to use the data to support a point.
3. Figure 5.7 (p. 136), another table from the Census Bureau, presents mean earnings by highest degree earned. First, be sure that you know the difference between mean and median (which is the number used in Figure 5.6). Study the data and reflect on the conclusions you can draw from the statistics. Consider: Of the various groups represented, which group most benefits from obtaining a college degree—as opposed to having only a high school diploma?

Year	Number of families (1,000)	Percent distribution							Median income (dollars)
		Under $15,000	$15,000 to $24,999	$25,000 to $34,999	$35,000 to $49,999	$50,000 to $74,999	$75,000 to $99,999	$100,000 and over	
ALL FAMILIES [1]									
1990	66,322	8.7	9.4	10.3	15.6	22.5	14.6	19.1	54,369
2000 [2]	73,778	7.0	8.6	9.3	14.3	19.8	15.1	26.2	61,063
2008	78,874	8.4	9.2	9.9	13.7	19.3	14.2	26.0	61,521
2009 [3]	76,867	8.7	9.1	10.0	13.8	19.4	13.5	25.6	60,088
WHITE									
1990	56,803	6.6	8.7	10.0	15.8	23.3	15.4	20.4	56,771
2000 [2]	61,330	5.7	7.9	9.0	14.2	20.1	15.8	27.7	63,849
2008 [4, 5]	64,183	6.9	8.5	9.5	13.4	19.8	15.0	27.5	65,000
2009 [3, 4, 5]	64,145	7.2	8.4	9.5	13.8	19.9	14.1	27.0	62,545
BLACK									
1990	7,471	23.9	14.7	12.5	14.4	17.5	8.8	8.2	32,946
2000 [2]	8,731	15.7	14.0	12.8	15.8	16.7	10.3	13.0	40,547
2008 [4, 5]	9,359	18.2	14.4	12.8	15.3	16.6	9.8	13.4	39,879
2009 [3, 4, 5]	9,367	18.0	14.5	13.3	15.2	16.4	10.6	12.1	38,409
ASIAN AND PACIFIC ISLANDER									
1990	1,536	8.1	7.8	8.2	11.6	21.2	15.0	28.5	64,969
2000 [2]	2,962	6.2	6.4	6.4	11.7	17.3	15.5	37.0	75,393
2008 [4, 7]	3,494	7.7	7.2	7.6	12.8	16.0	13.0	36.6	73,578
2009 [3, 4, 7]	3,592	6.9	7.0	7.9	10.4	17.7	12.3	37.7	75,027
HISPANIC ORIGIN [8]									
1990	4,961	17.0	16.3	13.6	17.3	19.1	8.5	8.2	36,034
2000 [2]	8,017	12.8	14.6	13.0	18.1	19.4	10.5	12.0	41,469
2008	10,503	15.5	14.6	14.1	16.8	17.2	9.6	12.5	40,466
2009 [3]	10,422	15.2	14.7	14.3	16.0	17.9	9.5	12.4	39,730

[Constant dollars based on CPI-U-RS deflator. Families as of March of following year, **(66,322 represents 66,322,000).** Based on Current Population Survey, Annual Social and Economic Supplement (ASEC); see text, this section, Section 1, and Appendix III. For data collection changes over time, see <http://www.census.gov/hhes/www/income/data/historical/history.html>. For definition of median, see Guide to Tabular Presentation]

[1] Includes other races not shown separately.   [2] Data reflect implementation of Census 2000-based population controls and a 28,000 household sample expansion to 78,000 households.   [3] Median income is calculated using $2,500 income intervals. Beginning with 2009 income data, the Census Bureau expanded the upper income intervals used to calculate medians to $250,000 or more. Medians falling in the upper open-ended interval are plugged with "$250,000." Before 2009, the upper open-ended interval was $100,000 and a plug of "$100,000" was used.   [4] Beginning with the 2003 Current Population Survey (CPS), the questionnaire allowed respondents to choose more than one race. For 2002 and later, data represent persons who selected this race group only and excludes persons reporting more than one race. The CPS in prior years allowed respondents to report only one race group. See also comments on race in the text for Section 1.   [5] Data represent White alone, which refers to people who reported White and did not report any other race category.   [6] Data represent Black alone, which refers to people who reported Black and did not report any other race category.   [7] Data represent Asian alone, which refers to people who reported Asian and did not report any other race category. [8] People of Hispanic origin may be any race.

Source: U.S. Census Bureau, *Income, Poverty and Health Insurance Coverage in the United States: 2009*, Current Population Reports, P60-238, and Historical Tables—Table F-23, September 2010. See also <http://www.census.gov/hhes/www/income/income. html> and <http://www.census.gov/hhes/www/income/data/historical/families/index.html>.

FIGURE 5.6 **Money Income of Families—Percent Distribution by Income Level in Constant (2009) Dollars: 1980 to 2009.**

WRITING THE INVESTIGATIVE ARGUMENT

The first step in writing an investigative argument is to select a topic to study. Composition students can write successful investigative essays on the media, on campus issues, and on various local concerns. Although you begin with a topic—not a claim—since you have to gather evidence before you can see what

Characteristic	Total persons	Not a high school graduate	High school graduate only	Some college, no degree	Associate's	Bachelor's	Master's	Professional	Doctorate
				Mean earnings by level of highest degree (dol.)					
All persons [1] . . .	**42,469**	**20,241**	**30,627**	**32,295**	**39,771**	**58,665**	**73,738**	**127,803**	**103,054**
Age:									
25 to 34 years old. . . .	35,595	19,415	30,627	31,392	35,544	45,662	58,997	86,440	74,628
35 to 44 years old. . . .	49,356	24,728	27,511	39,606	42,489	66,346	80,583	136,366	108,147
45 to 54 years old. . . .	51,956	23,725	36,090	44,135	45,145	69,548	86,532	146,808	112,134
55 to 64 years old. . . .	50,372	24,537	34,583	42,547	42,344	59,670	75,372	149,184	110,895
65 years old and over . .	37,544	19,395	28,469	29,602	33,541	44,147	45,138	95,440	95,585
Sex:									
Male.	50,180	23,036	35,468	39,204	47,572	69,479	90,954	150,310	114,347
Female	33,797	15,514	24,304	23,340	33,432	43,689	58,534	89,897	83,706
White [2].	43,337	20,457	31,429	33,119	40,632	57,762	73,771	127,942	104,533
Male.	51,287	23,353	36,416	40,352	48,521	71,286	81,776	149,149	115,497
Female	34,040	15,187	24,615	25,537	33,996	43,309	58,036	89,526	85,682
Black [2].	33,362	18,938	25,970	29,129	33,734	47,799	60,067	102,328	82,510
Male.	37,553	21,829	30,723	33,969	41,142	55,655	68,890	(B)	(B)
Female	29,831	15,644	22,954	25,433	29,464	42,567	54,523	(B)	(B)
Hispanic [3].	29,565	19,816	25,998	29,836	33,783	49,017	71,322	79,220	88,435
Male.	32,279	21,588	28,908	35,089	38,768	58,570	80,737	(B)	89,968
Female	25,713	16,170	21,473	24,281	29,785	39,568	61,843	(B)	(B)

[In dollars. For persons 18 years old and over with earnings. Persons as of March 2010. Based on Current Population Survey; see text, Section 1 and Appendix III. For definition of mean, see Guide to Tabular Presentation]

B Base figure too small to meet statistical standards for reliability of a derived figure.   [1] Includes other races not shown separately.   [2] For persons who selected this race group only. [3] Persons of Hispanic origin may be any race.

Source: U.S. Census Bureau, Current Population Survey, unpublished data, <http://www.census.gov/population/www/socdemo/educ-attn.html>.

FIGURE 5.7 Mean Earnings by Highest Degree Earned: 2009

it means, you should select a topic that holds your interest and that you may have given some thought to before choosing to write. For example, you may have noticed some clever ads for jeans or beer, or perhaps you are bothered by plans for another shopping area along a major street near your home. Either one of these topics can lead to an effective investigative, or inductive, argument.

Gathering and Analyzing Evidence

Let's reflect on strategies for gathering evidence for a study of magazine ads for a particular kind of product (the topic of the sample student paper that follows).

- Select a time frame and a number of representative magazines.
- Have enough magazines to render at least twenty-five ads on the product you are studying.
- Once you decide on the magazines and issues to be used, pull *all* ads for your product. Your task is to draw useful conclusions based on adequate data objectively collected. You can't leave some ads out and have a valid study.

- Study the ads, reflecting on the inferences they allow you to draw. The inferences become the claim of your argument. You may want to take the approach of classifying the ads, that is, grouping them into categories by the various appeals used to sell the product.

More briefly, consider your hunch that your area does not need another shopping mall. What evidence can you gather to support a claim to that effect? You could locate all existing strip or enclosed malls within a 10-mile radius of the proposed new mall site, visit each one, and count the number and types of stores already available. You may discover that there are plenty of malls but that the area really needs a grocery store or a bookstore. So instead of reading to find evidence to support a claim, you are creating the statistics and doing the analysis to guide you to a claim. Just remember to devise objective procedures for collecting evidence so that you do not bias your results.

Planning and Drafting the Essay

You've done your research and studied the data you've collected; how do you put this kind of argument together? Here are some guidelines to help you draft your essay.

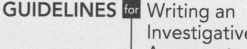
GUIDELINES for Writing an Investigative Argument

- **Begin with an opening paragraph that introduces your topic in an interesting way.** Possibilities include beginning with a startling statistic or explaining what impact the essay's facts will have on readers.
- **Devote space early in your paper to explaining your methods or procedures, probably in your second or third paragraph.** For example, if you have obtained information through questionnaires or interviews, recount the process: the questions asked, the number of people involved, the basis for selecting the people, and so on.
- **Classify the evidence that you present.** Finding a meaningful organization is part of the originality of your study and will make your argument more forceful. It is the way you see the topic and want readers to see it. If you are studying existing malls, you might begin by listing all of the malls and their locations. But then do not go store by store through each mall. Rather, group the stores by type and provide totals.
- **Consider presenting evidence in several ways, including in charts and tables as well as within paragraphs.** Readers are used to visuals, especially in essays containing statistics.
- **Analyze evidence to build your argument.** Do not ask your reader to do the thinking. No data dumps! Explain how your evidence *is* evidence by discussing the connection between facts and the inferences they support.

Analyzing Evidence: The Key to an Effective Argument

This is the thinking part of the process. Anyone can count stores or collect ads. What is your point? How does the evidence you have collected actually support your claim? You must guide readers through the evidence. Consider this example:

In a study of selling techniques used in computer ads in business magazines, a student, Brian, found four major selling techniques, one of which he classifies as "corporate emphasis." Brian begins his paragraph on corporate emphasis thus:

> In the technique of corporate emphasis, the advertiser discusses the whole range of products and services that the corporation offers, instead of specific elements. This method relies on the public's positive perception of the company, the company's accomplishments, and its reputation.

Brian then provides several examples of ads in this category, including an IBM ad:

> In one of its eight ads in the study, IBM points to the scientists on its staff who have recently won the Nobel Prize in physics.

But Brian does not stop there. He explains the point of this ad, connecting the ad to the assertion that this technique emphasizes the company's accomplishments:

> The inference we are to draw is that IBM scientists are hard at work right now in their laboratories developing tomorrow's technology to make the world a better place in which to live.

Preparing Graphics for Your Essay

Tables, bar charts, and pie charts are particularly helpful ways to present statistical evidence you have collected for an inductive argument. One possibility is to create a pie chart showing your classification of ads (or stores or questions on a questionnaire) and the relative amount of each item. For example, suppose you find four selling strategies. You can show in a pie chart the percentage of ads using each of the four strategies.

Computers help even the technically unsophisticated prepare simple charts. You can also do a simple table. When preparing graphics, keep these points in mind:

- Every graphic must be referred to in the text at the appropriate place—where you are discussing the information in the visual. Graphics are not disconnected attachments to an argument. They give a complete set of data in an easy-to-digest form, but some of that data must be discussed in the essay.
- Every graphic (except photographs) needs a label. Use Figure 1, Figure 2, and so forth. Then, in the text refer to each graphic by its label.
- Every graphic needs a title. Always place a title after Figure 1 (and so forth), on the same line, at the top or bottom of your visual.

- In a technically sophisticated world, hand-drawn graphics are not acceptable. Underline the graphic's title line, or place the visual within a box. (Check the tool bar at the top of your screen.) Type elements within tables. Use a ruler or compass to prepare graphics, or learn to use the graphics programs in your computer.

A CHECKLIST FOR REVISION ▪▪▪▪▪▪▪▪▪▪▪▪▪▪▪▪▪▪▪▪▪▪▪▪▪

- ☐ Have I stated a claim that is precise and appropriate to the data I have collected?
- ☐ Have I fully explained the methodology I used in collecting my data?
- ☐ Have I selected a clear and useful organization?
- ☐ Have I presented and discussed enough specifics to show readers how my data support my conclusions?
- ☐ Have I used graphics to present the data in an effective visual display?
- ☐ Have I revised, edited, and proofread my paper?

STUDENT ESSAY

BUYING TIME

Garrett Berger

Chances are you own at least one wristwatch. Watches allow us immediate access to the correct time. They are indispensable items in our modern world, where, as the saying is, time is money. Today the primary function of a wristwatch does not necessarily guide its design; like clothes, houses, and cars, watches have become fashion statements and a way to flaunt one's wealth.

Introduction connects to reader.

To learn how watches are being sold, I surveyed all of the full-page ads from the November issues of four magazines. The first two, *GQ* and *Vogue*, are well-known fashion magazines. *The Robb Report* is a rather new magazine that caters to the overclass. *Forbes* is of course a well-known financial magazine. I was rather surprised at the number of advertisements I found. After surveying 86 ads, marketing 59 brands, I have concluded that today watches are being sold through five main strategies: DESIGN/BRAND appeal, CRAFTSMANSHIP, ASSOCIATION, FASHION appeal, and EMOTIONAL appeal. The percentage of ads using each of these strategies is shown in Figure 1.

Student explains his methodology of collecting ads. Paragraph concludes with his claim.

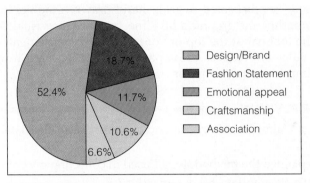

FIGURE 1 Percentage of Total Ads Using Each Strategy

Discussion of
first category.

In most DESIGN/BRAND appeal ads, only a picture and the brand name are used. A subset of this category uses the same basic strategy with a slogan or phrases to emphasize something about the brand or product. A Mont Blanc ad shows a watch profile with a contorted metal link band, asking the question "Is that you?" The reputation of the name and the appeal of the design sell the watch. Rolex, perhaps the best-known name in high-end watches, advertises, in *Vogue,* its "Oyster Perpetual Lady-Datejust Pearlmaster." A close-up of the watch face showcases the white, mother-of-pearl dial, sapphire bezel, and diamond-set band. A smaller, more complete picture crouches underneath, showing the watch on its side. The model name is displayed along a gray band that runs near the bottom. The Rolex crest anchors the bottom of the page. Forty-five ads marketing 29 brands use the DESIGN/BRAND strategy. A large picture of the product centered on a solid background is the norm.

Discussion of
second category.

CRAFTSMANSHIP, the second strategy, focuses on the maker, the horologer, and the technical sides of form and function. Brand heritage and a unique, hand-crafted design are major selling points. All of these ads are targeted at men, appearing in every magazine except *Vogue.* Collector pieces and limited editions were commonly sold using this strategy. The focus is on accuracy and technical excellence. Pictures of the inner works and cutaways, technical information, and explanations of movements and features are popular. Quality and exclusivity are all-important.

Detailed examples
to illustrate second
category.

A Cronoswiss ad from *The Robb Report* is a good example. The top third pictures a horologer, identified as "Gerd-R Lange, master watchmaker and founder of Cronoswiss in Munich," directly below. The middle third of the ad shows a watch, white-faced with a black leather band. The logo and slogan appear next to the watch. The bottom third contains copy beginning with the words "My watches are a hundred years behind the times." The rest explains what that statement means. Mr. Lange apparently believes that technical perfection in horology has already been attained. He also offers his book, *The Fascination of Mechanics,* free of charge along with the "sole distributor for North America" at the bottom. A "Daniel Roth" ad from the same magazine displays the name across the top of a white page; toward the top, left-hand corner a gold buckle and black band lead your eye to the center, where a gold watch with a transparent face displays its inner works exquisitely. Above and to the right, copy explains the exclusive and unique design accomplished by inverting the movement, allowing it to be viewed from above.

The third strategy is to sell the watch by establishing an ASSOCIATION with an object, experience, or person, implying that its value and quality are beyond question. In the six ads I found using this approach, watches are associated with violins, pilots, astronauts, hot air balloons, and a hero of the free world. This is similar to the first strategy, but relies on a reputation other than that of the maker. The watch is presented as being desirable for the connections created in the ad.

Discussion of third category.

Parmigiani ran an ad in *The Robb Report* featuring a gold watch with a black face and band illuminated by some unseen source. A blue-tinted violin rises in the background; the rest of the page is black. The brief copy reads: "For those who think a Stradivarius is only a violin. The Parmigiani Toric Chronograph is only a wristwatch." "The Moon Watch" proclaims an Omega ad from *GQ*. Inset on a white background is a picture of an astronaut on the moon saluting the American flag. The silver watch with a black face lies across the lower part of the page. The caption reads: "Speedmaster Professional. The first and only watch worn on the moon." Omega's logo appears at the bottom. Figure 2 shows another Omega use of this strategy.

FIGURE 2 Example of Association Advertising

The fourth strategy is to present the watch simply as a FASHION statement. In this line of attack, the ads appeal to our need to be current, accepted, to fit in and be like everyone else, or to make a statement, setting us apart from others as hip and cool. The product is presented as a necessary part of our wardrobes. The watch is fashionable and will send the "right" message. Design and style are the foremost concerns; "the look" sells the watch.

Discussion of fourth category.

Techno Marine has an ad in *GQ* which shows a large close-up of a watch running down the entire length of the left side of the page. Two alternate color schemes are pictured on the right, separating small bits of copy. At the bottom on the right are the name and logo. The first words at the top read: "Keeping time—you keep your closet up to the minute, why not your wrist? The latest addition to your watch wardrobe should be the AlphaSport." Longines uses a similar strategy in *Vogue.* Its ad is divided in half lengthwise. On the left is a black-and-white picture of Audrey Hepburn. The right side is white with the Longines' logo at the top and two ladies' watches in the center. Near the bottom is the phrase "Elegance is an Attitude." Retailers appear at the bottom. The same ad ran in *GQ*, but with a man's watch and a picture of Humphrey Bogart. A kind of association is made, but quality and value aren't the overriding concerns. The point is to have an elegant attitude like these fashionable stars did, one that these watches can provide and enhance.

The fifth and final strategy is that of EMOTIONAL appeal. The ads using this approach strive to influence our emotional responses and allege to influence the emotions of others towards us. Their power and appeal are exerted through the feelings they evoke in us. Nine out of ten ads rely on a picture as the main device to trigger an emotional link between the product and the viewer. Copy is scant; words are used mainly to guide the viewer to the advertiser's desired conclusions.

Discussion of fifth category.

A Frederique Constant ad pictures a man, wearing a watch, mulling over a chess game. Above his head are the words "Inner Passion." The man's gaze is odd; he is looking at something on the right side of the page, but a large picture of a watch superimposed over the picture hides whatever it is that he is looking at. So we are led to the watch. The bottom third is white and contains the maker's logo and the slogan "Live your Passion." An ad in *GQ* shows a man holding a woman. He leans against a rock; she reclines in his arms. Their eyes are closed, and both have peaceful, smiling expressions. He is wearing a Tommy Hilfiger watch. The ad spans two pages; a close-up of the watch is presented on the right half of the second page. The only words are the ones in the logo. This is perhaps one of those pictures that are worth a thousand words. The message is he got the girl because he's got the watch.

Strong conclusion; the effect of watch ads.

Even more than selling a particular watch, all of these ads focus on building the brand's image. I found many of the ads extremely effective at conveying their messages. Many of the better-known brands favor the comparatively simple DESIGN/BRAND appeal strategy, to reach a broader audience. Lesser-known, high-end makers contribute many of the more specialized strategies. We all count and mark the passing hours and minutes. And society places great importance on time, valuing punctuality. But these ads strive to convince us that having "the right time" means so much more than "the time."

FOR READING AND ANALYSIS

EVERY BODY'S TALKING | JOE NAVARRO

Joe Navarro spent more than twenty-five years in the FBI, specializing in counterintelligence and profiling. He is recognized as an authority on nonverbal messages, especially given off by those who are lying, and he continues to consult to government and industry. He has also turned his expertise to poker and has published, with Marvin Karlines, *Read 'Em and Reap* (2006), a guide to reading the nonverbal messages from poker opponents. The following essay appeared in the *Washington Post* on June 24, 2008.

PREREADING QUESTIONS What does the term "counterintelligence" mean? How much attention do you give to body language messages from others?

Picture this: I was sailing the Caribbean for three days with a group of friends and their spouses, and everything seemed perfect. The weather was beautiful, the ocean diaphanous blue, the food exquisite; our evenings together were full of laughter and good conversation.

Things were going so well that one friend said to the group, "Let's do this again next year." I happened to be across from him and his wife as he spoke those words. In the cacophony of resounding replies of "Yes!" and "Absolutely!" I noticed that my friend's wife made a fist under her chin as she grasped her necklace. This behavior stood out to me as powerfully as if someone had shouted, "Danger!"

I watched the words and gestures of the other couples at the table, and everyone seemed ecstatic—everyone but one, that is. She continued to smile, but her smile was tense.

Her husband has treated me as a brother for more than 15 years, and I consider him the dearest of friends. At that moment I knew that things between him and his wife were turning for the worse. I did not pat myself on the back for making these observations. I was saddened.

For 25 years I worked as a paid observer. I was a special agent for the FBI specializing in counterintelligence—specifically, catching spies. For me, observing human behavior is like having software running in the background, doing its job—no conscious effort needed. And so on that wonderful cruise, I made a "thin-slice assessment" (that's what we call it) based on just a few significant behaviors. Unfortunately, it turned out to be right: Within six months of our return, my friend's wife filed for divorce, and her husband discovered painfully that she had been seeing someone else for quite a while.

When I am asked what is the most reliable means of determining the health of a relationship, I always say that words don't matter. It's all in the language of the body. The nonverbal behaviors we all transmit tell others, in real time, what we think, what we feel, what we yearn for or what we intend.

Now I am embarking on another cruise, wondering what insights I will have about my travel companions and their relationships. No matter what, this promises to be a fascinating trip, a journey for the mind and the soul. I am with a handful of dear friends and 3,800 strangers, all headed for Alaska; for an observer it does not get any better than this.

While lining up to board on our first day, I notice just ahead of me a couple who appear to be in their early 30s. They are obviously Americans (voice, weight and demeanor).

Not so obvious is their dysfunctional relationship. He is standing stoically, shoulders wide, looking straight ahead. She keeps whispering loudly to him, but she is not facing forward. She violates his space as she leans into him. Her face is tense and her lips are narrow slivers each time she engages him with what clearly appears to be a diatribe. He occasionally nods his head but avoids contact with her. He won't let his hips near her as they start to walk side by side. He reminds me of Bill and Hillary Clinton walking toward the Marine One helicopter immediately after the Monica Lewinsky affair: looking straight ahead, as much distance between them as possible.

TORSO	ARMS	HANDS AND FINGERS	FEET AND LEGS
LEANING AWAY FROM SOMEONE: Means we dislike or disagree with them.	FINGERTIPS SPREAD APART ON A SURFACE:	THUMBS UP:	JIGGLING/KICKING FOOT:
LEANING TOWARD SOMEONE: Means we like or agree with them.	A display of confidence and authority.	A good indication of positive thoughts.	Indicates discomfort.
SPLAYING OUT:	ARMS AKIMBO:	STEEPLING: (FINGERTIP TO FINGERTIP)	CROSSING LEGS:
A sign of comfort becomes a territorial or dominance display when there are serious issues being discussed.	Establishes dominance or communicates there are 'issues.'	A powerful display of confidence.	Indicates we are comfortable.
CROSSED ARMS:	ARMS BEHIND THE BACK:	NECK TOUCHING:	TOE POINTS UPWARD:
Suddenly crossing arms tightly is a sign of discomfort.	Says "don't draw near" —keeps people at bay.	Indicates emotional discomfort, doubt or insecurity.	Signals a good mood.

Illustrations by Peter Arkle. Reprinted by permission.

10   I think everyone can decipher this one from afar because we have all seen situations like this. What most people will miss is something I have seen this young man do twice now, which portends poorly for both of them. Every time she looks away, he "disses" her. He smirks and rolls his eyes, even as she stands beside him. He performs his duties, pulling their luggage along; I suspect he likes to have her luggage nearby as a barrier between them. I won't witness the dissolution of their marriage, but I know it will happen, for the research behind this is fairly robust. When two people in a relationship have contempt for each other, the marriage will not last.

When it comes to relationships and courtship behaviors, the list of useful 11 cues is long. Most of these behaviors we learned early when interacting with our mothers. When we look at loving eyes, our own eyes get larger, our pupils dilate, our facial muscles relax, our lips become full and warm, our skin becomes more pliable, our heads tilt. These behaviors stay with us all of our lives.

I watched two lovers this morning in the dining room. Two young people, 12 perhaps in their late 20s, mirror each other, staring intently into each other's eyes, chin on hand, head slightly tilted, nose flaring with each breath. They are trying to absorb each other visually and tactilely as they hold hands across the table.

Over time, those who remain truly in love will show even more indicators 13 of mirroring. They may dress the same or even begin to look alike as they adopt each other's nonverbal expressions as a sign of synchrony and empathy. They will touch each other with kind hands that touch fully, not with the fingertips of the less caring.

They will mirror each other in ways that are almost imperceptible; they will 14 have similar blink rates and breathing rates, and they will sit almost identically. They will look at the same scenery and not speak, merely look at each other and take a deep breath to reset their breathing synchrony. They don't have to talk. They are in harmony physically, mentally and emotionally, just as a baby is in exquisite synchrony with its mother who is tracing his every expression and smile.

As I walk through the ship on the first night, I can see the nonverbals of 15 courtship. There is a beautiful woman, tall, slender, smoking a cigarette outside. Two men are talking to her, both muscular, handsome, interested. She has crossed her legs as she talks to them, an expression of her comfort. As she holds her cigarette, the inside of her wrist turns toward her newfound friends. Her interest and comfort with them resounds, but she is favoring one of them. As he speaks to her, she preens herself by playing with her hair. I am not sure he is getting the message that she prefers him; in the end, I am sure it will all get sorted out.

At the upscale lounge, a man is sitting at the bar talking animatedly to the 16 woman next to him and looking at everyone who walks by. The woman has begun the process of ignoring him, but he does not get it. After he speaks to her a few times, she gathers her purse and places it on her lap. She has turned slightly away from him and now avoids eye contact. He has no clue; he thinks he is cool by commenting on the women who pass by. She is verbally and nonverbally indifferent.

The next night it is more of the same. This time, I see two people who just 17 met talking gingerly. Gradually they lean more and more into each other. She is now dangling her sandal from her toes. I am not sure he knows it. Perhaps he sees it all in her face, because she is smiling, laughing and relaxed. Communication is fluid, and neither wants the conversation to end. She is extremely interested.

18   All of these individuals are carrying on a dialogue in nonverbals. The socially adept will learn to read and interpret the signs accurately. Others will make false steps or pay a high price for not being observant. They may end up like my friend on the Caribbean cruise, who missed the clues of deceit and indifference.

19   This brings me back to my friend and his new wife, who are on this wonderful voyage. They have been on board for four days, and they are a delight individually and together. He lovingly looks at her; she stares at him with love and admiration. When she holds his hand at dinner, she massages it ever so gently. Theirs is a strong marriage. They don't have to tell me. I can sense it and observe it. I am happy for them and for myself. I can see cues of happiness, and they are unmistakable. You can't ask for more.

Source: *Washington Post*, June 24, 2008. Reprinted by permission of the author.

QUESTIONS FOR READING

1. What is Navarro's subject? (Do not answer "taking cruises"!)
2. What clues are offered to support the conclusion that the two cruise couples' relationships are about to dissolve?
3. What are the nonverbal messages that reveal loving relationships?
4. What nonverbal messages should the man in the lounge be observing?

QUESTIONS FOR REASONING AND ANALYSIS

5. What is Navarro's claim?
6. What kind of evidence does he provide?
7. How do the illustrations contribute to the argument? What is effective about the author's opening?

QUESTIONS FOR REFLECTION AND WRITING

8. Has the author convinced you that nonverbal language reveals our thoughts and feelings? Why or why not?
9. Can you "read" the nonverbal language of your instructors? Take some time to analyze each of your instructors. What have you learned? (You might also reflect on what messages you may be sending in class.)

For all investigative essays—inductive arguments—follow the guidelines in this chapter and use the student essay as your model. Remember that you will need to explain your methods for collecting data, to classify evidence and present it in several formats, and also to explain its significance for readers. Just collecting data does not create an argument. Here are some possible topics to explore:

1. Study print ads for one type of product (e.g., cars, cosmetics, cigarettes) to draw inferences about the dominant techniques used to sell that product. Remember that the more ads you study, the more support you have for your inferences. You should study at least twenty-five ads.

2. Study print ads for one type of product as advertised in different types of magazines clearly directed to different audiences to see how (or if) selling techniques change with a change in audience. (Remember: To demonstrate no change in techniques can be just as interesting a conclusion as finding changes.) Study at least twenty-five ads, in a balanced number from the different magazines.

3. Select a major figure currently in the news and conduct a study of bias in one of the newsmagazines (e.g., *Time, U.S. News & World Report,* or *Newsweek*) or a newspaper. Use at least eight issues of the magazine or newspaper from the last six months and study all articles on your figure in each of those issues. To determine bias, look at the amount of coverage, the location (front pages or back pages), the use of photos (flattering or unflattering), and the language of the articles.

4. Conduct a study of amounts of violence on TV by analyzing, for one week, all prime-time programs that may contain violence. (That is, eliminate sitcoms and decide whether you want to include or exclude news programs.) Devise some classification system for types of violence based on your prior TV viewing experience before beginning your study—but be prepared to alter or add to your categories based on your viewing of shows. Note the number of times each violent act occurs. You may want to consider the total length of time (per program, per night, per type of violent act) of violence during the week you study. Give credit to any authors in this text or other publications for any ideas you borrow from their articles.

5. As an alternative to topic 4, study the number and types of violent acts in children's programs on Saturday mornings. (This and topic 4 are best handled if you can record and then replay the programs several times.)

6. Conduct a survey and analyze the results on some campus issue or current public policy issue. Prepare questions that are without bias and include questions to get information about the participants so that you can correlate answers with the demographics of your participants (e.g., age, gender, race, religion, proposed major in college, political affiliation, or whatever else you think is important to the topic studied). Decide whether you want to survey students only or both students and faculty. Plan how you are going to reach each group.

CHAPTER 6

Learning More about Argument: Induction, Deduction, Analogy, and Logical Fallacies

PEARLS BEFORE SWINE

BY STEPHAN PASTIS

READ: What is the situation? What are Pig's reactions to what he is told?

REASON: Who are the only creatures who can never lie? What is Pig's solution to what he has been told? Are we invited to accept Pig's solution?

REFLECT/WRITE: What makes the cartoon amusing? What is its more serious message?

You can build on your knowledge of the basics of argument, examined in Chapter 3, by understanding some traditional forms of argument: induction, deduction, and analogy. It is also important to recognize arguments that do not meet the standards of good logic.

INDUCTION

Induction is the process by which we reach inferences—opinions based on facts, or on a combination of facts and less debatable inferences. The inductive process moves from particular to general, from support to assertion. We base our inferences on the facts we have gathered and studied. In general, the more evidence, the more convincing the argument. No one wants to debate tomorrow's sunrise; the evidence for counting on it is too convincing. Most inferences, though, are drawn from less evidence, so we need to examine these arguments closely to judge their reasonableness.

The pattern of induction looks like this:

EVIDENCE: There is the dead body of Smith. Smith was shot in his bedroom between the hours of 11:00 P.M. and 2:00 A.M., according to the coroner. Smith was shot by a .32-caliber pistol. The pistol left in the bedroom contains Jones's fingerprints. Jones was seen, by a neighbor, entering the Smith home at around 11:00 the night of Smith's death. A coworker heard Smith and Jones arguing in Smith's office the morning of the day Smith died.

CLAIM: Jones killed Smith.

The facts are presented. The jury infers that Jones is a murderer. Unless there is a confession or a trustworthy eyewitness, the conclusion is an inference, not a fact. This is the most logical explanation. The conclusion meets the standards of simplicity and frequency while accounting for all of the known evidence.

The following paragraph illustrates the process of induction. In their book *Discovering Dinosaurs,* authors Mark Norell, Eugene Gaffney, and Lowell Dingus answer the question "Did dinosaurs really rule the world?"

> For almost 170 million years, from the Late Triassic to the end of the Cretaceous, there existed dinosaurs of almost every body form imaginable: small carnivores, such as *Compsognathus* and *Ornitholestes,* ecologically equivalent to today's foxes and coyotes; medium-sized carnivores, such as *Velociraptor* and the troödontids, analogous to lions and tigers; and the monstrous carnivores with no living analogs, such as *Tyrannosaurus* and *Allosaurus.* Included among the ornithischians and the elephantine sauropods are terrestrial herbivores of diverse body form. By the end of the Jurassic, dinosaurs had even taken to the skies. The only habitats that dinosaurs did not dominate during the Mesozoic were aquatic. Yet, there were marine representatives, such as the primitive toothed bird *Hesperornis.* Like penguins, these birds were flightless, specialized for diving, and probably had to return to land to reproduce. In light of this broad morphologic diversity [number of

body forms], dinosaurs did "rule the planet" as the dominant life form on Earth during most of the Mesozoic [era that includes the Triassic, Jurassic, and Cretaceous periods, 248 to 65 million years ago].

Observe that the writers organize evidence by type of dinosaur to demonstrate the range and diversity of these animals. A good inductive argument is based on a sufficient volume of *relevant* evidence. The basic shape of this inductive argument is illustrated in Figure 6.1.

CLAIM:	Dinosaurs were the dominant life form during the Mesozoic era.
GROUNDS:	The facts presented in the paragraph.
ASSUMPTION (WARRANT):	The facts are representative, revealing dinosaur diversity.

FIGURE 6.1 The Shape of an Inductive Argument

COLLABORATIVE EXERCISE: Induction

With your class partner or in small groups, make a list of facts that could be used to support each of the following inferences:

1. Fido must have escaped under the fence during the night.
2. Sue must be planning to go away for the weekend.
3. Students who do not hand in all essay assignments fail Dr. Bradshaw's English class.
4. The price of Florida oranges will go up in grocery stores next year.
5. Yogurt is a better breakfast food than bread.

DEDUCTION

Although induction can be described as an argument that moves from particular to general, from facts to inference, deduction cannot accurately be described as the reverse. Deductive arguments are more complex. *Deduction is the reasoning process that draws a conclusion from the logical relationship of two assertions, usually one broad judgment or definition and one more specific assertion, often an inference.* Suppose, on the way out of American history class, you say, "Abraham Lincoln certainly was a great leader." Someone responds with the expected question "Why do you think so?" You explain: "He was great because he performed with courage and a clear purpose in a time of crisis." Your explanation contains a conclusion and an assertion about Lincoln (an inference) in support. But behind your explanation rests an idea about leadership, in the terms of deduction, *a premise.* The argument's basic shape is illustrated in Figure 6.2.

CLAIM:	Lincoln was a great leader.
GROUNDS:	1. People who perform with courage and clear purpose in a crisis are great leaders.
	2. Lincoln was a person who performed with courage and a clear purpose in a crisis.
ASSUMPTION (WARRANT):	The relationship of the two reasons leads, logically, to the conclusion.

FIGURE 6.2 The Shape of a Deductive Argument

Traditionally, the deductive argument is arranged somewhat differently from these sentences about Lincoln. The two reasons are called *premises;* the broader one, called the *major premise,* is written first and the more specific one, the *minor premise,* comes next. The premises and conclusion are expressed to make clear that assertions are being made about categories or classes. To illustrate:

MAJOR PREMISE:	All people who perform with courage and a clear purpose in a crisis are great leaders.
MINOR PREMISE:	Lincoln was a person who performed with courage and a clear purpose in a crisis.
CONCLUSION:	Lincoln was a great leader.

If these two premises are correctly, that is, logically, constructed, then the conclusion follows logically, and the deductive argument is *valid.* This does not mean that the conclusion is necessarily *true.* It does mean that if you accept the truth of the premises, then you must accept the truth of the conclusion, because in a valid argument the conclusion follows logically, necessarily. How do we know that the conclusion must follow if the argument is logically constructed? Let's think about what each premise is saying and then diagram each one to represent each assertion visually. The first premise says that all people who act a particular way are people who fit into the category called "great leaders":

The second premise says that Lincoln, a category of one, belongs in the category of people who act in the same particular way that the first premise describes:

If we put the two diagrams together, we have the following set of circles, demonstrating that the conclusion follows from the premises:

We can also make negative and qualified assertions in a deductive argument. For example:

PREMISE:	No cowards can be great leaders.
PREMISE:	Falstaff was a coward.
CONCLUSION:	Falstaff was not a great leader.

Or, to reword the conclusion to make the deductive pattern clearer: No Falstaff (no member of this class) is a great leader. Diagramming to test for validity, we find that the first premise says no A's are B's:

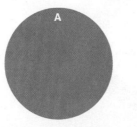 

The second premise asserts all C's are A's:

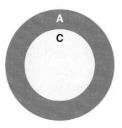

Put together, we see that the conclusion follows necessarily from the premises: No C's can possibly be members of class B.

Some deductive arguments merely look right, but the two premises do not lead logically to the conclusion that is asserted. We must read each argument carefully or diagram each one to make certain that the conclusion follows from the premises. Consider the following argument: *Unions must be communistic because they want to control wages.* The sentence contains a conclusion and one reason, or premise. From these two parts of a deductive argument we can also determine the unstated premise, just as we could with the Lincoln argument: *Communists want to control wages.* If we use circles to represent the three categories of people in the argument and diagram the argument, we see a different result from the previous diagrams:

Diagramming the argument reveals that it is invalid; that is, it is not logically constructed because the statements do not require that the union circle be placed inside the communist circle. We cannot draw the conclusion we want from any two premises, only from those that provide a logical basis from which a conclusion can be reached.

We must first make certain that deductive arguments are properly constructed or valid. But suppose the logic works and yet you do not agree with the claim? Your complaint, then, must be with one of the premises, a judgment or inference that you do not accept as true. Consider the following argument:

MAJOR PREMISE:	(All) dogs make good pets.
MINOR PREMISE:	Fido is a dog.
CONCLUSION:	Fido will make a good pet.

This argument is valid. (Diagram it; your circles will fit into one another just as with the Lincoln argument.) However, you are not prepared to agree, necessarily, that Fido will make a good pet. The problem is with the major premise. For the argument to work, the assertion must be about *all* dogs, but we know that not all dogs will be good pets.

When composing a deductive argument, your task will be to defend the truth of your premises. Then, if your argument is valid (logically constructed), readers will have no alternative but to agree with your conclusion. If you disagree with someone else's logically constructed argument, then you must show why one of the premises is not true. Your counterargument will seek to discredit one (or both) of the premises. The Fido argument can be discredited by your producing examples of dogs that have not made good pets.

A deductive argument can serve as the core of an essay, an essay that supports the argument's claim by developing support for each of the premises. Since the major premise is either a broad judgment or a definition, it will need to be defended on the basis of an appeal to values or beliefs that the writer expects readers to share. The minor premise, usually an inference about a particular situation (or person), would be supported by relevant evidence, as with any inductive argument. You can see this process at work in the Declaration of Independence. Questions follow the Declaration to guide your analysis of this famous example of the deductive process.

THE DECLARATION OF INDEPENDENCE

In Congress, July 4, 1776
The unanimous declaration of the thirteen
United States of America

1 When in the course of human events, it becomes necessary for one people to dissolve the political bands which have connected them with another, and to assume among the powers of the earth, the separate and equal station to which the Laws of Nature and of Nature's God entitle them, a decent respect

to the opinions of mankind requires that they should declare the causes which impel them to the separation.

We hold these truths to be self-evident, that all men are created equal, 2 that they are endowed by their Creator with certain unalienable rights, that among these are life, liberty and the pursuit of happiness. That to secure these rights, governments are instituted among men, deriving their just powers from the consent of the governed. That whenever any form of government becomes destructive of these ends, it is the right of the people to alter or to abolish it, and to institute new government, laying its foundation on such principles and organizing its powers in such form, as to them shall seem most likely to effect their safety and happiness. Prudence, indeed, will dictate that governments long established should not be changed for light and transient causes; and accordingly all experience hath shown, that mankind are more disposed to suffer, while evils are sufferable, than to right themselves by abolishing the forms to which they are accustomed. But when a long train of abuses and usurpations, pursuing invariably the same object evinces a design to reduce them under absolute despotism, it is their right, it is their duty, to throw off such government, and to provide new guards for their future security. Such has been the patient sufferance of these Colonies; and such is now the necessity which constrains them to alter their former systems of government. The history of the present King of Great Britain is a history of repeated injuries and usurpations, all having in direct object the establishment of an absolute tyranny over these States. To prove this, let facts be submitted to a candid world.

He has refused his assent to laws, the most wholesome and necessary for 3 the public good.

He has forbidden his Governors to pass laws of immediate and pressing 4 importance, unless suspended in their operation till his assent should be obtained; and when so suspended, he has utterly neglected to attend to them.

He has refused to pass other laws for the accommodation of large districts 5 of people, unless those people would relinquish the right of representation in the Legislature, a right inestimable to them and formidable to tyrants only.

He has called together legislative bodies at places unusual, uncomfort- 6 able, and distant from the depository of their public records, for the sole purpose of fatiguing them into compliance with his measures.

He has dissolved representative houses repeatedly, for opposing with 7 manly firmness his invasions on the rights of the people.

He has refused for a long time, after such dissolutions, to cause others to 8 be elected; whereby the legislative powers, incapable of annihilation, have returned to the people at large for their exercise; the State remaining in the meantime exposed to all the dangers of invasion from without and convulsions within.

He has endeavoured to prevent the population of these States; for that 9 purpose obstructing the laws of naturalization of foreigners; refusing to pass others to encourage their migration hither, and raising the conditions of new appropriations of lands.

10   He has obstructed the administration of justice, by refusing his assent to laws for establishing judiciary powers.

11   He has made judges dependent on his will alone, for the tenure of their offices, and the amount and payment of their salaries.

12   He has erected a multitude of new offices, and sent hither swarms of officers to harass our people, and eat out their substance.

13   He has kept among us, in times of peace, standing armies without the consent of our legislatures.

14   He has affected to render the military independent of and superior to the civil power.

15   He has combined with others to subject us to a jurisdiction foreign to our constitution, and unacknowledged by our laws; giving his assent to their acts of pretended legislation:

16   For quartering large bodies of armed troops among us:

17   For protecting them, by a mock trial, from punishment for any murders which they should commit on the inhabitants of these States:

18   For cutting off our trade with all parts of the world:

19   For imposing taxes on us without our consent:

20   For depriving us, in many cases, of the benefits of trial by jury:

21   For transporting us beyond seas to be tried for pretended offences:

22   For abolishing the free system of English laws in a neighbouring Province, establishing therein an arbitrary government, and enlarging its boundaries so as to render it at once an example and fit instrument for introducing the same absolute rule into these Colonies:

23   For taking away our Charters, abolishing our most valuable laws, and altering fundamentally the forms of our governments:

24   For suspending our own Legislatures, and declaring themselves invested with power to legislate for us in all cases whatsoever.

25   He has abdicated government here, by declaring us out of his protection and waging war against us.

26   He has plundered our seas, ravaged our coasts, burnt our towns, and destroyed the lives of our people.

27   He is at this time transporting large armies of foreign mercenaries to complete the works of death, desolation and tyranny, already begun with circumstances of cruelty and perfidy scarcely paralleled in the most barbarous ages, and totally unworthy the head of a civilized nation.

28   He has constrained our fellow citizens taken captive on the high seas to bear arms against their country, to become the executioners of their friends and brethren, or to fall themselves by their hands.

29   He has excited domestic insurrections amongst us, and has endeavoured to bring on the inhabitants of our frontiers, the merciless Indian savages, whose known rule of warfare, is an undistinguished destruction of all ages, sexes, and conditions.

30   In every stage of these oppressions we have petitioned for redress in the most humble terms; our repeated petitions have been answered only by repeated injury. A prince whose character is thus marked by every act which may define a tyrant is unfit to be the ruler of a free people.

Nor have we been wanting in attention to our British brethren. We have 31 warned them from time to time of attempts by their legislature to extend an unwarrantable jurisdiction over us. We have reminded them of the circumstances of our emigration and settlement here. We have appealed to their native justice and magnanimity, and we have conjured them by the ties of our common kindred to disavow these usurpations, which would inevitably interrupt our connections and correspondence. They too have been deaf to the voice of justice and of consanguinity. We must, therefore, acquiesce in the necessity, which denounces our separation, and hold them, as we hold the rest of mankind, enemies in war, in peace friends.

We, therefore, the Representatives of the United States of America, in 32 General Congress assembled, appealing to the Supreme Judge of the world for the rectitude of our intentions, do, in the name, and by the authority of the good people of these Colonies, solemnly publish and declare, That these United Colonies are, and of right ought to be Free and Independent States; that they are absolved from all allegiance to the British Crown, and that all political connection between them and the State of Great Britain, is and ought to be totally dissolved; and that as Free and Independent States, they have full power to levy war, conclude peace, contract alliances, establish commerce, and to do all other acts and things which Independent States may of right do. And for the support of this declaration, with a firm reliance on the protection of Divine Providence, we mutually pledge to each other our lives, our fortunes, and our sacred honor.

QUESTIONS FOR ANALYSIS

1. What is the Declaration's central deductive argument? State the argument in the shape illustrated above: major premise, minor premise, conclusion. Construct a valid argument. If necessary, draw circles representing each of the three terms in the argument to check for validity. (*Hint:* Start with the claim "George III's government should be overthrown.")

2. Which paragraphs are devoted to supporting the major premise? What kind of support has been given?

3. Which paragraphs are devoted to supporting the minor premise? What kind of support has been given?

4. Why has more support been given for one premise than the other?

EXERCISES: Completing and Evaluating Deductive Arguments

Turn each of the following statements into valid deductive arguments. (You have the conclusion and one premise, so you will have to determine the missing premise that would complete the argument. Draw circles if necessary to test for validity.) Then decide which arguments have premises that could be supported. Note the kind of support that might be provided. Explain why you think some arguments have insupportable premises. Here is an example:

PREMISE:	All Jesuits are priests.
PREMISE:	No women are priests.
CONCLUSION:	No women are Jesuits.

Since the circle for women must be placed outside the circle for priests, it must also be outside the circle for Jesuits. Hence the argument is valid. The first premise is true by definition; the term *Jesuit* refers to an order of Roman Catholic priests. The second premise is true for the Roman Catholic Church, so if the term *priest* is used only to refer to people with a religious vocation in the Roman Catholic Church, then the second premise is also true by definition.

1. Mrs. Ferguson is a good teacher because she can explain the subject matter clearly.
2. Segregated schools are unconstitutional because they are unequal.
3. Michael must be a good driver because he drives fast.
4. The media clearly have a liberal bias because they make fun of religious fundamentalists.

ANALOGY

The argument from analogy is an argument based on comparison. Analogies assert that since A and B are alike in several ways, they must be alike in another way as well. The argument from analogy concludes with an inference, an assertion of a significant similarity in the two items being compared. The other similarities serve as evidence in support of the inference. The shape of an argument by analogy is illustrated in Figure 6.3.

Although analogy is sometimes an effective approach to an issue because clever, imaginative comparisons are often moving, analogy is not as rigorously logical as either induction or deduction. Frequently, an analogy is based on only two or three points of comparison, whereas a sound inductive argument presents many examples to support its conclusion. Further, to be convincing, the points of comparison must be fundamental to the two items being compared. An argument for a county leash law for cats developed by analogy with dogs may cite the following similarities:

GROUNDS:	A has characteristics 1, 2, 3, and 4.
	B has characteristics 1, 2, and 3.
CLAIM:	B has characteristic 4 (as well).
ASSUMPTION	If B has three characteristics in common with A, it must have
(WARRANT):	the key fourth characteristic as well.

FIGURE 6.3 The Shape of an Argument by Analogy

- Cats are pets, just like dogs.
- Cats live in residential communities, just like dogs.
- Cats can mess up other people's yards, just like dogs.
- Cats, if allowed to run free, can disturb the peace (fighting, howling at night), just like dogs.

Does it follow that cats should be required to walk on a leash, just like dogs? If such a county ordinance were passed, would it be enforceable? Have you ever tried to walk a cat on a leash? In spite of legitimate similarities brought out by the analogy, the conclusion does not logically follow because the arguer is overlooking a fundamental difference in the two animals' personalities. Dogs can be trained to a leash; most cats (Siamese are one exception) cannot be so trained. Such thinking will produce sulking cats and scratched owners. But the analogy, delivered passionately to the right audience, could lead community activists to lobby for a new law.

Observe that the problem with the cat-leash-law analogy is not in the similarities asserted about the items being compared but rather in the underlying assumption that the similarities logically support the argument's conclusion. A good analogy asserts many points of comparison and finds likenesses that are essential parts of the nature or purpose of the two items being compared. The best way to challenge another's analogy is to point out a fundamental difference in the nature or purpose of the compared items. For all of their similarities, when it comes to walking on a leash, cats are *not* like dogs.

EXERCISES: Analogy

Analyze the following analogies. List the stated and/or implied points of comparison and the conclusion in the pattern illustrated in Figure 6.3. Then judge each argument's logic and effectiveness as a persuasive technique. If the argument is not logical, state the fundamental difference in the two compared items. If the argument could be persuasive, describe the kind of audience that might be moved by it.

1. College newspapers should not be under the supervision or control of a faculty sponsor. Fortunately, no governmental sponsor controls the *New York Times,* or we would no longer have a free press in this country. We need a free college press, too, one that can attack college policies when they are wrong.

2. Let's recognize that college athletes are really professional and start paying them properly. College athletes get a free education, and spending money from boosters. They are required to attend practices and games, and—if they play football or basketball—they bring in huge revenues for their "organization." College coaches are also paid enormous salaries, just like professional coaches, and often college coaches are tapped to coach professional teams. The only difference: The poor college athletes don't get those big salaries and huge signing bonuses.

3. Just like any business, the federal government must be made to balance its budget. No company could continue to operate in the red as the government does and expect to be successful. A constitutional amendment requiring a balanced federal budget is long overdue.

LOGICAL FALLACIES

A thorough study of argument needs to include a study of logical fallacies because so many "arguments" fail to meet standards of sound logic and good sense. Why do people offer arguments that aren't sensible?

Causes of Illogic

Ignorance

One frequent cause for illogical debate is a lack of knowledge of the subject. Some people have more information than others. The younger you are, the less you can be expected to know about complex issues. On the other hand, if you want to debate a complex or technical issue, then you cannot use ignorance as an excuse. Instead, read as much as you can, listen carefully to discussions, ask questions, and select topics about which you have knowledge or will research before writing.

Egos

Ego problems are another cause of weak arguments. Those with low self-esteem often have difficulty in debates because they attach themselves to their ideas and then feel personally attacked when someone disagrees with them. Remember: Self-esteem is enhanced when others applaud our knowledge and thoughtfulness, not our irrationality.

Prejudices

The prejudices and biases that we carry around, having absorbed them "ages ago" from family and community, are also sources of irrationality. Prejudices range from the worst ethnic, religious, or sexist stereotypes to political views we have adopted uncritically (Democrats are all bleeding hearts; Republicans are all rich snobs) to perhaps less serious but equally insupportable notions (if it's in print, it must be right). People who see the world through distorted lenses cannot possibly assess facts intelligently and reason logically from them.

A Need for Answers

Finally, many bad arguments stem from a human need for answers—any answers—to the questions that deeply concern us. We want to control our world because that makes us feel secure, and having answers makes us feel in control. This need can lead to illogic from oversimplifying issues.

Based on these causes of illogic, we can usefully divide fallacies into (1) oversimplifying the issue and (2) ignoring the issue by substituting emotion for reason.

Fallacies That Result from Oversimplifying

Errors in Generalizing

Errors in generalizing include overstatement and hasty or faulty generalization. All have in common an error in the inductive pattern of argument. The inference drawn from the evidence is unwarranted, either because too broad a generalization is made or because the generalization is drawn from incomplete or incorrect evidence.

Overstatement occurs when the argument's assertion is unqualified—referring to all members of a category. Overstatements often result from stereotyping, giving the same traits to everyone in a group. Overstatements are frequently signaled by words such as *all, every, always, never,* and *none.* But remember that assertions such as "children love clowns" are understood to refer to "all children," even though the word *all* does not appear in the sentence. It is the writer's task to qualify statements appropriately, using words such as *some, many,* or *frequently,* as appropriate.

Overstatements are discredited by finding only one exception to disprove the assertion. One frightened child who starts to cry when the clown approaches will destroy the argument. Here is another example:

- Lawyers are only interested in making money.

  (What about lawyers who work to protect consumers, or public defenders who represent those unable to pay for a lawyer?)

Hasty or faulty generalizations may be qualified assertions, but they still oversimplify by arguing from insufficient evidence or by ignoring some relevant evidence. For example:

- Political life must lead many to excessive drinking. In the last six months the paper has written about five members of Congress who either have confessed to alcoholism or have been arrested on DUI charges.

  (Five is not a large enough sample from which to generalize about *many* politicians. Also, the five in the newspaper are not a representative sample; they have made the news because of their drinking.)

Forced Hypothesis

The *forced hypothesis* is also an error in inductive reasoning. The explanation (hypothesis) offered is "forced," or illogical, because either (1) sufficient evidence does not exist to draw any conclusion or (2) the evidence can be explained more simply or more sensibly by a different hypothesis. This fallacy often results from not considering other possible explanations. You discredit a forced hypothesis by providing alternative conclusions that are more sensible than or just as sensible as the one offered. Consider this example:

- Professor Redding's students received either A's or B's last semester. He must be an excellent teacher.

  (The grades alone cannot support this conclusion. Professor Redding could be an excellent teacher; he could have started with excellent students; he could be an easy grader.)

Non Sequitur

The term *non sequitur,* meaning literally "it does not follow," could apply to all illogical arguments, but the term is usually reserved for those in which the conclusions are not logically connected to the reasons. In a hasty generalization, for example, there is a connection between support (five politicians in the news) and conclusion (many politicians with drinking problems), just not a convincing connection. With the *non sequitur* there is no recognizable connection, either because (1) whatever connection the arguer sees is not made clear to others or because (2) the evidence or reasons offered are irrelevant to the conclusion. For example:

- Donna will surely get a good grade in physics; she earned an A in her biology class.

   (Doing well in one course, even one science course, does not support the conclusion that the student will get a good grade in another course. If Donna is not good at math, she definitely will not do well in physics.)

Slippery Slope

The *slippery slope* argument asserts that we should not proceed with or permit A because, if we do, the terrible consequences X, Y, and Z will occur. This type of argument oversimplifies by assuming, without evidence and usually by ignoring historical examples, existing laws, or any reasonableness in people, that X, Y, and Z will follow inevitably from A. This kind of argument rests on the belief that most people will not want the final, awful Z to occur. The belief, however accurate, does not provide a sufficiently good reason for avoiding A. One of the best-known examples of slippery slope reasoning can be found in the gun-control debate:

- If we allow the government to register handguns, next it will register hunting rifles; then it will prohibit all citizen ownership of guns, thereby creating a police state or a world in which only outlaws have guns.

   (Surely no one wants the final dire consequences predicted in this argument. However, handgun registration does not mean that these consequences will follow. The United States has never been a police state, and its system of free elections guards against such a future. Also, citizens have registered cars, boats, and planes for years without any threat of their confiscation.)

False Dilemma

The *false dilemma* oversimplifies by asserting only two alternatives when there are more than two. The either–or thinking of this kind of argument can be an effective tactic if undetected. If the arguer gives us only two choices and one of those is clearly unacceptable, then the arguer can push us toward the preferred choice. For example:

- The Federal Reserve System must lower interest rates, or we will never pull out of the recession.

   (Clearly, staying in a recession is not much of a choice, but the alternative may not be the only or the best course to achieve a healthy economy. If interest rates go too low, inflation can result. Other options include the government's creating new jobs and patiently letting market forces play themselves out.)

False Analogy

When examining the shape of analogy, we also considered the problems with this type of argument. (See pp. 160–61.) Remember that you challenge a false analogy by noting many differences in the two items being compared or by noting a significant difference that has been ignored.

Post Hoc Fallacy

The term *post hoc,* from the Latin *post hoc, ergo propter hoc* (literally, "after this, therefore because of it") refers to a common error in arguments about cause. One oversimplifies by confusing a time relationship with cause. Reveal the illogic of *post hoc* arguments by pointing to other possible causes:

- We should throw out the entire city council. Since the members were elected, the city has gone into deficit spending.

  (Assuming that deficit spending in this situation is bad, was it caused by the current city council? Or did the current council inherit debts? Or is the entire region suffering from a recession?)

EXERCISES: Fallacies That Result from Oversimplifying

1. Here is a list of the fallacies we have examined so far. Make up or collect from your reading at least one example of each fallacy.
    a. Overstatement
    b. Stereotyping
    c. Hasty generalization
    d. Forced hypothesis
    e. *Non sequitur*
    f. Slippery slope
    g. False dilemma
    h. False analogy
    i. *Post hoc* fallacy

2. Explain what is illogical about each of the following arguments. Then name the fallacy represented. (Sometimes an argument will fit into more than one category. In that case name all appropriate terms.)
    a. Everybody agrees that we need stronger drunk-driving laws.
    b. The upsurge in crime on Sundays is the result of the reduced rate of church attendance in recent years.
    c. The government must create new jobs. A factory in Illinois has laid off half its workers.
    d. Steve has joined the country club. Golf must be one of his favorite sports.
    e. Blondes have more fun.
    f. You'll enjoy your Volvo; foreign cars never break down.
    g. Gary loves jokes. He would make a great comedian.
    h. The economy is in bad shape because of the Federal Reserve Board. Ever since it expanded the money supply, the stock market has been declining.
    i. Either we improve the city's street lighting, or we will fail to reduce crime.
    j. DNA research today is just like the study of nuclear fission. It seems important, but it's just another bomb that will one day explode on us. When will we learn that government must control research?

k. To prohibit prayer in public schools is to limit religious practice solely to internal belief. The result is that an American is religiously "free" only in his or her own mind.

l. Professor Johnson teaches in the political science department. I'll bet she's another socialist.

m. Coming to the aid of any country engaged in civil war is a bad idea. Next we'll be sending American troops, and soon we'll be involved in another Vietnam.

n. We must reject affirmative action in hiring or we'll have to settle for incompetent employees.

■ ■

Fallacies That Result from Avoiding the Real Issue

There are many ways to divert attention from the issue under debate. Of the six discussed here, the first three try to divert attention by introducing a separate issue or "sliding by" the actual issue. The following three divert by appealing to the audience's emotions or prejudices. In the first three the arguer tries to give the impression of good logic. In the last three the arguer charges forward on emotional manipulation alone.

Begging the Question

To assume that part of your argument is true without supporting it is to *beg the question*. Arguments seeking to pass off as proof statements that must themselves be supported are often introduced with such phrases as "the fact is" (to introduce opinion), "obviously," and "as we can see." For example:

- Clearly, lowering grading standards would be bad for students, so a pass/fail system should not be adopted.

  (Does a pass/fail system lower standards? No evidence has been given. If so, is that necessarily bad for students?)

Red Herring

The *red herring* is a foul-smelling argument indeed. The debater introduces a side issue, some point that is not relevant to the debate:

- The senator is an honest woman; she loves her children and gives to charities.

  (The children and charities are side issues; they do not demonstrate honesty.)

Straw Man

The *straw man* argument attributes to opponents incorrect and usually ridiculous views that they do not hold so that their position can be easily attacked. We can challenge this illogic by demonstrating that the arguer's opponents do not hold those views or by demanding that the arguer provide some evidence that they do:

- Those who favor gun control just want to take all guns away from responsible citizens and put them in the hands of criminals.

  (The position attributed to proponents of gun control is not only inaccurate but actually the opposite of what is sought by gun-control proponents.)

Ad Hominem

One of the most frequent of all appeals to emotion masquerading as argument is the *ad hominem* argument (literally, argument "to the man"). When someone says that "those crazy liberals at the ACLU just want all criminals to go free," or a pro-choice demonstrator screams at those "self-righteous fascists" on the other side, the best retort may be silence, or the calm assertion that such statements do not contribute to meaningful debate.

Common Practice or Bandwagon

To argue that an action should be taken or a position accepted because "everyone is doing it" is illogical. The majority is not always right. Frequently, when someone is defending an action as ethical on the ground that everyone does it, the action isn't ethical and the defender knows it isn't. For example:

- There's nothing wrong with fudging a bit on your income taxes. After all, the superrich don't pay any taxes, and the government expects everyone to cheat a little.

  (First, not everyone cheats on taxes; many pay to have their taxes done correctly. And if it is wrong, it is wrong regardless of the number who do it.)

Ad Populum

Another technique for arousing an audience's emotions and ignoring the issue is to appeal *ad populum*, "to the people," to the audience's presumed shared values and beliefs. Every Fourth of July, politicians employ this tactic, appealing to God, mother, apple pie, and "traditional family values." Simply reject the argument as illogical.

- Good, law-abiding Americans must be sick of the violent crimes occurring in our once godly society. But we won't tolerate it anymore; put the criminals in jail and throw away the key.

  (This does not contribute to a thoughtful debate on criminal justice issues.)

EXERCISES: Fallacies That Result from Ignoring the Issue

1. Here is a list of fallacies that result from ignoring the issue. Make up or collect from your reading at least one example of each fallacy.
    a. Begging the question
    b. Red herring
    c. Straw man

d. *Ad hominem*

e. Common practice or bandwagon

f. *Ad populum*

2. Explain what is illogical about each of the following arguments. Then name the fallacy represented.

   a. Gold's book doesn't deserve a Pulitzer Prize. She had been married four times.

   b. I wouldn't vote for him; many of his programs are basically socialist.

   c. Eight out of ten headache sufferers use Bayer to relieve headache pain. It will work for you, too.

   d. We shouldn't listen to Colman McCarthy's argument against liquor ads in college newspapers because he obviously thinks young people are ignorant and need guidance in everything.

   e. My roommate Joe does the craziest things; he must be neurotic.

   f. Since so many people obviously cheat the welfare system, it should be abolished.

   g. She isn't pretty enough to win the contest, and besides she had her nose "fixed" two years ago.

   h. Professors should chill out; everybody cheats on exams from time to time.

   i. The fact is that bilingual education is a mistake because it encourages students to use only their native language and that gives them an advantage over other students.

   j. Don't join those crazy liberals in support of the American Civil Liberties Union. They want all criminals to go free.

   k. Real Americans understand that free-trade agreements are evil. Let your representatives know that we want American goods protected.   ▪ ▪

EXERCISE: Analyzing Arguments

Examine the following letter to the editor by Christian Brahmstedt that appeared in the *Washington Post* on January 2, 1989. If you think it contains logical fallacies, identify the passages and explain the fallacies.

Help Those Who Help, Not Hurt, Themselves

1   In the past year, and repeatedly throughout the holiday season, the *Post* has devoted an abnormally large share of newsprint to the "plight" of the vagrants who wander throughout the city in search of free handouts: i.e., the "homeless."

2   As certain as taxes, the poor shall remain with civilization forever. Yet these "homeless" are certainly not in the same category as the poor. The poor of civilization, of which we have all been a part at one time in our lives, are proud and work hard until a financial independence frees them from the category.

The "homeless" do not seek work or pride. They are satisfied to beg and survive on others' generosity.

The best correlation to the "homeless" I have witnessed are the gray squirrels on Capitol Hill. After feeding several a heavy dose of nuts one afternoon, I returned the next day to see the same squirrels patiently waiting for a return feeding. In the same fashion, the "homeless" are trained by Washington's guilt-ridden society to continue begging a sustenance rather than learning independence.   3

The *Post* has preached that these vagrants be supported from the personal and federal coffers—in the same manner as the squirrels on Capitol Hill. This support is not helping the homeless; it is only teaching them to rely on it. All of our parents struggled through the depression as homeless of a sort, to arise and build financial independence through hard work.   4

The "homeless" problem will go away when, and only when, Washingtonians refuse to feed them. They will learn to support themselves and learn that society demands honest work for an honest dollar.   5

It would be better for Washington citizens to field their guilt donations to the poor, those folks who are holding down two or more jobs just to make ends meet, rather than throwing their tribute to the vagrants on the sewer grates. The phrase "help those who help themselves" has no more certain relevance than to the "homeless" issue.   6

Source: © *The Washington Post*.

FOR READING AND ANALYSIS

DECLARATION OF SENTIMENTS | ELIZABETH CADY STANTON

Elizabeth Cady Stanton (1815–1902) was one of the most important leaders of the women's rights movement. Educated at the Emma Willard Seminary in Troy, New York, Stanton studied law with her father before her marriage. At the Seneca Falls Convention in 1848 (the first women's rights convention), Stanton gave the opening speech and read her "Declaration of Sentiments." She founded and became president of the National Women's Suffrage Association in 1869.

PREREADING QUESTION As you read, think about the similarities and differences between this document and the Declaration of Independence. What significant differences in wording and content do you find?

1   When, in the course of human events, it becomes necessary for one portion of the family of man to assume among the people of the earth a position different from that which they have hitherto occupied, but one to which the laws of nature and of nature's God entitle them, a decent respect to the opinions of mankind requires that they should declare the causes that impel them to such a course.

Elizabeth Cady Stanton and her daughter, Harriot. from a daguerreotype 1856.

2   We hold these truths to be self-evident: that all men and women are created equal; that they are endowed by their Creator with certain inalienable rights; that among these are life, liberty, and the pursuit of happiness; that to secure these rights governments are instituted, deriving their just powers from the consent of the governed. Whenever any form of government becomes destructive of these ends, it is the right of those who suffer from it to refuse allegiance to it, and to insist upon the institution of a new government, laying its foundation on such principles, and organizing its powers in such form, as to them shall seem most likely to effect their safety and happiness. Prudence, indeed, will dictate that governments long established should not be changed for light and transient causes; and accordingly all experience hath shown that mankind are more disposed to suffer, while evils are sufferable, than to right themselves by abolishing the forms to which they were accustomed. But when a long train of abuses and usurpations, pursuing invariably the same object evinces a design to reduce them under absolute despotism, it is their duty to throw off such government, and to provide new guards for their future security. Such has been the patient sufferance of the women under this government, and such is now the necessity which constrains them to demand the equal station to which they are entitled.

3   The history of mankind is a history of repeated injuries and usurpations on the part of man toward woman, having in direct object the establishment of an absolute tyranny over her. To prove this, let facts be submitted to a candid world.

4   He has never permitted her to exercise her inalienable right to the elective franchise.

5   He has compelled her to submit to laws, in the formation of which she had no voice.

6   He has withheld from her rights which are given to the most ignorant and degraded men—both natives and foreigners.

7   Having deprived her of this first right of a citizen, the elective franchise, thereby leaving her without representation in the halls of legislation, he has oppressed her on all sides.

He has made her, if married, in the eye of the law, civilly dead. 8

He has taken from her all right in property, even to the wages she earns. 9

He has made her, morally, an irresponsible being, as she can commit many 10 crimes with impunity, provided they be done in the presence of her husband. In the covenant of marriage, she is compelled to promise obedience to her husband, he becoming, to all intents and purposes, her master—the law giving him power to deprive her of her liberty, and to administer chastisement.

He has so framed the laws of divorce, as to what shall be the proper 11 causes, and in case of separation, to whom the guardianship of the children shall be given, as to be wholly regardless of the happiness of women—the law, in all cases, going upon a false supposition of the supremacy of man, and giving all power into his hands.

After depriving her of all rights as a married woman, if single, and the 12 owner of property, he has taxed her to support a government which recognizes her only when her property can be made profitable to it.

He has monopolized nearly all the profitable employments, and from those 13 she is permitted to follow, she receives but a scanty remuneration. He closes against her all the avenues to wealth and distinction which he considers most honorable to himself. As a teacher of theology, medicine, or law, she is not known.

He has denied her the facilities for obtaining a thorough education, all col- 14 leges being closed against her.

He allows her in Church, as well as State, but a subordinate position, claim- 15 ing Apostolic authority for her exclusion from the ministry, and, with some exceptions, from any public participation in the affairs of the Church.

He has created a false public sentiment by giving to the world a different 16 code of morals for men and women, by which moral delinquencies which exclude women from society, are not only tolerated, but deemed of little account in man.

He has usurped the prerogative of Jehovah himself, claiming it as his right 17 to assign for her a sphere of action, when that belongs to her conscience and to her God.

He has endeavored, in every way that he could, to destroy her confidence 18 in her own powers, to lessen her self-respect, and to make her willing to lead a dependent and abject life.

Now in view of this entire disfranchisement of one-half the people of this 19 country, their social and religious degradation—in view of the unjust laws above mentioned, and because women do feel themselves aggrieved, oppressed, and fraudulently deprived of their most sacred rights, we insist that they have immediate admission to all the rights and privileges which belong to them as citizens of the United States.

In entering upon the great work before us, we anticipate no small amount 20 of misconception, misrepresentation, and ridicule; but we shall use every instrumentality within our power to effect our object. We shall employ agents, circulate tracts, petition the State and National legislatures, and endeavor to enlist the pulpit and the press in our behalf. We hope this Convention will be followed by a series of Conventions embracing every part of the country.

QUESTIONS FOR READING

1. Summarize the ideas of paragraphs 1 and 2. Be sure to use your own words.
2. What are the first three facts given by Stanton? Why are they presented first?
3. How have women been restricted by law if married or owning property? How have they been restricted in education and work? How have they been restricted psychologically?
4. What, according to Stanton, do women demand? How will they seek their goals?

QUESTIONS FOR REASONING AND ANALYSIS

5. What is Stanton's claim? With what does she charge men?
6. Most—but not all—of Stanton's charges have been redressed, however slowly. Which continue to be legitimate complaints, in whole or in part?

QUESTIONS FOR REFLECTION AND WRITING

7. Do we need a new declaration of sentiments for women? If so, what specific charges would you list? If not, why not?
8. Do we need a declaration of sentiments for other groups—children, minorities, the elderly, animals? If so, what specific charges should be listed? Select one group (that concerns you) and prepare a declaration of sentiments for that group. If you do not think any group needs a declaration, explain why.

THINGS PEOPLE SAY | NEIL DEGRASSE TYSON

An astrophysicist whose research interests include star formation and the structure of the Milky Way, Neil Tyson is director of the Hayden Planetarium in New York City. He is also one of today's most important figures in bringing science to the nonspecialist. He has been *Natural History* magazine's columnist, and since 2006 he has been the host of the PBS show *NOVAScienceNow*. A popular public speaker, Tyson is the author of nine books, including a collection of his essays. The following column from *Natural History* was originally published in the July/August 1998 issue.

PREREADING QUESTIONS Given your knowledge of the author and the title of his essay, what do you expect his subject to be? How often do you observe the physical universe and think about what you see?

1   Aristotle once declared that while the planets moved against the background stars, and while shooting stars, comets, and eclipses represented intermittent variability in the atmosphere and the heavens, the stars themselves were fixed and unchanging on the sky and that Earth was the center of all motion in the universe. From our enlightened perch, 25 centuries later, we chuckle at the folly of these ideas, but the claims were the consequence of legitimate, albeit simple, observations of the natural world.

Neil deGrasse Tyson with the "tools of his trade."

Aristotle also made other kinds of claims. He said that heavy things fall faster than light things. Who could argue against that? Rocks obviously fall to the ground faster than tree leaves. But Aristotle went further and declared that heavy things fall faster than light things in direct proportion to their own weight, so that a 10-pound object would fall ten times faster than a 1-pound object.

Aristotle was badly mistaken.

To test him, simply release a small rock and a big rock simultaneously from the same height. Unlike fluttering leaves, neither rock will be much influenced by air resistance and both will hit the ground at the same time. This experiment does not require a grant from the National Science Foundation to execute. Aristotle could have performed it but didn't. Aristotle's teachings were later adopted into the doctrines of the Catholic Church. And through the Church's power and influence Aristotelian philosophies became lodged in the common knowledge of the Western world, blindly believed and repeated. Not only did people repeat to others that which was not true, but they also ignored things that clearly happened but were not supposed to be true.

When scientifically investigating the natural world, the only thing worse than a blind believer is a seeing denier. In A.D. 1054, a star in the constellation Taurus abruptly increased in brightness by a factor of a million. The Chinese astronomers wrote about it. Middle Eastern astronomers wrote about it. Native Americans of what is now the southwestern United States made rock engravings of it. The star became bright enough to be plainly visible in the daytime for weeks, yet we have no record of anybody in all of Europe recording the event. (The bright new star in the sky was actually a supernova explosion that occurred in space some 7,000 years earlier but its light had only just reached Earth.) True, Europe was in the Dark Ages, so we cannot expect that acute data-taking skills were common, but cosmic events that were "allowed" to happen were routinely recorded. For example, 12 years later, in 1066, what ultimately became known as Halley's comet was seen and duly depicted—complete with agape onlookers—in a section of the famous Bayeux tapestry, circa 1100. An exception indeed. The Bible says the stars don't change. Aristotle said the stars don't change. The Church, with its unmatched authority, declares the stars don't change. The population then falls victim to a collective delusion that was stronger than its members' own powers of observation.

6   We all carry some blindly believed knowledge because we cannot realistically test every statement uttered by others. When I tell you that the proton has an antimatter counterpart (the antiproton), you would need $1 billion worth of laboratory apparatus to verify my statement. So it's easier to just believe me and trust that, at least most of the time, and at least with regard to the astrophysical world, I know what I am talking about. I don't mind if you remain skeptical. In fact, I encourage it. Feel free to visit your nearest particle accelerator to see antimatter for yourself. But how about all those statements that don't require fancy apparatus to prove? One would think that in our modern and enlightened culture, popular knowledge would be immune from falsehoods that were easily testable.

7   It is not.

8   Consider the following declarations. The North Star is the brightest star in the nighttime sky. The Sun is a yellow star. What goes up must come down. On a dark night you can see millions of stars with the unaided eye. In space there is no gravity. A compass points north. Days get shorter in the winter and longer in the summer. Total solar eclipses are rare.

9   Every statement in the above paragraph is false.

10   Many people (perhaps most people) believe one or more of these statements and spread them to others even when a firsthand demonstration of falsehood is trivial to deduce or obtain. Welcome to my things-people-say rant:

11   The North Star is not the brightest star in the nighttime sky. It's not even bright enough to earn a spot in the celestial top 40. Perhaps people equate popularity with brightness. But when gazing upon the northern sky, three of the seven stars of the Big Dipper, including its "pointer" star, are brighter than the North Star, which is parked just three fist-widths away. There is no excuse.

12   And I don't care what else anyone has ever told you, the Sun is white, not yellow. Human color perception is a complicated business, but if the Sun were yellow, like a yellow lightbulb, then white stuff such as snow would reflect this light and appear yellow—a snow condition confirmed to happen only near fire hydrants. What could lead people to say that the Sun is yellow? In the middle of the day, a glance at the Sun can damage your eyes. Near sunset, however, with the Sun low on the horizon and when the atmospheric scattering of blue light is at its greatest, the Sun's intensity is significantly diminished. The blue light from the Sun's spectrum, lost to the twilight sky, leaves behind a yellow-orange-red hue for the Sun's disk. When people glance at this color-corrupted setting Sun, their misconceptions are fueled.

13   What goes up need not come down. All manner of golf balls, flags, automobiles, and crashed space probes litter the lunar surface. Unless somebody goes up there to bring them back, they will never return to Earth. Not ever. If you want to go up and not come down, all you need to do is travel at any speed faster than about seven miles per second. Earth's gravity will gradually slow you down but it will never succeed in reversing your motion and forcing you back to Earth.

Unless your eyes have pupils the size of binocular lenses, no matter your 14 seeing conditions and no matter your location on Earth, you will not resolve any more than about five or six thousand stars in the entire sky out of the 100 billion (or so) stars of our Milky Way galaxy. Try it one night. Things get much, much worse when the Moon is out. And if the Moon happens to be full, it will wash out the light of all but the brightest few hundred stars.

During the Apollo space program, while one of the missions was en route 15 to the Moon, a noted television news anchor announced the exact moment when the "astronauts left the gravitational field of Earth." Since the astronauts were still on their way to the Moon, and since the Moon orbits Earth, then Earth's gravity must extend into space *at least as far as the Moon*. Indeed, Earth's gravity, and the gravity of every other object in the universe, extends without limit—albeit with ever-diminishing strength. Every spot in space is teeming with countless gravitational tugs in the direction of every other object in the universe. What the announcer meant was that the astronauts crossed the point in space where the force of the Moon's gravity exceeds the force of Earth's gravity. The whole job of the mighty three-stage *Saturn V* rocket was to endow the command module with enough initial speed to just reach this point in space because thereafter you can passively accelerate toward the Moon— and they did. Gravity is everywhere.

Everybody knows that when it comes to magnets, opposite poles attract 16 while similar poles repel. But a compass needle is designed so that the half that has been magnetized "North" points to Earth's magnetic north pole. The only way a magnetized object can align its north half to Earth's magnetic north pole is if Earth's magnetic north pole is actually in the south and the magnetic south pole is actually in the north. Furthermore, there is no particular law of the universe that requires the precise alignment of an object's magnetic poles with its geographic poles. On Earth the two are separated by about 800 miles, which makes navigation by compass a futile exercise in northern Canada.

Since the first day of winter is the shortest "day" of the year, then every 17 succeeding day in the winter season must get longer and longer. Similarly, since the first day of summer is the longest "day" of the year, then every suc- ceeding day in the summer must get shorter and shorter. This is, of course, the opposite of what is told and retold.

On average, every couple years, somewhere on Earth's surface, the Moon 18 passes completely in front of the Sun to create a total solar eclipse. This event is more common than the Olympics, yet you don't read newspaper headlines declaring "a rare Olympics will take place this year." The perceived rarity of eclipses may derive from a simple fact: for any chosen spot on Earth, you can wait up to a half-millennium before you see a total solar eclipse. True, but lame as an argument because there are spots on Earth (like the middle of the Sahara Desert or any region of Antarctica) that have never, and will not likely ever, host the Olympics.

Want a few more? At high noon, the Sun is directly overhead. The Sun 19 rises in the east and sets in the west. The Moon comes out at night. On the equinox there are 12 hours of day and 12 hours of night. The Southern Cross is a beautiful constellation. All of these statements are wrong too.

20   There is no time of day, nor day of the year, nor place in the continental United States where the Sun ascends to directly overhead. At "high noon," straight vertical objects cast no shadow. The only people on the planet who see this live between 23.5 degrees south latitude and 23.5 degrees north latitude. And even in that zone, the Sun reaches directly overhead on only two days per year. The concept of high noon, like the brightness of the North Star and the color of the Sun, is a collective delusion.

21   For every person on Earth, the Sun rises due east and sets due west on only two days of the year: the first day of spring and the first day of fall. For every other day of the year, and for every person on Earth, the Sun rises and sets someplace else on the horizon. On the equator, sunrise varies by 47 degrees across the eastern horizon. From the latitude of New York City (41 degrees north—the same as that of Madrid and Beijing) the sunrise spans more than 60 degrees. From the latitude of London (51 degrees north) the sunrise spans nearly 80 degrees. And when viewed from either the Arctic or Antarctic circles, the Sun can rise due north and due south, spanning a full 180 degrees.

22   The Moon also "comes out" with the Sun in the sky. By invoking a small extra investment in your skyward viewing (like looking up in broad daylight) you will notice that the Moon is visible in the daytime nearly as often as it is visible at night.

23   The equinox does not contain exactly 12 hours of day and 12 hours of night. Look at the sunrise and sunset times in the newspaper on the first day of either spring or fall. They do not split the day into two equal 12-hour blocks. In all cases, daytime wins. Depending on your latitude, it can win by as few as seven minutes at the equator up to nearly half an hour at the Arctic and Antarctic circles. Who or what do we blame? Refraction of sunlight as it passes from the vacuum of interplanetary space to Earth's atmosphere enables an image of the Sun to appear above the horizon several minutes before the actual Sun has actually risen. Equivalently, the actual Sun has set several minutes before the Sun that you see. The convention is to measure sunrise by using the upper edge of the Sun's disk as it peeks above the horizon; similarly, sunset is measured by using the upper edge of the Sun's disk as it sinks below the horizon. The problem is that these two "upper edges" are on opposite halves of the Sun thereby providing an extra solar width of light in the sunrise/sunset calculation.

24   The Southern Cross gets the award for the greatest hype among all eighty-eight constellations. By listening to Southern Hemisphere people talk about this constellation, and by listening to songs written about it, and by noticing it on the national flags of Australia, New Zealand, Western Samoa, and Papua New Guinea, you would think we in the North were somehow deprived. Nope. Firstly, one needn't travel to the Southern Hemisphere to see the Southern Cross. It's plainly visible (although low in the sky) from as far north as Miami, Florida. This diminutive constellation is the smallest in the sky—your fist at

arm's length would eclipse it completely. Its shape isn't very interesting either. If you were to draw a rectangle using a connect-the-dots method you would use four stars. And if you were to draw a cross you would presumably include a fifth star in the middle to indicate the cross-point of the two beams. But the Southern Cross is composed of only four stars, which more accurately resemble a kite or a crooked box. The constellation lore of Western cultures owes its origin and richness to centuries of Babylonian, Chaldean, Greek, and Roman imaginations. Remember, these are the same imaginations that gave rise to the endless dysfunctional social lives of the gods and goddesses. Of course, these were all Northern Hemisphere civilizations, which means the constellations of the southern sky (many of which were named only within the last 250 years) are mythologically impoverished. In the North we have the Northern Cross, which is composed of all five stars that a cross deserves. It forms a subset of the larger constellation Cygnus the swan, which is flying across the sky along the Milky Way. Cygnus is nearly twelve times larger than the Southern Cross.

When people believe a tale that conflicts with self-checkable evidence it 25 tells me that people undervalue the role of evidence in formulating an internal belief system. Why this is so is not clear, but it enables many people to hold fast to ideas and notions based purely on supposition. But all hope is not lost. Occasionally, people say things that are simply true no matter what. One of my favorites is, "Wherever you go, there you are" and its Zen corollary, "If we are all here, then we must not be all there."

Source: Reprinted with permission from *Natural History*, July/August 1998. This article appears in Neil deGrasse Tyson's book *Death by Black Hole: And Other Cosmic Quandaries* (New York: W. W. Norton, 2007), pp. 291–297.

QUESTIONS FOR READING

1. What happened in 1054? Who wrote about the event? Who did not? What happened in 1066? Why did Europeans record this year's event?

2. What *kinds* of knowledge do we usually have to accept from experts? What *kinds* of falsehoods should we not hold on to?

3. Why do people believe that the sun is yellow? Or that it rises in the east and sets in the west?

4. How does Tyson account for people believing statements that conflict with evidence?

QUESTIONS FOR REASONING AND ANALYSIS

5. What does Tyson accomplish in his opening four paragraphs?

6. The author provides a list of well-known "truths" and then explains why each one is a false fact. Has he provided sufficient evidence to make his point? If not, why not?

7. What is Tyson's claim, the main point he wants to establish with readers?

8. Has Tyson convinced you that it is important to observe the natural world and use logic to test what we assume to be true? If not, why not?

9. What are some of the sources of false facts? Where does Tyson put most of the blame—on those who pass on false facts or those who embrace them by ignoring evidence to the contrary? Do you agree with his view on where to place the blame? Why or why not?

10. How many of Tyson's false facts did you believe to be true? Have you now adjusted your fact list? Are you sharing your new knowledge with family and friends? Reflect on your reactions to Tyson's essay.

Studying Some Arguments by Genre

Definition Arguments

READ: How does the cat respond to the big dog's questions?

REASON: Does the big dog expect the responses he gets to his questions? How do you know?

REFLECT/WRITE: What is a rhetorical question? What is the risk of using one?

"Define your terms!" someone yells in the middle of a heated debate. Although yelling may not be the best strategy, the advice is sound for writers of argument. People do disagree over the meaning of words. Although we cannot let words mean whatever we want and still communicate, we do recognize that many words have more than one meaning. In addition, some words carry strong connotations, the emotional associations we attach to them. For this reason, realtors never sell *houses;* they always sell *homes.* They want you to believe that the house they are showing will become the home in which you will feel happy and secure.

Many important arguments turn on the definition of key terms. If you can convince others that you have the correct definition, then you are well on your way to winning your argument. The civil rights movement, for example, really turned on a definition of terms. Leaders argued that some laws are unjust, that because it is the law does not necessarily mean it is right. Laws requiring separate schools and separate drinking fountains and seats at the back of the bus for blacks were, in the view of civil rights activists, unjust laws, unjust because they are immoral and as such diminish us as humans. If obeying unjust laws is immoral, then it follows that we should not obey such laws. And when we recognize that obeying such laws hurts us, then we have an obligation to act to remove unjust laws. Civil disobedience—illegal behavior to some—becomes, by definition, the best moral behavior.

Attorney Andrew Vachss has argued that there are no child prostitutes, only prostituted children. Yes, there are children who engage in sex for money. But, Vachss argues, that is not the complete definition of a prostitute. A prostitute chooses to exchange sex for money. Children do not choose; they are exploited by adults, beaten and in other ways abused if they do not work for the adult controlling them. If we agree with his definition, Vachss expects that we will also agree that the adults must be punished for their abuse of those prostituted children.

DEFINING AS PART OF AN ARGUMENT

There are two occasions for defining words as a part of your argument:

- You need to define any technical terms that may not be familiar to readers— or that readers may not understand as fully as they think they do. David Norman, early in his book on dinosaurs, writes:

  Nearly everyone knows what some dinosaurs look like, such as *Tyrannosaurus, Triceratops,* and *Stegosaurus.* But they may be much more vague about the lesser known ones, and may have difficulty in distinguishing between dinosaurs and other types of prehistoric creatures. It is not at all unusual to overhear an adult, taking a group of children around a museum display, being reprimanded sharply by the youngsters for failing to realize that a woolly mammoth was not a dinosaur, or—more forgivably—that a giant flying reptile such as *Pteranodon,* which lived at the time of the dinosaurs, was not a dinosaur either.

So what exactly is a dinosaur? And how do paleontologists decide on the groups they belong to?

Norman answers his questions by explaining the four characteristics that all dinosaurs have. He provides what is often referred to as a *formal definition.* He places the dinosaur in a class, established by four criteria, and then distinguishes this animal from other animals that lived a long time ago. His definition is not open to debate. He is presenting the definition and classification system that paleontologists, the specialists, have established.

• You need to define any word you are using in a special way. If you were to write: "We need to teach discrimination at an early age," you should add: "by *discrimination* I do not mean prejudice. I mean discernment, the ability to see differences." (*Sesame Street* has been teaching children this good kind of discrimination for many years.) The word *discrimination* used to have only a positive connotation; it referred to an important critical thinking skill. Today, however, the word has been linked to prejudice; to discriminate is to act on one's prejudice against some group. Writing today, you need to clarify if you are using the word in its original, positive meaning.

WHEN DEFINING *IS* THE ARGUMENT

We also turn to definition because we believe that a word is being used incorrectly or is not fully understood. Columnist George Will once argued that we should forget *values* and use instead the word *virtues*—that we should seek and admire virtues, not values. His point was that the term *values,* given to us by today's social scientists, is associated with situational ethics, or with an "if it feels good do it" approach to action. He wants people to return to the more old-fashioned word *virtues* so that we are reminded that some behavior is right and some is wrong, and that neither the situation nor how we might "feel" about it alters those truths. In discussions such as Will's the purpose shifts. Instead of using definition as one step in an argument, definition becomes the central purpose of the argument. Will rejects the idea that *values* means the same thing as *virtues* and asserts that it is virtue—as he defines it—that must guide our behavior. An extended definition *is* the argument.

STRATEGIES FOR DEVELOPING AN EXTENDED DEFINITION

Arguing for your meaning of a word provides your purpose in writing. But, it may not immediately suggest ways to develop such an argument. Let's think in terms of what definitions essentially do: They establish criteria for a class or category and then exclude other items from that category. (A pen is a writing instrument that uses ink.) Do you see your definition as drawing a line or as setting up two entirely separate categories? For example:

When does interrogation   become   torture?

One might argue that some strategies for making the person questioned uncomfortable are appropriate to interrogation (reduced sleep or comforts, loud noise). But, at some point (stretching on a rack or waterboarding) one crosses a line to torture. To define torture, you have to explain where that line is—and how the actions on one side of the line are different from those on the other side.

What are the characteristics of wisdom as opposed to knowledge?

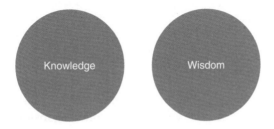

Do we cross a line from knowledge to become wise? Many would argue that wisdom requires traits or skills that are not found simply by increasing one's knowledge. The categories are separate. Others might argue that, while the categories are distinct, one does need knowledge to also be wise.

Envisioning these two approaches supports the abstract thinking that defining requires. Then what? Use some of the basic strategies of good writing:

- *Descriptive details.* Illustrate with specifics. List the traits of a leader or a courageous person. Explain the behaviors that we find in a wise person, or the behaviors that should be called torture. Describe the situations in which liberty can flourish, or the situations that result from unjust laws. Remember to use negative traits as well as positive ones. That is, show what is *not* covered by the word you are defining.

- *Examples.* Develop your definition with actual or hypothetical examples. Churchill, Lincoln, and FDR can all be used as examples of leaders. The biblical Solomon is generally acknowledged as a good example of a wise person. You can also create a hypothetical wise or courteous person, or a person whose behavior you would consider virtuous.

- *Comparison and/or contrast.* Clarify and limit your definition by contrasting it with words of similar—but not exactly the same—meanings. For example, what are the differences between knowledge and wisdom or interrogation and torture? The goal of your essay is to establish subtle but important differences so that your readers understand precisely what you want a given word to mean. In an essay at the end of this chapter, Robin Givhan distinguishes among *glamour, charisma,* and *cool* as a way to develop her definition of *glamour.*

- *History of usage or word origin.* The word's original meanings can be instructive. If the word has changed meaning over time, explore these changes as clues to how the word can (or should) be used. If you want readers to reclaim *discrimination* as a positive trait, then show them how that was part of the word's original meaning before the word became tied to prejudice. Word origin—etymology—can also give us insight into a word's meaning. Many words in English come from another language, or they are a combination of two words. The words *liberty* and *freedom* can usefully be discussed by examining etymology. Most dictionaries provide some word origin information, but the best source is, always, the *Oxford English Dictionary.*

- *Use or function.* A frequent strategy for defining is explaining an item's use or function: A pencil is a writing instrument. A similar approach can give insight into more general or abstract words as well. For example, what do we have—or gain—by emphasizing virtues instead of values? Or, what does a wise person *do* that a non-wise person does not do?

- *Metaphors.* Consider using figurative comparisons. When fresh, not clichés, they add vividness to your writing while offering insight into your understanding of the word.

In an essay titled "Why I Blog," Andrew Sullivan, one of the Internet's earliest bloggers, uses many of these strategies for developing a definition of the term *blog:*

- *Word origin.* "The word *blog* is a conflation of two words: *Web* and *log.* . . . In the monosyllabic vernacular of the Internet, *Web log* soon became the word *blog.*"

- *One-sentence definition.* "It contains in its four letters a concise and accurate self-description: it is a log of thoughts and writing posted publicly on the World Wide Web."

- *Descriptive details.* "This form of instant and global self-publishing . . . allows for no retroactive editing. . . . [I]ts truth [is] inherently transitory."

- *Contrast.* "The wise panic that can paralyze a writer . . . is not available to a blogger. You can't have blogger's block."

- *Metaphors.* "A blog . . . bobs on the surface of the ocean but has its anchorage in waters deeper than those print media is technologically able to exploit."

These snippets from Sullivan's lengthy essay give us a good look at defining strategies in action.

GUIDELINES for Evaluating Definition Arguments

When reading definition arguments, what should you look for? The basics of good argument apply to all arguments: a clear statement of claim, qualified if appropriate, a clear explanation of reasons and evidence, and enough relevant evidence to support the claim. How do we recognize these qualities in a definition argument? Use the following points as guides to evaluating:

- **Why is the word being defined?** Has the writer convinced you of the need to understand the word's meaning or change the way the word is commonly used?
- **How is the word defined?** Has the writer established his or her definition, clearly distinguishing it from what the writer perceives to be objectionable definitions? It is hard to judge the usefulness of the writer's position if the differences in meaning remain fuzzy. If George Will is going to argue for using *virtues* instead of *values*, he needs to be sure that readers understand the differences he sees in the two words.
- **What strategies are used to develop the definition?** Can you recognize the different types of evidence presented and see what the writer is doing in his or her argument? This kind of analysis can aid your evaluation of a definition argument.
- **What are the implications of accepting the author's definition?** Why does George Will want readers to embrace *virtues* rather than *values*? Will's argument is not just about subtle points of language. His argument is also about attitudes that affect public policy issues. Part of any evaluation of a definition argument must include our assessment of the author's definition.
- **Is the definition argument convincing?** Do the reasons and evidence lead you to agree with the author, to accept the idea of the definition and its implications as well?

PREPARING A DEFINITION ARGUMENT

In addition to the guidelines for writing arguments presented in Chapter 4, you can use the following advice specific to writing definition arguments.

Planning

1. *Think:* Why do you want to define your term? To add to our understanding of a complex term? To challenge the use of the word by others? If you don't have a good reason to write, find a different word to examine.
2. *Think:* How are you defining the word? What are the elements/parts/steps in your definition? Some brainstorming notes are probably helpful to keep your definition concrete and focused.

3. *Think:* What strategies will you use to develop and support your definition? Consider using several of these possible strategies for development:
    - *Word origin or history of usage*
    - *Descriptive details*
    - *Comparison and/or contrast*
    - *Examples*
    - *Function or use*
    - *Metaphors*

Drafting

1. Begin with an opening paragraph or two that introduces your subject in an interesting way. Possibilities include the occasion that has led to your writing—explain, for instance, a misunderstanding about your term's meaning that you want to correct.

2. Do *not* begin by quoting or paraphrasing a dictionary definition of the term. "According to Webster . . ." is a tired approach lacking reader interest. If the dictionary definition were sufficient, you would have no reason to write an entire essay to define the term.

3. State your claim—your definition of the term—early in your essay, if you can do so in a sentence or two. If you do not state a brief claim, then establish your purpose in writing early in your essay. (You may find that there are too many parts to your definition to combine into one or two sentences.)

4. Use several specific strategies for developing your definition. Select strategies from the list above and organize your approach around these strategies. That is, you can develop one paragraph of descriptive details, another of examples, another of contrast with words that are not exactly the same in meaning.

5. Consider specifically refuting the error in word use that led to your decision to write your own definition. If you are motivated to write based on what you have read, then make a rebuttal part of your definition argument.

6. Consider discussing the implications of your definition. You can give weight and value to your argument by explaining the larger significance of your definition.

A CHECKLIST FOR REVISION ▪▪▪▪▪▪▪▪▪▪▪▪▪▪▪▪▪▪▪▪▪▪▪▪▪▪▪▪▪▪

☐ Do I have a good understanding of my purpose? Have I made this clear to readers?

☐ Have I clearly stated my definition? Or clearly established the various parts of the definition that I discuss in separate paragraphs?

☐ Have I organized my argument, building the parts of my definition into a logical, coherent structure?

☐ Have I used specifics to clarify and support my definition?

☐ Have I used the basic checklist for revision in Chapter 4 (see p. 111)?

STUDENT ESSAY

PARAGON OR PARASITE?

Laura Mullins

Do you recognize this creature? He is low maintenance and often unnoticeable, a favorite companion of many. Requiring no special attention, he grows from the soil of pride and rejection, feeding regularly on a diet of ignorance and insecurity, scavenging for hurt feelings and defensiveness, gobbling up dainty morsels of lust and scandal. Like a cult leader clothed in a gay veneer, disguising himself as blameless, he wields power. Bewitching unsuspecting but devoted groupies, distracting them from honest self-examination, deceiving them into believing illusions of grandeur or, on the other extreme, unredeemable worthlessness, he breeds jealousy, hate, and fear; thus, he thrives. He is Gossip.

One of my dearest friends is a gossip. She is an educated, honorable, compassionate, loving woman whose character and judgment I deeply admire and respect. After sacrificially raising six children, she went on to study medicine and become a doctor who graciously volunteers her expertise. How, you may be wondering, could a gossip deserve such praise? Then you do not understand the word. My friend is my daughter's godmother; she is my gossip, or *godsib,* meaning sister-in-god. Derived from Middle English words *god,* meaning spiritual, and *sip/ sib/syp,* meaning kinsman, this term was used to refer to a familiar acquaintance, close family friend, or intimate relation, according to the *Oxford English Dictionary.* As a male, he would have joined in fellowship and celebration with the father of the newly born; if a female, she would have been a trusted friend, a birth-attendant or midwife to the mother of the baby. The term grew to include references to the type of easy, unrestrained conversation shared by these folks.

As is often the case with words, the term's meaning has certainly evolved, maybe eroded from its original idea. Is it harmless, idle chat, innocuous sharing of others' personal news, or back-biting, rumor-spreading,

Attention-getting introduction.

Clever extended metaphor.

Subject introduced.

Etymology of gossip and early meanings.

Current meanings.

and manipulation? Is it a beneficial activity worthy of pursuit, or a deplorable danger to be avoided?

Good use of sources
to develop definition.

In her article "Evolution, Alienation, and Gossip" (for the Social Issues Research Centre in Oxford, England), Kate Fox writes that "gossip is not a trivial pastime; it is essential to human social, psychological, and even physical well-being." Many echo her view that gossip is a worthy activity, claiming that engaging in gossip produces endorphins, reduces stress, and aids in building intimate relationships. Gossip, seen at worst as a harmless outlet, is encouraged in the workplace. Since much of its content is not inherently critical or malicious, it is viewed as a positive activity. However, this view does nothing to encourage those speaking or listening to evaluate or examine motive or purpose; instead, it seems to reflect the "anything goes" thinking so prevalent today.

Conversely, writer and high school English and geography teacher Lennox V. Farrell of Toronto, Canada, in his essay titled "Gossip: An Urban Form of Sorcery," presents gossip as a kind of "witchcraft . . . based on using unsubstantiated accusations by those who make them, and on uncritically accepting these by those enticed into listening." Farrell uses gossip in its more widely understood definition, encompassing the breaking of confidences, inappropriate sharing of indiscretions, destructive tale-bearing, and malicious slander.

Good use of
metaphor to depict
gossip as negative.

What, then, is gossip? We no longer use the term to refer to our children's godparents. Its current definition usually comes with derogatory implications. Imagine a backyard garden: you see a variety of greenery, recognizing at a glance that you are looking at different kinds of plants. Taking a closer look, you will find the gossip vine; inconspicuously blending in, it doesn't appear threatening, but ultimately it destroys. If left in the garden it will choke and then suck out life from its host. Zoom in on the garden scene and follow the creeping vine up trees and along a fence where two neighbors visit. You can overhear one woman saying to the other, "I know I should be the last to tell you, but your husband is being unfaithful to me." (Caption from a cartoon by Alan De la Nougerede.)

The current popular movement to legitimize gossip seems an excuse to condone the human tendency to puff-up oneself. Compared in legal terms, gossip is to conversation as hearsay is to eyewitness testimony; it's not credible. Various religious doctrines abhor the idea and practice of gossip. An old Turkish proverb says, "He who gossips to you will gossip of you." From the Babylonian Talmud, which calls gossip the three-pronged tongue, destroying the one talking, the one listening, and the one being spoken of, to the Upanishads, to the Bible, we can conclude that no good fruit is born from gossip. Let's tend our gardens and check our motives when we have the urge to gossip. Surely we can find more noble pursuits than the self-aggrandizement we have come to know as gossip.

> Conclusion states view that gossip is to be avoided—the writer's thesis.

FOR ANALYSIS AND DEBATE

GLAMOUR, THAT CERTAIN SOMETHING | ROBIN GIVHAN

Robin Givhan is a graduate of Princeton and holds a master's degree in journalism from the University of Michigan. When she was fashion editor at the *Washington Post,* she won a Pulitzer Prize (2006) for criticism, the first time the prize has been awarded to a fashion writer. In 2010 she moved to *The Daily Beast* and *Newsweek,* but was laid off by these publications in December 2012, when *Newsweek* gave up print journalism. Givhan's coverage of the world of fashion frequently becomes a study of culture, as we see in the following column, published February 17, 2008, shortly before the 2008 Academy Awards show.

PREREADING QUESTIONS What is the difference between glamour and good looks? What famous people do you consider glamorous?

Glamour isn't a cultural necessity, but its usefulness can't be denied.   1

It makes us feel good about ourselves by making us believe that life can 2 sparkle. Glamorous people make difficult tasks seem effortless. They appear to cruise through life shaking off defeat with a wry comment. No matter how hard they work for what they have, the exertion never seems to show. Yet the cool confidence they project doesn't ever drift into lassitude.

Hollywood attracts people of glamour—as well as the misguided souls 3 who confuse it with mere good looks—because that is where it is richly rewarded. And the Academy Awards are the epicenter of it all. We'll watch the Oscars next Sunday to delight in the stars who glide down the red carpet like graceful swans or who swagger onto the stage looking dashing.

4   Of course, we'll watch for other reasons, too. There's always the possibility of a supremely absurd fashion moment or an acceptance speech during which the winner becomes righteously indignant—Michael Moore–style—or practically hyperventilates like Halle Berry. While Moore, a nominee, is not glamorous, he is compelling for the sheer possibility of an impolitic eruption. Berry isn't glamorous either, mostly because nothing ever looks effortless with her. (She has even expressed anguish over her beauty.) Mostly, though, we will watch in search of "old Hollywood" glamour. But really, is there any other kind?

5   Among the actors who consistently manage to evoke memories of Cary Grant or Grace Kelly are George Clooney and Cate Blanchett. There's something about the way they present themselves that speaks to discretion, sex appeal and glossy perfection. As an audience, we think we know these actors but we really don't. We know their image, the carefully crafted personality they display to the public. If they have been to rehab, they went quietly and without a crowd of paparazzi.

6   Their lives appear to be an endless stream of lovely adventures, minor mishaps that turn into cocktail party banter, charming romances and just enough gravitas to keep them from floating away on a cloud of frivolity.

7   These actors take pretty pictures because they seem supremely comfortable with themselves. It's not simply their beauty we're seeing; it's also an unapologetic pleasure in being who they are.

8   Oscar nominee Tilda Swinton has the kind of striking, handsome looks of Anjelica Huston or Lauren Bacall. But Swinton doesn't register as glamorous as much as cool. She looks a bit androgynous and favors the eccentric Dutch design team of Viktor & Rolf, which once populated an entire runway show with Swinton doppelgangers. Coolness suggests that the person knows

something or understands something that average folks haven't yet figured out. Cool people are a step ahead. Glamour is firmly situated in the now.

There's nothing particularly intimate about glamour, which is why it 9 plays so well on the big screen and why film actors who embody it can sometimes be disappointing in real life. Glamour isn't like charisma, which is typically described as the ability to make others feel important or special.

Neither quality has much to do with a person's inner life. Glamour is no 10 measure of soulfulness or integrity. It isn't about truth, but perception. *Redbook* traffics in truth. *Vogue* promotes glamour.

Although Hollywood is the natural habitat for the glitterati, they exist 11 everywhere: politics, government, sports, business. Tiger Woods brought glamour to golf with his easy confidence and his ability to make the professional game look as simple as putt-putt. Donald Trump aspires to glamour with his flashy properties and their gold-drenched decor. But his efforts are apparent, his yearning obvious. The designer Tom Ford is glamorous. The man never rumples.

In the political world, Barack Obama has glamour. Bill Clinton has cha- 12 risma. And Hillary Clinton has an admirable work ethic. Bill Clinton could convince voters that he felt their pain. Hillary Clinton reminds them detail by detail of how she would alleviate it. Glamour has a way of temporarily making you forget about the pain and just think the world is a beautiful place of endless possibilities.

Ronald Reagan evoked glamour. His white-tie inaugural balls and 13 morning-coat swearing-in were purposefully organized to bring a twinkle back to the American psyche. George W. Bush has charisma, a.k.a. the likability factor, although it does not appear to be helping his approval rating now. Still, he remains a back-slapper and bestower of nicknames.

Charisma is personal. Glamour taps into a universal fairy tale. It's uncon- 14 cerned with the nitty-gritty. Instead, it celebrates the surface gloss. And sometimes, a little shimmer can be hard to resist.

QUESTIONS FOR READING

1. How does glamour make us feel?
2. Where do we usually find glamour? Why?
3. Which celebrities today best capture Hollywood's glamour of the past?
4. What traits do the glamorous have?
5. Explain the differences among glamour, charisma, and cool.

QUESTIONS FOR REASONING AND ANALYSIS

6. Examine the opening three sentences in paragraph 12. What makes them effective?

7. What are the specific strategies Givhan uses to develop her definition?

8. What is Givhan's claim?

QUESTIONS FOR REFLECTION AND WRITING

9. Givhan asserts that glamour is in the present but "cool people are a step ahead." Does this contrast make sense to you? Why or why not?

10. Do we ever really know the glamorous, charismatic, and cool celebrities? Explain.

11. Some young people aspire to be cool. How would you advise them? What should one do, how should one behave, to be cool? Is "cool" a trait that we can "put on" if we wish? Why or why not?

SUGGESTIONS FOR DISCUSSION AND WRITING

1. In the student essay, Laura Mullins defines the term *gossip*. Select one of the following words to define and prepare your own extended definition argument, using at least three of the strategies for defining described in this chapter. For each word in the list, you see a companion word in parentheses. Use that companion word as a word that you contrast with the word you are defining. (For example, how does gossip differ from conversation?) The idea of an extended definition argument is to make fine distinctions among words similar in meaning.

   courtesy (manners)   hero (star)

   wisdom (knowledge)   community (subdivision)

   patriotism (chauvinism)   freedom (liberty)

2. Select a word you believe is currently misused. It can be misused because it has taken on a negative (or positive) connotation that it did not originally have, or because it has changed meaning and lost something in the process. A few suggestions include *awful, fabulous, exceptional* (in education), *propaganda*.

3. Define a term that is currently used to label people with particular traits or values. Possibilities include *nerd, yuppie, freak, jock, redneck, bimbo, wimp*. Reflect, before selecting this topic, on why you want to explain the meaning of the word you have chosen. One purpose might be to explain the word to someone from another culture. Another might be to defend people who are labeled negatively by a term; that is, you want to show why the term should not have a negative connotation.

CHAPTER 8

Evaluation Arguments

READ: What is the situation? Where are we?

REASON: Look at the faces; what do you infer to be the attitude of the participants?

REASON/WRITE: What is the photo's message?

"I really love Ben's Camaro; it's so much more fun to go out with him than to go with Gregory in his Volvo wagon," you confide to a friend. "On the other hand, Ben always wants to see the latest horror movie—and boy are they horrid! I'd much rather watch one of our teams play—whatever the season; sports events are so much more fun than horror movies!"

"Well, at least you and Ben agree not to listen to Amy Winehouse CDs. Her life was so messed up; why would anyone admire her music?" your friend responds.

CHARACTERISTICS OF EVALUATION ARGUMENTS

Evaluations. How easy they are to make. We do it all the time. So, surely an evaluation argument should be easy to prepare. Not so fast. Remember at the beginning of the discussion of argument in Chapter 3, we observed that we do not argue about personal preferences because there is no basis for building an argument. If you don't like horror movies, then don't go to them—even with Ben! However, once you assert that sporting events are more fun than horror movies, you have shifted from personal preference to the world of argument, the world in which others will judge the effectiveness of your logic and evidence. On what basis can you argue that one activity is more fun than the other? And, always more fun? And, more fun for everyone? You probably need to qualify this claim and then you will need to establish the criteria by which you have made your evaluation. Although you might find it easier to defend your preference for a car for dates, you, at least in theory, can build a convincing argument for a qualified claim in support of sporting events. Your friend, though, will have great difficulty justifying her evaluation of Winehouse based on Winehouse's lifestyle. An evaluation of her music needs to be defended based on criteria about music—unless she wants to try to argue that any music made by people with unconventional or immoral lifestyles will be bad music, a tough claim to defend.

In a column for *Time* magazine, Charles Krauthammer argues that Tiger Woods is the greatest golfer ever to play the game. He writes:

> How do we know? You could try Method 1: Compare him directly with the former greatest golfer, Jack Nicklaus. . . . But that is not the right way to compare. You cannot compare greatness directly across the ages. There are so many intervening variables: changes in technology, training, terrain, equipment, often rules and customs.
>
> How then do we determine who is greatest? Method 2: The Gap. Situate each among his contemporaries. Who towers? . . . Nicklaus was great, but he ran with peers: Palmer, Player, Watson. Tiger has none.

Krauthammer continues with statistics to demonstrate that there is no one playing now with Tiger who comes close in number of tournaments won, number of majors won, and number of strokes better in these events than the next player. He then applies the Gap Method to Babe Ruth in baseball, Wayne

Gretzky in hockey, and Bobby Fischer in chess to demonstrate that it works to reveal true greatness in competition among the world's best.

Krauthammer clearly explains his Gap Method, his basic criterion for judging greatness. Then he provides the data to support his conclusions about who are or were the greatest in various fields. His is a convincing evaluation argument.

These examples suggest some key points about evaluation arguments:

- **Evaluation arguments are arguments, not statements of personal preferences.** As such, they need a precise, qualified claim and reasons and evidence for support, just like any argument.

- **Evaluation arguments are about "good" and "bad," "best" and "worst."** These arguments are not about what we should or should not do or why a situation is the way it is. The debate is not whether one should select a boyfriend based on the kind of car he drives or why horror movies have so much appeal for many viewers. The argument is that sports events are great entertainment, or better entertainment than horror movies.

- **Evaluation arguments need to be developed based on a clear statement of the criteria for evaluating.** Winehouse won Grammys for her music—why? By what standards of excellence do we judge a singer? A voice with great musicality and nuance? The selection of songs with meaningful lyrics? The ability to engage listeners—the way the singer can "sell" a song? The number of recordings sold and awards won? All of these criteria? Something else?

- **Evaluation arguments, to be successful, may need to defend the criteria, not just to list them and show that the subject of the argument meets those criteria.** Suppose you want to argue that sporting events are great entertainment because it is exciting to cheer with others, you get to see thrilling action, and it is good, clean fun. Are sports always "good, clean fun"? Some of the fighting in hockey matches is quite vicious. Some football players get away with dirty hits. Krauthammer argues that his Gap Method provides the better criterion for judging greatness and then shows why it is the better method. Do not underestimate the challenge of writing an effective evaluation argument.

TYPES OF EVALUATION ARGUMENTS

The examples we have examined above are about people or items or experiences in our lives. Tiger Woods is the greatest golfer ever, based on the Gap Method strategy. Sports events are more fun to attend than horror movies. We can (and do!) evaluate just about everything we know or do or buy. This is one type of evaluation argument. In this category we would place the review—of a book, movie, concert, or something similar.

A second type of evaluation is a response to another person's argument. We are not explaining why the car or college, sitcom or singer, is good or great or the best. Instead, we are responding to one specific argument we have read (or listened to) that we think is flawed, flawed in many ways or in one significant way that essentially destroys the argument. This type of evaluation argument is called a rebuttal or refutation argument.

Sometimes our response to what we consider a really bad argument is to go beyond the rebuttal and write a counterargument. Rather than writing about the limitations and flaws in our friend's evaluation of Winehouse as a singer not to be listened to, we decide to write our own argument evaluating Winehouse's strengths as a contemporary singer. This counterargument is best described as an evaluation argument, not a refutation. Similarly, we can disagree with someone's argument defending restrictions placed by colleges on student file sharing. But, if we decide to write a counterargument defending students' rights to share music files, we have moved from rebuttal to our own position paper, our own argument based on values. Counterarguments are best seen as belonging to one of the other genres of argument discussed in this section of the text.

GUIDELINES for Analyzing an Evaluation Argument

The basics of good argument apply to all arguments: a clear statement of claim, qualified as appropriate, a clear explanation of reasons and evidence, and enough relevant evidence to support the claim. When reading evaluation arguments, use the following points as additional guides:

- **What is the writer's claim?** Is it clear, qualified if necessary, and focused on the task of evaluating?

- **Has the writer considered audience as a basis for both claim and criteria?** Your college may be a good choice for you, given your criteria for choosing, but is it a good choice for others? Qualifications need to be based on audience: College A is a great school for young people in need of B and with X amount of funds. Or: *The Da Vinci Code* is an entertaining read for those with some understanding of art history and knowledge of the Roman Catholic Church.

- **What criteria are presented as the basis for evaluation?** Are they clearly stated? Do they seem reasonable for the topic of evaluation? Are they defended if necessary?

- **What evidence and/or reasons are presented to show that the item under evaluation meets the criteria?** Specifics are important in any evaluation argument.

- **What are the implications of the claim?** If we accept the Gap Method for determining greatness, does that mean that we can never compare stars from different generations? If we agree with the rebuttal argument, does that mean that there are no good arguments for the claim in the essay being refuted?

- **Is the argument convincing?** Does the evidence lead you to agree with the author? Do you want to buy that car, listen to that CD, read that book, see that film as a result of reading the argument?

PREPARING AN EVALUATION ARGUMENT

In addition to the guidelines for writing arguments presented in Chapter 4, you can use the following advice specific to writing evaluation arguments.

Planning

1. **Think:** Why do you want to write this evaluation? Does it matter, or are you just sharing your personal preferences? Select a topic that requires you to think deeply about how we judge that item (college, book, CD, etc.).

2. **Think about audience:** Try to imagine writing your evaluation for your classmates, not just your instructor. Instead of thinking about an assignment to be graded, think about why we turn to reviews, for example. What do readers want to learn? They want to know if they should see that film. Your job is to help them make that decision.

3. **Think:** What are my criteria for evaluation? And, how will I measure my topic against them to show that my evaluation is justified? You really must know how you would determine a great singer or a great tennis player before you write, or you risk writing only about personal preferences.

4. **Establish a general plan:** If you are writing a review, be sure to study the work carefully. Can you write a complete and accurate summary? (It is easier to review a CD than a live concert because you can replay the CD to get all the details straight.) You will need to balance summary, analysis, and evaluation in a review—and be sure that you do not mostly write summary or reveal the ending of a novel or film! If you are evaluating a college or a car, think about how to order your criteria. Do you want to list all criteria first and then show how your item connects to them, point by point? Or, do you want the criteria to unfold as you make specific points about your item?

    To analyze a film, consider the plot, the characters, the actors who play the lead characters, any special effects used, and the author's (and director's) "take" on the story. If the "idea" of the film is insignificant, then it is hard to argue that it is a great film. Analysis of style in a book needs to be connected to that book's intended audience. Style and presentation will vary depending on the knowledge and sophistication of the intended reader. If, for example, you have difficulty understanding a book aimed at a general audience, then it is fair to say that the author has not successfully reached his or her audience. But if you are reviewing a book intended for specialists, then your difficulties in reading are not relevant to a fair evaluation of that book. You can point out, though, that the book is tough going for a nonspecialist—just as you could point out that a movie sequel is hard to follow for those who did not see the original film.

Drafting

1. Begin with an opening paragraph or two that engages your reader while introducing your subject and purpose in writing. Is there a specific occasion that has led to your writing? And what, exactly, are you evaluating?

2. Either introduce your criteria next and then show how your item for evaluation meets the criteria, point by point, through the rest of the essay; or, decide on an order for introducing your criteria and use that order as your structure. Put the most important criterion either first or last. It can be effective to put the most controversial point last.

3. If you are writing a review, then the basic criteria are already established. You will need some combination of summary, analysis, and evaluation. Begin with an attention-getter that includes a broad statement of the work's subject or subject category: This is a *biography* of Benjamin Franklin; this is a *female action-hero film.* An evaluation in general terms can complete the opening paragraph. For example:

    Dr. Cynthia Pemberton's new book, *More Than a Game: One Woman's Fight for Gender Equity in Sport,* is destined to become a classic in sport sociology, sport history, and women's studies.

4. The rest of the review will then combine summary details, analysis of presentation, and a final assessment of the work in the concluding paragraph. From the same review, after learning specifics of content, we read:

    The target audience for this book includes educators, coaches, athletes, and administrators at any level. Additionally, anyone interested in studying women's sports or pursuing a Title IX case will love this book.

5. Consider discussing the implications of your evaluation. Why is this important? Obviously for a book or film or art show, for example, we want to know if this is a "must read" or "must see." For other evaluation arguments, let us know why we should care about your subject and your perspective. Charles Krauthammer does not just argue that Tiger Woods is the greatest golfer ever; he also argues that his Gap Method is the best strategy for evaluation. That's why he shows that it works not just to put Woods ahead of Nicklaus but also to put other greats in their exalted place in other sports.

A CHECKLIST FOR REVISION

☐ Do I have a good understanding of my purpose? Have I made my evaluation purpose clear to readers?

☐ Have I clearly stated my claim?

☐ Have I clearly stated my criteria for evaluation—or selected the appropriate elements of content, style, presentation, and theme for a review?

☐ Have I organized my argument into a coherent structure by some pattern that readers can recognize and follow?

☐ Have I provided good evidence and logic to support my evaluation?

☐ Have I used the basic checklist for revision in Chapter 4? (See p. 111.)

STUDENT REVIEW

WINCHESTER'S ALCHEMY: TWO MEN AND A BOOK

Ian Habel

One can hardly imagine a tale promising less excitement for a general audience than that of the making of the *Oxford English Dictionary* (*OED*). The sensationalism of murder and insanity would have to labor intensely against the burden of lexicography in crafting a genuine page-turner on the subject. Much to my surprise, Simon Winchester, in writing *The Professor and the Madman: A Tale of Murder, Insanity, and the Making of the Oxford English Dictionary,* has succeeded in producing so compelling a story that I was forced to devour it completely in a single afternoon, an unprecedented personal feat.

The Professor and the Madman is the story of the lives of two apparently very different men and the work that brought them together. Winchester begins by recounting the circumstances that led to the incarceration of Dr. W. C. Minor, a well-born, well-educated, and quite insane American ex-Army surgeon. Minor, in a fit of delusion, had murdered a man whom he believed to have crept into his Lambeth hotel room to torment him in his sleep. The doctor is tried and whisked off to the Asylum for the Criminally Insane, Broadmoor.

The author then introduces readers to the other two main characters: the *OED* itself and its editor James Murray, a lowborn, self-educated Scottish philologist. The shift in narrative focus is used to dramatic effect. The natural assumption on the part of the reader that these two seemingly unrelated plots must eventually meet urges us to read on in anticipation of that connection. As each chapter switches focus from one man to the other, it is introduced by a citation from the *OED*, reminding us that the story is ultimately about the dictionary. The citations also serve to foreshadow and provide a theme for the chapter. For example, the *OED* definition of *murder* heads the first chapter, relating to the details of Minor's crime.

Winchester acquaints us with the shortcomings of seventeenth- and eighteenth-century attempts at compiling a comprehensive dictionary of the English language. He takes us inside the meetings of the Philological Society, whose members proposed the compilation of the dictionary to end all dictionaries. The *OED* was to include examples of usage illustrating every shade of meaning for every word in the English language. Such a mammoth feat would require enlisting thousands of volunteer readers to comb the corpus of English literature in search of illustrative quotations to be submitted on myriad slips of paper. These slips of paper on each word would in turn be studied by a small army of editors preparing the definitions.

It is not surprising that our Dr. Minor, comfortably tucked away at Broadmoor, possessing both a large library and seemingly infinite free time, should become one of those volunteer readers. After all, we are still rightfully assuming some connection of the book's two plot lines. Yet what sets Dr. Minor apart from his fellow volunteers (aside from the details of his incarceration) is the remarkable efficiency with which he approached his task. Not content merely to fill out slips of paper for submission, Minor methodically indexed every possibly useful mention of any word appearing in his personal library. He then asked to be kept informed of the progress of the work, submitting quotations that would be immediately useful to editors. In this way he managed to "escape" his cell and plunge himself into the work of contemporaries, to become a part of a major event of his time.

Minor's work proved invaluable to the *OED*'s staff of editors, led by James Murray. With the two plot lines now intertwined, readers face such questions as "Will they find out that Minor is insane?" "Will Minor and Murray ever meet?" and "How long will they take to complete the dictionary?" The author builds suspense regarding a meeting of Minor and Murray by providing a false account of their first encounter, as reported by the American press, only to shatter us with the fact that this romantic version did not happen. I'll let Winchester give you the answers to these questions, while working his magic on you, drawing you into this fascinating tale of the making of the world's most famous dictionary.

EVALUATING AN ARGUMENT: THE REBUTTAL OR REFUTATION ESSAY

When your primary purpose in writing is to challenge someone's argument rather than to present your own argument, you are writing a *rebuttal* or *refutation*. A good refutation demonstrates, in an orderly and logical way, the weaknesses of logic or evidence in the argument. Study the following guidelines to prepare a good refutation essay and then study the sample refutation that follows. It has been annotated to show you how the author has structured his rebuttal.

GUIDELINES for Preparing a Refutation or Rebuttal Argument

1. **Read accurately.** Make certain that you have understood your opponent's argument. If you assume views not expressed by the writer and accuse the writer of holding those illogical views, you are guilty of the straw man fallacy, of attributing and then attacking a position that the person does not hold. Look up terms and references you do not know and examine the logic and evidence thoroughly.

2. **Pinpoint the weaknesses in the original argument.** Analyze the argument to determine, specifically, what flaws the argument contains. If the argument contains logical fallacies, make a list of the ones you plan to discredit. Examine the evidence presented. Is it insufficient, unreliable, or irrelevant? Decide, before drafting your refutation, exactly what elements of the argument you intend to challenge.

3. **Write your claim.** After analyzing the argument and deciding on the weaknesses to be challenged, write a claim that establishes that your disagreement is with the writer's logic, assumptions, or evidence, or a combination of these.

4. **Draft your essay, using the following three-part organization:**

   a. *The opponent's argument.* Usually you should not assume that your reader has read or remembered the argument you are refuting. Thus at the beginning of your essay, you need to state, accurately and fairly, the main points of the argument to be refuted.

   b. *Your claim.* Next make clear the nature of your disagreement with the argument you are rebutting.

   c. *Your refutation.* The specifics of your rebuttal will depend on the nature of your disagreement. If you are challenging the writer's evidence, then you must present the evidence that will show why the evidence used is unreliable or misleading. If you are challenging assumptions, then you must explain why they do not hold up. If your claim is that the piece is filled with logical fallacies, then you must present and explain each fallacy.

MIND OVER MASS MEDIA | STEVEN PINKER

A professor of psychology at Harvard University, Steven Pinker is the author of significant articles and books on visual cognition and the psychology of language—his areas of research. These include *The Language Instinct* (2007) and *How the Mind Works* (2009). *Time* magazine has listed Pinker as one of the "100 most influential people in the world." His contribution to the ongoing debate over the impact of the Internet and social media was published on June 12, 2010.

PREREADING QUESTIONS Given Pinker's title and the headnote information, what do you expect him to write about? Can you anticipate his position—or will you have to read to discover it?

1 New forms of media have always caused moral panics: the printing press, newspapers, paperbacks and television were all once denounced as threats to their consumers' brainpower and moral fiber.

Attention-getting opening.

2 So too with electronic technologies. PowerPoint, we're told, is reducing discourse to bullet points. Search engines lower our intelligence, encouraging us to skim on the surface of knowledge rather than dive to its depths. Twitter is shrinking our attention spans.

3 But such panics often fail basic reality checks. When comic books were accused of turning juveniles into delinquents in the 1950s, crime was falling to record lows, just as the denunciations of video games in the 1990s coincided with the great American crime decline. The decades of television, transistor radios and rock videos were also decades in which I.Q. scores rose continuously.

1st point of refutation: Reality check, past and present.

4 For a reality check today, take the state of science, which demands high levels of brainwork and is measured by clear benchmarks of discovery. These days scientists are never far from their email, rarely touch paper and cannot lecture without PowerPoint. If electronic media were hazardous to intelligence, the quality of science would be plummeting. Yet discoveries are multiplying like fruit flies, and progress is dizzying. Other activities in the life of the mind, like philosophy, history and cultural criticism, are likewise flourishing, as anyone who has lost a morning of work to the Website *Arts & Letters Daily* can attest.

5 Critics of new media sometimes use science itself to press their case, citing research that shows how "experience can change the brain." But cognitive

2nd point: How the brain really works.

neuroscientists roll their eyes at such talk. Yes, every time we learn a factor skill the wiring of the brain changes; it's not as if the information is stored in the pancreas. But the existence of neural plasticity does not mean the brain is a blob of clay pounded into shape by experience.

6   Experience does not revamp the basic information-processing capacities of the brain. Speed-reading programs have long claimed to do just that, but the verdict was rendered by Wood Allen after he read *War and Peace* in one sitting: "It was about Russia." Genuine multitasking, too, has been exposed as a myth, not just by laboratory studies but by the familiar sight of an S.U.V. undulating between lanes as the driver cuts a deal on his cellphone.

7   Moreover, as the psychologists Christopher Chabris and Daniel Simons show in their new book *The Invisible Gorilla: And Other Ways Our Intuitions Deceive Us*, the effects of experience are highly specific to the experiences themselves. If you train people to do one thing (recognize shapes, solve math puzzles, find hidden words), they get better at doing that thing, but almost nothing else. Music doesn't make you better at math, conjugating Latin doesn't make you more logical, brain-training games don't make you smarter. Accomplished people don't bulk up their brains with intellectual calisthenics; they immerse themselves in their fields. Novelists read lots of novels, scientists read lots of science.

8   The effects of consuming electronic media are also likely to be far more limited than the panic implies. Media critics write as if the brain takes on the qualities of whatever it consumes, the informational equivalent of "you are what you eat." As with primitive peoples who believe that eating fierce animals will make them fierce, they assume that watching quick cuts in rock videos turns your mental life into quick cuts or that reading bullet points and Twitter turns your thoughts into bullet points and Twitter postings.

9   Yes, the constant arrival of information packets can be distracting or addictive, especially to people with attention deficit disorder. But distraction is not a new phenomenon. The solution is not to bemoan technology but to develop strategies of self-control, as we do with every other temptation in life. Turn off email or Twitter when you work, put away your BlackBerry at dinner time, ask your spouse to call you to bed at a designated hour.

3rd point: Control use and understand what makes us smart.

10   And to encourage intellectual depth, don't rail at PowerPoint or Google. It's not as if habits of deep reflection, thorough research and rigorous reasoning ever came naturally to people. They must be acquired in special institutions, which we call universities, and maintained with constant upkeep, which we call analysis, criticism and debate. They are not granted by propping a heavy encyclopedia on your lap, nor are they taken away by efficient access to information on the Internet.

11   The new media have caught on for a reason. Knowledge is increasing exponentially; human brainpower and waking hours are not. Fortunately, the Internet and information technologies are helping us manage, search and retrieve our collective intellectual output at different scales, from Twitter and previews to e-books and online encyclopedias. Far from making us stupid, these technologies are the only things that will keep us smart.

Source: *New York Times/International Herald Tribune*, June 12, 2010. Reprinted by permission of the author.

QUESTIONS FOR READING

1.   What is Pinker's subject? (Be precise.)
2.   What happened to the crime rate during the 1990s?
3.   What happened during the years of heavy TV use and the publication of rock videos?
4.   What changes occur in the brain when we learn new information? What does not change?
5.   What do people do to be successful in their fields?

QUESTIONS FOR REASONING AND ANALYSIS

6.   What is Pinker's response to those who complain about the new electronic technologies? What is his claim?
7.   What kinds of evidence does Pinker provide?

QUESTIONS FOR REFLECTION AND WRITING

8.   Pinker asserts that speed reading and multitasking have been shown to be myths. Is this idea new to you? Are you surprised? Do you believe that you can multitask successfully? If so, how would you seek to refute Pinker?
9.   Is the author convincing in his refutation of those who argue that electronic technologies will make us stupid? If so, why? If not, why not?

FOR ANALYSIS AND DEBATE

CHRISTMAS-TREE TOTALITARIANS | THOMAS SOWELL

A former professor of economics with a PhD from the University of Chicago, Thomas Sowell is currently a Senior Fellow at the Hoover Institution at Stanford University. He is the author of numerous books and articles, including *Intellectuals and Society* (2009). The following column was posted December 25, 2012, on the *National Review Online*.

PREREADING QUESTIONS Does the title give you any clue as to the subject of Sowell's essay—beyond connecting it to its publication date? What might be his general subject or approach?

When I was growing up, an older member of the family used to say, "What 1 you don't know would make a big book." Now that I am an older member of the family, I would say to anyone, "What you don't know would fill more books than the *Encyclopaedia Britannica*." At least half of society's trouble come from know-it-alls, in a world where nobody knows even 10 percent of it all.

Some people seem to think that, if life is not fair, then the answer is to turn 2 more of the nation's resources over to politicians—who will, of course, then spend these resources in ways that increase the politicians' chance of getting reelected.

The annual outbursts of intolerance toward any display of traditional Christmas 3 scenes, or even daring to call a Christmas tree by its name, show that today's liberals are by no means liberal. Behind the mist of their lofty words, the totalitarian mindset shows through.

4   If you don't want to have a gun in your home or in your school, that's your choice. But don't be such a damn fool as to advertise to the whole world that you are in "a gun-free environment" where you are a helpless target for any homicidal fiend who is armed. Is it worth a human life to be a politically correct moral exhibitionist?

Thomas Sowell

5   The more I study the history of intellectuals, the more they seem like a wrecking crew, dismantling civilization bit by bit—replacing what works with what sounds good.

6   Some people are wondering what takes so long for the negotiations about the "fiscal cliff." Maybe both sides are waiting for supplies. Democrats may be waiting for more cans to kick down the road. Republicans may be waiting for more white flags to hold up in surrender.

7   If I were rich, I would have a plaque made up, and sent to every judge in America, bearing a statement made by Adam Smith more than two-and-a-half centuries ago: "Mercy to the guilty is cruelty to the innocent."

8   If someone wrote a novel about a man who was raised from childhood to resent the successful and despise the basic values of America—and who then went on to become president of the United States—that novel would be considered too unbelievable, even for a work of fiction. Yet that is what has happened in real life.

9   Many people say, "War should be a last resort." Of course it should be a last resort. So should heart surgery, divorce, and many other things. But that does not mean that we should just continue to hope against hope indefinitely that things will work out, somehow, until catastrophe suddenly overtakes us.

10   Everybody is talking about how we are going to pay for the huge national debt, but nobody seems to be talking about the runaway spending that created that record-breaking debt. In other words, the big spenders get political benefits from handing out goodies, while those who resist giving them more money to spend will be blamed for sending the country off the "fiscal cliff."

11   When Barack Obama refused to agree to a requested meeting with Israeli prime minister Benjamin Netanyahu—the leader of a country publically and repeatedly threatened with annihilation by Iran's leaders, as the Iranians move toward creating nuclear bombs—I thought of a line from the old movie classic Citizen Kane: "Charlie wasn't cruel. He just did cruel things."

12   There must be something liberating about ignorance. Back when most members of Congress had served in the military, there was a reluctance of politicians to try to tell military leaders how to run the military services. But,

now that few members of Congress have ever served in the military, they are ready to impose all sorts of fashionable notions on the military.

After watching a documentary about 13 the tragic story of Jonestown, I was struck by the utterly unthinking way that so many people put themselves completely at the mercy of a glib and warped man, who led them to degradation and destruction. And I could not help thinking of the parallel with the way we put a glib and warped man in the White House.

There are people calling for the banning of assault weapons who could not define an "assault weapon" if their lives depended on it. Yet the ignorant expect others to take them seriously.

Source: *National Review Online*, December 25, 2012. Reprinted by permission of Thomas Sowell and Creators Syndicate, Inc. © 2012 Creators Syndicate, Inc.

QUESTIONS FOR READING

1. Who, in Sowell's view, are totalitarians?
2. Who are "politically correct moral exhibitionist[s]"?
3. What action leads the author to write that Obama does "cruel things"? What else does Sowell call Obama?

QUESTIONS FOR REASONING AND ANALYSIS

4. Sowell writes about Christmas trees, the fiscal cliff, Obama, guns, and the national debt; how do these topics connect to give Sowell his general subject?
5. What, then, is the author's claim? Do you see a general theme that unites the many issues Sowell includes?
6. How does the author develop and support his claim?
7. Examine Sowell's style and tone. How would you characterize his tone? Is his approach likely to be effective for his primary audience? Explain.

QUESTIONS FOR REFLECTION AND WRITING

8. Do you find any logical fallacies in Sowell's argument? If so, how would you challenge them?
9. Has Sowell supported his general claim and specific generalizations to your satisfaction? Why or why not?

1. Think about sports stars you know. Write an argument defending one player as the best in his or her field of play. Think about whether you want to use Krauthammer's "Method 1" or "Method 2" or your own method for your criteria. (Remember that you can qualify your argument; you could write about the best college football player this year, for example.)

2. If you like music, think about what you might evaluate from this field. Who is the best rock band? Hip-hop artist? Country-western singer? And so forth. Be sure to make your criteria for evaluation clear.

3. You have had many instructors—and much instruction—in the last 12+ years. Is there one teacher who is/was the best? If so, why? Is there a teaching method that stands out in your memory for the excellence of its approach? Find an evaluation topic from your educational experiences.

4. Select an editorial, op-ed column, letter to the editor, or one of the essays in this text as an argument with which you disagree. Prepare a refutation of the work's logic or evidence or both. Follow the guidelines for writing a refutation or rebuttal in this chapter.

5. What is your favorite book? Movie? Television show? Why is it your favorite? Does it warrant an argument that it is really good, maybe even the best, in some way or in some category (sitcoms, for example)? Write a review, following the guidelines for this type of evaluation argument given in this chapter.

The Position Paper: Claims of Values

READ: Who are the speakers? What is the situation?

REASON: What is the point of the cartoon? What does Dana Summers, the cartoonist, want readers to think about?

REFLECT/WRITE: Why does this cartoon make a good opening for a chapter on arguments based on values?

As we established in Chapter 4, all arguments involve values. Evaluation arguments require judgment—thoughtful judgment, one hopes, based on criteria—but judgment nonetheless. If you believe that no one should spend more than $25,000 for a car, then you will not appreciate the qualities that attract some people to Mercedes. When one argues that government tax rates should go up as income goes up, it is because one believes that it is *right* for government to redistribute income to some degree: The rich pay more in taxes, the poor get more in services. When countries ban the importing of ivory, they do so because they believe it is *wrong* to destroy the magnificent elephant just so humans can use their ivory tusks for decorative items. (Observe that the word *magnificent* expresses a value.)

Some arguments, though, are less about judging what is good or best, or less about how to solve specific problems, than they are about stating a position on an issue. An argument that defends a general position (segregated schools are wrong) may imply action that should result (schools should be integrated), but the focus of the argument is first to state and defend the position. It is helpful to view these arguments, based heavily on values and a logical sequencing of ideas with less emphasis on specifics, as a separate type—genre—of argument. These claims of values are often called position papers.

CHARACTERISTICS OF THE POSITION PAPER

The position paper, or claim of values, may be the most difficult of arguments simply because it is often perceived to be the easiest. Let's think about this kind of argument:

- A claim based on values and argued more with logic than specifics is usually more general or abstract or philosophical than other types of argument. Greenpeace objects to commercial fishing that uses large nets that ensnare dolphins along with commercial fish such as tuna. Why? Because we ought not to destroy such beautiful and highly developed animals. Because we ought not to destroy more than we need, to waste part of nature because we are careless or in a hurry. For Greenpeace, the issue is about values—though it may be about money for the commercial fishermen.

- The position paper makes a claim about what is right or wrong, good or bad, for us as individuals or as a society. Topics can range from capital punishment to pornography to reducing the amount of trash we toss.

- Although a claim based on values is often developed in large part by a logical sequencing of reasons, support of principles also depends on relevant facts. Remember the long list of specific abuses listed in the Declaration of Independence (see pp. 156–59). If Greenpeace can show that commercial fisheries can be successful using a different kind of net or staying away from areas heavily populated by dolphins, it can probably get more support for its general principles.

- A successful position paper requires more than a forceful statement of personal beliefs. If we can reason logically from principles widely shared by our audience, we are more likely to be successful. If we are going to challenge their beliefs or values, then we need to consider the conciliatory approach as a strategy for getting them to at least listen to our argument.

GUIDELINES for Analyzing a Claim of Value

When reading position papers, what should you look for? Again, the basics of good argument apply here as well as with definition arguments. To analyze claims of values specifically, use these questions as guides:

- **What is the writer's claim?** Is it clear?
- **Is the claim qualified if necessary?** Some claims of value are broad philosophical assertions ("Capital punishment is immoral and bad public policy"). Others are qualified ("Capital punishment is acceptable only in crimes of treason").
- **What facts are presented?** Are they credible? Are they relevant to the claim's support?
- **What reasons are given in support of the claim?** What assumptions are necessary to tie reasons to claim? Make a list of reasons and assumptions and analyze the writer's logic. Do you find any fallacies?
- **What are the implications of the claim?** For example, if you argue for the legalization of all recreational drugs, you eliminate all "drug problems" by definition. But what new problems may be created by this approach? Consider more car accidents and reduced productivity for openers.
- **Is the argument convincing?** Does the evidence provide strong support for the claim? Are you prepared to agree with the writer, in whole or in part?

PREPARING A POSITION PAPER

In addition to the guidelines for writing arguments presented in Chapter 4, you can use the following advice specific to writing position papers or claims of value.

Planning

1. **Think:** What claim, exactly, do you want to support? Should you qualify your first attempt at a claim statement?
2. **Think:** What grounds (evidence) do you have to support your claim? You may want to make a list of the reasons and facts you would consider using to defend your claim.

3. **Think:** Study your list of possible grounds and identify the assumptions (warrants) and backing for your grounds.

4. **Think:** Now make a list of the grounds most often used by those holding views that oppose your claim. This second list will help you prepare counterarguments to possible rebuttals, but first it will help you test your commitment to your position. If you find the opposition's arguments persuasive and cannot think how you would rebut them, you may need to rethink your position. Ideally, your two lists will confirm your views but also increase your respect for opposing views.

5. **Consider:** How can I use a conciliatory approach? With an emotion-laden or highly controversial issue, the conciliatory approach can be an effective strategy. Conciliatory arguments include

    - the use of nonthreatening language,
    - the fair expression of opposing views, and
    - a statement of the common ground shared by opposing sides.

    You may want to use a conciliatory approach when (1) you know your views will be unpopular with at least some members of your audience; (2) the issue is highly emotional and has sides that are "entrenched" so that you are seeking some accommodations rather than dramatic changes of position; (3) you need to interact with members of your audience and want to keep a respectful relationship going. The sample student essay on gun control (at the end of this chapter) illustrates a conciliatory approach.

Drafting

1. Begin with an opening paragraph or two that introduces your topic in an interesting way. Possibilities include a statement of the issue's seriousness or reasons why the issue is currently being debated—or why we should go back to reexamine it. Some writers are spurred by a recent event that receives media coverage; recounting such an event can produce an effective opening. You can also briefly summarize points of the opposition that you will challenge in supporting your claim. Many counterarguments are position papers.

2. Decide where to place your claim statement. Your best choices are either early in your essay or at the end of your essay, after you have made your case. The second approach can be an effective alternative to the more common pattern of stating one's claim early.

3. Organize evidence in an effective way. One plan is to move from the least important to the most important reasons, followed by rebuttals to potential counterarguments. Another possibility is to organize by the arguments of the opposition, explaining why each of their reasons fails to hold up. A third approach is to organize logically. That is, if some reasons build on the accepting of other reasons, you want to begin with the necessary underpinnings and then move forward from those.

4. Maintain an appropriate level of seriousness for an argument of principle. Of course, word choice must be appropriate to a serious discussion, but in addition be sure to present reasons that are also appropriately serious. For example, if you are defending the claim that music CDs should not be subject to content labeling because such censorship is inconsistent with First Amendment rights, do not trivialize your argument by including the point that young people are tired of adults controlling their lives. (This is another issue for another paper.)

5. Provide a logical defense of or specifics in support of each reason. You have not finished your task by simply asserting several reasons for your claim. You also need to present facts or examples for or a logical explanation of each reason. For example, you have not defended your views on capital punishment by asserting that it is right or just to take the life of a murderer. Why is it right or just? Executing the murderer will not bring the victim back to life. Do two wrongs make a right? These are some of the thoughts your skeptical reader may have unless you explain and justify your reasoning. *Remember:* Quoting another writer's opinion on your topic does not provide proof for your reasons. It merely shows that someone else agrees with you.

A CHECKLIST FOR REVISION

☐ Do I have a clear statement of my claim? Is it qualified, if appropriate?

☐ Have I organized my argument, building the parts of my support into a clear and logical structure that readers can follow?

☐ Have I avoided logical fallacies?

☐ Have I found relevant facts and examples to support and develop my reasons?

☐ Have I paid attention to appropriate word choice, including using a conciliatory approach if that is a wise strategy?

☐ Have I used the basic checklist for revision in Chapter 4 (see p. 111)?

STUDENT ESSAY

EXAMINING THE ISSUE OF GUN CONTROL

Chris Brown

The United States has a long history of compromise. Issues such as representation in government have been resolved because of compromise, forming some of the bases of American life. Americans, however, like to feel

Introduction connects ambivalence in American character to conflict over gun control.

that they are uncompromising, never willing to surrender an argument. This attitude has led to a number of issues in modern America that are unresolved, including the issue of gun control. Bickering over the issue has slowed progress toward legislation that will solve the serious problem of gun violence in America, while keeping recreational use of firearms available to responsible people. To resolve the conflict over guns, the arguments of both sides must be examined, with an eye to finding the flaws in both. Then perhaps we can reach some meaningful compromises.

Student organizes
by arguments for
no gun control.

Gun advocates have used many arguments for the continued availability of firearms to the public. The strongest of these defenses points to the many legitimate uses for guns. One use is protection against violence, a concern of some people in today's society. There are many problems with the use of guns for protection, however, and these problems make the continued use of firearms for protection dangerous. One such problem is that gun owners are not always able to use guns responsibly. When placed in a situation in which personal injury or loss is imminent, people often do not think intelligently. Adrenaline surges through the body, and fear takes over much of the thinking process. This causes gun owners to use their weapons, firing at whatever threatens them. Injuries and deaths of innocent people, including family members of the gun owner, result. Removing guns from the house may be the best solution to these sad consequences.

1. Guns for
protection.

Responding to this argument, gun advocates ask how they are to defend themselves without guns. But guns are needed for protection from other guns. If there are no guns, people need only to protect themselves from criminals using knives, baseball bats, and other weapons. Obviously the odds of surviving a knife attack are greater than the odds of surviving a gun attack. One reason is that a gun is an impersonal weapon. Firing at someone from 50 feet away requires much less commitment than charging someone with a knife and stabbing repeatedly. Also, bullet wounds are, generally, more severe than knife wounds. Guns are also more likely to be misused when a dark figure is in one's house. To kill with the gun requires only to point and shoot; no recognition of the figure is needed. To kill with a knife, by contrast, requires getting within arm's reach of the figure, and knowing, for sure, the identity of your presumed opponent.

There are other uses of guns, including recreation. Hunting and target shooting are valid, responsible uses of guns. How do we keep guns available for recreation? The answer is in the form of gun clubs and hunting clubs. Many are already established; more can be constructed. These clubs can provide recreational use of guns for responsible people while keeping guns off the streets and out of the house.

2. Recreational uses.

The last argument widely used by gun advocates is the constitutional right to bear arms. The fallacies in this argument are that the Constitution was written in a vastly different time. This different time had different uses for guns, and a different type of gun. Firearms were defended in the Constitution because of their many valid uses and fewer problems. Guns were mostly muskets, guns that were not very accurate beyond close range. Also, guns took more than 30 seconds to load in the eighteenth century and could fire only one shot before reloading. These differences with today's guns affect the relative safety of guns then and now. In addition, those who did not live in the city at the time used hunting for food as well as for recreation; hunting was a necessary component of life. That is not true today. Another use of guns in the eighteenth century was as protection from animals. Wild animals such as bears and cougars were much more common. Settlers, explorers, and hunters needed protection from these animals in ways not comparable with modern life.

3. Second Amendment rights.

Finally, Revolutionary America had no standing army. Defense of the nation and of one's home from other nations relied on local militia. The right to bear arms granted in the Constitution was inspired by the need for national protection as well as by the other outdated needs previously discussed. Today America has a standing army with enough weaponry to adequately defend itself from outside aggressors. There is no need for every citizen to carry a musket, or an AK-47, for the protection of the nation. It would seem, then, that the Second Amendment does not fully apply to modern society. While it justifies gun ownership, it is open to restrictions and controls based on the realities of today's world.

Student establishes
a compromise
position.

To reach a compromise, we also have to examine the other side of the issue. Some gun-control advocates argue that all guns are unnecessary and should be outlawed. The problem with this argument is that guns will still be available to those who do not mind breaking the law. Until an economically sound and feasible way of controlling illegal guns in America is found, guns cannot be totally removed, no matter how much legislation is passed. This means that if guns are to be outlawed for uses other than recreational uses, a way must be found to combat the illegal gun trade that will evolve. Tough criminal laws and a large security force are all that can be offered to stop illegal uses of guns until better technology is available. This means that, perhaps, a good resolution would involve gradual restrictions on guns, until eventually guns were restricted only to recreational uses in a controlled setting for citizens not in the police or military.

Conclusion restates
student's claim.

Both sides on this issue have valid points. Any middle ground needs to offer something to each side. It must address the reasons people feel they need guns for protection and allow for valid recreational use, but keep military-style guns off the street, except when in the hands of properly trained police officers. Time and money will be needed to move toward the removal of America's huge gun arsenal. But, sooner or later a compromise on the issue of gun control must be made to make America a safer, better place to live.

TO TRACK MY THIEF | DAVID POGUE

A graduate of Yale University with an interesting blend of study in music, English, and computer science, David Pogue writes a weekly column for the *New York Times* and a monthly column for *Scientific American*, focusing on technology issues. He has hosted *NOVA ScienceNow* shows on PBS and is a CBS News correspondent. Before becoming a columnist, he arranged and conducted a number of Broadway musicals and wrote a number of the books "for Dummies." The following column comes from the November 2012 issue of *Scientific American*.

PREREADING QUESTIONS Knowing that this is a technology column and considering the title, what do you expect Pogue's subject to be? What makes Pogue's title clever and catchy?

When I boarded an Amtrak 1 train this summer, I had no idea what kind of ride I was in for.

Upon arrival at my home stop 2 in Connecticut, I realized that my iPhone was missing. I still had hope, though. Apple's free Find My iPhone service uses GPS, Wi-Fi and cellular information to locate lost i-gadgets on a map. After a couple of days, Find My iPhone emailed me to announce that it had found my phone—a map revealed it to be at a house in Seat Pleasant, MD.

Well, great. How was I going 3 to retrieve a phone five states away? On a nutty whim, I posted a note to my Twitter followers about my lost phone. "Find My iPhone shows it in MD. Anyone want to help me track it down? ADVENTURE!" And I included a map showing the green locator dot over a satellite image of a nondescript house.

Within an hour the quest to recover my phone was on blogs, Twitter, and 4 even national newspapers and television shows. "Where's Pogue's phone?" became a high-tech treasure hunt.

Using the address provided by Find My iPhone, local police got involved. 5 The homeowner confessed to stealing the phone—no doubt baffled as to how the police had known exactly how to find him. And a day later I had the phone back. (I decided not to press charges.)

To me, that was that. Modern tech + good old-fashioned police work = 6 happy ending, right?

Not for everyone. Lots of people were disturbed by the affair. They saw 7 my posting the thief's address as a gross violation of his privacy.

"Are there to be ANY limits in this country?" wrote one reader. "Mr. Pogue 8 . . . not only . . . crowdsourced instant 'deputies,' giving [them] detailed maps of the device's location but got the police to go to that location. That location is someone's home. What's the presumption of privacy there?"

My initial thought was: "Wait a minute—we're expressing sympathy for 9 the *thief*?" When you steal something, don't you risk giving up some rights? How was my Twitter post any different from the "wanted" posters of suspects' photographs that still hang in post offices?

Of course, the difference in this case is that I, not law enforcement, posted 10 the map and began the chase. Does that constitute a breach of the thief's rights? Is this a slippery slope into a world where the Internet's citizens become digital vigilantes?

11   Those are tricky questions. Even when the government or law-enforcement agencies want to get cell location information, the law is not always clear-cut. Sometimes the police require a warrant to obtain such information from cell phone companies; in other instances, they do not. In my case, there's not even much law to guide us, says Chris Soghoian, a privacy researcher at Indiana University Bloomington. A bill proposed last year in Congress, nicknamed the "GPS Act," would have addressed "find my phone" services, saying that it's "not unlawful" for the owner of a stolen phone to use geolocation information to help an investigation.

12   It is possible, Soghoian says, that I violated some kind of state harassment or stalking statute. For the most part, however, both the legal and ethical ramifications of my crowdsourced phone quest are nothing but murk. It would have been better if I had been able to recover the phone without blasting a photograph of the guy's home to the Internet at large. It would have been better if he hadn't taken my phone at all or had responded to the "Reward if found" messages I sent to its screen. Yet combining the powers of geotracking and social networking seemed such an obvious tactic that, at the time, I hardly gave it a second thought.

13   In the end, maybe what society really needs is an app called Find My Moral Compass.

QUESTIONS FOR READING

1. What happened to the author on his train ride home?
2. What app found his phone?
3. What did he do with this information?

QUESTIONS FOR REASONING AND ANALYSIS

4. What sequence of thoughts and discussions did Pogue go through as he listened to others and reflected on his actions?
5. What is the ethical issue created by Pogue's actions?
6. What position does he reach on the issue? Does he offer a specific claim statement or imply one?

QUESTIONS FOR REFLECTION AND WRITING

7. How might we classify Pogue's essay, based on style and approach? Would you still assert that the author has presented an argument—one that explores an ethical issue created by modern technology? Why or why not? Explain.
8. If you had been one of the author's Twitter followers, how would you have responded to his "ADVENTURE"? Does Pogue need a moral compass, or did he act ethically? Be prepared to defend your view.
9. Does our digital world come with a loss of privacy? If so, is it worth the trade-off? Be prepared to discuss or write about this issue.

TRASH TALK: REFLECTIONS ON OUR THROWAWAY SOCIETY
GREGORY M. KENNEDY, SJ

The author of *An Ontology of Trash* (2007), Greg Kennedy is currently a student of theology at Regis College in Toronto, Canada. His essay originally appeared May 7, 2012, in *America*, a national weekly journal for Roman Catholics. He chose to modify the original article somewhat to reach out to this text's more diverse readership.

PREREADING QUESTIONS Knowing that the author is a Jesuit seminarian, would you necessarily expect his position on trash to be different from that of any other writer on this topic? How might his education and training influence his approach or writing style?

Every morning my colleague's desk captured my passing eye. Nestled beneath the computer screen, between her cup of pens and a stapler, she kept her mid-morning snack. Sometimes it was two chocolates in gold foil, or a pair of sugar biscuits bound together in cellophane, sometimes rose-colored paper enveloping a candy from the Philippines. And always fruit. One day it was an apple, another an orange, a third day a banana. Regardless of the variety, the fruit was invariably as meticulously wrapped as its companion foodstuffs.

Now plastic wrap around an apple struck me as redundant. Plastic wrap around a banana or orange still snug in its peel struck me as downright ridiculous. I could not help staring incredulously each morning at these doubly embedded specimens, but never gathered the gumption to query my colleague about her logic.

Why, I wondered, would a person spend time, energy, and money to shroud a banana in plastic, which would later require more time, energy and money to get rid of? After all, the good Creator already outfitted the banana with an effective, protective cover. What purpose does that extra layer of petrochemical veneer serve?

By no means would my colleague stand alone in the dock before such questions. Nearly every retailer and almost as many customers in this country suspect that no licit commercial transaction has occurred if, in the end, there isn't a bag, or a box, a bottle, or a blister pack to pitch into the garbage pail.

In *Gone Tomorrow: The Hidden Life of Garbage*, Heather Rogers estimates that 80% of U.S. products, like plastic wrap, are discarded after a single use. Of course, it takes a special kind of person to use a banana more than once. Food, the quintessential consumer good, has become a Grade-A disposable in the overstocked market. A supersized portion of comestibles in this country does not receive even the fleeting honor of a single use. The average American household wastes a quarter of all the food it presumably worked hard to bring home. Add to that the other waste occurring along the entire length of the production and distribution line—from the farm to the supermarket deli—and the total percentage of food wasted before tasted approaches a shocking and shaming forty percent.

Except in rare instances, for example, pie-throwing contests, food is not intentionally produced in order to be tossed. The same does not hold for food's innumerable, protective accessorizing. Of all municipal solid waste, the single largest share goes to containers and packaging at 30%. Juice boxes, polystyrene clamshells, tin cans, plastic this, that and the other thing—nary a bite comes to our lips that has not recently emerged from an artificial peel.

7   At first glance, it may seem that the plastic cling wrap and the organic banana peel differ only chemically, since they share the same function: packaging. Ever since Aristotle, philosophers have looked to an object's putative purpose in seeking to define its particular essence. This technique often succeeds with manufactured objects, but always stumbles over natural things. Only the consumer conveniently regards the banana peel as packaging. From the standpoint of the banana tree, the peel plays a vital part in procreation. To the soil the peel means future nutrients and increased fertility.

8   Irreducible to a single purpose, natural things exist as waste only temporarily and conditionally. When out one evening picking saskatoon berries, a friend expressed his anxiety to me about the coming nightfall. "If we don't pick these bushes clean, all their berries will go to waste." I conceded a limited truth to this statement. As far as our stomachs were concerned, the berries would not fulfill their function if they never reached our mouths.

9   Had we consulted the bush and berries, however, we might have slowed our hurried harvest. With respect to reproduction, the berries existed as ingeniously designed aerial seed-distribution units. In boyishly biological terms: birds eat the berries, fly a while and poop out the seeds across all the various kinds of soils one hears about in parables. However, we, the civilized consumers, would, by eating the seeds, destine them to destruction in the sewage treatment plant. So where exactly was the waste, on the bush or in our plumbing?

10   Plastic wrap does not enjoy this multiplicity of purpose, nor the redemptive ambiguity of "waste." Its design is much less intelligent. Once the wrap fulfills its single function, it is good for nothing. In fact, it is about as good *as* nothing, because it has no more to achieve. If function and essence do go together in manufactured objects, then a consumer item deprived of function will also be devoid of essence. It becomes waste unconditionally and forever, since it no longer serves any possible end.

11   Since it was originally conceived and produced to lose its function after a single use, the object was in a sense already wasted even before it performed its purpose. So here we have an object that already existed as waste. Planned obsolescence, you could say, renders objects presently obsolete. Such absolute waste, waste considered from all possible angles, waste built right into the conception of an object, I philosophically classify as "trash."

12   The word "trash" has a modern ring. The reality began littering history only after the Industrial Revolution, when the mass production of goods took off, leaving the ground piled up with discarded, worn out bags. Albert Borgmann,

philosopher of technology at the University of Montana, locates the key to modern industry in its division of labor. This is standard history. What moves Borgmann's interpretation well beyond mediocrity is where he draws the most basic lines of division: not between human workers, but within technology itself.

The genius of modern technology, he demonstrates, lies in its unprece- 13 dented ability to split the product from its production. Consumers desire commodities, such as tasty food, amusing entertainment, easy transportation. Devices deliver these desirables. Their delivery advances toward perfection the closer they come to providing products in demand without demanding anything in return. Thus the perfect device remains completely hidden behind the convenience of the consumable commodity.

Convenience, the rock on which we have built the consumer world, relies 14 absolutely on the division between commodity and device. Digging your own potatoes is not terribly convenient, especially when compared to dashing into 7-11 for a sealed-fresh bag of salt-and-vinegar chips. A complex, technological and all but invisible industrial food system is the globalized device feeding our hunger for fast-food convenience items. Packaging, of course, is an essential ingredient for making food convenient.

As part of the device, packaging has a sole function: to deliver the com- 15 modity of food as safely and conveniently as possible. Its single function necessitates its single use. If the consumer had to fold the plastic wrap and bring it home for tomorrow's snack, or had to wash and dry the take-away cup in preparation for the next injection of java, or had to return the aluminum can to the cola company for refills, then these devices would be delivering their goods inconveniently. But by definition, the device can't make such demands; its whole point is to disappear. As soon as it has accomplished its mission of delivery, the packaging device exhausts the conditions of its existence. It is trash, pure and simple. Into the void of the trash or recycling bin it vanishes.

So the banana peel and the plastic wrap differ much more than just chemi- 16 cally. The peel, not limited to a single purpose, exists and functions within an integrated web of relationships. Each relationship lets it be in a unique way. The peel exists as waste only within a limited subset of its total interconnections.

The plastic wrap, on the other hand, was expressly designed to deliver just 17 one value: the protection of goods from air, dirt and germs. Once the food is gone then so goes the plastic's *raison d'etre*. The wrap has nothing left to live for; it is curled up and buried. Materially, the object has the same qualities as it had when it first spooled off the roll. But as far as the consumer is concerned, it has instantly become irredeemable waste. How many of us would entrust another sandwich to it? No, it simply must be trashed. It belongs nowhere in our consumer world.

We all know that, despite our worst intentions, the disposables we discard 18 do not really disappear. Yet we like to pretend that they do. As consumers we have precious little business with the trash we generate. Our elaborate system of garbage collection, incineration, disposal and recycling is a sophisticated device that delivers to most urban consumers the commodities of sanitation and cleanliness. Undoubtedly, swept streets and clean homes count as real blessings. But hiding our trash within the technological division of commodity and device allows us to consume without concerning ourselves about consequences.

19   And the consequences keep piling up. In spite of all our roused environmental consciousness and the de-materialization of the digital age, our quantity of trash compounds. According to the EPA, Americans generated 2.68 lbs of municipal solid waste per person per day in 1960. By 2010 that total had bloated to 4.43 lbs. The fatter the wedge we drive between the commodity and its device, the more trash we inevitably stuff into the gap.

20   We can and must do otherwise. Some years after WWII, French philosopher Jean-Paul Sartre said: "We were never more free than during German occupation." Sartre had a flair for paradox. Under occupation, every act took on significance; every act, no matter how prosaic, held out the chance for bravery and non-conformity. In a throw-away society, analogous opportunities prevail. Every shopping bag you refuse, every coffee cup you reuse, every piece of plastic you eschew is an act of freedom and conscience against our thoughtless slavery to trash.

Source: *America: The National Catholic Weekly*, May 7, 2012. Reprinted by permission of the author.

QUESTIONS FOR READING

1. What percentage of food is wasted?
2. What percentage of solid waste is composed of packaging? How does packaging's purpose differ from food's purpose?
3. How does plastic covering differ from organic covering—such as the banana peel?
4. What do modern consumers want? How does plastic packaging help to deliver this?

QUESTIONS FOR REASONING AND ANALYSIS

5. Explain why plastic packaging is "trash" whereas organic "waste" is not.
6. Our digital age has presumably resulted in less paper, and yet our volume of solid waste continues to increase. What—implies Kennedy—is contributing to the increased tonnage of trash?
7. Review elements of style in Chapter 2 and then analyze Kennedy's writing, focusing on three characteristics that you select to study. How does his style contribute to his argument?

QUESTIONS FOR REFLECTION AND WRITING

8. What specific suggestions for wasting less food and tossing less trash do you have to add to Kennedy's discussion? Explain and defend your suggestions. If you don't think that wasting food along the way or filling solid waste dumps are really that big a problem, prepare your rebuttal of Kennedy's argument.
9. Kennedy concludes his essay by quoting Sartre. Explain Sartre's point and how Kennedy uses it to support his concluding point. Contemplate other ways in which we could use these ideas as guides to living.

1. Chris Brown, in the student essay, writes a conciliatory argument seeking common ground on the volatile issue of gun control. Write your own conciliatory argument on this issue, offering a different approach than Brown, but citing Brown for any ideas you borrow from his essay. Alternatively, write a counterargument of his essay.

2. There are other "hot issues," issues that leave people entrenched on one side or the other, giving expression to the same arguments again and again without budging many, if any, readers. Do not try to write on any one of these about which you get strongly emotional. Select one that you can be calm enough over to write a conciliatory argument, seeking to find common ground. Some of these issues include same-sex marriage, legalizing recreational drugs, capital punishment, mainstreaming students with disabilities, the use of torture to interrogate terrorists. Exclude abortion rights from the list—it is too controversial for most writers to handle successfully.

3. Other issues that call for positions based on values stem from First Amendment rights. Consider a possible topic from this general area. Possibilities include:

   Hate speech should (or should not) be a crime.
   Obscenity and pornography on the Internet should (or should not) be restricted.
   Hollywood films should (or should not) show characters smoking.

4. Consider issues related to college life. Should all colleges have an honor code—or should existing codes be eliminated? Should students be automatically expelled for plagiarism? Should college administrators have any control over what is published in the college newspaper?

CHAPTER 10

Arguments about Cause

READ: Who is the person in the ad? Why is she posed with the draped net?

REASON: What argument does the ad make? What visual strategies are used? What assumption about audience is made?

REFLECT/WRITE: Is the ad effective? Why or why not?

Because we want to know *why* things happen, arguments about cause are both numerous and important to us. We begin asking why at a young age, pestering adults with questions such as "Why is the sky blue?" and "Why is the grass green?" And, to make sense of our world, we try our hand at explanations as youngsters, deciding that the first-grade bully is "a bad boy." The bully's teacher, however, will seek a more complex explanation because an understanding of the causes is the place to start to guide the bully to more socially acceptable behavior.

As adults we continue the search for answers. We want to understand past events: Why was President Kennedy assassinated? We want to explain current situations: Why do so many college students binge drink? And of course we also want to predict the future: Will the economy improve if there is a tax cut? All three questions seek a causal explanation, including the last one. If you answer the last question with a yes, you are claiming that a tax cut is a cause of economic improvement.

CHARACTERISTICS OF CAUSAL ARGUMENTS

Causal arguments vary not only in subject matter but in structure. Here are the four most typical patterns:

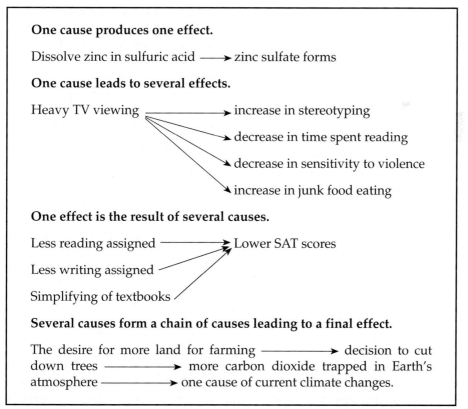

One cause produces one effect.

Dissolve zinc in sulfuric acid ⟶ zinc sulfate forms

One cause leads to several effects.

Heavy TV viewing ⟶ increase in stereotyping
⟶ decrease in time spent reading
⟶ decrease in sensitivity to violence
⟶ increase in junk food eating

One effect is the result of several causes.

Less reading assigned ⟶ Lower SAT scores
Less writing assigned
Simplifying of textbooks

Several causes form a chain of causes leading to a final effect.

The desire for more land for farming ⟶ decision to cut down trees ⟶ more carbon dioxide trapped in Earth's atmosphere ⟶ one cause of current climate changes.

These models lead to several key points about causal arguments:

- **Most causal arguments are highly complex.** Except for some simple chemical reactions, most arguments about cause are difficult, can involve many steps, and are often open to challenge. Even arguments based in science lead to shrill exchanges. Think, then, how much more open to debate are arguments about the worldwide economic downturn or arguments about human behavior. Many people think that "it's obvious" that violent TV and video games lead to more aggressive behavior. And yet, psychologists, in study after study, have not demonstrated conclusively that there is a clear causal connection. One way to challenge this causal argument is to point to the majority of people who do not perform violent acts even though they have watched television and played video games while growing up.

- **Because of the multiple and intertwined patterns of causation in many complex situations, the best causal arguments keep focused on their purpose.** For example, you are concerned with global warming. Cows contribute to global warming. Are we going to stop cattle farming? Not likely. Factories contribute to global warming. Are we going to tear down factories? Not likely—but we can demand that smokestacks have filters to reduce harmful emissions. Focus your argument on the causes that readers are most likely to accept because they are most likely to accept the action that the causes imply.

- **Learn and use the specific terms and concepts that provide useful guides to thinking about cause.** First, when looking for the cause of an event, we look for an *agent*—a person, situation, another event that led to the effect. For example, a lit cigarette dropped in a bed caused the house fire—the lit cigarette is the agent. But why, we ask, did someone drop a lit cigarette on a bed? The person, old and ill, took a sleeping pill and dropped the cigarette when he fell asleep. Where do we stop in the chain of causes?

  Second, most events do not occur in a vacuum with a single cause. There are *conditions* surrounding the event. The man's age and health were conditions. Third, we can also look for *influences.* The sleeping pill certainly influenced the man to drop the cigarette. Some conditions and influences may qualify as *remote causes. Proximate causes* are more immediate, usually closer in time to the event or situation. The man's dozing off is a proximate cause of the fire. Finally, we come to the *precipitating cause,* the triggering event—in our example, the cigarette's igniting the combustible mattress fabric. Sometimes we are interested primarily in the precipitating cause; in other situations, we need to go further back to find the remote causes or conditions that are responsible for what has occurred.

- **Be alert to the difference between cause and correlation.** First, be certain that you can defend your pattern of cause and effect as genuine causation, not as correlation only. Married people are better off financially, are healthier, and report happier sex lives than singles or cohabiting couples. Is this a correlation only? Or, does marriage itself produce these effects? Linda Waite is one sociologist who argues that marriage is the cause. Another example: Girls who participate in after-school activities are much less likely to get pregnant. Are the activities a cause? Probably not. But there are surely conditions and influences that have led to both the decision to participate in activities and the decision not to become pregnant.

An Example of Causal Complexity: Lincoln's Election and the Start of the Civil War

If Stephen Douglas had won the 1860 presidential election instead of Abraham Lincoln, would the Civil War have been avoided? An interesting question posed to various American history professors and others, including Waite Rawls, president of the Museum of the Confederacy. Their responses were part of an article that appeared in the *Washington Post* on November 7, 2010.

Obviously, this is a question that cannot be answered, but it led Rawls to discuss the sequence of causes leading to the breakout of the war. Rawls organizes his brief causal analysis around a great metaphor: the building and filling and then lighting of a keg of powder. Let's look at his analysis.

Existing Conditions

"The wood for the keg was shaped by the inability of the founding fathers to solve the two big problems of state sovereignty and slavery in the shaping of the Constitution."

More Recent Influences

1. "[T]he economics of taxes and the politics of control of the westward expansion were added to those two original issues as the keg was filled with powder."
2. "By the time of the creation of the Republican Party in 1856, the powder keg was almost full and waiting for a fuse. And the election of any candidate from the Republican Party—a purely sectional party—put the fuse in the powder keg, and the Deep South states seceded. But there was still no war."

Proximate Causes

"Two simultaneous mistakes in judgment brought the matches out of the pocket—the Deep South mistakenly thought that Lincoln, now elected, would not enforce the Union, and Lincoln mistakenly thought that the general population of the South would not follow the leadership" of the Deep South states.

Precipitating Causes

1. "Lincoln struck the match when he called the bluff of the South Carolinians and attempted to reinforce Fort Sumter, but that match could have gone out without an explosion."
2. "Lincoln struck a second, more fateful match, when he called for troops to put down the 'insurrection.' That forced the Upper South and Border States into a conflict that they had vainly attempted to avoid." (Reprinted by permission of Waite Rawls.)

Rawls concludes that the election of Lincoln did not start the war; it was only one step in a complex series of causes that led to America's bloodiest war. His analysis helps us see the complexity of cause/effect analysis.

Mill's Methods for Investigating Causes

John Stuart Mill, a nineteenth-century British philosopher, explained in detail some important ways of investigating and demonstrating causal relationships: commonality, difference, and process of elimination. We can benefit in our study of cause by understanding and using his methods.

1. **Commonality.** One way to isolate cause is to demonstrate that one agent is *common* to similar outcomes. For instance, twenty-five employees attend a company luncheon. Late in the day, ten report to area hospitals, and another four complain the next day of having experienced vomiting the night before. Public health officials will soon want to know what these people ate for lunch. Different people during the same twelve-hour period had similar physical symptoms of food poisoning. The common factor may well have been the tuna salad they ate for lunch.

2. **Difference.** Another way to isolate cause is to recognize one key *difference.* If two situations are alike in every way but one, and the situations result in different outcomes, then the one way they differ must have caused the different outcome.

    Studies in the social sciences are often based on the single-difference method. To test for the best teaching methods for math, an educator could set up an experiment with two classrooms similar in every way except that one class devotes fifteen minutes three days a week to instruction by drill. If the class receiving the drill scores much higher on a standard test given to both groups of students, the educator could argue that math drills make a measurable difference in learning math. But the educator should be prepared for skeptics to challenge the assertion of only one difference between the two classes. Could the teacher's attitude toward the drills also make a difference in student learning? If the differences in student scores are significant, the educator probably has a good argument.

3. **Process of elimination.** We can develop a causal argument around a technique we all use for problem solving: *the process of elimination.* When something happens, we examine all possible causes and eliminate them, one by one, until we are satisfied that we have isolated the actual cause (or causes).

    When the Federal Aviation Administration has to investigate a plane crash, it uses this process, exploring possible causes such as mechanical failure, weather, human error, or terrorism. Sometimes the process isolates more than one cause or points to a likely cause without providing absolute proof.

EXERCISE: Understanding Causal Patterns

From the following events or situations, select the one you know best and list as many conditions, influences, and causes—remote, proximate, precipitating—as you can think of. You may want to do this exercise with your class partner or in small groups. Be prepared to explain your causal pattern to the class.

1. Decrease in marriage rates in the United States
2. Arctic ice melt
3. Increase in the numbers of women elected to public office
4. High salaries of professional athletes
5. Increased interest in soccer in the United States
6. Comparatively low scores by U.S. students on international tests in math and science
7. Majority of 2012 U.S. Olympians were women

GUIDELINES for Analyzing Causal Arguments

When analyzing causal arguments, what should you look for? The basics of good argument apply to all arguments: a clear statement of claim, qualified if appropriate; a clear explanation of reasons and evidence; and enough relevant evidence to support the claim. How do we recognize these qualities in a causal argument? Use these points as guides to analyzing:

- **Does the writer carefully distinguish among types of causes?** Word choice is crucial. Is the argument that A and A alone caused B or that A was one of several contributing causes?

- **Does the writer recognize the complexity of causation and not rush to assert only one cause for a complex event or situation?** The credibility of an argument about cause is quickly lost if readers find the argument oversimplified.

- **Is the argument's claim clearly stated, with qualifications as appropriate?** If the writer wants to argue for one cause, not the only cause, of an event or situation, then the claim's wording must make this limited goal clear to readers. For example, one can perhaps build the case for heavy television viewing as one cause of stereotyping, loss of sensitivity to violence, and increased fearfulness. But we know that the home environment and neighborhood and school environments also do much to shape attitudes.

- **What reasons and evidence are given to support the argument?** Can you see the writer's pattern of development? Does the reasoning seem logical? Are the data relevant? This kind of analysis of the argument will help you evaluate it.

- **Does the argument demonstrate causality, not just a time relationship or correlation?** A causal argument needs to prove *agency:* A is the cause of B, not just something that happened before B or something that is present when B is present. March precedes April, but March does not cause April to arrive.

- **Does the writer present believable causal agents, agents consistent with our knowledge of human behavior and scientific laws?** Most educated people do not believe that personalities are shaped by astrological signs or that scientific laws are suspended in the Bermuda Triangle, allowing planes and ships to vanish or enter a fourth dimension.

- **What are the implications for accepting the causal argument?** If A and B clearly are the causes of C, and we don't want C to occur, then we presumably must do something about A and B—or at least we must do something about either A or B and see if reducing or eliminating one of the causes significantly reduces the incidence of C.
- **Is the argument convincing?** After analyzing the argument and answering the questions given in the previous points, you need to decide if, finally, the argument works.

PREPARING A CAUSAL ARGUMENT

In addition to the guidelines for writing arguments presented in Chapter 4, you can use the following advice specific to writing causal arguments.

Planning

1. **Think:** What are the focus and limits of your causal argument? Do you want to argue for one cause of an event or situation? Do you want to argue for several causes leading to an event or situation? Do you want to argue for a cause that others have overlooked? Do you want to show how one cause is common to several situations or events? Diagramming the relationship of cause to effect may help you see what you want to focus on.

2. **Think:** What reasons and evidence do you have to support your tentative claim? Consider what you already know that has led to your choice of topic. A brainstorming list may be helpful.

3. **Think:** How, then, do you want to word your claim? As we have discussed, wording is crucial in causal arguments. Review the discussion of characteristics of causal arguments if necessary.

4. **Reality check:** Do you have a claim worth defending in a paper? Will readers care?

5. **Think:** What, if any, additional evidence do you need to develop a convincing argument? You may need to do some reading or online searching to obtain data to strengthen your argument. Readers expect relevant, reliable, current statistics in most arguments about cause. Assess what you need and then think about what sources will provide the needed information.

6. **Think:** What assumptions (warrants) are you making in your causal reasoning? Are these assumptions logical? Will readers be likely to agree with your assumptions, or will you need to defend them as part of your argument? For example: One reason to defend the effects of heavy TV watching on viewers is the commonsense argument that what humans devote considerable time to will have a significant effect on their lives. Will your readers be prepared to accept this commonsense reasoning, or will they remain skeptical, looking for stronger evidence of a cause/effect relationship?

Drafting

1. Begin with an opening paragraph or two that introduces your topic in an interesting way. Lester Thurow in "Why Women Are Paid Less Than Men" writes:

    In the 40 years from 1939 to 1979 white women who work full time have with monotonous regularity made slightly less than 60 percent as much as white men. Why?

    This opening establishes the topic and Thurow's purpose in examining causes. The statistics get the reader's attention.

2. Do not begin by announcing your subject. Avoid openers such as: In this essay I will explain the causes of teen vandalism.

3. Decide where to place your claim statement. You can conclude your opening paragraph with it, or you can place it in your conclusion, after you have shown readers how best to understand the causes of the issue you are examining.

4. Present reasons and evidence in an organized way. If you are examining a series of causes, beginning with background conditions and early influences, then your basic plan will be time sequence. Readers need to see the chain of causes unfolding. Use appropriate terms and transitional words to guide readers through each stage in the causal pattern. If you are arguing for an overlooked cause, begin with the causes that have been put forward and show what is flawed in each one. Then present and defend your explanation of cause. This process of elimination structure works well when readers are likely to know what other causes have been offered in the past. You can also use one of Mill's other two approaches, if one of them is relevant to your topic.

5. Address the issue of correlation rather than cause, if appropriate. After presenting the results of a study of marriage that reveals many benefits (emotional, physical, financial) of marriage, Linda Waite examines the question that she knows skeptical readers may have: Does marriage actually *cause* the benefits, or is the relationship one of *correlation* only—that is, the benefits of marriage just happen to come with being married; they are not caused by being married.

6. Conclude by discussing the implications of the causal pattern you have argued for, if appropriate. Lester Thurow ends by asserting that if he is right about the cause of the gender pay gap, then there are two approaches society can take to remove the pay gap. If, in explaining the causes of teen vandalism, you see one cause as "group behavior," a gang looking for something to do, it then follows that you can advise young readers to stay out of gangs. Often with arguments about cause, there are personal or public policy implications in accepting the causal explanation.

A CHECKLIST FOR REVISION ■·▩·▩·▩·▩·▩·▩·▩·▩·▩·▩·▩·▩·▩·▩·▩·▩·▩·▩

☐   Do I have a clear statement of my claim? Is it appropriately qualified and focused? Is it about an issue that matters?

☐ Have I organized my argument so that readers can see my pattern for examining cause?

☐ Have I used the language for discussing causes correctly, distinguishing among conditions and influences and remote and proximate causes? Have I selected the correct word—either *affect* or *effect*—as needed?

☐ Have I avoided the *post hoc* fallacy and the confusing of correlation and cause?

☐ Have I carefully examined my assumptions and convinced myself that they are reasonable and can be defended? Have I defended them when necessary to clarify and thus strengthen my argument?

☐ Have I found relevant facts and examples to support and develop my argument?

☐ Have I used the basic checklist for revision in Chapter 4 (see p. 111)?

FOR ANALYSIS AND DEBATE

| WHY YOUR OFFICE NEEDS MORE BRATTY MILLENNIALS | EMILY MATCHAR |

The author, a graduate of Yale University, is a freelance writer whose articles focus on culture, food, travel, and women's issues. Her first book is *Homeward Bound: The New Cult of Domesticity* (2013).

PREREADING QUESTIONS Who are the millennials? What do you think they might be able to contribute to the office?

1   Have you heard the one about the kid who got his mom to call his boss and ask for a raise? Or about the college student who quit her summer internship because it forbade Facebook in the office?

2   Yep, we're talking about Generation Y—loosely defined as those born between 1982 and 1999—also known as millennials. Perhaps you know them by their other media-generated nicknames: teacup kids, for their supposed emotional fragility; boomerang kids, who always wind up back home; trophy kids—everyone's a winner!; the Peter Pan generation, who'll never grow up.

3   Now this pampered, over-praised, relentlessly self-confident generation (at age 30, I consider myself a sort of older sister to them) is flooding the workplace. They'll make up 75 percent of the American workforce by 2025—and they're trying to change everything.

4   These are the kids, after all, who text their dads from meetings. They think "business casual" includes skinny jeans. And they expect the company president to listen to their "brilliant idea."

5   When will they adapt?

6   They won't. Ever. Instead, through their sense of entitlement and inflated self-esteem, they'll make the modern workplace adapt to them. And we should thank them for it. Because the modern workplace frankly stinks, and the changes wrought by Gen Y will be good for everybody.

Few developed countries demand as much from their workers as the United 7
States. Americans spend more time at the office than citizens of most other
developed nations. Annually, we work 408 hours more than the Dutch, 374 hours
more than the Germans and 311 hours more than the French. We even work 59
hours more than the stereotypically nose-to-the-grindstone Japanese. Though
women make up half of the American workforce, the United States is the only
country in the developed world without guaranteed paid maternity leave.

All this hard work is done for less and less reward. Wages have been stag- 8
nant for years, benefits shorn, opportunities for advancement blocked. While
the richest Americans get richer, middle-class workers are left to do more with
less. Because jobs are scarce and we're used to a hierarchical workforce, we
accept things the way they are. Worse, we've taken our overwork as a badge
of pride. Who hasn't flushed with a touch of self-importance when turning
down social plans because we're "too busy with work"?

Into this sorry situation strolls the self-esteem generation, printer-fresh 9
diplomas in hand. And they're not interested in business as usual.

The current corporate culture simply doesn't make sense to much of 10
middle-class Gen Y. Since the cradle, these privileged kids have been offered
autonomy, control and choices ("Green pants or blue pants today, sweetie?").
They've been encouraged to show their creativity and to take their extracurricular interests seriously. Raised by parents who wanted to be friends with
their kids, they're used to seeing their elders as peers rather than authority
figures. When they want something, they're not afraid to say so.

And what the college-educated Gen Y-ers entering the workforce want is 11
engaging, meaningful, flexible work that doesn't take over their lives. The
grim economy and lack of job opportunities don't seem to be adjusting their
expectations downward much, either. According to a recent AP analysis, more
than 53 percent of recent college grads are unemployed or underemployed,
but such numbers don't appear to keep these new grads from thinking their
job owes them something.

In a March MTV survey of about 500 millennials, called "No Collar 12
Workers," 81 percent of respondents said they should be able to set their own
hours, and 70 percent said they need "me time" on the job (compared with 39
percent of baby boomers). Ninety percent think they deserve their "dream
job." They expect to be listened to when they have an idea, even when they're
the youngest person in the room.

"Why do we have to meet in an office cross-country when we can call in 13
remotely via Skype?" asks Megan Broussard, a 25-year-old New Yorker who
worked at a large PR firm for three years before quitting to become a freelance writer and career adviser. "Why wouldn't my opinion matter as much as
someone else's who only has a few more years of experience than I do?"

These desires are not exactly radical. Who wouldn't want flexibility, auton- 14
omy and respect?

What's different, says Lindsey Pollak, the author of "Getting From College 15
to Career: Your Essential Guide to Succeeding in the Real World," is how Gen
Y-ers are asking for those things. Pollak, a consultant who advises companies
on how to deal with Gen Y, says these workers—at least, the well-educated

ones who can afford to make demands—want what everyone wants out of a job, they're just asking for it in a more aggressive way. "And they're the first ones to leave when they don't get it," Pollak says.

16   According to surveys, 50 percent of Gen Y-ers would rather be unemployed than stay in a job they hate. Unlike their child- and mortgage-saddled elders, many can afford to be choosy about their jobs, given their notorious reliance on their parents. After all, they can always move back in with Mom and Dad (40 percent of young people will move home at least once, per Pew research), who are likely to be giving them financial help well into their 20s (41 percent of Gen Y-ers receive financial support from their parents after college, according to research from Ameritrade).

17   In fact, it's possible that a bad economy can make being choosy even easier—if more people are struggling to find work and living at home, there's no stigma to it.

18   Nancy Sai, a 25-year-old who works at a nonprofit in Manhattan, spent a year living with her parents and working at a gas station while trying to snag her dream job. Her mom kept bugging her to look for something different— teaching! government! anything!—but Sai held firm. While it took her a year to find the ideal gig, she's glad she waited. Her job is meaningful, the office environment friendly and welcoming, her bosses forthcoming with feedback. Some of her friends have not been so lucky—one quit her job in politics when her boss refused to give her any time off.

19   "She couldn't separate her work life from her personal life at all," Sai says. "She quit without another job lined up. She said she felt the most liberated she had in two years."

20   Despite the recession, or perhaps because of it, corporations are eager to hire and retain the best, most talented Gen Y workers. "In this risky economic environment, the energy, insight and high-tech know-how of Gen Yers will be essential for all high-performing organizations," said a 2009 study on Gen Y from Deloitte, the professional services giant.

21   Companies are beginning to heed Gen Y's demands. Though flextime and job-sharing have been staples of the workforce for a few decades, they are becoming more accepted, even in rigid corporate culture, says Laura Schild-kraut, a career counselor specializing in the needs of Gen Y. There has also been a rise in new work policies, such as ROWE, or "results only work environment," a system in which employees are evaluated on their productivity, not the hours they keep. In a ROWE office, the whole team can take off for a 4 p.m. "Spider-Man" showing if they've gotten enough done that day.

22   Radical-sounding perks such as unlimited paid vacation—assuming you've finished your pressing projects—are more common among companies concerned with attracting and retaining young talent. By 2010, 1 percent of U.S. companies had adopted this previously unheard-of policy, largely in response to the demands of Generation Y.

23   The Deloitte study warns that, to retain Gen Y-ers, companies "must foster a culture of respect that extends to all employees, regardless of age or level in the organization." In other words: Treat your Gen Y workers nicely. But we should be treating everyone nicely already, shouldn't we?

Beyond that, Gen Y's demands may eventually help bring about the family- 24 friendly policies for which working mothers have been leading the fight. Though the Family and Medical Leave Act of 1993 afforded some protections for working parents, genuine flexibility is still a privilege of the lucky few, and parents who try to leave the office at 5:30 p.m. are often accused of not pulling their weight. Well, guess what? Now everybody wants to leave the office at 5:30. Because they've got band practice. Or dinner with their grandma. Or they need to walk their rescue puppy.

The American workplace has been transformed during economic upswings 25 and downturns. The weekend was a product of labor union demands during the relative boom of the early 20th century. The Great Depression led to the New Deal's Fair Labor Standards Act, which introduced the 40-hour workweek and overtime pay to most Americans. But now, workplace change is coming from unadulterated, unorganized worker pushiness.

So we could continue to roll our eyes at Gen Y, accuse them of being 26 spoiled and entitled and clueless little brats. We could wish that they'd get taken down a peg by the "school of hard knocks" and learn to accept that this is just the way things are.

But if we're smart, we'll cheer them on. Be selfish, Gen Y! Be entitled! 27 Demand what you want. Because we want it, too.

Source: *Washington Post*, August 19, 2012. Reprinted by permission of the author.

QUESTIONS FOR READING

1. What is the age range for millennials? What other term is used for this group?
2. How has this group been raised? How do they view their elders? Themselves?
3. What details describe the current middle-class work world in the United States?

QUESTIONS FOR REASONING AND ANALYSIS

4. What changes does Matchar want to see in the workplace?
5. What upbringing, according to the author, has caused the Gen Y-ers to hold their attitudes toward work?
6. What, then, is the author's claim? State it so that you have made a cause/effect statement.
7. What *kinds* of grounds does Matchar provide in support of her claim?

QUESTIONS FOR REFLECTION AND WRITING

8. Do you agree with the author that the Gen Y-ers' desired changes would be good for the workplace? Why or why not?
9. The descriptions of various generations are, of course, generalizations. (*You* might not be "bratty"!) Do you basically accept the characteristics of Gen Y-ers as described in the essay? And the upbringing that has shaped them? If you disagree, how would you challenge these generalizations? (Remember that these generalizations are not the author's alone; Matchar is expressing a widely shared analysis of this generation.)

"DARING TO DISCUSS WOMEN IN SCIENCE": A RESPONSE TO JOHN TIERNEY

CAROLINE SIMARD

Caroline Simard is a board member of the Ada Initiative and research consultant to the Anita Borg Institute for Women and Technology, at the Stanford University School of Medicine. She holds a PhD in communication and social science and works to find ways to increase the number of women and underrepresented minorities in science, technology, engineering, and mathematics (STEM), and business fields. Simard's essay, a response to an article by John Tierney, was posted at *Huffington Post,* June 9, 2010.

PREREADING QUESTIONS What type of argument do you anticipate, given the title and headnote information? What other type of argument should you anticipate, given the essay's location in this text?

1   On Monday [June 2010], John Tierney of the *New York Times* published a pro-vocative article, "Daring to Discuss Women in Science," in which he argues that biology may be a factor to explain why women are not reaching high-level posi-tions. He suggests that boys are innately more gifted at math and science and that the dearth of women in science may point to simple biological differences. If this is the case, why would we waste our time trying to get more women in science?

2   Mr. Tierney, let's indeed discuss women in science.

3   First, let me start by saying that I applaud the discussion—all potential explanations for a complex issue and all evidence need to be considered, even the ones that are not popular in the media or not "politically correct." I also believe that Larry Summer's now infamous comments about the possibil-ity that biological differences account for the dearth of women scientists and technologists was, similarly, in the spirit of intellectual debate.

4   The problem with the biology argument that "boys are just more likely to be born good at math and science" isn't that it's not "politically correct"—it's that it assumes that we can take away the power of societal influences, which have much more solid evidence than the biology hypothesis. Tierney makes the point himself in his article—in order to provide evidence for biological dif-ferences, he cites a longitudinal Duke [University] study which shows that the highest achievers in SAT math tests (above 750), which counted 13 boys for every girl in the early 80s, became a ratio of 4 boys to 1 girls in 1991, "presum-ably because of sociocultural factors." Hmm, isn't this actual evidence that biology is not what is at play here? If it is possible to reduce the gender achievement gap in math by 3 thanks to "sociocultural factors," I rest my case. Sociocultural factors are indeed extremely powerful.

5   The Duke study also notes that the 4/1 achievement gap at the highest score hasn't changed in the last 20 years despite ongoing programs to encourage girls in math and science, whereas the highest achievers in writing ability (SAT above 700) shows a ratio of 1.2 girls for every boy, slightly favoring girls. However, if the premise is that boys are inherently "better" at math, and girls are inherently better at writing, why would the achievement gap be so large in math and negligible in writing? The stagnant 4 to 1 ratio is not evidence that there is an innate biological difference in math aptitude, but rather confirmation that persistent sociocultural barriers remain—that is, science and math are still thought of as male domains.

Research shows that math and science are 6
indeed thought of as stereotypically male
domains. Project Implicit at Harvard University
studied half a million participants in 34 countries and found that 70 percent of respondents worldwide have implicit stereotypes
associating science with male more than with
female. Years of research by Claude Steele
and Joshua Aronson and their colleagues
show that implicit stereotypes affect girls'
performance in math—a phenomenon called
"stereotype threat." When girls receive cues
that "boys are better at math," their scores in
math suffer. One study in a classroom setting
showed that the difference in performance
between boys and girls in math SAT scores
was eliminated by simply having a mentor
telling them that math is learned over time rather is "innate."

The problem is, girls are routinely getting the message that they don't 7
belong in math and science, further undermining their performance (and Mr.
Tierney's article isn't exactly helping in changing the stereotype for the general public). The result of this implicit (unconscious) stereotype is that parents,
teachers, and school counselors are less likely to encourage girls to pursue
math and science than they are boys. These girls are then less likely to seek
advanced math classes and would be unlikely, without those opportunities, to
make it to the above 700 SAT math score regardless of ability.

Anecdotally, I had this experience with my daughter a couple of years ago. 8
At age 10, she had somehow decided that she wasn't good at math (despite
being raised in a household with 2 PhDs). With her self-confidence plummeting, math homework became very painful in our household. When I dug deeper,
I found that she mistakenly believed that you were either born with math ability
or you weren't—that this was an innate biological ability as opposed to something you could learn, and that somehow she hadn't been "born with it." Once
I actively dispelled that notion and provided her with additional mentoring, her
math performance significantly improved. I never hear her say that she isn't
good at math anymore, and her math homework is flawless.

The Duke article, and Tierney, raises an important question about prefer- 9
ence, however, that research suggests that boys are more interested in
"things" and girls are more interested in "people" and thus gravitate towards
fields reflecting that interest. In this research too, there is debate about what
in this difference is "nature" versus "nurture"—there are powerful socialization forces at play. Regardless, we have to dispel the notion that science is
only about "things" and not about people or somehow disconnected from all
social relevance. Indeed, some of the most successful interventions to increase
girls' interest in math and science have been to reframe the curriculum to provide examples and projects that are grounded in the interests of a diverse
population of students. The EPICS program at Purdue University is a great

example of grounding engineering disciplines in socially relevant contexts and has been shown to engage a diversity of students.

10   What we need, to put this debate to rest, is to replicate these findings in a country where science and math are not viewed as stereotypically male. The most recent cross-national comparison study, published in 2010 in *Psychological Bulletin* by Nicole Else-Quest and her colleagues and comparing 43 countries, shows that the achievement difference in math between girls and boys varies broadly across countries.

11   Their research shows that country-by-country variation is correlated with gender differences in self-confidence in math, which is compounded by stereotype threat. One of the strongest predictors of the gender gap in math achievement is a given country's level of gender equity in science jobs, consistent with socialization arguments: "if girls' mothers, aunts, and sisters do not have STEM careers, they will perceive that STEM is a male domain and thus feel anxious about math, lack the confidence to take challenging math courses, and underachieve on math tests."

12   Until girls stop getting the signal that math is for boys, the 4 to 1 gender gap in highest achievement categories of math and science will persist. This has nothing to do with innate ability.

13   Mr. Tierney, I look forward to your subsequent articles on this issue. Let's indeed dare to discuss women in science and continue to bring to bear the most relevant research on this issue.

Source: *HuffPostTech*, June 9, 2010. Reprinted by permission of the author.

QUESTIONS FOR READING

1.   What is the occasion for Simard's posting? What is her topic?
2.   What is Tierney's position on the issue?
3.   What sociocultural factors are the causes of the gender gap in math and science, in Simard's view?

QUESTIONS FOR REASONING AND ANALYSIS

4.   What is Simard's claim? (Try to state it with precision.)
5.   What *kinds* of grounds does Simard present? What point about Tierney's warrant does the author want to make with the evidence she includes?
6.   Examine Simard's style and tone; how do they help her argument?

QUESTIONS FOR REFLECTION AND WRITING

7.   In the debate over women in science, there are two related assumptions: (1) Math ability is inborn and (2) Boys are innately better at math than girls. Have you heard either one—or both—of these views? Has Simard convinced you that the evidence challenges these ideas? Why or why not?
8.   Why can stereotypes be a "threat"? How can ideas "threaten" us? Explain and illustrate to answer these questions.

1. Think about your educational experiences as a basis for generating a topic for a causal argument. For example: What are the causes of writer's block? Why do some apparently good students (based on class work, grades, etc.) do poorly on standardized tests? How does pass/fail grading affect student performance? What are the causes of high tuition and fees? What might be some of the effects of higher college costs? What are the causes of binge drinking among college students? What are the effects of binge drinking?

2. *Star Trek*, in its many manifestations, continues to play on television—why? What makes it so popular a series? Why are horror movies popular? What are the causes for the great success of the Harry Potter books? If you are familiar with one of these works, or another work that has been amazingly popular, examine the causes for that popularity.

3. The gender pay gap (see Figure 5.3 in Chapter 5) reflects earnings differences between all working men and all working women. It is not a comparison of earnings by job. What might be some of the causes for women continuing to earn less than men—in spite of the fact that more women than men now earn BA degrees? Consider what you know about women in the workforce who work full time. (The pay gap is also not about full- versus part-time work; both men and women work part time as well as full time.) Look at other graphics in Chapter 5 and think about what you have learned from Caroline Simard regarding women in STEM fields. Be prepared to discuss some causes of the pay gap or prepare an essay on the topic. (Be sure to qualify your claim as appropriate, based on what you know.)

CHAPTER 11

Presenting Proposals: The Problem/Solution Argument

READ: What is the subject of this cartoon?

REASON: How does the cartoon visualize the subject? What do you see between the primary sign and the "exit" sign?

REFLECT/WRITE: Toles illustrates a problem but not solutions. What have some states done to address the problem? What solutions can you suggest?

You think that there are several spots on campus that need additional lighting at night. You are concerned that the lake near your hometown is green, with algae floating on it. You believe that bikers on the campus need to have paths and a bike lane on the main roads into the college. These are serious local issues; you should be concerned about them. And, perhaps it is time to act on your concerns—how can you do that? You can write a proposal, perhaps a letter to the editor of your college or hometown newspaper.

These three issues invite a recommendation for change. And to make that recommendation is to offer a solution to what you perceive to be a problem. Public policy arguments, whether local and specific (lampposts or bike lanes), or more general and far-reaching (e.g., the federal government must stop the flow of illegal drugs into the country) can best be understood as arguments over solutions to problems. If there are only 10 students on campus who bike to class or only 200 Americans wanting to buy cocaine, then most people would not agree that we have two serious problems in need of debate over the best solutions. But, when the numbers become significant, then we see a problem and start seeking solutions.

Consider some of these issues stated as policy claims:

- The college needs bike lanes on campus roads and more bike paths across the campus.
- We need to spend whatever is necessary to stop the flow of drugs into this country.

Each claim offers a solution to a problem, as we can see:

- Bikers will be safer if there are bike lanes on main roads and more bike paths across the campus.
- The way to address the drug problem in this country is to eliminate the supply of drugs.

The basic idea of policy proposals looks like this:

Somebody	should (or should not)	do X – because:
(Individual, organization, government)		*(solve this problem)*

Observe that proposal arguments recommend action. They look to the future. And, they often advise the spending of someone's time and/or money.

CHARACTERISTICS OF PROBLEM/ SOLUTION ARGUMENTS

- *Proposal arguments may be about local and specific problems or about broader, more general public policy issues.* We need to "think globally" these days, but we still often need to "act locally," to address the problems we see around us in our classrooms, offices, and communities.

- *Proposal arguments usually need to define the problem.* How we define a problem has much to do with what kinds of solutions are appropriate. For example, many people are concerned about our ability to feed a growing world population. Some will argue that the problem is not an agricultural one—how much food we can produce. The problem is a political one—how we distribute the food, at what cost, and how competent or fair some governments are in handling food distribution. If the problem is agricultural, we need to worry about available farmland, water supply, and farming technology. If the problem is political, then we need to concern ourselves with price supports, distribution strategies, and embargoes for political leverage. To develop a problem/solution argument, you first need to define the problem.

- *How we define the problem also affects what we think are the causes of the problem.* Cause is often a part of the debate, especially with far-reaching policy issues, and may need to be addressed, particularly if solutions are tied to eliminating what we consider to be the causes. Why are illegal drugs coming into the United States? Because people want those drugs. Do you solve the problems related to drug addicts by stopping the supply? Or, do you address the demand for drugs in the first place?

- *Proposal arguments need to be developed with an understanding of the processes of government, from college administrations to city governments to the federal bureaucracy.* Is that dying lake near your town on city property or state land? Are there conservation groups in your area who can be called on to help with the process of presenting proposals to the appropriate people?

- *Proposal arguments need to be based on the understanding that they ask for change—and many people do not like change, period.* Probably all but the wealthiest Americans recognize that our health-care system needs fixing. That doesn't change the fact that many working people struggling to pay premiums are afraid of any changes introduced by the federal government.

- *Successful problem/solution arguments offer solutions that can realistically be accomplished.* Consider Prohibition, for example. This was a solution to problem drinking—except that it did not work, could not be enforced, because the majority of Americans would not abide by the law.

GUIDELINES for Analyzing Problem/Solution Arguments

When analyzing problem/solution arguments, what should you look for? In addition to the basics of good argument, use these points as guides to analyzing:

- **Is the writer's claim not just clear but also appropriately qualified and focused?** For example, if the school board in the writer's community is not doing a good job of communicating its goals as a basis for its funding package, the writer needs to focus just on that particular school board, not on school boards in general.

- **Does the writer show an awareness of the complexity of most public policy issues?** There are many different kinds of problems with American schools and many more causes for those problems. A simple solution—a longer school year, more money spent, vouchers—is not likely to solve the mixed bag of problems. Oversimplified arguments quickly lose credibility.

- **How does the writer define and explain the problem?** Is the way the problem is stated clear? Does it make sense to you? If the problem is being defined differently than most people have defined it, has the writer argued convincingly for looking at the problem in this new way?

- **What reasons and evidence are given to support the writer's solutions?** Can you see how the writer develops the argument? Does the reasoning seem logical? Are the data relevant? This kind of analysis will help you evaluate the proposed solutions.

- **Does the writer address the feasibility of the proposed solutions?** Does the writer make a convincing case for the realistic possibility of achieving the proposed solutions?

- **Is the argument convincing?** Will the solutions solve the problem as it has been defined? Has the problem been defined accurately? Can the solutions be achieved?

Read and study the following annotated argument. Complete your analysis by answering the questions that follow.

WANT MORE SCIENTISTS? TURN GRADE SCHOOLS INTO LABORATORIES

PRIYA NATARAJAN

A professor in both the astronomy and physics departments at Yale University, Priya Natarajan is a theoretical astrophysicist. Her areas of investigation include black hole physics and gravitational lensing. Interested as well in enhancing general science literacy, Natarajan serves on the Advisory Board of NOVA ScienceNow, speaks at conferences, and writes newspaper articles. The following op-ed essay was published on February 5, 2012.

PREREADING QUESTIONS When you were in grade school, did you like to "discover things" in the natural world? How would you encourage early study of science?

"What's your major?" Ask a college freshman this question, and the answer may be physics or chemistry. Ask a sophomore or a junior, however, and you're less likely to hear about plans to enter the "STEM" fields—science, technology, engineering and mathematics. America's universities are not graduating nearly enough scientists, engineers and other skilled professionals to keep our country globally competitive in the decades ahead. 1

Author states problem.

And this is despite evidence such as a recent Center on Education and the Workforce report that forecasts skill requirements through 2018 and clearly shows the importance of STEM fields. The opportunities for those with just a high school education are restricted, it says—many high-paying jobs are open only to people with STEM college degrees. 2

States seriousness of problem.

A cause author will refute.

3   Still, as many as 60 percent of students who enter college with the intention of majoring in science and math change their plans. Because so many students intend to major in a STEM subject but don't follow through, many observers have assumed that universities are where the trouble starts. I beg to differ.

Author's solution.

4   I am a professor of astronomy and physics at Yale University, where I teach an introductory class in cosmology. I see the deficiencies that first-year students show up with. My students may have dexterity with the equations they're required to know, but they lack the capacity to apply their knowledge to real-life problems. This critical shortcoming appears in high school and possibly in elementary grades—long before college. If we want more Americans to pursue careers in STEM professions, we have to intervene much earlier than we imagined.

Specific strategies for solving problem.

5   Many efforts are underway to get younger students interested in science and math. One example is the Tree of Life's online "treehouse" project, a collection of information about biodiversity compiled by hundreds of experts and amateurs. Students can use this tool to apply what they are learning in the classroom to the world around them. Starting early in children's education, we need to provide these types of engaging, interactive learning environments that link school curricula to the outside world.

6   My own schooling is an example. Growing up in Delhi, India, I did puzzles, explored numbers and searched for patterns in everyday settings long before I ever saw an equation. One assignment I vividly remember asked us to find examples of hexagons. I eagerly pointed out hexagons everywhere: street tiles, leaves, flowers, signs, buildings. I was taught equations only after I learned what they meant and how to think about them. As a result, I enjoyed math, and I became good at it.

7   Not all American children have this experience, but they can. The Khan Academy, for example, has pioneered the use of technology to encourage unstructured learning outside the classroom and now provides teaching supplements in 36 schools around the country. For instance, recent reports describe a San Jose charter school using Khan's instructional videos in ninth-grade math classes to tailor lessons to each student's pace.

8   Perhaps more than English or history, STEM subjects require an enormous amount of foundational learning before students can become competent. Students usually reach graduate school before they can hope to make an original contribution. They experiment in high school labs, but the U.S. schools' approach to math and science lacks, in large part, a creative element. We need to help students understand that math and science are cumulative

disciplines, and help them enjoy learning even as they gradually build a base of knowledge.

One way to do this is to encourage students to engage in self-guided or 9 collaborative research projects—something the Internet has made much more feasible. An example from my own field is Zooniverse, a collection of experimental projects in which students can classify galaxies and search for new planets or supernovae using real data collected by NASA. Taking part in such explorations early will help students understand that science and math aren't just abstract equations, but tools we use to understand our world. By the time they get to college, they will have mastered the rhythm of the scientific method—learn, apply, learn, apply—and enjoy the process.

Six years ago, I had a student in an introductory cosmology class for non– 10 science majors who had entered Yale as an economics major, a choice based primarily on pressure from his parents. After one summer researching gamma-ray bursts—the most energetic explosions in the universe—he is currently finishing up a PhD in physics at Berkeley. He was hooked by the opportunity to apply what he learned in the classroom to a challenging scientific problem. He loved the thrill of figuring something out.

Without firsthand experience of the scientific method and its eventual pay-11 off, students will continue to flock to other majors when their science and math courses become too demanding. If we want more scientists and engineers later, we need to teach children about the joys of hard work and discovery now.

Author states her claim.

Source: Washington Post, February 5, 2012. Reprinted by permission of the author.

QUESTIONS FOR READING

1. What are the STEM fields? Why are these fields important?
2. What percentage of college students planning to major in math or science end up changing fields?
3. What do many college students lack, leading them to have trouble in advanced STEM courses?

QUESTIONS FOR REASONING AND ANALYSIS

4. What is the problem Natarajan examines? What has caused this problem, in the author's view? What, then, is her claim?
5. How does the author support her claim?

QUESTIONS FOR REFLECTION AND WRITING

6. Few would question the reality of the problem Natarajan addresses; the issue is how to solve it. Do you agree that at least much of the cause rests with the early teaching of math and science? If yes, why? If no, why not?
7. From your experience, can you suggest other ways to improve early education in math and science?

PREPARING A PROBLEM/SOLUTION ARGUMENT

In addition to the guidelines for writing arguments presented in Chapter 4, you can use the following advice specific to defending a proposal.

Planning

1. **Think:** What should be the focus and limits of your argument? There's a big difference between presenting solutions to the problem of physical abuse of women by men and presenting solutions to the problem of date rape on your college campus. Select a topic that you know something about, one that you can realistically handle.

2. **Think:** What reasons and evidence do you have to support your tentative claim? Think through what you already know that has led you to select your particular topic. Suppose you want to write on the issue of campus rape. Is this choice due to a recent event on the campus? Was this event the first in many years or the last in a trend? Where and when are the rapes occurring? A brainstorming list may be helpful.

3. **Reality check:** Do you have a claim worth defending? Will readers care? Binge drinking and the polluting of the lake near your hometown are serious problems. Problems with your class schedule may not be—unless your experience reveals a college-wide problem.

4. **Think:** Is there additional evidence that you need to obtain to develop your argument? If so, where can you look for that evidence? Are there past issues of the campus paper in your library? Will the campus police grant you an interview?

5. **Think:** What about the feasibility of each solution you plan to present? Are you thinking in terms of essentially one solution with several parts to it or several separate solutions, perhaps to be implemented by different people? Will coordination be necessary to achieve success? How will this be accomplished? For the problem of campus rape, you may want to consider several solutions as a package to be coordinated by the counseling service or an administrative vice president.

Drafting

1. Begin by either reminding readers of the existing problem you will address or arguing that a current situation should be recognized as a problem. In many cases, you can count on an audience who sees the world as you do and recognizes the problem you will address. But in some cases, your first task will be to convince readers that a problem exists that should worry them. If they are not concerned, they won't be interested in your solutions.

2. Early in your essay define the problem—as you see it—for readers. Do not assume that they will necessarily accept your way of seeing the issue. You may need to defend your understanding of the problem before moving on to solutions.

3. If appropriate, explain the cause or causes of the problem. If your proposed solution is tied to removing the cause or causes of the problem, then you need to establish cause and prove it early in your argument. If cause is important, argue for it; if it is irrelevant, move to your solution.

4. Explain your solution. If you have several solutions, think about how best to order them. If several need to be developed in a sequence, then present them in that necessary sequence. If you are presenting a package of diverse actions that together will solve the problem, then consider presenting them from the simplest to the more complex. With the problem of campus rape, for example, you may want to suggest better lighting on campus paths at night plus an escort service for women who are afraid to walk home alone plus sensitivity training for male students. Adding more lampposts is much easier than getting students to take sensitivity classes.

5. Explain the process for achieving your solution. If you have not thought through the political or legal steps necessary to implement your solution, then this step cannot be part of your purpose in writing. However, anticipating a skeptical audience that says "How are we going to do that?" you would be wise to have precise steps to offer your reader. You may have obtained an estimate of costs for new lighting on your campus and want to suggest specific paths that need the lights. You may have investigated escort services at other colleges and can spell out how such a service can be implemented on your campus. Showing readers that you have thought ahead to the next steps in the process can be an effective method of persuasion.

6. Support the feasibility of your solution. Be able to estimate costs. Show that you know who would be responsible for implementation. Specific information strengthens your argument.

7. Show how your solution is better than others. Anticipate challenges by including reasons for adopting your program rather than another program. Explain how your solution will be more easily adopted or more effective when implemented than other possibilities. Of course, a less practical but still viable defense is that your solution is the right thing to do. Values also belong in public policy debates, not just issues of cost and acceptability.

A CHECKLIST FOR REVISION

☐ Do I have a clear statement of my policy claim? Is it appropriately qualified and focused?

☐ Have I clearly explained how I see the problem to be solved? If necessary, have I argued for seeing the problem my way?

☐ Have I presented my solutions—and argued for them—in a clear and logical structure? Have I explained how these solutions can be implemented and why they are better than other solutions that have been suggested?

☐ Have I used data that are relevant and current?

☐ Have I used the basic checklist for revision in Chapter 4? (See p. 111.)

FOR ANALYSIS AND DEBATE

POVERTY IN AMERICA: WHY CAN'T WE END IT? | PETER EDELMAN

A professor of law at Georgetown University, Peter Edelman is faculty director of the Center on Poverty, Inequality, and Public Policy at Georgetown and the author of numerous articles and books. His areas of specialty include constitutional law, legislation, and welfare law. His most recent book is *So Rich, So Poor: Why It's So Hard to End Poverty in America* (2012). The following essay appeared July 29, 2012 in the *New York Times*.

PREREADING QUESTIONS What percentage of Americans do you think live below the poverty line? Do you think the numbers are great enough to be considered a problem?

1   Ronald Reagan famously said, "We fought a war on poverty and poverty won." With 46 million Americans—15 percent of the population—now counted as poor, it's tempting to think he may have been right.

2   Look a little deeper and the temptation grows. The lowest percentage in poverty since we started counting was 11.1 percent in 1973. The rate climbed as high as 15.2 percent in 1983. In 2000, after a spurt of prosperity, it went back down to 11.3 percent, and yet 15 million more people are poor today.

3   At the same time, we have done a lot that works. From Social Security to food stamps to the earned-income tax credit and on and on, we have enacted programs that now keep 40 million people out of poverty. Poverty would be nearly double what it is now without these measures, according to the Center on Budget and Policy Priorities. To say that "poverty won" is like saying the Clean Air and Clean Water Acts failed because there is still pollution.

4   With all of that, why have we not achieved more? Four reasons: An astonishing number of people work at low-wage jobs. Plus, many more households are headed now by a single parent, making it difficult for them to earn a living income from the jobs that are typically available. The near disappearance of cash assistance for low-income mothers and children—i.e., welfare—in much of the country plays a contributing role, too. And persistent issues of race and gender mean higher poverty among minorities and families headed by single mothers.

5   The first thing needed if we're to get people out of poverty is more jobs that pay decent wages. There aren't enough of these in our current economy. The need for good jobs extends far beyond the current crisis; we'll need a full-employment policy and a bigger investment in 21st-century education and skill development strategies if we're to have any hope of breaking out of the current economic malaise.

6   This isn't a problem specific to the current moment. We've been drowning in a flood of low-wage jobs for the last 40 years. Most of the income of people in poverty comes from work. According to the most recent data available from the Census Bureau, 104 million people—a third of the population—have annual incomes below twice the poverty line, less than $38,000 for a family of three. They struggle to make ends meet every month.

This classic picture of poverty is old; sadly, as Edelman explains, poverty is still with us.

Half the jobs in the nation pay less than $34,000 a year, according to the Economic Policy Institute. A quarter pay below the poverty line for a family of four, less than $23,000 annually. Families that can send another adult to work have done better, but single mothers (and fathers) don't have that option. Poverty among families with children headed by single mothers exceeds 40 percent. 7

Wages for those who work on jobs in the bottom half have been stuck since 1973, increasing just 7 percent. 8

It's not that the whole economy stagnated. There's been growth, a lot of it, but it has stuck at the top. The realization that 99 percent of us have been left in the dust by the 1 percent at the top (some much further behind than others) came far later than it should have—Rip Van Winkle and then some. It took the Great Recession to get people's attention, but the facts had been accumulating for a long time. If we've awakened, we can act. 9

Low-wage jobs bedevil tens of millions of people. At the other end of the low-income spectrum we have a different problem. The safety net for single mothers and their children has developed a gaping hole over the past dozen years. This is a major cause of the dramatic increase in extreme poverty during those years. The census tells us that 20.5 million people earn incomes below half the poverty line, less than about $9,500 for a family of three—up eight million from 2000. 10

Why? A substantial reason is the near demise of welfare—now called Temporary Assistance for Needy Families, or TANF. In the mid-90s more than two-thirds of children in poor families received welfare. But that number has dwindled over the past decade and a half to roughly 27 percent. 11

One result: six million people have no income other than food stamps. Food stamps provide an income at a third of the poverty line, close to $6,300 for a family of three. It's hard to understand how they survive. 12

At least we have food stamps. They have been a powerful antirecession tool in the past five years, with the number of recipients rising to 46 million today from 26.3 million in 2007. By contrast, welfare has done little to counter the impact of the recession; although the number of people receiving cash assistance rose from 3.9 million to 4.5 million since 2007, many states actually reduced the size of their rolls and lowered benefits to those in greatest need. 13

Race and gender play an enormous part in determining poverty's continuing course. Minorities are disproportionately poor: around 27 percent of African-Americans, Latinos and American Indians are poor, versus 10 percent 14 of whites. Wealth disparities are even wider. At the same time, whites constitute the largest number among the poor. This is a fact that bears emphasis, since measures to raise income and provide work supports will help more whites than minorities. But we cannot ignore race and gender, both because they present particular challenges and because so much of the politics of poverty is grounded in those issues.

15   We know what we need to do—make the rich pay their fair share of running the country, raise the minimum wage, provide health care and a decent safety net, and the like. But realistically, the immediate challenge is keeping what we have. Representative Paul Ryan and his ideological peers would slash everything from Social Security to Medicare and on through the list, and would hand out more tax breaks to the people at the top. Robin Hood would turn over in his grave.

16   We should not kid ourselves. It isn't certain that things will stay as good as they are now. The wealth and income of the top 1 percent grows at the expense of everyone else. Money breeds power and power breeds more money. It is a truly vicious circle.

17   A surefire politics of change would necessarily involve getting people in the middle—from the 30th to the 70th percentile—to see their own economic self-interest. If they vote in their own self-interest, they'll elect people who are likely to be more aligned with people with lower incomes as well as with them. As long as people in the middle identify more with people on the top than with those on the bottom, we are doomed. The obscene amount of money flowing into the electoral process makes things harder yet.

18   But history shows that people power wins sometimes. That's what happened in the Progressive Era a century ago and in the Great Depression as well. The gross inequality of those times produced an amalgam of popular unrest, organization, muckraking journalism and political leadership that attacked the big—and worsening—structural problem of economic inequality. The civil rights movement changed the course of history and spread into the women's movement, the environmental movement and, later, the gay rights movement. Could we have said on the day before the dawn of each that it would happen, let alone succeed? Did Rosa Parks know?

19   We have the ingredients. For one thing, the demographics of the electorate are changing. The consequences of that are hardly automatic, but they create an opportunity. The new generation of young people—unusually distrustful of encrusted power in all institutions and, as a consequence, tending toward libertarianism—is ripe for a new politics of honesty. Lower-income people will participate if there are candidates who speak to their situations. The change has to come from the bottom up and from synergistic leadership that draws it out. When people decide they have had enough and there are candidates who stand for what they want, they will vote accordingly.

20   I have seen days of promise and days of darkness, and I've seen them more than once. All history is like that. The people have the power if they will use it, but they have to see that it is in their interest to do so.

Source: *New York Times*, July 29, 2012. Reprinted by permission of the author.

QUESTIONS FOR READING

1. How many Americans live in poverty today?
2. What programs keep more from living in poverty?
3. What are the four causes Edelman lists that account for this poverty?
4. What solutions does Edelman present?

QUESTIONS FOR REASONING AND ANALYSIS

5. What is Edelman's claim? (State it as a problem/solution issue.)
6. One cause of poverty is the continued low incomes of women and minorities. Why, in examining solutions, does the author point out that extending aid will actually help more whites than minorities? What does he want readers to start thinking about?
7. Edelman makes clear that his call for some specific changes won't happen unless there is a more general change of attitude among voters. What change in thinking is essential in his view? Why?
8. Does the author believe that change is possible, that we could "win a war" on poverty? How optimistic does he seem to you?

QUESTIONS FOR REFLECTION AND WRITING

9. What numbers surprise you the most in this essay? Why?
10. Do you agree with Edelman that the change in attitude must come before the country will be able to decrease the numbers of poor in America? If you disagree, how would you rebut Edelman—that is, how can we reduce poverty without the attitude change?
11. Do you think that our poverty rate is a problem that we should address? Why or why not? Explain your position.

A MODEST PROPOSAL | JONATHAN SWIFT

For Preventing the Children of Poor People in Ireland from Being a Burden to Their Parents or Country, and for Making Them Beneficial to the Public

Born in Dublin, Jonathan Swift (1667–1745) was ordained in the Anglican Church and spent many years as dean of St. Patrick's in Dublin. Swift was also involved in the political and social life of London for some years, and throughout his life he kept busy writing. His most famous imaginative work is *Gulliver's Travels* (1726). Almost as well known is the essay that follows, published in 1729. Here you will find Swift's usual biting satire but also his concern to improve humanity.

PREREADING QUESTIONS Swift was a minister, but he writes this essay as if he were in a different job. What "voice" or persona do you hear? Does Swift agree with the views of this persona?

1   It is a melancholy object to those who walk through this great town[1] or travel in the country, where they see the streets, the roads, and cabin doors crowded with beggars of the female sex, followed by three, four, or six children, all in rags, and importuning every passenger for an alms. These mothers, instead of being able to work for their honest livelihood, are forced to employ all their time in strolling to beg sustenance for their helpless infants, who, as they grow up, either turn thieves for want of work, or leave their dear native country to fight for the pretender[2] in Spain or sell themselves to the Barbados.

2   I think it is agreed by all parties that this prodigious number of children in the arms, or on the backs, or at the heels of their

Jonathan Swift

mothers, and frequently of their fathers, is in the present deplorable state of the kingdom a very great additional grievance; and therefore, whoever could find out a fair, cheap, and easy method of making these children sound and useful members of the commonwealth would deserve so well of the public as to have his statue set up for a preserver of the nation.

3   But my intention is very far from being confined to provide only for the children of professed beggars; it is of a much greater extent, and shall take in the whole number of infants at a certain age who are born of parents in effect as little able to support them as those who demand our charity in the streets.

4   As to my own part, having turned my thoughts for many years upon this important subject, and maturely weighed the several schemes of other projectors,[3] I have always found them grossly mistaken in the computation. It is true a child just dropped from its dam may be supported by her milk for a solar year with little other nourishment; at most not above the value of two shillings, which the mother may certainly get, or the value in scraps, by her lawful occupation of begging; and, it is exactly at one year that I propose to provide for them in such a manner as instead of being a charge upon their parents or the parish, or wanting food and raiment for the rest of their lives, they shall on the contrary contribute to the feeding, and partly to the clothing, of many thousands.

---

[1] Dublin.—Ed.

[2] James Stuart, claimant to the British throne lost by his father, James II, in 1688.—Ed.

[3] Planners.—Ed.

There is likewise another great advantage in my scheme, that it will pre- 5 vent those voluntary abortions, and that horrid practice of women murdering their bastard children, alas, too frequent among us, sacrificing the poor inno- cent babes, I doubt, more to avoid the expense than the shame, which would move tears and pity in the most savage and inhuman breast.

The number of souls in this kingdom being usually reckoned one million 6 and a half, of these I calculate there may be about two hundred thousand couples whose wives are breeders; from which number I subtract thirty thou- sand couples who are able to maintain their own children, although I appre- hend there cannot be so many, under the present distress of the kingdom; but this being granted, there will remain a hundred and seventy thousand breed- ers. I again subtract fifty thousand for those women who miscarry, or whose children die by accident or disease within the year. There only remain a hun- dred and twenty thousand children of poor parents annually born. The ques- tion therefore is, how this number shall be reared and provided for, which, as I have already said, under the present situation of affairs, is utterly impossible by all the methods hereto proposed. For we can neither employ them in handi- craft or agriculture; we neither build houses (I mean in the country) nor culti- vate land. They can very seldom pick up a livelihood by stealing until they arrive at six years old, except where they are of towardly parts[4]; although I confess they learn the rudiments much earlier, during which time they can, however, be properly looked upon only as probationers, as I have been informed by a principal gentleman in the country of Cavan, who protested to me that he never knew above one or two instances under the age of six, even in the part of the kingdom renowned for the quickest proficiency in that art.

I am assured by our merchants that a boy or girl before twelve years old is 7 no saleable commodity; and even when they come to this age they will not yield above three pounds, or three pounds and a half a crown at most, on the exchange; which cannot turn to account either to the parents or the kingdom, the charge of nutriment and rags having been at least four times that value.

I shall now therefore humbly propose my own thoughts, which I hope will 8 not be liable to the least objection.

I have been assured by a very knowing American of my acquaintance in 9 London that a young healthy child well nursed is at a year old a most delicious, nourishing, and wholesome food, whether stewed, roasted, baked, or boiled; and I make no doubt that it will equally serve in a fricassee or ragout.

I do therefore humbly offer it to public consideration that of the hundred 10 and twenty-thousand children, already computed, twenty thousand may be reserved for breed, whereof only one fourth part to be males, which is more than we allow to sheep, black cattle, or swine; and my reason is that these chil- dren are seldom the fruits of marriage, a circumstance not much regarded by our savages, therefore one male will be sufficient to serve four females. That the remaining hundred thousand may at a year old be offered in sale to the persons of quality and fortune, through the kingdom, always advising the

---

[4] Innate abilities.—Ed.

mother to let them suck plentifully in the last month, so as to render them plump and fat for the table. A child will make two dishes at an entertainment for friends; and when the family dines alone, the fore or hind quarter will make a reasonable dish, and seasoned with a little pepper or salt will be very good boiled on the fourth day, especially in winter.

11   I have reckoned upon a medium that a child just born will weigh twelve pounds, and in a solar year if tolerably nursed increaseth to twenty-eight pounds.

12   I grant this food will be somewhat dear, and therefore very proper for landlords, who, as they have already devoured most of the parents, seem to have the best title to the children.

13   Infant's flesh will be in season throughout the year, but more plentiful in March, and a little before and after. For we are told by a grave author, an eminent French physician,[5] that fish being a prolific diet, there are more children born in Roman Catholic countries about nine months after Lent than at any other season; therefore reckoning a year after Lent, the markets will be more gutted than usual, because the number of popish infants is at least three to one in this kingdom; and therefore it will have one other collateral advantage, by lessening the number of Papists among us.

14   I have already computed the charge of nursing a beggar's child (in which list I reckon all cottagers, laborers, and four-fifths of the farmers) to be about two shillings per annum, rags included; and I believe no gentleman would repine to give ten shillings for the carcass of a good fat child, which, as I have said, will make four dishes of excellent nutritive meat, when he hath only some particular friend or his own family to dine with him. Thus the squire will learn to be a good landlord, and grow popular among his tenants; the mother will have eight shillings net profit, and be fit for work until she produces another child.

15   Those who are more thrifty (as I must confess the times require) may flay the carcass; the skin of which artificially dressed will make admirable gloves for ladies and summer boots for fine gentlemen.

16   As to our city of Dublin, shambles[6] may be appointed for this purpose, in the most convenient parts of it, and butchers we may be assured will not be wanting; although I rather recommend buying the children alive, and dressing them hot from the knife as we do roasting pigs.

17   A very worthy person, a true lover of his country, and whose virtues I highly esteem, was lately pleased in discoursing on this matter to offer a refinement upon my scheme. He said that many gentlemen of this kingdom, having of late destroyed their deer, he conceived that the want of venison might be well supplied by the bodies of young lads and maidens, not exceeding fourteen years of age nor under twelve, so great a number of both sexes in every county being now ready to starve for want of work and service; and these to be disposed of by their parents, if alive, or otherwise by their nearest relations. But with due deference to so excellent a friend and so deserving a patriot, I

---

[5] François Rabelais.—Ed.
[6] Butcher shops.—Ed.

cannot be altogether in his sentiments. For as to the males, my American acquaintance assured me from frequent experience that their flesh was generally tough and lean, like that of our school-boys, by continual exercise, and their taste disagreeable; and to fatten them would not answer the charge. Then as to the females, it would, I think with humble submission, be a loss to the public, because they soon would become breeders themselves; and besides, it is not probable that some scrupulous people might be apt to censure such a practice (although indeed very unjustly) as a little bordering upon cruelty; which, I confess, hath always been with me the strongest objection against any project, how wellsoever intended.

But in order to justify my friend, he confessed that this expedient was put 18 into his head by the famous Psalmanazar,[7] a native of the island Formosa who came from thence to London above twenty years ago, and in conversation told my friend that in his country when any young person happened to be put to death, the executioner sold the carcass to persons of quality as a prime dainty; and that in his time the body of a plump girl of fifteen, who was crucified for an attempt to poison the emperor, was sold to his Imperial Majesty's prime minister of state, and other great mandarins of the court, in joints from the gibbet, at four hundred crowns. Neither indeed can I deny that if the same use were made of several plump young girls in this town, who without one single groat to their fortunes cannot stir abroad without a chair, and appear at the playhouse and assemblies in foreign fineries which they never will pay for, the kingdom would not be the worse.

Some persons of a desponding spirit are in great concern about that vast 19 number of poor people who are aged, diseased, or maimed, and I have been desired to employ my thoughts what course may be taken to ease the nation of so grievous an incumbrance. But I am not in the least pain upon that matter, because it is very well known that they are every day dying and rotting by cold and famine, and filth and vermin, as fast as can be reasonably expected. And as to the younger laborers, they are now in almost as hopeful a condition. They cannot get work, and consequently pine away for want of nourishment to a degree that if at any time they are accidentally hired to common labor, they have not strength to perform it; and thus the country and themselves are in a fair way of being soon delivered from the evils to come.

I have too long digressed, and therefore shall return to my subject. I think 20 the advantages by the proposal which I have made are obvious and many, as well as of the highest importance.

For, first, as I have already observed, it would greatly lessen the number of 21 Papists, with whom we are yearly overrun, being the principal breeders of the nation as well as our most dangerous enemies; and who stay at home on purpose with a design to deliver the kingdom to the pretender, hoping to take their advantage by the absence of so many good Protestants, who have chosen rather to leave their country than stay at home and pay tithes against their conscience to an idolatrous Episcopal curate.

---

[7] A known imposter who was French, not Formosan as he claimed.—Ed.

22   Secondly, the poorer tenants will have something valuable of their own, which by law may be made liable to distress,[8] and help their landlord's rent; their corn and cattle being already seized, and money a thing unknown.

23   Thirdly, whereas the maintenance of a hundred thousand children, from two years old upwards, cannot be computed at less than ten shillings a piece per annum, the nation's stock will be thereby increased fifty thousand pounds per annum, besides the profit of a new dish introduced to the tables of all gentlemen of fortune in the kingdom who have any refinement in taste. And the money will circulate among ourselves, the goods being entirely of our own growth and manufacture.

24   Fourthly, the constant breeders, besides the gain of eight shillings sterling per annum by the sale of their children, will be rid of the charge of maintaining them after the first year.

25   Fifthly, this food would likewise bring great custom to taverns, where the vintners will certainly be so prudent as to procure the best receipts for dressing it to perfection, and consequently have their houses frequented by all the fine gentlemen, who justly value themselves upon their knowledge in good eating; and a skillful cook, who understands how to oblige his guests, will contrive to make it as expensive as they please.

26   Sixthly, this would be a great inducement to marriage, which all wise nations have either encouraged by rewards or enforced by laws and penalties. It would increase the care and tenderness of mothers towards their children, when they were sure of a settlement for life to the poor babes, provided in some sort by the public; to their annual profit instead of expense. We should soon see an honest emulation among the married women, which of them could bring the fattest child to the market. Men would become as fond of their wives during the time of their pregnancy as they are now of their mares in foal, their cows in calf, or sows when they are ready to farrow; nor offer to beat or kick them (as it is too frequent a practice) for fear of a miscarriage.

27   Many other advantages might be enumerated. For instance, the addition of some thousand carcasses in our exportation of barrelled beef, the propagation of swine's flesh, and improvement in the art of making good bacon, so much wanted among us by the great destruction of pigs, too frequent at our tables, which are no way comparable in taste or magnificence to a well-grown fat, yearling child, which roasted whole will make a considerable figure at a lord mayor's feast or any other public entertainment. But this and many others I omit, being studious of brevity.

28   Supposing that one thousand families in this city would be constant customers for infants' flesh, besides others who might have it at merry meetings, particularly weddings and christenings, I compute that Dublin would take off annually about twenty thousand carcasses, and the rest of the kingdom (where probably they will be sold somewhat cheaper) the remaining eighty thousand.

29   I can think of no one objection that will possibly be raised against this proposal, unless it should be urged that the number of people will be thereby

---

[8] Can be seized by lenders.—Ed.

much lessened in the kingdom. This I freely own, and it was indeed one principal design in offering it to the world. I desire the reader will observe that I calculate my remedy for this one individual kingdom of Ireland and for no other that ever was, is, or I think ever can be upon earth. Therefore let no man talk to me of other expedients: of taxing our absentees at five shillings a pound: of using neither clothes nor household furniture except what is of our own growth and manufacture: of utterly rejecting the materials and instruments that promote foreign luxury: of curing the expensiveness or pride, vanity, idleness, and gaming in our women: of introducing a vein of parsimony, prudence and temperance: of learning to love our country, wherein we differ even from Laplanders and the inhabitants of Topinamboo[9]: of quitting our animosities and factions, nor act any longer like the Jews, who were murdering one another at the very moment their city was taken[10]: of being a little cautious not to sell our country and consciences for nothing: of teaching landlords to have at least one degree of mercy towards their tenants. Lastly, of putting a spirit of honesty, industry, and skill into our shopkeepers; who, if a resolution could now be taken to buy only our native goods, would immediately unite to cheat and exact upon us in the price, the measure, and the goodness, nor could ever yet be brought to make one fair proposal of just dealing, though often and earnestly invited to it.

Therefore I repeat, let no man talk to me of these and the like expedients, 30 till he hath at least a glimpse of hope that there will ever be some hearty and sincere attempt to put them in practice.

But as to myself, having been wearied out for many years with offering 31 vain, idle, visionary thoughts, and at length utterly despairing of success, I fortunately fell upon this proposal, which, as it is wholly new, so it hath something solid and real, of no expense and little trouble, full in our own power, and whereby we can incur no danger in disobliging England. For this kind of commodity will not bear exportation, the flesh being of too tender a consistence to admit a long continuance in salt, although perhaps I could name a country which would be glad to eat up our whole nation without it.

After all, I am not so violently bent upon my own opinion as to reject any 32 offer proposed by wise men, which shall be found equally innocent, cheap, easy, and effectual. But before something of that kind shall be advanced in contradiction to my scheme, and offering a better, I desire the author, or authors, will be pleased maturely to consider two points. First, as things now stand, how they will be able to find food and raiment for a hundred thousand useless mouths and backs. And secondly, there being a round million of creatures in human figure throughout this kingdom, whose whole subsistence put into a common stock would leave them in debt two million of pounds sterling, adding those who are beggars by profession to the bulk of farmers, cottagers, and laborers, with their wives and children who are beggars, in effect; I desire

---

[9] An area in Brazil.—Ed.

[10] Some Jews were accused of helping the Romans and were executed during the Roman siege of Jerusalem in A.D. 70—Ed.

those politicians who dislike my overture, and may perhaps be so bold to attempt an answer, that they will first ask the parents of these mortals whether they would not at this day think it a great happiness to have been sold for food at a year old in the manner I prescribe, and thereby have avoided such a perpetual scene of misfortunes as they have since gone through by the oppression of landlords, the impossibility of paying rent without money or trade, the want of common sustenance, with neither house nor clothes to cover them from the inclemencies of weather, and the most inevitable prospect of entailing the like or greater miseries upon their breed forever.

33   I profess, in the sincerity of my heart, that I have not the least personal interest in endeavoring to promote this necessary work, having no other motive than the public good of my country, by advancing our trade, providing for infants, relieving the poor, and giving some pleasure to the rich. I have no children by which I can propose to get a single penny, the youngest being nine years old, and my wife past childbearing.

QUESTIONS FOR READING

1.   How is the argument organized? What is accomplished in paragraphs 1–7? In paragraphs 8–16? In paragraphs 17–19? In paragraphs 20–28? In paragraphs 29–33?

2.   What specific advantages does the writer offer in defense of his proposal?

QUESTIONS FOR REASONING AND ANALYSIS

3.   What specific passages and connotative words make us aware that this is a satirical piece using irony as its chief device?

4.   After noting Swift's use of irony, what do you conclude to be his purpose in writing?

5.   What can you conclude to be some of the problems in eighteenth-century Ireland? Where does Swift offer direct condemnation of existing conditions in Ireland and attitudes of the English toward the Irish?

6.   What actual reforms would Swift like to see?

QUESTIONS FOR REFLECTION AND WRITING

7.   What are some of the advantages of using irony? What does Swift gain by this approach? What are possible disadvantages in using irony? Reflect on irony as a persuasive strategy.

8.   What are some current problems that might be addressed by the use of irony? Make a list. Then select one and think about what "voice" or persona you might use to bring attention to that problem. Plan your argument with irony as a strategy.

1. Think of a problem on your campus or in your community for which you have a workable solution. Organize your argument to include all relevant steps as described in this chapter. Although your primary concern will be to present your solution, depending on your topic you may need to begin by convincing readers of the seriousness of the problem or the causes of the problem—if your solutions involve removing those causes.

2. Think of a problem in education—K–12 or at the college level—that you have a solution for and that you are interested in. You may want to begin by brainstorming to develop a list of possible problems in education about which you could write—or look through Chapter 19 for ideas. Be sure to qualify your claim and limit your focus as necessary to work with a problem that is not so broad and general that your "solutions" become general and vague comments about "getting better teachers." (If one problem is a lack of qualified teachers, then what specific proposals do you have for solving that particular problem?) Include as many steps as are appropriate to develop and support your argument.

3. Think of a situation that you consider serious but that apparently many people do not take seriously enough. Write an argument in which you emphasize, by providing evidence, that the situation is a serious problem. You may conclude by suggesting a solution, but your chief purpose in writing will be to alert readers to a problem.

The Researched and Formally Documented Argument

CHAPTER 12

Locating, Evaluating, and Preparing to Use Sources

We do research all the time. You would not select a college or buy a car without doing research: gathering relevant information, analyzing that information, and drawing conclusions from your study. You may already have done some research in this course, using sources in this text or finding data online to strengthen an argument. Then you acknowledged your sources either informally in your essay or formally, following the documentation guidelines in this section. So, when you are assigned a more formal research essay, remember that you are not facing a brand-new assignment. You are just doing a longer paper with more sources, and you have this section to guide you to success.

SELECTING A GOOD TOPIC

To get started you need to select and limit a topic. One key to success is finding a workable topic. No matter how interesting or clever the topic, it is not workable if it does not meet the guidelines of your assignment. Included in those guidelines may be a required length, a required number of sources, and a due date. Understand and accept all of these guidelines as part of your writing context.

What Type of Paper Am I Preparing?

Study your assignment to understand the type of project. Is your purpose expository, analytic, or argumentative? How would you classify each of the following topics?

1. Explain the chief solutions proposed for increasing the Southwest's water supply.
2. Compare the Freudian and behavioral models of mental illness.
3. Find the best solutions to a current environmental problem.
4. Consider: What twentieth-century invention has most dramatically changed our personal lives?

Did you recognize that the first topic calls for a report? The second topic requires an analysis of two schools of psychology, so you cannot report on only one, but you also cannot argue that one model is better than the other. Both topics 3 and 4 require an argumentative paper: You must select and defend a claim.

Who Is My Audience?

If you are writing in a specific discipline, imagine your instructor as a representative of that field, a reader with knowledge of the subject area. If you are in a composition course, your instructor may advise you to write to a general reader, someone who reads newspapers but may not have the exact information and perspective you have. For a general reader, specialized terms and concepts need definition.

> **NOTE:** Consider the expectations of your readers. A research essay is not a personal essay. It is not about you; it is about a subject. Keep yourself in the background and carefully evaluate any use of the personal pronoun "I."

How Can I Select a Good Topic?

Choosing from assigned topics. At times students are unhappy with topic restriction. Looked at another way, your instructor has eliminated a difficult step in the research process and has helped you avoid the problem of selecting an unworkable topic. If topics are assigned, you will still have to choose from the list and develop your own claim and approach.

Finding a course-related topic. This guideline gives you many options and requires more thought about your choice. Working within the guidelines, try to write about what interests you. Here are examples of assignments turned into topics of interest to the student:

ASSIGNMENT	INTEREST	TOPIC
1. Trace the influence of any twentieth-century event, development, invention.	Music	The influence of the Jazz Age on modern music
2. Support an argument on some issue of pornography and censorship.	Computers	Censorship of pornography on the Internet
3. Demonstrate the popularity of a current myth and then discredit it.	Science fiction	The lack of evidence for the existence of UFOs

Selecting a topic without any guidelines. When you are free to write on any topic, you may need to use some strategies for topic selection.

- Look through your text's table of contents or index for subject areas that can be narrowed or focused.
- Look over your class notes and think about subjects covered that have interested you.
- Consider college-based or local issues.
- Do a subject search in an electronic database to see how a large topic can be narrowed—for example, type in "dinosaur" and observe such subheadings as *dinosaur behavior* and *dinosaur extinction*.
- Use one or more invention strategies to narrow and focus a topic:
  — Freewriting
  — Brainstorming
  — Asking questions about a broad subject, using the reporter's *who, what, where, when,* and *why.*

What Kinds of Topics Should I Avoid?

Here are several kinds of topics that are best avoided because they usually produce disasters, no matter how well the student handles the rest of the research process:

1. *Topics that are irrelevant* to your interests or the course. If you are not interested in your topic, you will not produce a lively, informative paper. If you select a topic far removed from the course content, you may create some hostility in your instructor, who will wonder why you are unwilling to become engaged in the course.
2. *Topics that are broad subject areas.* These result in general surveys that lack appropriate detail and support.
3. *Topics that can be fully researched with only one source.* You will produce a summary, not a research paper.
4. *Biographical studies.* Short undergraduate papers on a person's life usually turn out to be summaries of one or two major biographies.
5. *Topics that produce a strong emotional response in you.* If there is only one "right" answer to the abortion issue and you cannot imagine counterarguments, don't choose to write on abortion. Probably most religious topics are best avoided.
6. *Topics that are too technical for you* at this point in your college work. If you do not understand the complexities of the federal tax code, then arguing for a reduction in the capital gains tax may be an unwise topic choice.

WRITING A TENTATIVE CLAIM OR RESEARCH PROPOSAL

Once you have selected and focused a topic, write a tentative claim, research question, or research proposal. Some instructors will ask to see a statement—from a sentence to a paragraph long—to be approved before you proceed. Others may require a one-page proposal that includes a tentative claim, a basic organizational plan, and a description of types of sources to be used. Even if your instructor does not require anything in writing, you need to write something for your benefit—to direct your reading and thinking. Here are two possibilities:

1. **SUBJECT:** Computers

   TOPIC: The impact of computers on the twentieth century

   CLAIM: Computers had the greatest impact of any technological development in the twentieth century.

   RESEARCH PROPOSAL: I propose to show that computers had the greatest impact of any technological development in the twentieth century.

> I will show the influence of computers at work, in daily living, and in play to emphasize the breadth of influence. I will argue that other possibilities (such as cars) did not have the same impact as computers. I will check the library's book catalog and databases for sources on technological developments and on computers specifically. I will also interview a family friend who works with computers at the Pentagon.

This example illustrates several key ideas. First, the initial subject is both too broad and unfocused (*What* about computers?). Second, the claim is more focused than the topic statement because it asserts a position, a claim the student must support. Third, the research proposal is more helpful than the claim only because it includes some thoughts on developing the thesis and finding sources.

2. Less sure of your topic? Then write a research question or a more open-ended research proposal. Take, for example, a history student studying the effects of Prohibition. She is not ready to write a thesis, but she can write a research proposal that suggests some possible approaches to the topic:

TOPIC:	The effect of Prohibition
RESEARCH QUESTION:	What were the effects of Prohibition on the United States?
RESEARCH PROPOSAL:	I will examine the effects of Prohibition on the United States in the 1920s (and possibly consider some long-term effects, depending on the amount of material on the topic). Specifically, I will look at the varying effects on urban and rural areas and on different classes in society.

PREPARING A WORKING BIBLIOGRAPHY

To begin this next stage of your research, you need to know three things:

- *Your search strategy.* If you are writing on a course-related topic, your starting place may be your textbook for relevant sections and possible sources (if the text contains a bibliography). For this course, you may find some potential sources among the readings in this text. Think about what you already know or have in hand as you plan your search strategy.
- *A method for recording bibliographic information.* You have two choices: the always reliable 3 × 5 index cards or a bibliography file in your personal computer.
- *The documentation format you will be using.* You may be assigned the Modern Language Association (MLA) format, or perhaps given a choice

between MLA and the American Psychological Association (APA) documentation styles. Once you select the documentation style, skim the appropriate pages in Chapter 14 to get an overview of both content and style.

A list of possible sources is only a *working* bibliography because you do not yet know which sources you will use. (Your final bibliography will include only those sources you cite—actually refer to—in your paper.) A working bibliography will help you see what is available on your topic, note how to locate each source, and contain the information needed to document. Whether you are using cards or computer files, follow these guidelines:

1. Check all reasonable catalogs and indexes for possible sources. (Use more than one reference source even if you locate enough sources there; you are looking for the best sources, not the first ones you find.)
2. Complete a card or prepare an entry for every potentially useful source. You won't know what to reject until you start a close reading of sources.
3. Copy (or download from an online catalog) all information needed to complete a citation and to locate the source. (When using an index that does not give all needed information, leave a space to be filled in when you actually read the source.)
4. Put bibliographic information in the correct format for every possible source; you will save time and make fewer errors. Do not mix or blend styles. When searching for sources, have your text handy and use the appropriate models as your guide.

The following brief guide to correct form will get you started. Illustrations are for cards, but the information and order will be the same in your PC file. (Guidelines are for MLA style.)

Basic Form for Books

As Figure 12.1 shows, the basic MLA form for books includes the following information in this pattern:

1. The author's full name, last name first.
2. The title (and subtitle if there is one) of the book, in italics (underlined in handwriting).
3. The facts of publication: the city of publication (followed by a colon), the publisher (followed by a comma), and the date of publication.
4. The publication medium—Print.

Note that periods are placed after the author's name, after the title, and at the end of the citation. Other information, when appropriate (e.g., the number of volumes), is added to this basic pattern. (See pp. 318–29 for many sample citations.) Include, in your working bibliography, the book's classification number so that you can find it in the library.

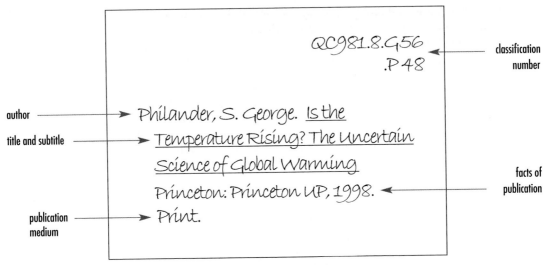

FIGURE 12.1 Bibliography Card for a Book

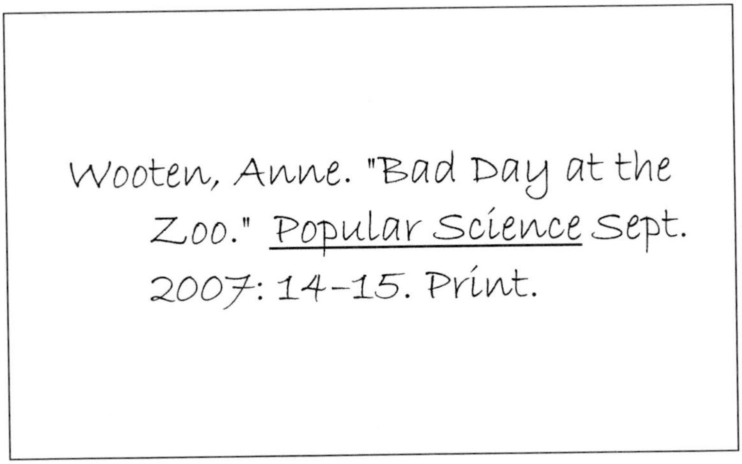

FIGURE 12.2 Bibliography Card for a Magazine Article

Basic Form for Articles

Figure 12.2 shows the simplest form for magazine articles. Include the following information, in this pattern:

1. The author's full name, last name first.
2. The title of the article, in quotation marks.
3. The facts of publication: the title of the periodical in italics (underlined in handwriting), the volume number (if the article is from a scholarly journal), the date (followed by a colon), and inclusive page numbers.
4. The publication medium—Print.

You will discover that indexes rarely present information in MLA format. Here, for example, is a source on problems with zoos, found in an electronic database:

BAD DAY AT THE ZOO.
Wooten, Anne. Popular Science, Sep2007, Vol. 271 Issue 3, p. 14–15, 2p.

If you read the article in the magazine itself, then the correct citation, for MLA, will look like that in the sample bibliography card in Figure 12.2. (Because *Popular Science* is a magazine, not a scholarly journal, you provide month and year but not volume and issue numbers.) However, if you obtain a copy of the article from one of your library's electronic databases, then your citation will need additional information to identify your actual source of the article:

Wooten, Anne. "Bad Day at the Zoo." *Popular Science* Sept. 2007: 14–15.
   Academic Search Complete. Web. 8 Sept. 2008.

Note that the medium of publication is now "Web," not "Print," and the name of the database is italicized as if it were a book containing the article.

NOTE: A collection of printouts, slips of paper, and backs of envelopes is not a working bibliography! You may have to return to the library for missing information, and you risk making serious errors in documentation. Know the basics of your documentation format and follow it faithfully when collecting possible sources.

LOCATING SOURCES

All libraries contain books and periodicals and a system for accessing them. A library's *book collection* includes the general collection, the reference collection, and the reserve book collection. Electronic materials such as tapes and CDs will also be included in the general "book" collection. The *periodicals collection* consists of popular magazines, scholarly journals, and newspapers. Electronic databases with texts of articles provide alternatives to the print periodicals collection.

REMEMBER: All works, regardless of their source or the format in which you obtain them—and this includes online sources—must be fully documented in your paper.

The Book Catalog

Your chief guide to books and audiovisual materials is the library catalog, usually an electronic database accessed from computer stations in the library or, with an appropriate password, from your personal computer.

One of the famous lions sitting in front of the New York Public Library.

In the catalog there will be at least four ways to access a specific book: the author entry, the title entry, one or more subject entries, and a keyword option. When you pull up the search screen, you will probably see that the keyword option is the default. If you know the exact title of the work you want, switch to the title option, type it in, and hit submit. If you want a list of all of the library's books on Hemingway, though, click on author and type in "Hemingway." Keep these points in mind:

- With a title search, do not type any initial article (a, an, the). To locate *The Great Gatsby,* type in "Great Gatsby."
- Use correct spelling. If you are unsure of spelling, use a keyword instead of an author or title search.
- If you are looking for a list of books on your subject, do a keyword or subject search.
- When screens for specific books are shown, either print screens of potential sources or copy all information needed for documentation—plus the call number for each book.

The Reference Collection

The research process often begins with the reference collection. You will find atlases, dictionaries, encyclopedias, general histories, critical studies, and biographies. In addition, various reference tools such as bibliographies and indexes are part of the reference collection.

Many tools in the reference collection once only in print form are now also online. Some are now only online. Yet online is not always the way to go. Let's consider some of the advantages of each of the formats:

Advantages of the Print Reference Collection

1. The reference tool may be only in print—use it.
2. The print form covers the period you are studying. (Most online indexes and abstracts cover only from 1980 to the present.)
3. In a book, with a little scanning of pages, you can often find what you need without getting spelling or commands exactly right.
4. If you know the best reference source to use and are looking for only a few items, the print source can be faster than the online source.

Advantages of Online Reference Materials

1. Online databases are likely to provide the most up-to-date information.
2. You can usually search all years covered at one time.
3. Full texts (with graphics) are sometimes available, as well as indexes with detailed summaries of articles. Both can be printed or e-mailed to your PC.
4. Through links to the Internet, you have access to an amazing amount of material. (Unless you focus your keyword search, however, you may be overwhelmed.)

Before using any reference work, take a few minutes to check its date, purpose, and organization. If you are new to online searching, take a few minutes to learn about each reference tool by working through the online tutorial.

A Word about Wikipedia

Many researchers go first to a general encyclopedia, in the past in print in the reference collection, today more typically online. This is not always the best strategy. Often you can learn more about your topic from a current book or a more specialized reference source—which your reference librarian can help you find. Both may give you additional sources for your project. If—or when—you turn to a general encyclopedia, make it a good one that is available online through your library. Some colleges have told their students that *Wikipedia* is not an acceptable source for college research projects.

Electronic Databases

You will probably access electronic databases by going to your library's home page and then clicking on the appropriate term or icon. (You may have found the book catalog by clicking on "library catalog"; you may find the databases by clicking on "library resources" or some other descriptive label.) You will need to choose a particular database and then type in your keyword for a basic

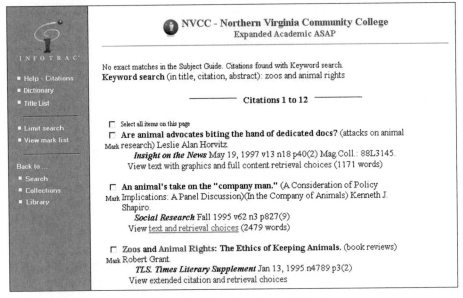

FIGURE 12.3 Partial List of Articles Found on Search Topic

search or select "advanced search" to limit that search by date or periodical or in some other way. Each library will create somewhat different screens, but the basic process of selecting among choices provided and then typing in your search commands remains the same. Figure 12.3 shows a partial list of articles that resulted from a keyword search for "zoos and animal rights."

GUIDELINES for Using Online Databases

Keep these points in mind as you use online databases:

- **Although some online databases provide full texts of all articles, others provide full texts of only some of the articles indexed.** The articles not in full text will have to be located in a print collection of periodicals.

- **Articles indexed but not available in full text often come with a brief summary or abstract.** This allows you to decide whether the article looks useful for your project. *Do not treat the abstract as the article. Do not use material from it and cite the author. If you want to use the article, find it in your library's print collection or obtain it from another library.*

- **The information you need for documenting material used from an article is not in correct format for any of the standard documentation styles.** You will have to reorder the information and use the correct style for writing titles. If your instructor wants to see a list of possible sources in MLA format, do not hand in a printout of articles from an online database.

- **Because no single database covers all journals, you may want to search several databases that seem relevant to your project.** Ask your reference librarian for suggestions of various databases in the sciences, social sciences, public affairs, and education.

The Internet

In addition to using electronic databases to find sources, you can search the Internet directly.

Keep in mind these facts about the Internet:

- The Internet is both disorganized and huge, so you can waste time trying to find information that is easily obtained in a library reference book or database.
- The Internet is best at providing current information, such as news and movie reviews. It is also a great source of government information.
- Because anyone can create a website and put anything on it, you will have to be especially careful in evaluating Internet sources. Remember that articles in magazines and journals have been selected by editors and are often peer reviewed as well, but no editor selects or rejects material on a personal website.

GUIDELINES for Searching the Web

The Internet will provide useful sources for many research projects. It will be much less useful than books or online databases for others. One task of the good researcher is to think about the best places to go to get the best material for a specific project. If you think the Internet will be useful for you, keep these general guidelines in mind to aid your research:

- Bookmark sites you expect to use often so that you do not have to remember a complex URL or do another Google search.
- Make your research terms as precise as possible to avoid getting overwhelmed with hits.
- If you are searching for a specific phrase, put quotation marks around the words. This will reduce the number of hits and lead to more useful sites. Example: "Rainforest depletion." Without the quotation marks, you will get lots of information about rainforests, but not necessarily about their depletion. You will also get information on the concept of depletion that has nothing to do with rainforests.
- Complete a bibliography card—including the date you accessed the source—for each separate site from which you take material (see Chapter 14 for documentation guidelines).

FIELD RESEARCH

Field research can enrich many projects. The following sections offer some suggestions.

Federal, State, and Local Government Documents

In addition to federal documents you may obtain through *PAIS* or *GPO Access*, department and agency websites, or the Library of Congress's good legislative site, *Thomas* (**http://thomas.loc.gov**), consider state and county archives, maps, and other published materials. Instead of selecting a national or global topic, consider examining the debate over a controversial bill introduced in your state legislature. Use online databases to locate articles on the bill and the debate and interview legislators and journalists who participated in or covered the debates or served on committees that worked with the bill.

You can also request specific documents from appropriate state or county agencies and nonprofit organizations. One student, given the assignment of examining solutions to an ecological problem, decided to study the local problem of preserving the Chesapeake Bay. She obtained issues of the Chesapeake Bay Foundation newsletter and brochures prepared by them advising homeowners about hazardous household waste materials that end up in the bay. Added to her sources were bulletins on soil conservation and landscaping tips for improving the area's water quality. Local problems can lead to interesting research topics because they are current and relevant to you and because they involve uncovering different kinds of source materials.

Correspondence

Business and government officials are usually willing to respond to written requests for information. Make your letter brief and well written. Either include a self-addressed, stamped envelope for the person's convenience or e-mail your request. If you are not e-mailing, write as soon as you discover the need for information and be prepared to wait several weeks for a reply. It is appropriate to indicate your deadline and ask for a timely response. Three guidelines for either letters or e-mails to keep in mind are:

1. Explain precisely what information you need.
2. Do not request information that can be found in your library's reference collection.
3. Explain how you plan to use the information. Businesses especially are understandably concerned with their public image and will be disinclined to provide information that you intend to use as a means of attacking them.

Use reference guides to companies and government agencies or their websites to obtain addresses and the person to whom your letter or e-mail should be sent.

Interviews

Some experts are available for personal interviews. Call or write for an appointment as soon as you recognize the value of an interview. Remember that interviews are more likely to be scheduled with state and local officials than with the president of General Motors. If you are studying a local problem, also consider leaders of the civic association with an interest in the issue. In many communities, the local historian or a librarian will be a storehouse of information about the community. Former teachers can be interviewed for papers on education. Interviews with doctors or nurses can add a special dimension to papers on medical issues.

If an interview is appropriate for your topic, follow these guidelines:

1. Prepare specific questions in advance.
2. Arrive on time, properly dressed, and behave in a polite, professional manner.
3. Take notes, asking the interviewee to repeat key statements so that your notes are accurate.
4. Take a tape recorder with you but ask permission to use it before taping.
5. If you quote any statements in your paper, quote accurately, eliminating only such minor speech habits as "you know's" and "uhm's." (See Chapter 14 for proper documentation of interviews.)
6. Direct the interview with your prepared questions, but also give the interviewee the chance to approach the topic in his or her own way. You may obtain information or views that had not occurred to you.
7. Do not get into a debate with the interviewee. You are there to learn.

Lectures

Check the appropriate information sources at your school to keep informed of visiting speakers. If you are fortunate enough to attend a lecture relevant to a current project, take careful, detailed notes. Because a lecture is a source, use of information or ideas from it must be presented accurately and then documented. (See Chapter 14 for documentation format.)

Films, DVDs, Television

Your library will have audiovisual materials that provide good sources for some kinds of topics. For example, if you are studying *Death of a Salesman,* view a videotaped version of the play. Also pay attention to documentaries on public television and to the many news and political talk shows on both public and commercial channels. In many cases transcripts of shows can be obtained from the TV station. Alternatively, tape the program while watching it so that you can view it several times. The documentation format for such nonprint sources is illustrated in Chapter 14.

Surveys, Questionnaires, and Original Research

Depending on your paper, you may want to conduct a simple survey or write and administer a questionnaire. Surveys can be used for many campus and local issues, for topics on behavior and attitudes of college students and/or faculty, and for topics on consumer habits. Explore surveymonkey.com for help administering an online survey. Simple ones are free! Remember: Surveying 50 of your Facebook friends will not produce a random sample. When writing questions, keep these guidelines in mind:

- Use simple, clear language.
- Devise a series of short questions rather than only a few that have several parts to them. (You want to separate information for better analysis.)
- Phrase questions to avoid wording that seeks to control the answer. For example, do *not* ask "Did you perform your civic duty by voting in the last election?" This is a loaded question.

In addition to surveys and questionnaires, you can incorporate some original research. As you read sources on your topic, be alert to reports of studies that you could redo and update in part or on a smaller scale. Many topics on advertising and television give opportunities for your own analysis. Local-issue topics may offer good opportunities for gathering information on your own, not just from your reading. One student, examining the controversy over a proposed new shopping mall on part of the Manassas Civil War Battlefield in Virginia, made the argument that the mall served no practical need in the community. He supported his position by describing existing malls, including the number and types of stores each contained and the number of miles each was from the proposed new mall. How did he obtain this information? He drove around the area, counting miles and stores. Sometimes a seemingly unglamorous approach to a topic turns out to be an imaginative one.

EVALUATING SOURCES, MAINTAINING CREDIBILITY

As you study your sources, keep rethinking your purpose and approach. Test your research proposal or tentative claim against what you are learning. Remember: You can always change the direction and focus of your paper as new approaches occur to you, and you can even change your position as you reflect on what you are learning.

You will work with sources more effectively if you keep in mind why you are using them. What you are looking for will vary somewhat, depending on your topic and purpose, but there are several basic approaches:

1. *Acquiring information and viewpoints firsthand.* Suppose that you are concerned about the mistreatment of animals kept in zoos. You do not want to just read what others have to say on this issue. First, visit a zoo, taking notes on what you see. Second, before you go, plan to interview at least one person on the zoo staff, preferably a veterinarian who can explain the zoo's guidelines for animal care. Only after gathering and thinking about these *primary sources* do you want to add to your knowledge by reading articles and books—*secondary sources.* Many kinds of topics require the use of both primary and secondary sources. If you want to study violence in children's TV shows, for example, you should first spend some time watching specific shows and taking notes.

2. *Acquiring new knowledge.* Suppose you are interested in breast cancer research and treatment, but you do not know much about the choices of

treatment and, in general, where we are with this medical problem. You will need to turn to sources first to learn about the topic. Begin with sources that will give you an overview, perhaps a historical perspective. Begin with sources that provide an overview of how knowledge and treatment have progressed in the last thirty years. Similarly, if your topic is the effects of Prohibition in the 1920s, you will need to read first for knowledge but also with an eye to ways to focus the topic and organize your paper.

3. *Understanding the issues.* Suppose you think that you know your views on illegal immigration, so you intend to read only to obtain some useful statistical information to support your argument. Should you scan sources quickly, looking for facts you can use? This approach may be too hasty. As explained in Chapter 3, good arguments are built on a knowledge of counterarguments. You are wise to study sources presenting a variety of attitudes on your issue so that you understand—and can refute—the arguments of others. *Remember: that with controversial issues often the best argument is a conciliatory one that presents a middle ground and seeks to bring people together.*

When you use facts and opinions from sources, you are saying to readers that the facts are accurate and the ideas credible. If you do not evaluate your sources before using them, you risk losing your credibility as a writer. (Remember Aristotle's idea of *ethos,* how your character is judged.) Just because they are in print does not mean that a writer's "facts" are reliable or ideas worthwhile. Judging the usefulness and reliability of potential sources is an essential part of the research process.

GUIDELINES for Evaluating Sources

Today, with access to so much material on the Internet, the need to evaluate is even more crucial. Here are some strategies for evaluating sources, with special attention to Internet sources:

- **Locate the author's credentials.** Periodicals often list their writers' degrees, current position, and other publications; books, similarly, contain an "about the author" section. If you do not see this information, check various biographical dictionaries (*Biography Index, Contemporary Authors*) or look for the author's website for information. For articles on the web, look for the author's e-mail address or a link to a home page. *Never use a web source that does not identify the author or the organization responsible for the material. Critical question:* Is this author qualified to write on this topic? How do I know?

- **Judge the credibility of the work.** For books, read how reviewers evaluated the book when it was first published. For articles, judge the respectability of the magazine or journal. Study the author's use of documentation as one measure of credibility. Scholarly works cite sources. Well-researched and reliable pieces in quality popular magazines will also make clear the sources of any statistics used or the credentials of any authority who is quoted. One good rule: Never use undocumented statistical information. Another judge of credibility is the quality of writing. Do not use sources filled with grammatical and mechanical errors. For web sources, find out what institution hosts the site. If you have not heard of the company or organization, find out more about it. *Critical question:* Why should I believe information/ideas from this source?

- **Select only those sources that are at an appropriate level for your research.** Avoid works that are either too specialized or too elementary for college research. You may not understand the former (and thus could misrepresent them in your paper), and you gain nothing from the latter. *Critical question:* Will this source provide a sophisticated discussion for educated adults?

- **Understand the writer's purpose.** Consider the writer's intended audience. Be cautious using works designed to reinforce biases already shared by the intended audience. Is the work written to persuade rather than to inform and analyze? Examine the writing for emotionally charged language. For Internet sources, ask yourself why this person or institution decided to have a website or contribute to a newsgroup. *Critical question:* Can I trust the information from this source, given the apparent purpose of the work?

- **In general, choose current sources.** Some studies published years ago remain classics, but many older works are outdated. In scientific and technical fields, the "information revolution" has outdated some works published only five years ago. So look at publication dates (When was the website page last updated?) and pass over outdated sources in favor of current studies. *Critical question:* Is this information still accurate?

PREPARING AN ANNOTATED BIBLIOGRAPHY

An annotated bibliography is a list of sources on a topic that includes a summary of each source. As part of your research process, you may be required to prepare either a partial or a complete annotated bibliography. Instructors include this assignment to keep you moving forward in your study of sources; it is a way of checking that you have found and read useful sources in good time to complete your project. Annotating each source also demands careful reading and analysis; it provides a check against skimming a source for some information without taking time to read and understand the context in which the information is presented and the author's position on the topic. You may find that your research paper is more focused and better written if you take the time to write a brief summary statement about each source you plan to use, even if an annotated bibliography is not required.

When preparing an annotated bibliography, list sources alphabetically and in correct MLA (or APA) format (see Chapter 14). Then, immediately after each citation, place a two-to-five-sentence summary of that source. Use hanging indentation, just as you would for your list of works cited at the end of your paper. *Warning: Do not confuse an annotated bibliography with a Works Cited list.* When you complete your research essay, list all sources used *without* the summaries.

A partial annotated bibliography follows, based on the sample student research essay in Chapter 13. Use this as your model.

Tell Us What You Really Are: The Debate over
Labeling Genetically Modified Food
Selected Annotated Bibliography
David Donaldson

MacDonald, Chris, and Melissa Whellams. "Corporate Decisions about Labeling
Genetically Modified Foods." *Journal of Business Ethics* 75.2 (2007): 181–89.
JSTOR. Web. 8 June 2011. MacDonald and Whellams examine the ethical obligation
of companies to label genetically modified foods. The authors explain that there is no
evidence that such products pose a health risk and that the FDA sees no reason to
require special labeling. The authors explain that such labeling would impose a hardship on the companies preparing GM foods. Although the authors assert that they
do not necessarily oppose required labeling, they conclude that food companies are
not ethically obligated to voluntarily label GM foods.

U.S. Chamber of Commerce. "Precautionary Principle." U.S. Chamber of Commerce. 2011.
Web. 9 June 2011. The U.S. Chamber of Commerce has posted on its website a
statement regarding the "precautionary principle." The Chamber asserts that it has
always supported regulatory decisions based on good science and sound risk assessment.
The Chamber opposes the use of the "precautionary principle"—assume the worst and
regulate risks that are uncertain or unknown—as a guide for U.S. regulatory decisions.

U.S. Food and Drug Administration. "Bioengineered Foods." Statement of Robert E. Brackett to
the FDA. U.S. Food and Drug Administration. 12 July 2009. Web. 18 June 2011. Robert E.
Brackett's statement to the Senate Committee on Agriculture, Nutrition, and Forestry is a
lengthy, detailed review of the FDA's responsibilities in determining food safety in general and
its specific procedures for approving foods developed by hybridization and bioengineering.
Brackett explains that GM foods could conceivably create one of three problems: cause new
allergies, cause toxicity, or produce anti-nutrients (e.g., result in a decrease in Vitamin C). The
FDA has the power to screen new foods for all three potential problems and to disapprove or
require labeling, as appropriate. Brackett assures the Committee that the FDA works closely
with companies developing GM foods and that they carefully test for all three potential
problems to maintain a safe food supply for consumers.

CHAPTER 13

Writing the Researched Essay

You have agonized over your topic choice, searched for good sources, read and thought about your topic, seeking a way to put together a compelling argument—while not forgetting documentation. Whew! Don't rush now. Study this chapter's writing points and apply the guidelines to the writing of a convincing essay. Here are some general guidelines for studying sources.

GUIDELINES for Studying Sources

1. **Read first; take notes later.** First, do background reading, selecting the most general sources that provide an overview of the topic.

2. **Skim what appear to be your chief sources.** Learn what other writers on the topic consider the important facts, issues, and points of debate.

3. **Annotate photocopies**—do not highlight endlessly. Instead, carefully bracket material you want to use. Then write a note in the margin indicating how and where you might use that material.

4. **Either download Internet sources or take careful notes on the material.** Before preparing a note on content, be sure to copy all necessary information for documenting the material—including the date you accessed the website.

5. **Initially mark key passages in books with Post-Its.** Write on the Post-It how and where you might use the material. Alternatively, photocopy book pages and then annotate them. Be sure to record for yourself the source of all copied pages.

6. **As you study and annotate, create labels for source materials that will help you organize your essay.** For example, if you are writing about the problem of campus rape, you might label passages as: "facts showing there is a problem," "causes of the problem," and "possible solutions to the problem."

7. **Recognize that when you are working with many sources, note taking rather than annotating copies of sources is more helpful.** Notes, whether on cards or typed on separate sheets of paper, provide an efficient method for collecting and organizing lots of information.

AVOIDING PLAGIARISM

Documenting sources accurately and fully is required of all researchers. Proper documentation distinguishes between the work of others and your ideas, shows readers the breadth of your research, and strengthens your credibility. In Western culture, copyright laws support the ethic that ideas, new information, and wording belong to their author. To borrow these without acknowledgment is against the law and has led to many celebrated lawsuits. For students who plagiarize, the consequences range from an F on the paper to suspension from college. Be certain, then, that you know what the requirements for correct documentation are; accidental plagiarism is still plagiarism and will be punished.

> **NOTE:** MLA documentation requires precise page references for all ideas, opinions, and information taken from sources—except for common knowledge. Author and page references provided in the text are supported by complete bibliographic citations on the Works Cited page.

In sum, you are required to document the following:

- Direct quotations from sources
- Paraphrased ideas and opinions from sources
- Summaries of ideas from sources
- Factual information, except common knowledge, from sources

Understand that putting an author's ideas in your own words in a paraphrase or summary does not eliminate the requirement of documentation. To illustrate, consider the following excerpt from Thomas R. Schueler's report *Controlling Urban Runoff* (Washington Metropolitan Water Resources Planning Board, 1987: 3–4) and a student paragraph based on the report.

SOURCE

The aquatic ecosystems in urban headwater streams are particularly susceptible to the impacts of urbanization. . . . Dietemann (1975), Ragan and Dietemann (1976), Klein (1979) and WMCOG (1982) have all tracked trends in fish diversity and abundance over time in local urbanizing streams. Each of the studies has shown that fish communities become less diverse and are composed of more tolerant species after the surrounding watershed is developed. Sensitive fish species either disappear or occur very rarely. In most cases, the total number of fish in urbanizing streams may also decline.

Similar trends have been noted among aquatic insects which are the major food resource for fish. . . . Higher post-development sediment and trace metals can interfere in their efforts to gather food. Changes in water temperature, oxygen levels, and substrate composition can further reduce the species diversity and abundance of the aquatic insect community.

PLAGIARIZED STUDENT PARAGRAPH

Studies have shown that fish communities become less diverse as the amount of runoff increases. Sensitive fish species either disappear or occur very rarely, and, in most cases, the total number of fish declines. Aquatic insects, a major source of food for fish, also decline because sediment and trace metals interfere with their food-gathering efforts. Increased water temperature and lower oxygen levels can further reduce the species diversity and abundance of the aquatic insect community.

The student's opening words establish a reader's expectation that the student has taken information from a source, as indeed the student has. But where is the documentation? The student's paraphrase is a good example of plagiarism: an unacknowledged paraphrase of borrowed information that even collapses into copying the source's exact wording in two places. For MLA style, the author's name and the precise page numbers are needed throughout the paragraph. Additionally, most of the first sentence and the final phrase must be put into the student's own words or placed within quotation marks. The following revised paragraph shows an appropriate acknowledgment of the source used.

REVISED STUDENT PARAGRAPH TO REMOVE PLAGIARISM

In *Controlling Urban Runoff*, Thomas Schueler explains that studies have shown "that fish communities become less diverse as the amount of runoff increases" (3). Sensitive fish species either disappear or occur very rarely and, in most cases, the total number of fish declines. Aquatic insects, a major source of food for fish, also decline because sediment and trace metals interfere with their food-gathering efforts. Increased water temperature and lower oxygen levels, Schueler concludes, "can further reduce the species diversity and abundance of the aquatic insect community" (4).

What Is Common Knowledge?

In general, common knowledge includes

- undisputed dates,
- well-known facts, and
- generally known facts, terms, and concepts in a field of study when you are writing in that field

So, do not cite a source for the dates of the American Revolution. If you are writing a paper for a psychology class, do not cite your text when using terms such as *ego* or *sublimation*. However, you must cite a historian who analyzes the causes of England's loss to the Colonies or a psychologist who disputes Freud's ideas. *Opinions* about well-known facts must be documented. *Discussions* of debatable dates, terms, or concepts must be documented. When in doubt, defend your integrity and document.

USING SIGNAL PHRASES TO AVOID CONFUSION

If you are an honest student, you do not want to submit a paper that is plagiarized, even though that plagiarism was unintentional on your part. What leads to unintentional plagiarism?

- A researcher takes careless notes, neglecting to include precise page numbers on the notes, but uses the information anyway, without documentation.
- A researcher works in material from sources in such a way that, even with page references, readers cannot tell what has been taken from the sources.

Good note-taking strategies will keep you from the first pitfall. Avoiding the second problem means becoming skilled in ways to include source material in your writing while still making your indebtedness to sources absolutely clear to readers. The way to do this: Give the author's name in the essay. You can also include, when appropriate, the author's credentials ("According to Dr. Hays, a geologist with the Department of Interior, . . ."). These *introductory tags* or *signal phrases* give readers a context for the borrowed material, as well as serving as part of the required documentation of sources. *Make sure that each signal phrase clarifies rather than distorts an author's relationship to his or her ideas and your relationship to the source.*

GUIDELINES for Appropriately Using Sources

Here are three guidelines to follow to avoid misrepresenting borrowed material:

- **Pay attention to verb choice in signal phrases.** When you vary such standard wording as "Smith says" or "Jones states," be careful that you do not select verbs that misrepresent "Smith's" or "Jones's" attitude toward his or her own work. Do not write "Jones wonders" when in fact Jones has strongly asserted her views. (See pp. 294–95 for a discussion of varying word choice in signal phrases.)

- **Pay attention to the location of signal phrases.** If you mention Jones after you have presented her views, be sure that your reader can tell precisely which ideas in the passage belong to Jones. If your entire paragraph is a paraphrase of Jones's work, you are plagiarizing to conclude with "This idea is presented by Jones." Which of the several ideas in your paragraph comes from Jones? Your reader will assume that only the last idea comes from Jones.

- **Paraphrase properly.** Be sure that paraphrases are truly *in your own words*. To use Smith's words and sentence style in your writing is to plagiarize.

NOTE: Putting a parenthetical page reference at the end of a paragraph is not sufficient if you have used the source throughout the paragraph. Use introductory tags or signal phrases to guide the reader through the material.

EXERCISES: Acknowledging Sources to Avoid Plagiarism

1. The following paragraph (from Franklin E. Zimring's "Firearms, Violence and Public Policy" [*Scientific American*, Nov. 1991]) provides material for the examples that follow of adequate and inadequate acknowledgment of sources. After reading Zimring's paragraph, study the three examples with these questions in mind: (1) Which example represents adequate acknowledgment? (2) Which examples do not represent adequate acknowledgment? (3) In exactly what ways is each plagiarized paragraph flawed?

SOURCE

Although most citizens support such measures as owner screening, public opinion is sharply divided on laws that would restrict the ownership of handguns to persons with special needs. If the U.S. does not reduce handguns and current trends continue, it faces the prospect that the number of handguns in circulation will grow from 35 million to more than 50 million within 50 years. A national program limiting the availability of handguns would cost many billions of dollars and meet much resistance from citizens. These costs would likely be greatest in the early years of the program. The benefits of supply reduction would emerge slowly because efforts to diminish the availability of handguns would probably have a cumulative impact over time. (page 54)

STUDENT PARAGRAPH 1

One approach to the problem of handgun violence in America is to severely limit handgun ownership. If we don't restrict ownership and start the costly task of removing handguns from our society, we may end up with around 50 million handguns in the country by 2040. The benefits will not be apparent right away but will eventually appear. This idea is emphasized by Franklin Zimring (54).

STUDENT PARAGRAPH 2

One approach to the problem of handgun violence in America is to restrict the ownership of handguns except in special circumstances. If we do not begin to reduce the number of handguns in this country, the number will grow from 35 million to more than 50 million within 50 years. We can agree with Franklin Zimring that a program limiting handguns will cost billions and meet resistance from citizens (54).

STUDENT PARAGRAPH 3

According to law professor Franklin Zimring, the United States needs to severely limit handgun ownership or face the possibility of seeing handgun ownership increase "from 35 million to more than 50 million within 50 years" (54). Zimring points out that Americans disagree significantly on restricting handguns and that enforcing such laws would be very expensive. He concludes that the benefits would not be seen immediately but that the restrictions "would probably have a cumulative impact over time" (54). Although Zimring paints a gloomy picture of high costs and little immediate relief from gun violence, he also presents the shocking possibility of 50 million guns by the year 2040. Can our society survive so much fire power?

Clearly, only the third student paragraph demonstrates adequate acknowledgment of the writer's indebtedness to Zimring. Notice that the placement of the last parenthetical page reference acts as a visual closure to the student's borrowing. She then turns to her response to Zimring and her own views on the problem of handguns.

2.   Read the following passage and then the three plagiarized uses of the passage. Explain why each one is plagiarized and how it can be corrected.

Original Text: Stanley Karnow, Vietnam, A History. The First Complete Account of Vietnam at War. New York: Viking, 1983, 319.

Lyndon Baines Johnson, a consummate politician, was a kaleidoscopic personality, forever changing as he sought to dominate or persuade or placate or frighten his friends and foes. A gigantic figure whose extravagant moods matched his size, he could be cruel and kind, violent and gentle, petty, generous, cunning, naïve, crude, candid, and frankly dishonest. He commanded the blind loyalty of his aides, some of whom worshipped him, and he sparked bitter derision or fierce hatred that he never quite fathomed.

a. LBJ's vibrant and changing personality filled some people with adoration and others with bitter derision that he never quite fathomed (Karnow 319).

b. LBJ, a supreme politician, had a personality like a kaleidoscope, continually changing as he tried to control, sway, appease, or intimidate his enemies and supporters (Karnow 319).

c. Often, figures who have had great impact on America's history have been dynamic people with powerful personalities and vibrant physical presence. LBJ, for example, was a huge figure who polarized those who worked for and with him. "He commanded the blind loyalty of his aides, some of whom worshipped him, and he sparked bitter derision or fierce hatred" from many others (Karnow 319).

3.   Read the following passage and then the four sample uses of the passage. Judge each of the uses for how well it avoids plagiarism and if it is documented correctly. Make corrections as needed.

Original Text: Stanley Karnow, *Vietnam, A History. The First Complete Account of Vietnam at War.* New York: Viking, 1983, 327.

On July 27, 1965, in a last-ditch attempt to change Johnson's mind, Mansfield and Russell were to press him again to "concentrate on finding a way out" of Vietnam—"a place where we ought not be," and where "the situation is rapidly going out of control." But the next day, Johnson announced his decision to add forty-four American combat battalions to the relatively small U.S. contingents already there. He had not been deaf to Mansfield's pleas, nor had he simply swallowed the Pentagon's plans. He had waffled and agonized during his nineteen months in the White House, but eventually this was his final judgment. As he would later explain: "There are many, many people who can recommend and advise, and a few of them consent. But there is only one who has been chosen by the American people to decide."

a. Karnow writes that Senators Mansfield and Russell continued to try to convince President Johnson to avoid further involvement in Vietnam, "a place where we ought not to be" they felt. (327).

b. Though Johnson received advice from many, in particular Senators Mansfield and Russell, he believed the weight of the decision to become further engaged in Vietnam was solely his as the one " 'chosen by the American people to decide' "(Karnow 327).

c. On July 28, 1965, Johnson announced his decision to add forty-four battalions to the troops already in Vietnam, ending his waffling and agonizing of the past nineteen months of his presidency. (Karnow 357)

d. Karnow explains that LBJ took his responsibility to make decisions about Vietnam seriously (327). Although Johnson knew that many would offer suggestions, only he had " 'been chosen by the American people to decide' " (Karnow 327).   ■ ■

ORGANIZING THE PAPER

Armed with an understanding of writing strategies to avoid plagiarism, you are now almost ready to draft your essay. Follow these steps to get organized to write:

1. *Arrange notes (or your annotated sources) by the labels you have used and read them through.* You may discover that some notes or marked sections of sources now seem irrelevant. Set them aside, but do not throw them away yet. Some further reading and note taking may also be necessary to fill in gaps that have become apparent.

2. *Reexamine your tentative claim or research proposal.* As a result of reading and reflection, do you need to alter or modify your claim in any way? Or, if you began with a research question, what now is your answer to the question? Is, for example, TV violence harmful to children?

3. *Decide on the claim that will direct your writing.* To write a unified essay with a "reason for being," you need a claim that meets these criteria:

   • It is a complete sentence, not a topic or statement of purpose.

   TOPIC: Rape on college campuses.

   CLAIM: There are steps that both students and administrators can take to reduce incidents of campus rape.

- It is limited and focused.

UNFOCUSED:	Prohibition affected the 1920s in many ways.
FOCUSED:	Prohibition was more acceptable to rural than urban areas because of differences in values, social patterns, cultural backgrounds, and the economic result of prohibiting liquor sales.

- It establishes a new or interesting approach to the topic that makes your research meaningful.

NOT INVENTIVE:	A regional shopping mall should not be built next to the Manassas Battlefield.
INVENTIVE:	Putting aside an appeal to our national heritage, one can say, simply, that there is no economic justification for the building of a shopping mall next to the Manassas Battlefield.

4. *Write down the organization that emerges from your labels and grouping of sources, and compare this with your preliminary plan.* If there are differences, justify those changes to yourself. Consider: Does the new, fuller plan provide a complete and logical development of your claim?

DRAFTING THE ESSAY

Plan Your Time

How much time will you need to draft your essay? Working with sources and taking care with documentation make research paper writing more time-consuming than writing an undocumented essay. You also need to allow time between completing the draft and revising. Do not try to draft, revise, and proof an essay all in one day.

Handle In-Text Documentation as You Draft

The Modern Language Association (MLA) recommends that writers prepare their Works Cited page(s) *before* drafting their essay. With this important information prepared correctly and next to you as you draft, you will be less likely to make errors in documentation that will result in a plagiarized essay. Although you may believe that stopping to include parenthetical documentation as you write will cramp your writing, you really cannot try to insert the documentation after completing the writing. The risk of failing to document accurately is too great to chance. Parenthetical documentation is brief; listen to the experts and take the time to include it as you compose.

You saw some models of documentation in Chapter 12. In Chapter 14, you have complete guidelines and models for in-text (parenthetical) documentation and then many models for the complete citations of sources. Study the information in Chapter 14 and then draft your Works Cited page(s) as part of your preparation for writing.

Choose an Appropriate Writing Style

Specific suggestions for composing the parts of your paper follow, but first here are some general guidelines for research essay style.

Use the Proper Person

Research papers are written primarily in the third person *(she, he, it, they)* to create objectivity and to direct attention to the content of the paper. The question is over the appropriateness of the first person *(I, we)*. Although you want to avoid writing "as *you* can see," do not try to avoid the use of *I* if you need to distinguish your position from the views of others. It is better to write "I" than "it is the opinion of this writer" or "the researcher learned" or "this project analyzed." On the other hand, avoid qualifiers such as "I think." Just state your ideas.

Use the Proper Tense

When you are writing about people, ideas, or events of the past, the appropriate tense is the past tense. When writing about current times, the appropriate tense is the present. Both tenses may occur in the same paragraph, as the following paragraph illustrates:

> Fifteen years ago "personal" computers were all but unheard of. Computers were regarded as unknowable, building-sized mechanized monsters that required a precise 68 degree air-conditioned environment and eggheaded technicians with thick glasses and white lab coats scurrying about to keep the temperamental and fragile egos of the electronic brains mollified. Today's generation of computers is accessible, affordable, commonplace, and much less mysterious. The astonishing progress made in computer technology in the last few years has made computers practical, attainable, and indispensable. Personal computers are here to stay.

In the above example, when the student moves from computers in the past to computers in the present, he shifts tenses accurately.

When writing about sources, the convention is to use the present tense *even* for works or authors from the past. The idea is that the source, or the author, *continues* to make the point or use the technique into the present—that is, every time there is a reader. So, write "Lincoln selects the biblical expression 'Fourscore and seven years ago'" and "King echoes Lincoln when he writes 'five score years ago.'"

Avoid Excessive Quoting

Many students use too many direct quotations. Plan to use your own words most of the time for these good reasons:

- Constantly shifting between your words and the language of your sources (not to mention all those quotation marks) makes reading your essay difficult.
- This is your paper and should sound like you.
- When you take a passage out of its larger context, you face the danger of misrepresenting the writer's views.
- When you quote endlessly, readers may begin to think either that you are lazy or that you don't really understand the issues well enough to put them in your own words. You don't want to present either image to your readers.
- You do not prove any point by quoting another person's opinion. All you indicate is that there is someone else who shares your views. Even if that person is an expert on the topic, your quoted material still represents the view of only one person. You support a claim with reasons and evidence, both of which can usually be presented in your own words.

When you must quote, keep the quotations brief, weave them carefully into your own sentences, and be sure to identify the author in a signal phrase. Study the guidelines for handling quotations on pages 25–28 for models of correct form and style.

Write Effective Beginnings

The best introduction is one that presents your subject in an interesting way to gain the reader's attention, states your claim, and gives the reader an indication of the scope and limits of your paper. In a short research essay, you may be able to combine an attention-getter, a statement of subject, and a claim in one paragraph. More typically, especially in longer papers, the introduction will expand to two or three paragraphs. In the physical and social sciences, the claim may be withheld until the conclusion, but the opening introduces the subject and presents the researcher's hypothesis, often posed as a question. Since students sometimes have trouble with research paper introductions in spite of knowing these general guidelines, several specific approaches are illustrated here:

1. In the opening to her study of car advertisements, a student, relating her topic to what readers know, reminds readers of the culture's concern with image:

    > Many Americans are highly image conscious. Because the "right" look is
    >
    > essential to a prosperous life, no detail is too small to overlook. Clichés about
    >
    > first impressions remind us that "you never get a second chance to make a
    >
    > first impression," so we obsessively watch our weight, firm our muscles, sculpt

our hair, select our friends, find the perfect houses, and buy our automobiles. Realizing the importance of image, companies compete to make the "right" products, that is, those that will complete the "right" image. Then advertisers direct specific products to targeted groups of consumers. Although targeting may be labeled as stereotyping, it has been an effective strategy in advertising.

2. Terms and concepts central to your project need defining early in your paper, especially if they are challenged or qualified in some way by your study. This opening paragraph demonstrates an effective use of definition:

> William Faulkner braids a universal theme, the theme of initiation, into the fiber of his novel *Intruder in the Dust*. From ancient times to the present, a prominent focus of literature, of life, has been rites of passage, particularly those of childhood to adulthood. Joseph Campbell defines rites of passage as "distinguished by formal, and usually very severe, exercises of severance." A "candidate" for initiation into adult society, Campbell explains, experiences a shearing away of the "attitudes, attachments and life patterns" of childhood (9). This severe, painful stripping away of the child and installation of the adult is presented somewhat differently in several works by American writers.

3. Begin with a thought-provoking question. A student, arguing that the media both reflect and shape reality, started with these questions:

> Do the media just reflect reality, or do they also shape our perceptions of reality? The answer to this seemingly "chicken-and-egg" question is: They do both.

4. Beginning with important, perhaps startling, facts, evidence, or statistics is an effective way to introduce a topic, provided the details are relevant to the topic. Observe the following example:

> Teenagers are working again, but not on their homework. Over 40 percent of teenagers have jobs by the time they are juniors (Samuelson A22). And their jobs do not support academic learning since almost two-thirds of teenagers are employed in sales and service jobs that entail mostly carrying, cleaning, and wrapping (Greenberger and Steinberg 62–67), not reading, writing, and computing. Unfortunately, the negative effect on learning is not offset by improved opportunities for future careers.

Avoid Ineffective Openings

Follow these rules for avoiding openings that most readers find ineffective or annoying.

1. *Do not restate the title* or write as if the title were the first sentence in paragraph 1. It is a convention of writing to have the first paragraph stand independent of the title.
2. *Do not begin with "clever" visuals* such as artwork or fancy lettering.
3. *Do not begin with humor* unless it is part of your topic.
4. *Do not begin with a question that is just a gimmick, or one that a reader may answer in a way you do not intend.* Asking "What are the advantages of solar energy?" may lead a reader to answer "None that I can think of." A straightforward research question ("Is *Death of a Salesman* a tragedy?") is appropriate.
5. *Do not open with an unnecessary definition quoted from a dictionary.* "According to Webster, solar energy means . . ." is a tired, overworked beginning that does not engage readers.
6. *Do not start with a purpose statement:* "This paper will examine . . ." Although a statement of purpose is a necessary part of a report of empirical research, a report still needs an interesting introduction.

Compose Solid, Unified Paragraphs

As you compose the body of your paper, keep in mind that you want to (1) maintain unity and coherence, (2) guide readers clearly through source material, and (3) synthesize source material and your own ideas. Do not settle for paragraphs in which facts from notes are just loosely run together. Review the following discussion and study the examples to see how to craft effective body paragraphs.

Provide Unity and Coherence

You achieve paragraph unity when every sentence in a paragraph relates to and develops the paragraph's main idea. Unity, however, does not automatically produce coherence; that takes attention to wording. Coherence is achieved when readers can follow the connection between one sentence and another and between each sentence and the main idea. Strategies for achieving coherence include repetition of key words, the use of pronouns that clearly refer to those key words, and the use of transition and connecting words. Observe these strategies at work in the following paragraph:

> Perhaps the most important differences between the initiations of Robin
>
> and Biff and that experienced by Chick are the facts that Chick's epiphany does
>
> not come all at once and it does not devastate him. Chick
>
> learns about adulthood —and enters adulthood —piecemeal and with support.

His first eye-opening experience occurs as he tries to pay Lucas for dinner and

is rebuffed (15–16). Chick learns, after trying again to buy a clear conscience,

the impropriety and affront of his actions (24). Lucas teaches Chick how he

should resolve his dilemma by setting him "free" (26–27). Later, Chick feels out-

rage at the adults crowding into the town, presumably to see a lynching, then

disgrace and shame as they eventually flee (196–97, 210).

Coherence is needed not only within paragraphs but between paragraphs as well. You need to guide readers through your paper, connecting paragraphs and showing relationships by the use of transitions. The following opening sentences of four paragraphs from a paper on solutions to rape on the college campus illustrate smooth transitions:

¶ 3 Specialists have provided a number of reasons why men rape.

¶ 4 Some of the causes of rape on the college campus originate with the

colleges themselves and with how they handle the problem.

¶ 5 Just as there are a number of causes for campus rapes, there are a

number of ways to help solve the problem of these rapes.

¶ 6 If these seem like commonsense solutions, why, then, is it so difficult to

significantly reduce the number of campus rapes?

Without awkwardly writing "Here are some of the causes" and "Here are some of the solutions," the student guides her readers through a discussion of causes for and solutions to the problem of campus rape.

Guide Readers Through Source Material

To understand the importance of guiding readers through source material, consider first the following paragraph from a paper on the British coal strike in the 1970s:

The social status of the coal miners was far from good. The country

blamed them for the dimmed lights and the three-day workweek. They had

been placed in the position of social outcasts and were beginning to "con-

sider themselves another country." Some businesses and shops had even

gone so far as to refuse service to coal miners (Jones 32).

Who has learned that the coal miners felt ostracized or that the country blamed them? As readers we cannot begin to judge the validity of these assertions without some context provided by the writer. Most readers are put off by an unattached direct quotation or some startling observation that is documented

correctly but given no context within the paper. Using signal phrases that identify the author of the source and, when useful, the author's credentials helps
guide readers through the source material. The following revision of the paragraph above provides not only context but also sentence variety:

> The social acceptance of coal miners, according to Peter Jones, British
>
> correspondent for *Newsweek*, was far from good. From interviews both in
>
> London shops and in pubs near Birmingham, Jones concluded that Britishers
>
> blamed the miners for the dimmed lights and three-day workweek. Several
>
> striking miners, in a pub on the outskirts of Birmingham, asserted that some
>
> of their friends had been denied service by shopkeepers and that they
>
> "consider[ed] themselves another country" (32).

Select Appropriate Signal Phrases

When you use signal phrases, try to vary both the words you use and their
place in the sentence. Look, for example, at the first sentence in the sample
paragraph above. The signal phrase is placed in the middle of the sentence and
is set off by commas. The sentence could have been written two other ways:

> The social acceptance of coal miners was far from good, according to Peter
>
> Jones, British correspondent for *Newsweek*.

OR

> According to Peter Jones, British correspondent for *Newsweek*, the social
>
> acceptance of coal miners was far from good.

Whenever you provide a name and perhaps credentials for your source, you
have these three sentence patterns to choose from. Make a point to use all three
options in your paper. Word choice can be varied as well. Instead of writing
"Peter Jones says" throughout your paper, consider some of these verb choices:

Jones *asserts*	Jones *contends*	Jones *attests to*
Jones *states*	Jones *thinks*	Jones *points out*
Jones *concludes*	Jones *stresses*	Jones *believes*
Jones *presents*	Jones *emphasizes*	Jones *agrees with*
Jones *argues*	Jones *confirms*	Jones *speculates*

NOTE: Not all the words in this list are synonyms; you cannot substitute
confirms for *believes*. First, select the verb that most accurately conveys
the writer's relationship to his or her material. Then, when appropriate, vary
word choice as well as sentence structure.

Readers need to be told how to respond to the sources used. They need to know which sources you accept as reliable and which you disagree with, and they need you to distinguish clearly between fact and opinion. Ideas and opinions from sources need signal phrases and then some discussion from you.

Synthesize Source Material and Your Own Ideas

A smooth synthesis of source material is aided by signal phrases and parenthetical documentation because they mark the beginning and ending of material taken from a source. But a complete synthesis requires something more: your ideas about the source and the topic. To illustrate, consider the problems in another paragraph from the British coal strike paper:

> Some critics believed that there was enough coal in Britain to maintain
>
> enough power to keep industry at a near-normal level for thirty-five weeks
>
> (Jones 30). Prime Minister Heath, on the other hand, had placed the coun-
>
> try's usable coal supply at 15.5 million tons (Jones 30). He stated that this
>
> would have fallen to a critical 7 million tons within a month had he not
>
> declared a three-day workweek (Jones 31).

This paragraph is a good example of random details strung together for no apparent purpose. How much coal did exist? Whose figures were right? And what purpose do these figures serve in the paper's development? Note that the entire paragraph is developed with material from one source. Do sources other than Jones offer a different perspective? This paragraph is weak for several reasons: (1) It lacks a controlling idea (topic sentence) to give it purpose and direction; (2) it relies for development entirely on one source; (3) it lacks any discussion or analysis by the writer.

By contrast, the following paragraph demonstrates a successful synthesis:

> Of course, the iridium could have come from other extraterrestrial
>
> sources besides an asteroid. One theory, put forward by Dale Russell, is that
>
> the iridium was produced outside the solar system by an exploding star (500).
>
> Such an explosion, Russell states, could have blown the iridium either off the
>
> surface of the moon or directly from the star itself (500–01), while also pro-
>
> ducing a deadly blast of heat and gamma rays (Krishtalka 19). This theory seems
>
> to explain the traces of iridium in the mass extinction, but it does not explain
>
> why smaller mammals, crocodiles, and birds survived (Wilford 220).
>
> So the supernova theory took a backseat to the other extraterrestrial theories:
>
> those of asteroids and comets colliding with the Earth. The authors of the

book *The Great Extinction,* Michael Allaby and James Lovelock, subtitled their work *The Solution to . . . the Disappearance of the Dinosaurs.* Their theory: an asteroid or comet collided with Earth around sixty-five million years ago, killing billions of organisms, and thus altering the course of evolution (157). The fact that the theory of collision with a cosmic body warrants a book calls for some thought: Is the asteroid or comet theory merely sensationalism, or is it rooted in fact? Paleontologist Leonard Krishtalka declares that few paleontologists have accepted the asteroid theory, himself calling "some catastrophic theories . . . small ideas injected with growth hormone" (22). However, other scientists, such as Allaby and Lovelock, see the cosmic catastrophic theory as a solid one based on more than guesswork (10–11).

This paragraph's synthesis is accomplished by several strategies: (1) The paragraph has a controlling idea; (2) the paragraph combines information from several sources; (3) the information is presented in a blend of paraphrase and short quotations; (4) information from the different sources is clearly indicated to readers; and (5) the student explains and discusses the information.

You might also observe the different lengths of the two sample paragraphs just presented. Although the second paragraph is long, it is not unwieldy because it achieves unity and coherence. By contrast, body paragraphs of only three sentences are probably in trouble.

Write Effective Conclusions

Sometimes ending a paper seems even more difficult than beginning one. You know you are not supposed to just stop, but every ending that comes to mind sounds more corny than clever. If you have trouble, try one of these types of endings:

1. Do not just repeat your claim exactly as it was stated in paragraph 1, but expand on the original wording and emphasize the claim's significance. Here is the conclusion of the solar energy paper:

    > The idea of using solar energy is not as far-fetched as it seemed years ago. With the continued support of government plus the enthusiasm of research groups, environmentalists, and private industry, solar energy may become a household word quite soon. With the increasing cost of fossil fuel, the time could not be better for exploring this use of the sun.

2. End with a quotation that effectively summarizes and drives home the point of your paper. Researchers are not always lucky enough to find the

ideal quotation for ending a paper. If you find a good one, use it. Better
yet, present the quotation and then add your comment in a sentence or
two. The conclusion to a paper on the dilemma of defective newborns is a
good example:

> Dr. Joseph Fletcher is correct when he says that "every advance in medi-
> cal capabilities is an increase in our moral responsibility" (48). In a world of
> many gray areas, one point is clear. From an ethical point of view, medicine is
> a victim of its own success.

3. If you have researched an issue or problem, emphasize your proposed
    solutions in the concluding paragraph. The student opposing a mall
    adjacent to the Manassas Battlefield concluded with several solutions:

> Whether the proposed mall will be built is clearly in doubt at the
> moment. What are the solutions to this controversy? One approach is, of
> course, not to build the mall at all. To accomplish this solution, now, with the
> re-zoning having been approved, probably requires an act of Congress to buy
> the land and make it part of the national park. Another solution, one that
> would please the county and the developer and satisfy citizens objecting to
> traffic problems, is to build the needed roads before the mall is completed.
> A third approach is to allow the office park of the original plan to be built,
> but not the mall. The local preservationists had agreed to this original devel-
> opment proposal, but now that the issue has received national attention,
> they may no longer be willing to compromise. Whatever the future of the
> William Center, the present plan for a new regional mall is not acceptable.

Avoid Ineffective Conclusions

Follow these rules to avoid conclusions that most readers consider ineffective
and annoying.

1. *Do not introduce a new idea.* If the point belongs in your paper, you should
    have introduced it earlier.
2. *Do not just stop or trail off,* even if you feel as though you have run out of
    steam. A simple, clear restatement of the claim is better than no conclusion.
3. *Do not tell your reader what you have accomplished:* "In this paper I have
    explained the advantages of solar energy by examining the costs. . . ." If
    you have written well, your reader knows what you have accomplished.

4. *Do not offer apologies or expressions of hope.* "Although I wasn't able to find as much on this topic as I wanted, I have tried to explain the advantages of solar energy, and I hope that you will now understand why we need to use it more" is a disastrous ending.

Choose an Effective Title

Give some thought to your paper's title since that is what your reader sees first and what your work will be known by. A good title provides information and creates interest. Make your title informative by making it specific. If you can create interest through clever wording, so much the better. But do not confuse "cutesiness" with clever wording. Review the following examples of acceptable and unacceptable titles:

VAGUE:	A Perennial Issue Unsolved
	(There are many; which one is this paper about?)
BETTER:	The Perennial Issue of Press Freedom Versus Press Responsibility
TOO BROAD:	Earthquakes
	(What about earthquakes? This title is not informative.)
BETTER:	The Need for Earthquake Prediction
TOO BROAD:	*The Scarlet Letter*
	(Never use just the title of the work under discussion; you can use the work's title as a part of a longer title of your own.)
BETTER:	Color Symbolism in *The Scarlet Letter*
CUTESY:	Babes in Trouble
	(The slang "Babes" makes this title seem insensitive rather than clever.)
BETTER:	The Dilemma of Defective Newborns

REVISING THE PAPER: A CHECKLIST

After completing a first draft, catch your breath and then gear up for the next step in the writing process: revision. Revision actually involves three separate steps: *rewriting*—adding or deleting text, or moving parts of the draft around; *editing*—a rereading to correct errors from misspellings to incorrect documentation format; and then *proofreading* the typed copy. If you treat these as separate steps, you will do a more complete job of revision—and get a better grade on your paper!

Rewriting

Read your draft through and make changes as a result of answering the following questions:

Purpose and Audience
- ☐ Is my draft long enough to meet assignment requirements and my purpose?
- ☐ Are terms defined and concepts explained appropriately for my audience?

Content
- ☐ Do I have a clearly stated thesis—the claim of my argument?
- ☐ Have I presented sufficient evidence to support my claim?
- ☐ Are there any irrelevant sections that should be deleted?

Structure
- ☐ Are paragraphs ordered to develop my topic logically?
- ☐ Does the content of each paragraph help develop my claim?
- ☐ Is everything in each paragraph on the same subtopic to create paragraph unity?
- ☐ Do body paragraphs have a balance of information and analysis, of source material and my own ideas?
- ☐ Are there any paragraphs that should be combined? Are there any very long paragraphs that should be divided? (Check for unity.)

Editing

Make revisions guided by your responses to the questions, make a clean copy, and read again. This time, pay close attention to sentences, words, and documentation format. Use the following questions to guide editing.

Coherence
- ☐ Have connecting words been used and key terms repeated to produce paragraph coherence?
- ☐ Have transitions been used to show connections between paragraphs?

Sources
- ☐ Have I paraphrased instead of quoted whenever possible?
- ☐ Have I used signal phrases to create a context for source material?
- ☐ Have I documented all borrowed material, whether quoted or paraphrased?
- ☐ Are parenthetical references properly placed after borrowed material?

Style
- ☐ Have I varied sentence length and structure?
- ☐ Have I avoided long quotations?
- ☐ Do I have correct form for quotations? For titles?

☐ Is my language specific and descriptive?

☐ Have I avoided inappropriate shifts in tense or person?

☐ Have I removed any wordiness, deadwood, trite expressions, or clichés?

☐ Have I used specialized terms correctly?

☐ Have I avoided contractions as too informal for most research papers?

☐ Have I maintained an appropriate style and tone for academic work?

Proofreading

When your editing is finished, prepare a completed draft of your paper according to the format described and illustrated below. Then proofread the completed copy, making any corrections neatly in ink. If a page has several errors, print a corrected copy. Be sure to make a copy of the paper for yourself before submitting the original to your instructor.

THE COMPLETED PAPER

Your research paper should be double-spaced throughout (including the Works Cited page) with 1-inch margins on all sides. Your project will contain the following parts, in this order:

1. *A title page,* with your title, your name, your instructor's name, the course name or number, and the date, neatly centered, if an outline follows. If there is no outline, place this information at the top left of the first page.

2. *An outline,* or statement of purpose, if required.

3. *The body or text of your paper.* Number all pages consecutively, including pages of works cited, using arabic numerals. Place numbers in the upper right-hand corner of each page. Include your last name before each page number.

4. *A list of works cited,* placed on a separate page(s) after the text. Title the first page "Works Cited." (Do not use the title "Bibliography.")

SAMPLE STUDENT ESSAY IN MLA STYLE

The following paper illustrates an argumentative essay using sources documented in MLA style.

Donaldson 1

David Donaldson

Professor Princiotto-Gorrell/Professor Stevens

English 203U—Research Process

7 July 2011

Tell Us What You Really Are: The Debate over

Labeling Genetically Modified Food

The decision to eat—or not to eat—genetically modified (GM) food is a relatively new dilemma for consumers. People have been going to the grocery store for years, and up until the mid-1990s there was little question as to what they were buying. Consumers knew that when they picked up a tomato, that product was in fact a tomato, not a tomato that had been spliced, or merged, with the genes of some other organism in an attempt to get it to behave like an entirely different fruit. There were most definitely food additives, preservatives, and other questionable ingredients up until then, but before 1994, a tomato was still a tomato. Food additives, preservatives, potentially allergenic ingredients, and possibly toxic ingredients must be labeled on each product. Until GM food is proven to be safe it is essential that the federal government also require labeling to denote the presence of genetically modified organisms (GMOs). Safety is not the only factor in the GM food debate. Religious and cultural concerns, as well as the consumer's freedom of choice, must be considered when deciding whether to label GM foods.

The genetic modification of food is defined by MacDonald and Whellams as "any change to the heritable traits of an organism achieved by intentional manipulation" (181). Or, more specifically, defined by Sarah Kirby as "the process of removing individual genes from one organism and transplanting them into another organism," it is the basis of contemporary bioengineering (352). Although there are scientists and government officials who want to equate genetic modification with genetic hybridization, the

Provide last name with page number at top right of each page.

Use heading on top left when a separate title page is not used.

Center title.

Indent paragraphs 5 spaces.

Double-space throughout.

Clear opening leads to student's thesis.

Key term defined.

Donaldson 2

definitions given for genetic modification do not match the definition of genetic hybridization.

It is true that plant and animal hybridization has been going on for a long time. That is how many of the flora and fauna here today were conceived. They did not just show up as they are today; rather, over time they evolved into what they are now due to progressive variations in their genes. As explained by Gundorf and Huchingson, scientists used selective breeding to achieve a desired trait, or to suppress a trait deemed undesirable (233). Kirby expands on Gudorf and Huchingson's idea by adding that selective breeding was more natural since "it was restricted to two organisms that are able to breed together" (352). In "A Defense of the U.S. Position on Labeling Genetically Modified Organisms," Sally Kirsch adds that the United States Food and Drug Administration (FDA) even cites the longevity of selective breeding to justify their stance that nothing is wrong or unsafe about GM food (25).

Bioengineering has been seen as the answer to many of the environmental issues related to climate change, to help feed growing populations in developing countries. Scientists have created "drought resistant corn and soybeans," rice with increased nutrients, and "pest resistant plants" (Kirsch 21). However, for more cosmetic reasons, they have also created the FLAVR SAVR™ tomato. This tomato would eventually become the first GM food available to consumers. The *Gale Encyclopedia of Science* article "Plant Breeding" explains that it was not until 1992 that "a tomato with delayed ripening became the first genetically modified (GM) commercial food crop" (3375). Two years later, the company Calgene received approval from the FDA to sell their FLAVR SAVR™ tomatoes (Martineau 189). Kirsch notes that there was a lukewarm public greeting for Calgene's tomato, and the underwhelming sales further emphasized that the general public was apprehensive about GM food (21). However, in their article, "'Does Contain' vs. 'Does Not Contain': Does it Matter Which GMO Label is Used?" Crespi

Paragraph developed using paraphrase and direct quotations from several sources.

Donaldson 3

and Marette argue that "Americans are much more accepting of GMOs than the rest of the world" (328).

This is no longer a process simply by which plants are being spliced with plant genes and animals are being spliced with animal genes. Today, bioengineers can create a plant that has been spliced with animal genes (Kirby 357). The health and safety results of the GM process are still relatively unknown as this technology is still new. The uncertainty of this process is fueling the public outcry for GMO labeling in the United States. Anne MacKenzie builds on Kirby's point, arguing that because consumers have become more knowledgeable about food and health, more concerned about the safety of the food supply, have developed a greater desire to know about how their food is made, and have mounted a growing distrust of biotech companies and the government, they want more information about what is going into their food (52).

Student establishes difference between hybridization and genetic modification.

The most noted possible health hazard linked to GM foods is the potential for new or heightened food allergies. MacKenzie, Gudorf and Huchingson, and Kirby all mention new food allergies as one of the more obvious reasons to require the mandatory labeling of GM food. MacKenzie states: "Allergenicity is an important consideration for foods derived through biotechnology because of the possibility of a new protein introduced into a food could be an allergen" (51). She adds that when a food such as soy, a common allergen, is used in the genetic modification process, "life-threatening" results are more likely to occur (51). Gudorf and Huchingson suggest that GM food could be held responsible for the increase in the number of people who have developed food-related allergies in the last decade (233). They also point out that, for example, people do not know specifically which peanut gene may spark their allergy (233). It could be the gene for color, the gene for oil production, or the gene that makes peanuts viable underground that contains the protein that sets off their allergy. If a

Here and below student examines possible problems with GM foods.

Donaldson 4

scientist wants to make a strawberry that grows underground, and inserts
that gene from the peanut into a strawberry's DNA, the same individuals who
are allergic to peanuts could now become allergic to that particular
strawberry (Gudorf and Huchingson 233).

Kirby acknowledges that GM foods may "set-off" allergies, but she adds
that genetic modification could also "produce dangerous toxins, increase
cancer risks, produce antibiotic-resistant pathogens, and damage food quality"
(359). Specifically related to allergies, Kirby explains that "people have never
before been exposed to several of the foreign proteins currently being
genetically spliced into foods" (360). Conversely, Robert Bracket, Director of
the Center for Food Safety and Applied Nutrition, testified before the FDA
that if the genetic modification process were to merge one organism with an
organism that is considered a common food allergen, soy, milk, egg, etc., then
that product would indeed be labeled as containing a common food allergen
as is required by law (FDA). Otherwise, Bracket says, "GM food is safe and
no different than its conventionally grown counterpart," which echoes the
FDA spokesman quoted by MacDonald and Whellams (FDA).

Aside from health concerns, there are also religious and cultural
motives that should be considered when deciding whether to label GM food.
Theologically speaking, Christianity does not necessarily reject GM food. In
"Some Christian Reflections on GM Food," Donald Bruce suggests that the
concern within Christianity is more a moral obligation to God's creation
rather than a dietary issue (119). However, multiple interpretations are
present. Genesis 1: 26–28 basically states that "Christian thinking has
generally seen intervention in the natural world as ordained by God in the
creation of ordinances that grant humans dominion over all the rest of
creation" (Bruce 119). Conversely, there are also Christians who think
that GM food is the result of humans "playing God in wrongly changing what
God has created" (Bruce 121). For Christians who believe that genetically

Donaldson 5

modifying food is wrong, mandatory labeling of GM food would guide them in
their food choices.

For those of the Muslim or Jewish faith, GM food presents dietary
concerns as well as potential moral objections. Ebrahim Moosa cites the splicing
of animal genes into plants as one of the biggest worries Muslims face from GM
food (135). He says that "a tomato containing a gene harvested from a flounder
may not generate repugnance in an observant Muslim, since fish is permissible
for adherents of this tradition, but a potato with a pig gene may well trigger
visceral repugnance" (135). This is the same reason cited by Kirby (357).
To emphasize his point, Moosa tells a story of Muhammad when he lived in
Medina. In the story, Muhammad comes across farmers splicing different
species of date-palm seedlings to increase their crop yields. Muhammad asks
why they did it that way, and they reply: "That was the way they had always
done it." The prophet then replies: "Well, perhaps, it would be better if you
did not" (138). Kirby suggests that animal to plant genetic splicing is also the
reason for those of the Jewish faith, or any vegetarian or vegan, to be
concerned about the absence of mandatory GM food labeling (357). Peter
Sand concurs, stating that providing consumers with information "irrespective
of health concerns," such as labeling halal or kosher food, is essential in
allowing consumers to have genuine freedom of choice (190).

Currently, although about "80% of processed food in the United States
has a component from a genetically modified crop, a new survey finds that
only 26% of Americans think they have ever eaten such food" (Krebs). This
same United States Department of Agriculture (USDA) poll found that 94% of
respondents felt that labeling items that contained GMOs would be a good
idea (Krebs). This figure is up from a 2000 MSNBC poll that shows that "81%
of people who responded were in favor of labeling genetically engineered
products" (Kirsch 21). Kirsch follows that statement by confirming that the
FDA and the biotech industry feel the opposite (21). Kirby repeats this view,

Current FDA position
on GM foods.

Donaldson 6

adding that the FDA recognizes "no material difference in nutrition, composition, or safety between genetically modified food and food that has not been genetically modified" (qtd. in Kirby 353). Additionally, as long as the plant or animal that DNA is taken from and the plant or animal that the DNA is being spliced into are generally recognized as safe (GRAS), then the product is not subject to any sort of review prior to being released to consumers (Kirby 354). The FDA assumes that all products in the current food supply are GRAS. However, the current system does not take into account that the end result of tomato DNA and trout DNA is not simply a "tomato fish," but rather an entirely new entity that could bring with it unforeseen health risks ranging from food allergies to death.

Currently, according to Crespi and Marette, the United States has no mandatory GMO labeling requirement (328). Sand adds that the United States is not alone (187). He lists Canada and Argentina specifically, because combined the three countries are responsible for approximately 80% of the world's GM crops (187). Crespi and Marette add that much of the rest of the world currently recognizes the "precautionary principle," and the potentially deleterious effects of GMOs, and those governments do not want their citizens to be exposed to what might result from the consumption of GMOs (328).

To date, there have been no documented health risks related to GM foods. Proponents of GM food, such as the FDA, use this as the basis for their argument that GM foods pose no threat to consumers, and why mandatory labeling of GM food is unnecessary. An FDA spokesman says: "We have seen no evidence that the bioengineered foods now on the market pose any human health concerns or that they are in any way less safe than crops produced through traditional breeding" (qtd. in MacDonald and Whellams 184–185). While the tone throughout their article suggests that they disagree, MacDonald and Whellams argue that there is nothing unethical about GM foods that should result in mandatory labeling (184). Anne MacKenzie, the Associate Vice-

Donaldson 7

President of Science Evaluation for The Canadian Food Inspection Agency, concurs by saying that regulators have not yet noticed a "significant toxic or allergenic harm" (52). However, as stated by MacDonald and Whellams, many other countries choose to adopt the "precautionary principle" (185). This principle states that if something, like GM food, presents a potential threat to health or the environment, it is best to be cautious and to take action even if science hasn't demonstrated harmful effects (MacDonald and Whellams 185).

Because there may be serious, long-term negative implications on consumer health as a result of the continued consumption of GMOs, biotech companies, governments, and consumers should all be more wary of GM foods (MacDonald and Whellams 185). The "precautionary principle" is law in the European Union, as they consider unknown risk sufficient to require further study before approval. The United States takes the position that if something is not demonstrated to be harmful, then there is no problem in moving forward with implementation ("Precautionary Principle"). There is strong opposition from the United States's Chamber of Commerce to the Precautionary Principle; the Chamber argues that potential but unknown risk should not stand in the way of progress ("Precautionary Principle").

The United States currently operates under a voluntary labeling program (Sand 187), including labeling of foods with GMOs and those without GMOs. However, when Marion Nestle searched for labeling of foods with GMOs, she was not surprised that her search was unsuccessful. Nestle states: "Scientifically based or not, the motivation of the biotechnology companies for opposing labeling is obvious: if the foods are labeled as GM, you might choose not to buy them" (57). The FDA's voluntary labeling program for products that do not contain GMOs can be seen at the grocery store today in products that carry a GMO-free label. The question that remains is whether "GMO-free" labels offer consumers a fully informed choice.

Donaldson 8

The lack of a mandatory labeling system in the U.S. is not because no

Attempts to get GM
foods labeled.
one has tried. In 1999, Congressman Dennis Kucinich (D-OH) introduced into

Congress the "Genetically Engineered Food Right to Know Act" (Kirsch

26–27). The aim of this bill was to require food that contained GM material,

or was comprised of GM material, to be labeled as such (Kirsch 27). Kirby

explains that this bill would have required that "food produced with GM

material be labeled at each stage of the food production process," in order to

mitigate cross contamination (367). This bill would have made it necessary to

put a label on GM products that reads: "GENETICALLY ENGINEERED

UNITED STATES GOVERNMENT NOTICE: THIS PRODUCT CONTAINS A

GENETICALLY ENGINEERED MATERIAL OR WAS PRODUCED WITH A

GENETICALLY ENGINEERED MATERIAL" (Kirsch 27). Heather Carr adds

that Congressman Kucinich has introduced this bill into multiple sessions of

Congress, including as recently as 2010, never to make it out of committee.

Although support increased in the House of Representatives, it has never

been enough to move the bill through.

In 2000, Senator Barbara Boxer (D-CA) introduced a similar bill that

would have required a label stating: "GENETICALLY ENGINEERED. THIS

PRODUCT CONTAINS A GENETICALLY ENGINEERED MATERIAL"

(Kirsch 27). Like the House bill, this bill never came to fruition. The FDA

maintains that GM food is safe, and because of this, biotech companies say

that there is no need to liken their products to potentially dangerous

products (such as cigarettes or alcohol) with what resembles a warning label.

Anne MacKenzie disagrees with the biotech companies, arguing that

"consumers have a right to know" what they are eating, and how it was made

(50). She suggests that mandatory consumer-friendly labeling be used, but

that the labels should communicate in a way that does not mislead consumers

into thinking that GM food is any different from non-GM food (50–52). She

also asserts that the label "should not imply that the consumption of food

Donaldson 9

derived through biotechnology has implications for public health," since currently there is no concrete evidence that GM food is either good or bad for human consumption (52). MacDonald and Whellams proffer that if this were done properly, it would be possible to label GM food while at the same time addressing the biotech companies' concern that GM food labels would "be seen as a warning" (183).

While MacKenzie is in favor of mandatory labeling, Lars Bracht Andersen remains apprehensive. Andersen, while supporting a consumer's right to know, also understands the biotech industry's view that "mandatory labeling, given predominantly negative consumer perceptions, is likely to effectively remove GM foods from the market" (143). He argues for voluntary labeling, stating that it would have the "least negative impact on the diversity of the market" (143). However, since voluntary labeling alone seems unlikely to protect consumers and provide adequate choice, mandatory labeling of GMO-free products and of those products that contain GMOs is essential.

Student rejects voluntary labeling and repeats his thesis that GM foods need mandatory labeling.

Donaldson 10

Works Cited

Andersen, Lars Bracht. "The EU Rules on Labeling of Genetically Modified

Foods: Mission Accomplished?" *European Food & Feed Law Review* 5.3

(2010): 136–43. *Academic Search Complete.* Web. 2 June 2011.

Bruce, Donald. "Some Christian Reflections on GM Food." *Boundaries:*

Religious Traditions And Genetically Modified Foods. Ed. Conrad G. Brunk and

Harold Coward. Albany: State U of New York P, 2009. Print.

Carr, Heather. "Genetically Engineered Organism Liability Act of 2010 H.R. 5579."

Eat Drink Better. Important Media Network, 4 Aug. 2010. Web. 18 June 2011.

Clemmitt, M. "Global Food Crisis: What's Causing the Rising Prices?" *CQ*

Researcher 18.24 (2008): 553–76. *CQ Researcher.* Web. 29 May 2011.

Crespi, John M., and Stephan Marette. "'Does Contain' vs. 'Does Not

Contain': Does It Matter Which GMO Label Is Used?" *European Journal of*

Law and Economics 16.3 (2003): 327–44. *SpringerLink.* Web. 12 June 2011.

Davison, John. "GM Plants: Science, Politics, and EC Regulations." *Plant*

Science 178.2 (2010): 94–98. *ScienceDirect.* Web. 8 June 2011.

Gudorf, Christine E., and James E. Huchingson. *Boundaries: A Casebook in*

Environmental Ethics. Washington D.C.: Georgetown UP, 2010. Print.

Kirby, Sarah. "Genetically Modified Foods: More Reasons to Label Than Not."

Drake Journal of Agricultural Law 6.2 (2001): 351–68. *HeinOnline.* Web. 12 June

2011.

Kirsch, Sally R. "A Defense of the U.S. Position on Labeling Genetically

Modified Organisms." *International and Comparative Environmental Law* 1.1

(2000): 21–28. *HeinOnline.* Web. 9 June 2011.

Krebs, Al. "New Poll—94% of Americans Want Labels on GE Food." *Organic*

Consumers Association. Oct. 2003. Web. 9 June 2011.

MacDonald, Chris, and Melissa Whellams. "Corporate Decisions about

Labeling Genetically Modified Foods." *Journal of Business Ethics* 75.2

(2007): 181–89. *JSTOR.* Web. 8 June 2011.

Continue to number pages consecutively.

Start a new page for Works Cited.

Double-space throughout.

List sources alphabetically.

Use hanging indentation.

Donaldson 11

Mackenzie, Anne A. "International Efforts to Label Food Derived Through
     Biotechnology." *Governing Food: Science, Safety, and Trade.* Ed. Peter W. B.
     Phillips and Robert Wolfe. Montreal: McGill–Queen's UP, 2001.
     49–61. Print.

Martineau, Belinda. *First Fruit: The Creation of the Flavr Savr™ Tomato and the
     Birth of Genetically Engineered Food.* New York: McGraw, 2001. Print.

Moosa, Ebrahim. "Genetically Modified Foods and Muslim Ethics." *Boundaries:
     Religious Traditions and Genetically Modified Foods.* Ed. Conrad G. Brunk and
     Harold Coward. Albany: State U of New York P, 2009. Print.

Nestle, Marion. *What to Eat.* New York: North Point, 2006. Print.

"Plant Breeding." *The Gale Encyclopedia of Science.* Ed. K. Lee Lerner and
     Brenda Wilmoth Lerner. 4th ed. Vol. 4. Detroit: Gale, 2008. 3370–75.
     Gale Virtual Reference Library. Web. 29 May 2011.

Sand, Peter H. "Labelling Genetically Modified Food: The Right to Know."
     Review of European Community & International Environmental Law 15.2
     (2006): 185–92. *Wiley Online Library.* Web. 9 June 2011.

U.S. Chamber of Commerce. "Precautionary Principle." U.S. Chamber of
     Commerce, 2011. Web. 9 June 2011.

U.S. Food and Drug Administration. "Bioengineered Foods." Statement of
     Robert E. Brackett to the FDA. U.S. Food and Drug Administration. 15
     July 2009. Web. 18 June 2011.

Weasel, Lisa H. *Food Fray.* New York: AMACOM, 2009. Print.

CHAPTER 14

Formal Documentation:
MLA Style, APA Style

n Chapter 12 you were shown, in sample bibliography cards, what information about a source you need to prepare the documentation for a researched essay. In Chapter 13 you were shown in-text documentation patterns as part of the discussion of avoiding plagiarism and writing effective paragraphs. The format shown is for MLA (Modern Language Association) style, the documentation style used in the humanities. APA (American Psychological Association) style is used in the social sciences. The sciences and other disciplines also have style sheets, but the most common documentation patterns used by undergraduates are MLA and APA, the two patterns explained in this chapter.

Remember that MLA recommends that writers prepare their Works Cited list—a list of all sources they have used—before drafting the essay. This list can then be used as an accurate guide to the in-text/parenthetical documentation that MLA requires along with the Works Cited list at the end of the essay. Heed this good advice. This chapter begins with guidelines for in-text documentation and then provides many models of full documentation for a Works Cited list.

REMEMBER: Never guess at documentation! Always consult this chapter to make each in-text citation and your Works Cited page(s) absolutely correct.

As you now know, MLA documentation style has two parts: in-text references to author and page number and then complete information about each source in a Works Cited list. Because parenthetical references to author and page are incomplete—readers could not find the source with such limited information—all sources referred to by author and page number in the essay require the full details of publication in a Works Cited list that concludes the essay. General guidelines for in-text citations are given below.

NOTE: You need a 100 percent correspondence between the sources listed in your Works Cited and the sources you actually cite (refer to) in your essay. Do not omit from your Works Cited any sources you refer to in your essay. Do not include in your Works Cited any sources not referred to in your paper.

GUIDELINES for Using Parenthetical Documentation

- **The purpose of documentation is to make clear exactly what material in a passage has been borrowed and from what source the borrowed material has come.**
- **Parenthetical in-text documentation requires specific page references for borrowed material—unless the source is not a print one.**

- **Parenthetical documentation is required for both quoted and paraphrased material and for both print and nonprint sources.**
- **Parenthetical documentation provides as brief a citation as possible consistent with accuracy and clarity.**

THE SIMPLEST PATTERNS OF PARENTHETICAL DOCUMENTATION

The simplest in-text citation can be prepared in one of three ways:

1. Give the author's last name (full name in your first reference to the writer) in the text of your essay and put the appropriate page number(s) in parentheses following the borrowed material.

    Frederick Lewis Allen observes that, during the 1920s, urban tastes spread

    to the country (146).

2. Place the author's last name and the appropriate page number(s) in parentheses immediately following the borrowed material.

    During the 1920s, "not only the drinks were mixed, but the company as well"

    (Allen 82).

3. On the rare occasion that you cite an entire work rather than borrowing from a specific passage, give the author's name in the text and omit any page numbers.

    Leonard Sax explains, to both parents and teachers, the specific ways in

    which gender matters.

    Each one of these in-text references is complete *only* when the full citation is placed in the Works Cited section of your paper:

    Allen, Frederick Lewis. *Only Yesterday: An Informal History of the Nineteen-*

    Twenties. New York: Harper, 1931. Print.

    Sax, Leonard. *Why Gender Matters.* New York: Random, 2005. Print.

The three patterns just illustrated should be used in each of the following situations:

1. The source referred to is not anonymous—the author is known.
2. The source referred to is by one author.
3. The source cited is the only work used by that author.
4. No other author in your list of sources has the same last name.

PLACEMENT OF PARENTHETICAL DOCUMENTATION

The simplest placing of an in-text reference is at the end of the sentence *before* the period. When you are quoting, place the parentheses *after* the final quotation mark but still before the period that ends the sentence.

> During the 1920s, "not only the drinks were mixed, but the company as well"
>
> (Allen 82).

> **NOTE:** Do not put any punctuation between the author's name and the page number.

If the borrowed material forms only a part of your sentence, place the parenthetical reference *after* the borrowed material and *before* any subsequent punctuation. This placement more accurately shows readers what is borrowed and what are your own words.

> Sport, Allen observes about the 1920s, had developed into an obsession (66),
>
> another similarity between the 1920s and the 1980s.

If a quoted passage is long enough to require setting off in display form (block quotation), then place the parenthetical reference at the end of the passage, *after* the final period. Remember: Long quotations in display form *do not* have quotation marks.

> It is hard to believe that when he writes about the influence of science Allen
>
> is describing the 1920s, not the 1980s:
>
> > The prestige of science was colossal. The man in the street and the
> >
> > woman in the kitchen, confronted on every hand with new machines and
> >
> > devices which they owed to the laboratory, were ready to believe that
> >
> > science could accomplish almost anything. (164)

And to complete the documentation for all three examples:

Works Cited

Allen, Frederick Lewis. *Only Yesterday: An Informal History of the Nineteen-*

   Twenties. New York: Harper, 1931. Print.

PARENTHETICAL CITATIONS OF COMPLEX SOURCES

Not all sources can be cited in one of the three patterns illustrated above, for not all meet the four criteria listed on p. 314. Works by two or more authors, for example, will need somewhat fuller references. Each sample form of in-text documentation given below must be completed with a full Works Cited reference, as shown above.

Two Authors, Mentioned in the Text

Richard Herrnstein and Charles Murray contend that it is "consistently . . .

advantageous to be smart" (25).

Two Authors, Not Mentioned in the Text

The advantaged smart group forms a "cognitive elite" in our society

(Herrnstein and Murray 26–27).

A Book in Two or More Volumes

Sewall analyzes the role of Judge Lord in Dickinson's life (2: 642–47).

OR

Judge Lord was also one of Dickinson's preceptors (Sewall 2: 642–47).

 NOTE: The number before the colon always signifies the volume number. The number(s) after the colon represents the page number(s).

A Book Listed by Title—Author Unknown

According to *The Concise Dictionary of American Biography,* William Jennings

Bryan's 1896 campaign stressed social and sectional conflicts (117).

The *New York Times*' editors were not pleased with some of the changes in

welfare programs ("Where Welfare Stands" 4: 16).

Always cite the title of the article, not the title of the journal, if the author is unknown. In the second example, the number before the page number is the newspaper's section number.

A Work by a Corporate Author

A report by the Institute of Ecology's Global Ecological Problems Workshop

argues that the civilization of the city can lull us into forgetting our

relationship to the total ecological system on which we depend (13).

Although corporate authors may be cited with the page number within the parentheses, your writing will be more graceful if corporate authors are introduced in the sentence. Then only page numbers go in parentheses.

Two or More Works by the Same Author

During the 1920s, "not only the drinks were mixed, but the company as well"

(Allen, *Only Yesterday* 82).

Frederick Lewis Allen contends that the early 1900s were a period of

complacency in America (*The Big Change* 4–5).

In *The Big Change*, Allen asserts that the early 1900s were a period of

complacency (4–5).

If your list of sources contains two or more works by the same author, the fullest parenthetical citation includes the author's last name, followed by a comma, the work's title, shortened if possible, and the page number. If the author's name appears in the text—or the author and title both appear as in the third example above—omit these items from the parenthetical citation. When you have to include the title to distinguish among sources, it is best to put the author's name in the text.

Two or More Works in One Parenthetical Reference

Several writers about the future agree that big changes will take place in

work patterns (Toffler 384–87; Naisbitt 35–36).

Separate each author with a semicolon. But, if the parenthetical reference becomes disruptively long, cite the works in a "See also" note rather than in the text.

A Source Without Page Numbers

It is usually a good idea to name the nonprint source within your sentence so that readers will not expect to see page numbers.

Although some still disagree, the *Oxford English Dictionary Online* defines

global warming as "thought to be caused by various side-effects of modern

energy consumption."

Complete Publication Information in Parenthetical Reference

At times you may want to give complete information about a source within parentheses in the text of your essay. Then a Works Cited list is not used. Use square brackets for parenthetical information within parentheses. This approach may be a good choice when you use only one source that you refer to several times. Literary analyses are one type of essay for which this approach to citation may be a good choice. For example:

> Edith Wharton establishes the bleakness of her setting, Starkfield, not just
> through description of place but also through her main character, Ethan,
> who is described as "bleak and unapproachable" (*Ethan Frome* [New York:
> Scribner's, 1911, Print] 3. All subsequent references are to this edition). Later
> Wharton describes winter as "shut[ting] down on Starkfield" and negating
> life there (7).

Additional-Information Footnotes or Endnotes

At times you may need to provide additional information that is not central to your argument. These additions belong in a content note. However, use these sparingly and never as a way of advancing your thesis. Many instructors object to content notes and prefer only parenthetical citations.

"See Also" Footnotes or Endnotes

More acceptable is the note that refers to other sources of evidence for or against the point to be established. These notes are usually introduced with "See also" or "Compare," followed by the citation. For example:

> Chekhov's debt to Ibsen should be recognized, as should his debt to other
> playwrights of the 1890s who were concerned with the inner life of their
> characters.[1]

---

[1] See also Eric Bentley, *In Search of Theater* (New York: Vintage, 1959) 330; Walter Bruford, *Anton Chekhov* (New Haven: Yale UP, 1957) 45.

PREPARING MLA CITATIONS FOR A WORKS CITED LIST

The partial in-text citations described and illustrated above must be completed by a full reference in a list given at the end of the essay. To prepare your Works Cited list, alphabetize, by author last name, the sources you have actually referred to and complete each citation according to the forms explained and illustrated in the following pages. The key is to find the appropriate model for each of your sources and then follow the model exactly. (Guidelines for formatting a finished Works Cited page are found on pp. 310–11.) But, you will make fewer errors if you also understand the basic pieces of information needed in citations and the order of that information.

Books require the following information, in the order given, with periods after each of the four major elements:

- Author, last name first.
- Title—and subtitle if there is one—in italics.
- Facts of publication: city of publication, followed by a colon, shortened publisher's name (Norton for W. W. Norton, for example), followed by a comma, and the year of publication, followed by a period.
- Medium of publication: Print.

Author	Title	Facts of Publication	Medium of Publication
Bellow, Saul.	*A Theft*.	New York: Viking-Penguin, 1989.	Print.

Forms for Books: Citing the Complete Book

A Book by a Single Author

Schieff, Stacy. *Cleopatra: A Life*. New York: Little, Brown, 2010. Print.

The subtitle is included, preceded by a colon, even if there is no colon on the book's title page.

A Book by Two or Three Authors

Adkins, Lesley, and Ray Adkins. *The Keys of Egypt: The Race to Crack the*

   Hieroglyph Code. New York: HarperCollins, 2000. Print.

Second (and third) authors' names appear in normal signature order.

A Book with More Than Three Authors

Baker, Susan P., et al. *The Injury Fact Book*. Oxford: Oxford UP, 1992. Print.

Use the name of the first person listed on the title page. The English "and others" may be used instead of "et al." Shorten "University Press" to "UP."

Two or More Works by the Same Author

Goodall, Jane. *In the Shadow of Man*. Boston: Houghton, 1971. Print.

---. *Through a Window: My Thirty Years with the Chimpanzees of Gombe*. Boston:

   Houghton, 1990. Print.

Give the author's full name with the first entry. For the second (and additional works), begin the citation with three hyphens followed by a period. Alphabetize the entries by the books' titles.

A Book Written Under a Pseudonym with Name Supplied

Wrighter, Carl P. [Paul Stevens]. *I Can Sell You Anything*. New York: Ballantine,

1972. Print.

An Anonymous Book

Beowulf: A New Verse Translation. Trans. Seamus Heaney. New York: Farrar,

2000. Print.

An Edited Book

Hamilton, Alexander, James Madison, and John Jay. *The Federalist Papers*. Ed.

Isaac Kramnick. New York: Viking-Penguin, 1987. Print.

Lynn, Kenneth S., ed. *Huckleberry Finn: Text, Sources, and Critics*. New York:

Harcourt, 1961. Print.

If you cite the author's work, put the author's name first and the editor's name after the title, preceded by "Ed." If you cite the editor's work (an introduction or notes), then place the editor's name first, followed by a comma and "ed."

A Translation

Schulze, Hagen. *Germany: A New History*. Trans. Deborah Lucas Schneider.

Cambridge: Harvard UP, 1998. Print.

Cornford, Francis MacDonald, trans. *The Republic of Plato*. New York: Oxford

UP, 1945. Print.

If the author's work is being cited, place the author's name first and the translator's name after the title, preceded by "Trans." If the translator's work is the important element, place the translator's name first, as in the second example above. If the author's name does not appear in the title, give it after the title. For example: By Plato.

A Book in Two or More Volumes

Spielvogel, Jackson J. *Western Civilization*. 2 vols. Minneapolis: West,

1991. Print.

A Book in Its Second or Subsequent Edition

O'Brien, David M. *Storm Center: The Supreme Court and American Politics.*

2nd ed. New York: Norton, 1990. Print.

A Book in a Series

Parkinson, Richard. *The Rosetta Stone.* British Museum Objects in Focus.

London: British Museum, 2005. Print.

The series title—and number, if there is one—follows the book's title but is not put in italics.

A Reprint of an Earlier Work

Twain, Mark. *Adventures of Huckleberry Finn.* 1885. Centennial Facsimile

Edition. Introd. Hamlin Hill. New York: Harper, 1962. Print.

Faulkner, William. *As I Lay Dying.* 1930. New York: Vintage-Random, 1964. Print.

Provide the original date of publication as well as the facts of publication for the reprinted version. Indicate any new material, as in the first example. The second example illustrates citing a reprinted book, by the same publisher, in a paperback version. (Vintage is a paperback imprint of the publisher Random House.)

A Book with Two or More Publishers

Green, Mark J., James M. Fallows, and David R. Zwick. *Who Runs Congress?* Ralph

Nader Congress Project. New York: Bantam; New York: Grossman, 1972. Print.

Separate the publishers with a semicolon.

A Corporate or Governmental Author

California State Department of Education. *American Indian Education*

Handbook. Sacramento: California Department of Education, Indian

Education Unit, 1991. Print.

The Bible

The Bible [Always refers to the King James Version.] Print.

The Reader's Bible: A Narrative. Ed. with introd. Roland Mushat Frye. Princeton:

Princeton UP, 1965. Print.

In the first example do not put the title in italics. Indicate the version if it is not the King James Version. Provide facts of publication for versions not well known.

Forms for Books: Citing Part of a Book

A Preface, Introduction, Foreword, or Afterword

Sagan, Carl. Introduction. *A Brief History of Time: From the Big Bang to Black Holes.* By Stephen Hawking. New York: Bantam, 1988, ix–x. Print.

Use this form if you are citing the author of the Preface, Introduction, Foreword, or the like. Use an identifying word after the author's name and give inclusive page numbers for the part of the book by the author you are citing.

An Encyclopedia Article

Ostrom, John H. "Dinosaurs." *McGraw-Hill Encyclopedia of Science and Technology.* 1957 ed. Print.

"Benjamin Franklin." *Concise Dictionary of American Biography.* Ed. Joseph E. G. Hopkins. New York: Scribner's, 1964. Print.

Give complete publication facts for less well-known works or first editions.

One or More Volumes in a Multivolume Work

James, Henry. *The Portrait of a Lady.* Vols. 3 and 4 of *The Novels and Tales of Henry James.* New York: Scribner's, 1908. Print.

A Work in an Anthology or Collection

Hurston, Zora Neale. *The First One. Black Female Playwrights: An Anthology of Plays Before 1950.* Ed. Kathy A. Perkins. Bloomington: Indiana UP, 1989. 80–88. Print.

Comstock, George. "The Medium and the Society: The Role of Television in American Life." *Children and Television: Images in a Changing Sociocultural World.* Ed. Gordon L. Berry and Joy Keiko Asamen. Newbury Park, CA: Sage, 1993. 117–31. Print.

Give inclusive page numbers for the particular work you have used.

An Article in a Collection, Casebook, or Sourcebook

MacKenzie, James J. "The Decline of Nuclear Power." *engage/social* April 1986. Rpt. as "America Does Not Need More Nuclear Power" in *The Environmental Crisis: Opposing Viewpoints.* Ed. Julie S. Bach and Lynn Hall. Opposing Viewpoints Series. St. Paul: Greenhaven, 1986. 136–41. Print.

Many articles in collections have been previously published, so a complete citation needs to include the original facts of publication (excluding page numbers if they are not readily available) as well as the facts of publication for the collection. Include inclusive page numbers for the article used.

Cross-References

If you are citing several articles from one collection, you can cite the collection and then provide only the author and title of specific articles used, with a cross-reference to the editor(s) of the collection.

> Head, Suzanne, and Robert Heinzman, eds. *Lessons of the Rainforest.* San
>
> Francisco: Sierra Club, 1990. Print.

> Bandyopadhyay, J., and Vandana Shiva. "Asia's Forest, Asia's Cultures." Head
>
> and Heinzman 66–77. Print.

Forms for Periodicals: Articles in Journals and Magazines Accessed in Print

Articles from the various forms of periodicals, when read in their print format, require the following information, in the order given, with periods after each of the four major elements:

- Author, last name first.
- Title of the article, in quotation marks.
- Facts of publication: title of the journal (magazine or newspaper) in italics, volume and issue number *for scholarly journals only,* date followed by a colon and inclusive page numbers, and then a period.
- Medium of publication: Print.

The following models show the variations in the details of publication, depending on the type of publication.

Article in a Journal Paged by Year

> Brown, Jane D., and Carol J. Pardun. "Little in Common: Racial and Gender
>
> Differences in Adolescents' Television Diets." *Journal of Broadcasting and*
>
> *Electronic Media* 48.2 (2004): 266–78. Print.

Note that there is *no* punctuation between the title of the periodical and the volume number and date.

Article in a Journal Paged by Issue

> Lewis, Kevin. "Superstardom and Transcendence." *Arete: The Journal of Sport*
>
> *Literature* 2.2 (1985): 47–54. Print.

Provide both volume and issue number regardless of the journal's choice of paging.

Article in a Monthly Magazine

> Wegner, Mary-Ann Pouls. "Gateway to the Netherworld." *Archaeology* Jan./
>
> Feb. 2013: 50–53. Print.

Do not use volume or issue number. Cite the month(s) and year followed by a colon and inclusive page numbers. Abbreviate all months except May, June, and July.

Article in a Weekly Magazine

> Stein, Joel. "Eat This, Low Carbers." *Time* 15 Aug. 2005: 78. Print.

Provide the complete date, using the order of day, month, year.

An Anonymous Article

> "Death of Perestroika." *Economist* 2 Feb. 1991: 12–13. Print.

The missing name indicates that the article is anonymous. Alphabetize under D.

A Published Interview

> Angier, Natalie. "Ernst Mayr at 93." Interview. *Natural History* May 1997: 8–11. Print.

Follow the pattern for a published article, but add the descriptive label "Interview" (followed by a period) after the article's title.

A Review

> Whitehead, Barbara D. "The New Segregation." Rev. of *Coming Apart: The*
>
> *State of White America, 1960–2010,* by Charles Murrary. *Commonweal* 4
>
> May 2012. Print.

If the review is signed, begin with the author's name and then the title of the review article. Also provide the title of the work being reviewed and its author, preceded by "Rev. of." For reviews of art shows, videos, or computer software, provide place and date or descriptive label to make the citation clear.

Forms for Periodicals: Articles in Newspapers Accessed in Print

An Article from a Newspaper

> Arguila, John. "What Deep Blue Taught Kasparov—and Us." *Christian Science*
>
> *Monitor* 16 May 1997: 18. Print.

A newspaper's title should be cited as it appears on the masthead, excluding any initial article, thus *New York Times,* not *The New York Times.*

An Article from a Newspaper with Lettered Sections

Ferguson, Niall. "Rough Week, but America's Era Goes On." *Washington Post*

21 Sept. 2008: B1 +. Print.

Place the section letter immediately before the page number without any spacing. If the paging is not consecutive, give the first page and the plus sign.

An Article from a Newspaper with a Designated Edition

Pereria, Joseph. "Women Allege Sexist Atmosphere in Offices Constitutes

Harassment." *Wall Street Journal* 10 Feb. 1988, eastern ed.: 23. Print.

Cite the edition used after the date and before the page number.

An Editorial

"Japan's Two Nationalisms." Editorial. *Washington Post* 4 June 2000: B6. Print.

Add the descriptive label "Editorial" after the article title.

A Letter to the Editor

Wiles, Yoko A. "Thoughts of a New Citizen." Letter. *Washington Post* 27 Dec.

1995: A22. Print.

Forms for Web Sources

Remember that the purpose of a citation is to allow readers to obtain the source you have used. To locate online sources, more information is usually needed than for printed sources. Include as many of the items listed below, in the order given here, as are relevant—and available—for each source. Take time to search a website's home page to locate as much of the information as possible. AND: Always include the date you accessed the source, as the web remains ever fluid and changing.

- Author (or editor, compiler, translator), last name first.
- Title of the work, in quotation marks if it is part of a site, in italics if it is a complete and separate work, such as an online novel.
- Facts of publication of the print version if the item was originally published in print.
- Title of the website, in italics—unless it is the same as item 2 above.
- Publisher or sponsor of the site (possibly a university, company, or organization).

- Date of publication. (If none is available, use n.d.)
- Medium of publication: Web.
- Your date of access: day, month, and year.

NOTE: MLA discourages the use of URLs as a way to access a web source. URLs invite errors by both writers and readers. A search for the title of the website is both faster and safer.

Study this annotated citation as a general model:

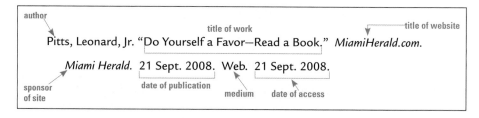

A Published Article from an Online Database

Shin, Michael S. "Redressing Wounds: Finding a Legal Framework to Remedy

Racial Disparities in Medical Care." *California Law Review* 90.6 (2002):

2047–2100. *JSTOR.* Web. 10 Sept. 2008.

Kumar, Sanjay. "Scientists Accuse Animal Rights Activists of Stifling Research."

British Medical Journal 23 Nov. 2002: 1192. *EBSCOhost.* Web. 12 Sept. 2008.

No posting date is used with databases of printed articles. Postings are ongoing.

An Article from a Reference Source

"Prohibition." *Encyclopaedia Britannica Online.* Encyclopaedia Britannica, 2007.

Web. 16 July 2008.

An Online News Source

Associated Press. "Parents: Work Hinders Quality Time with Kids." *CNN.com.*

Cable News Network. 31 July 2003. Web. 31 July 2003.

An Article in an Online Magazine

Kinsley, Michael. "Politicians Lie. Numbers Don't." *Slate.com.* Washington Post

Company. 16 Sept. 2008. Web. 21 Sept. 2008.

A Poem from a Scholarly Project

> Keats, John. "Ode to a Nightingale." *Poetical Works.* 1884. *Bartleby.com: Great*
>
> *Books.* Ed. Steven van Leeuwen. Web. 2 Oct. 2008.

Information from a Government Site

> United States Department of Health and Human Services. "The 2008 HHS
>
> Poverty Guidelines." 23 Jan. 2008. Web. 23 Sept. 2008.

Information from a Professional Site

> "Music Instruction Aids Verbal Memory." APA Press Release. Reporter: Agnes
>
> S. Chan. *APA Online.* American Psychological Association. 27 July 2003. Web.
>
> 16 Sept. 2008.

Information from a Professional Home Page or Blog

> Sullivan, Andrew. "America: The Global Pioneer of Torture." *The Daily Dish.*
>
> The Atlantic Monthly Group. 14 Sept. 2008. Web. 23 Sept. 2008.

For information from an untitled personal home page, use the label "Home page" (but not in italics or quotation marks).

Forms for Other Print and Nonprint Sources

The materials in this section, although often important to research projects, do not always lend themselves to documentation by the forms illustrated above. Follow the basic order of author, title, facts of publication, and medium of publication as much as possible. Add more information as needed to make the citation clear and useful to a reader.

An Article Published in Print and on CD or DVD

> Detweiler, Richard A. "Democracy and Decency on the Internet." *Chronicle of*
>
> *Higher Education* 28 June 1996: A40. *General Periodicals Ondisc. UMI-*
>
> *ProQuest.* Apr. 1997. CD.

A Work or Part of a Work on CD-ROM, DVD-ROM, Etc.

> Eseiolonis, Karyn. "Georgio de Chirico's *Mysterious Bathers.*" *A Passion for Art:*
>
> *Renoir, Cezanne, Matisse and Dr. Barnes.* Corbis Productions, 1995. CD.

Kloss, William. "Donatello and Padua." *Great Artists of the Italian Renaissance.*

DVD. Chantilly, VA: The Teaching Company, 2004.

An Audio (or Video) from a Website

Vachss, Andrew. "Dead and Gone." Interview by Bill Thompson. Aired on *Eye*

on Books, 24 Oct. 2000. *The Zero.* Home page. Web. 25 Sept. 2008.

A Recording

Stein, Joseph. *Fiddler on the Roof.* Jerry Bock, composer. Original-Cast

Recording with Zero Mostel. RCA, LSO-1093. 1964. LP.

The conductor and/or performers help identify a specific recording.

Plays or Concerts

Mourning Becomes Electra. By Eugene O'Neill. Shakespeare Theater.

Washington, DC. 16 May 1997. Performance.

Principal actors, singers, musicians, and/or the director can be added as appropriate.

A Television or Radio Program

"Breakthrough: Television's Journal of Science and Medicine." PBS series

hosted by Ron Hendren. 10 June 1997. Television.

An Interview

Plum, Kenneth. Personal interview. 5 Mar. 2012.

A Lecture

Bateson, Mary Catherine. "Crazy Mixed-Up Families." Northern Virginia

Community College, 26 Apr. 1997. Lecture.

An Unpublished Letter or E-mail

Usick, Patricia. Message to the author. 26 June 2005. E-mail.

Maps and Charts

Hampshire and Dorset. Map. Kent, UK: Geographers' A–Z, n.d. Print.

Cartoons and Advertisements

Halleyscope. "Halleyscopes Are for Night Owls." Advertisement. *Natural*

History Dec. 1985: 15. Print.

United Airlines Advertisement. ESPN. 8 Aug. 2008. Television.

A Published Dissertation

Brotton, Joyce D. *Illuminating the Present Through Literary Dialogism: From the*

Reformation Through Postmodernism. Diss. George Mason U, 2002. Ann

Arbor: UMI, 2002. Print.

Government Documents

United States. Senate. Committee on Energy and Natural Resources.

Subcommittee on Energy Research and Development. *Advanced Reactor*

Development Program: Hearing. Washington: GPO, 24 May 1988. Print.

---. Environmental Protection Agency. *The Challenge of the Environment: A*

Primer on EPA's Statutory Authority. Washington: GPO, 1972. Print.

If the author is not given, cite the name of the government first followed by the name of the department or agency. If you cite more than one document published by the same government, use the standard three hyphens followed by a period. If you cite a second document prepared by the EPA, use another three hyphens and period. Abbreviate the U.S. Government Printing Office: GPO.

If the author is known, follow this pattern:

Geller, William. *Deadly Force.* U.S. Dept. of Justice National Institute of Justice

Crime File Study Guide. Washington: Dept. of Justice, n.d. Print.

Legal Documents

U.S. Const. Art. 1, sec. 3. Print.

The Constitution is referred to by article and section. Abbreviations are used. Do not use italics.

When citing a court case, give the name of the case, the volume, name, and page of the report cited, and the date. Italicize the name of the case in your text but not in the Works Cited.

Turner v. Arkansas. 407 U.S. 366. 1972. Print.

AUTHOR/YEAR OR APA STYLE

The *author/year system* identifies a source by placing the author's last name and the publication year of the source within parentheses at the point in the text where the source is cited. The in-text citations are supported by complete citations in a list of sources at the end of the paper. Most disciplines in the social sciences, biological sciences, and earth sciences use some version of the author/year style. The guidelines given here follow the style of the *Publication Manual of the American Psychological Association* (6th ed., 2010).

APA Style: In-Text Citations

The simplest parenthetical reference can be presented in one of three ways:

1. Place the year of publication within parentheses immediately following the author's name in the text.

    > In a typical study of preference for motherese, Fernald (1985) used an
    >
    > operant auditory preference procedure.

Within the same paragraph, additional references to the source do not need to repeat the year, if the researcher clearly establishes that the same source is being cited.

Because the speakers were unfamiliar subjects, Fernald's work eliminates the

possibility that it is the mother's voice per se that accounts for the preference.

2. If the author is not mentioned in the text, place the author's last name followed by a comma and the year of publication within parentheses after the borrowed information.

> The majority of working women are employed in jobs that are at least
>
> 75 percent female (Lawrence & Matsuda, 1997).

3. Cite a specific passage by providing the page, chapter, or figure number following the borrowed material. *Always* give specific page references for quoted material.

- A brief quotation:

> Deuzen-Smith (1988) believes that counselors must be involved with cli-
>
> ents and "deeply interested in piecing the puzzle of life together" (p. 29).

- A quotation in display form:

> Bartlett (1932) explains the cyclic process of perception:
>
>> Suppose I am making a stroke in a quick game, such as tennis or cricket.
>>
>> How I make the stroke depends on the relating of certain new experi-
>>
>> ences, most of them visual, to other immediately preceding visual experi-
>>
>> ences, and to my posture, or balance of posture, at the moment. (p. 201)

Indent a block quotation five spaces from the left margin, do not use quotation marks, and double-space throughout. To show a new paragraph within the block quotation, indent the first line of the new paragraph an additional five spaces. Note the placing of the year after the author's name, and the page number at the end of the direct quotation.

More complicated in-text citations should be handled as follows:

Two Authors, Mentioned in the Text

> Kuhl and Meltzoff (1984) tested 4- to 5-month-olds in an experiment . . .

Two Authors, Not Mentioned in the Text

> . . . but are unable to show preference in the presence of two mismatched
>
> modalities (e.g., a face and a voice; see Kuhl & Meltzoff, 1984).

Give both authors' last names each time you refer to the source. Connect their names with "and" in the text. Use an ampersand (&) in the parenthetical citation.

More Than Two Authors

For works coauthored by three, four, or five people, provide all last names in the first reference to the source. Thereafter, cite only the first author's name followed by "et al."

> As Price-Williams, Gordon, and Ramirez have shown (1969), . . .

OR

> Studies of these children have shown (Price-Williams, Gordon, & Ramirez, 1969) . . .

THEN

> Price-Williams et al. (1969) also found that . . .

If a source has six or more authors, use only the first author's last name followed by "et al." every time the source is cited.

Corporate Authors

In general, spell out the name of a corporate author each time it is used. If a corporate author has well-known initials, the name can be abbreviated after the first citation.

FIRST IN-TEXT CITATION:	(National Institutes of Health [NIH], 1989)
SUBSEQUENT CITATIONS:	(NIH, 1989)

Two or More Works Within the Same Parentheses

When citing more than one work by the same author in a parenthetical reference, use the author's name only once and arrange the years mentioned in order, thus:

> Several studies of ego identity formation (Marcia, 1966, 1983) . . .

When an author, or the same group of coauthors, has more than one work published in the same year, distinguish the works by adding the letters *a, b, c,* and so on, as needed, to the year. Give the last name only once, but repeat the year, each one with its identifying letter; thus:

> Several studies (Smith, 1990a, 1990b, 1990c) . . .

When citing several works by different authors within the same parentheses, list the authors alphabetically; alphabetize by the first author when citing coauthored works. Separate authors or groups of coauthors with semicolons, thus:

> Although many researchers (Archer & Waterman, 1983; Grotevant, 1983; Grotevant & Cooper, 1986; Sabatelli & Mazor, 1985) study identity formation . . .

Personal Communication

Cite information obtained via interview, phone, letter, and e-mail communication.

> According to Sandra Haun (personal interview, September 7, 2008) . . .

Because readers cannot retrieve information from these personal sources, do *not* include a citation in your list of references.

APA STYLE: PREPARING A LIST OF REFERENCES

Every source cited parenthetically in your paper needs a complete bibliographic citation. These complete citations are placed on a separate page (or pages) after the text of the paper and before any appendices included in the paper. Sources are arranged alphabetically, and the first page is titled "References." Begin each source flush with the left margin and indent second and subsequent lines five spaces. Double-space throughout the list of references. Follow these rules for alphabetizing:

1. Organize two or more works by the same author, or the same group of coauthors, chronologically.

   Beck, A. T. (1991).

   Beck, A. T. (1993).

2. Place single-author entries before multiple-author entries when the first of the multiple authors is the same as the single author.

   Grotevant, H. D. (1983).

   Grotevant, H. D., & Cooper, C. R. (1986).

3. Organize multiple-author entries that have the same first author but different second or third authors alphabetically by the name of the second author or third and so on.

   Gerbner, G., & Gross, L.

   Gerbner, G., Gross, L., Jackson-Beeck, M., Jeffries-Fox, S., & Signorielli, N.

   Gerbner, G., Gross, L., Morgan, M., & Signorielli, N.

4. Organize two or more works by the same author(s) published in the same year alphabetically by title.

Form for Books

A book citation contains these elements in this form:

author	date	title	place of publication	publisher

Seligman, (M. E. P.) (1991). *Learned optimism.* New York: Knopf.

Authors

Give all authors' names, last name first, and initials. Separate authors with commas, use the ampersand (&) before the last author's name, and end with a period. For edited books, place the abbreviation "Ed." or "Eds." in parentheses following the last editor's name.

Date of Publication

Place the year of publication in parentheses followed by a period.

Title

Capitalize only the first word of the title and of the subtitle, if there is one, and any proper nouns. Italicize the title and end with a period. Place additional information such as number of volumes or an edition in parentheses after the title, before the period.

Burleigh, N. (2007). *Mirage: Napoleon's scientists and the unveiling of Egypt.*

Publication Information

Cite the city of publication; add the state (using the Postal Service abbreviation) or country if necessary to avoid confusion; then give the publisher's name, after a colon, eliminating unnecessary terms such as *Publisher, Co.,* and *Inc.* End the citation with a period.

Mitchell, J.V. (Ed.). (1985). *The ninth mental measurements yearbook.* Lincoln:

University of Nebraska Press.

National Institute of Drug Abuse. (1993, April 13). *Annual national high school*

senior survey. Rockville, MD: Author.

Newton, D. E. (1996). *Violence and the media.* Santa Barbara, CA: ABC-Clio.

Give a corporate author's name in full. When the organization is both author and publisher, place the word *Author* after the place of publication.

Form for Articles

An article citation contains these elements in this form:

author	date	title of article	title of journal

Changeaux, J.P. (1993). Chemical signaling in the brain. *Scientific American,*

volume 269, 58–62. page

Date of Publication

Place the year of publication for articles in scholarly journals in parentheses, followed by a period. For articles in newspapers and popular magazines, give the year followed by month and day (if appropriate).

(1997, March).

Title of Article

Capitalize only the title's first word, the first word of any subtitle, and any proper nouns. Place any necessary descriptive information in square brackets immediately after the title.

> Scott, S. S. (1984, December 12). Smokers get a raw deal [Letter to the Editor].

Publication Information

Cite the title of the journal in full, capitalizing according to conventions for titles. Italicize the title and follow it with a comma. Give the volume number, italicized, followed by a comma, and then inclusive page numbers followed by a period. *If* a journal begins each issue with a new page 1, then also cite the issue number in parentheses immediately following the volume number. Do not use "p." or "pp." before page numbers when citing articles from scholarly journals; do use "p." or "pp." in citations to newspaper and magazine articles.

> Martin, C. L., Wood, C. H., & Little, J. K. (1990). The development of gender
>
> stereotype components. *Child Development, 61,* 1891–1904.
>
> Leakey, R. (2000, April/May). Extinctions past and present. *Time,* p. 35.

An Article or Chapter in an Edited Book

> Goodall, J. (1993). Chimpanzees—bridging the gap. In P. Cavalieri & P. Singer
>
> (Eds.), *The great ape project: Equality beyond humanity* (pp. 10–18). New
>
> York: St. Martin's.

Cite the author(s), date, and title of the article or chapter. Then cite the name(s) of the editor(s) in signature order after "In," followed by "Ed." or "Eds." in parentheses; the title of the book; the inclusive page numbers of the article or chapter, in parentheses, followed by a period. End with the city of publication and the publisher of the book.

A Report

> U.S. Merit Systems Protection Board. (1988). *Sexual harassment in the federal*
>
> *workplace: An update.* Washington, DC: U.S. Government Printing Office.

Form for Electronic Sources

As a minimum, an APA reference for any type of Internet source should include the following information: a document title or description, the date of publication, a way to access the document online, and, when possible, an author name.

When the Internet address (URL) is likely to be stable, you can cite that address. For example: www.nytimes.com. However, a good source that you find during your research may not be found later by your readers with the URL that you used. APA recommends, therefore, that such sources be documented with the item's DOI (digital object identifier) instead of its URL.

Do not place URLs within angle brackets (< >). Do not place a period at the end of the URL, even though it concludes the citation. If you have to break a URL at the end of a line, break only after a slash. Introduce the URL at the end of the citation this way: Retrieved from www.nytimes.com

DOIs are a series of numbers and letters that provide a link to a specific item, and this link does not change with time. Although DOIs are often on the first page of a document, they can, at times, be hard to locate. APA prefers that you always choose a source's DOI over its URL, if you can find it. Place the DOI at the end of the citation, and introduce the number thus: doi: [number]. Do not end the citation with a period.

Here are a few examples of citations for Internet sources:

Journal Article Retrieved Online, with DOI Information

Habernas, Jurgen. (2006). Political communication in media society.

Communication Theory 16(4), 411–426. doi: 10.1111/

j.1468-2885.2006.00280.x

Gardiner, K., Herault, Y., Lott, I., Antonarakis, S., Reeves, R., & Dierssen, M.

(2010). Down syndrome: From understanding the neurobiology to ther-

apy. Journal of Neuroscience 30(45), 14943–14945. doi: 10.1523/

JNEUROSCI.3728-10.2010

Electronic Daily Newspaper Article Available by Search

Schwartz, J. (2002, September 13). Air pollution con game. Washington Times.

Retrieved from http://www.washtimes.com

Journal Article Available from a Periodical Database

Note that no URL is necessary; just provide the name of the database.

Dixon, B. (2001, December). Animal emotions. Ethics & the Environment, 6(2),

22. Retrieved from Academic Search Premier database/EBSCOhost

Research Databases.

U.S. Government Report on a Government Website

U.S. General Accounting Office. (2002, March). Identity theft: Prevalence and

cost appear to be growing. Retrieved from http://www.consumer.gov/

idtheft/reports/gao-d02363.pdf

Cite a message posted to a newsgroup or electronic mailing list in the reference list. Cite an e-mail from one person to another *only* in the essay, not in the list of references.

SAMPLE STUDENT ESSAY IN APA STYLE

The following student essay illustrates APA style. Use 1-inch margins and double-space throughout, including any block quotations. Block quotations should be indented *five* spaces from the left margin (in contrast to the ten spaces required by MLA style). Observe the following elements: title page, running head, abstract, author/year in-text citations, subheadings within the text, and a list of references.

APA Style

Note placement of running head and page number.

Running Head: Depression and Marital Status 1

Sample title page for a paper in APA style.

The Relationship Between Depression and Marital Status

Carissa Ervine

Sociology of Mental Disorder: SOC 4714

Virginia Tech University

Depression and Marital Status 2

Abstract

Many studies have examined the relationship between mental disorders, specifically depression, and marital status. From the studies, several theories have developed to explain this relationship. An examination of the studies' findings and of the theories tested demonstrates that no one theory accounts for all patterns of marital status and mental health or disorder.

Papers in APA style
usually begin with
an abstract.

Depression and Marital Status 3

Many studies have evaluated the relationship between mental disorders, more specifically depression, and marital status. These studies consistently find that people who are divorced or have never been married have more depressive symptoms than those who are married. This paper explores both the causes of and the theories that seek to explain these findings.

Definition and Description of Depression

Subheadings are often used in papers in the social sciences.

Depression is a mood disorder in which individuals experience loss of interest or of pleasure in nearly all activities. They feel extreme sadness, despair, and hopelessness. These feelings lead to a lack of motivation to do simple, daily tasks. Many people with depression also have low self-esteem. According to the *Diagnostic and Statistical Manual of Mental Disorders* (DSM), a person must experience at least four of the symptoms listed in order to have depression: changes in appetite or weight, sleep, or psychomotor activity; decreased energy; feelings of worthlessness or guilt; difficulty concentrating or making decisions; or recurrent thoughts of death or suicide ideas or attempts.

Prevalence of Depression According to Marital Status

Throughout epidemiological research, studies have consistently shown that those who are married have fewer depressed symptoms than those who are not married (Kim & McKenry, 2005; Wade & Pevalin, 2004), and many studies have sought to find the reasons. Some think it is because marriage offers certain benefits; therefore, married people have better overall health and less depression (Kim & McKenry, 2002). When a marriage dissolves, so does that person's mental health. Marital disruption causes a significant increase in depression, even three years after a divorce (Aseltine & Kessler, 1993). It has also been found that people who are depressed before marriage have improved mental health once they are married (Lucas et al., 2003). Those who do get divorced have more depressive symptoms that may or may not disappear over time (Kim & McKenry, 2002; Lucas et al., 2003). Kim and McKenry (2002) demonstrate, though, that getting remarried after a divorce leads to a decrease in depressive symptoms.

Depression and Marital Status 4

Studies have also evaluated whether people in marriages were happier because those who were not married, or who became divorced, got selected out of marriage due to psychological problems that make them undesirable partners. This idea is referred to as the social selection theory. Four years prior to getting divorced, people show higher rates of psychological problems than those who stayed married, although those who were widowed did not (Wade & Pevalin, 2004). People who get married and stay married have fewer depressive symptoms and better psychological well-being years before they ever got married (Lucas et al., 2003).

Some researchers assert that marriage itself is good for mental health, but that it is the quality of the marriage that matters. High marital stress causes depressive symptoms that tend to dissipate after divorce (Aseltine & Kessler, 1993; Johnson & Wu, 2002). Gove, Hughes, and Style (1983) demonstrated that marital quality and happiness are strong predictors of mental health. Actually, remaining unmarried can be more beneficial to one's psychological health than being in a continuously unhappy marriage.

> Use ampersand within parentheses; use "and" in sentences.

Last, some studies suggest that marriage does not increase psychological well-being at all. These studies suggest that life satisfaction does change when major events ensue, and then people gradually adapt over time until their psychological health reaches their baseline (Lucas et al., 2003). Initially, people react strongly to both good and bad events, but as time passes, their emotional reactions lessen, and they return to normal (Lucas et al., 2003). Booth and Amato (1991) found that before a divorce occurs there is a rise in stress, but then stress levels return to normal two years after the divorce.

Evaluation of the Evidence

All these findings play some part in explaining why the married tend to have fewer depressive symptoms than their counterparts, but some studies were better conducted than others and used longitudinal data to explain

Depression and Marital Status 5

some of the differences found. The fact that married people have better health because they get benefits from marriage seems to be the best explanation. In many instances, the social selection perspective did not hold up. For example, some studies showed that the psychological health of divorced persons improved once they remarried (Johnson & Wu, 2002). If the selection perspective held, those who remarried would not likely experience a decrease in depressive symptoms. The selection perspective would support the idea that those selected out of marriage would not even be likely to remarry. Johnson and Wu's (2002) results consistently show that marriage is better for people because of the benefits they receive from it.

Frech and Williams (2007) found that those who were depressed before marriage had a decrease in depressive symptoms once they were married, supporting the idea that marriage offers benefits. This may occur because marriage provides economic and psychosocial benefits. Those who are married may have two incomes, resulting in less stress over financial matters. Marriage also offers day-to-day companionship, decreasing social isolation (Frech & Williams, 2007). These benefits do not support the fact that marital quality matters, because they are based on marital status per se.

Some researchers who favor the social selection theory believe that high rates of distress prior to a divorce indicate psychological problems in the individual (Wade & Pevalin, 2004), although this may not necessarily be the case. Higher stress levels are common in the years preceding a divorce. After all, divorce is not a discrete event; many problems lead up to it. Higher levels of distress in the years before a divorce may reflect anticipation of the marital disruption (Mastekaasa, 1995). While marriage can bring many benefits, the quality of the marriage is important. High stress levels because of an unhappy marriage are likely to explain the higher stress levels leading up to divorce.

Booth and Amato (1991) also found a pre-divorce rise in stress, but then they also found that levels of stress in the individuals return to normal two years after the divorce. While this finding does appear to challenge the selection

APA Style

perspective, it is not consistent with many other findings that marriage is better for psychological well-being. Johnson and Wu (2002) used the same waves of people in their study; they did not find that those remaining divorced experienced a decrease in depressive symptoms over time. Nor did satisfaction levels return to the original baselines after divorce. This difference in findings is likely to be caused by a difference in the number of times the participants were studied. Booth and Amato studied their respondents only every three years, whereas Johnson and Wu studied them more often. Johnson and Wu did not find that those remaining divorced experienced a decrease in depressive symptoms over time. Lucas (2005) argues that although some adaption does occur, normally it is not complete. Many people are likely to establish new baselines of psychological well-being that are slightly lower than they were before they were divorced (Lucas et al., 2003).

While many studies find fewer depressive symptoms in married people, discrepancies in explanations still exist. The strongest evidence indicates that married people have less depression because marriage offers many benefits and social supports that the unmarried do not have. But marital quality is just as important as marital status, and this can account for why distress levels go up right before divorce occurs. A bad marriage creates stress, and distress levels increase because of this, not because of poor psychological health that an individual brings to a marriage.

Review of Theories Relating to Marital Status and Depression

As noted, several theories explain why people who are married have better mental health than those who are not. First, the social selection theory asserts that those who are married have better psychological well-being than those who do not and that the unmarried have been "selected" out of marriage. That is, those who aren't married have more mental illness, such as depression, so they are not considered to be suitable mates (Johnson & Wu, 2002). These people either never marry or get married and then divorce. Their psychological characteristics predispose them to divorce (Mastekaasa, 1992).

Depression and Marital Status 7

The crisis theory asserts that having a divorce is a life crisis that temporarily changes mental health. People encounter many stressors while going through a divorce. One of these is the adjustment to role changes. Once the transition is completed, stress levels go down and psychological well-being returns to normal (Booth & Amato, 1991). Lucas et al. (2003) also found that after the marital transition of divorce, people adapted to their new set of circumstances. Depression went down and their psychological well-being returned.

Last, role theory asserts that the stress that the divorced experience is chronic. The new social role they must take on will cause them higher levels of distress because they have less social support, more economic responsibilities, and possibly more stress associated with raising children alone (Johnson & Wu, 2002). This theory also asserts that these chronic stress levels will not go down as long as the divorced remain single. If a divorced person decides to remarry, then his or her stress levels begin to dissipate because there are now fewer stressful roles to fulfill. The social causation perspective also ties into this. With fewer stressful roles to take on, married people can enjoy many of the benefits that marriage offers. When a marriage dissolves, however, they no longer have these benefits.

Evaluation of Theories

Role theory gives a good explanation of why married people have better psychological well-being and fewer depressive symptoms. It is well-known that stress increases the likelihood that someone will have a mental illness. It is also true that levels of depression increase when marital disruption occurs (Wade & Pevalin, 2004). The divorced are used to having a partner who can offer benefits such as greater financial security and a strong social network. With fewer resources to draw upon and more roles to take on, the divorced person is susceptible to depressive symptoms (Kim & McKerry, 2002). However, symptoms of distress and depression do decrease once a divorced person remarries and undergoes another role transition. With the new marriage, the

Depression and Marital Status 8

number of required roles decreases and the increased resources of the new marriage ease depression.

In contrast, crisis theory asserts that depressive symptoms and distress decrease with time after a divorce. But crisis theory does not seem to hold up, since studies demonstrate that marriage and remarriage increase psychological well-being. The fact that remarriage increases psychological well-being also contradicts the social selection perspective. If social selection did occur, people would be selected out from remarrying at all. None of these theories, however, effectively examines the effect of marital quality, an issue important to understanding the relationship between depression and marital status.

The best conclusion is that no one theory is complex enough to explain the relationship between marital status and mental health. It is likely that all theories have valid points and that the reason married people experience better mental health stems from a combination of causes. Further research should focus on finding a theory that can account for more, if not all, of the forces shaping the mental health of married people.

References

Aseltine, R. H., & Kessler, R.C. (1993). Marital disruption and depression in a community sample. *Journal of Health and Social Behavior, 34,* 237–251.

Booth, A., & Amato, P. (1991). Divorce and psychological stress. *Journal of Health and Social Behavior, 32,* 396–407.

Frech, A., & Williams, K. (2007). Depression and the psychological benefits of entering marriage. *Journal of Health and Social Behavior, 48,* 149–163.

Gove, W. R., Hughes, M., & Style, B. S. (1983). Does marriage have positive effects on the psychological well-being of the individual? *Journal of Health and Social Behavior, 24,* 122–131.

Johnson, D. R., & Wu, J. (2002). An empirical test of crisis, social selection, and role explanations of the relationship between marital disruption and psychological distress: A pooled time-series analysis of four wave panel data. *Journal of Marriage and Family, 64,* 211–224.

Kim, K. H., & McKenry, P. C. (2002). The relationship between marriage and psychological well-being. *Journal of Family Issues, 23*(8), 885–911.

Lucas, R. E. (2005). Time does not heal all wounds: A longitudinal study of reaction and adaption to divorce. *Psychological Science, 16*(12), 945–950.

Lucas, R. E., Clark, A. E., Georgellis, Y., & Diener, E. (2003). Reexamining adaptation and the set point model of happiness: Reactions to changes in marital status. *Journal of Personality and Social Psychology, 84*(3), 527–538.

Mastekaasa, A. (1992). Marriage and psychological well-being: Some evidence on selection into marriage. *Journal of Marriage and the Family, 54,* 901–911.

Mastekaasa, A. (1995). Marital dissolution and subjective distress: Panel evidence. *European Sociological Review, 11*(20), 173–185.

Wade, T. J., & Pevalin, D. J (2004). Marital transitions and mental health. *Journal of Health and Social Behavior, 45,* 155–170.

APA Style

Title the page "References."

Double-space throughout. In each citation, indent all lines, after the first, five spaces. Note APA style in placing dates.

For two or more sources by the same author, order by the year of publication.

Chapter 15

Eco-Composition:
A Term Long Inquiry

What specific aspects of contemporary reality warrant, indeed insist upon, investigation as part of a liberatory education in which knowledge generated within the classroom is not an end in itself, but a precondition for its application beyond the classroom, at the point of contact with reality: with the advocates who perpetuate it, with other investigators seeking to transform it, or with the public—whose collective opinion regarding the problem either perpetuates it or fuels the possibilities for altering it, by altering the material conditions that sustain it. To the problematics of race, gender, and class, which continue to insist upon critical inquiry and collective intervention, I would add the problematics of capitalism, the war on terror, the environment, the mass media, health care, and education, as aspects of reality that warrant inquiry and intervention, analysis and application of that analysis, if those realities are to be transformed in the interest of the common good and social justice. Inquiry could focus on these "generative themes" individually or in combination, as part of a problem-posing investigation of reality, in which students self-select the "generative theme" to be investigated, and in which the teacher models inquiry in one of these "generative themes" as part of a term-long, collective investigation (or models aspects of the inquiry into a handful of these "generative themes") with primary and secondary readings to focus and inaugurate the inquiry: to provide a signifying

context and a polemical springboard for the investigation.

More specifically, how might inquiry into each of these problematic aspects of reality be

framed in a central question for investigation, as a point of departure for the dialogic "unveiling"

of the problem? After modeling one or two of these central questions for inquiry, the teacher

could invite students to choose the problem they wish to investigate/unveil, and devise their own

inaugural question to shape the inquiry, to define the "generative theme," as follows:

- *The Economy:* Is "free-market" capitalism compatible with democracy? Is

  "consumerism the only form of citizenship being offered young people?" (Giroux

  xxii). Analyze and assess the recent economic "melt-down" (causes, effects,

  implications, and solutions, then devise a means of applying the analysis beyond

  the classroom. Assess the causes, effects, and implications for democracy of

  consumerism and the commodity fetishism that drives it, then devise an action

  plan for applying the analysis beyond the classroom.

- *The War on Terrorism*: Was the invasion of Iraq justified? Are practices and

  policies associated with war compatible with democracy (warrantless wire-

  tapping, imprisonment without trial, torture, biological warfare, embedded media,

  exposure of CIA operatives etc); What role did signification play in the

  manufacture of consent for the war? Analyze and assess the problem, then devise

  a means of applying the analysis beyond the classroom.

- *The Environment:* Is combating global warming in the nation's best interest?

  Does chemical contamination of our air, water, and food sources pose a problem

  as immediate as the threat of nuclear annihilation? Is banning pesticides/

herbicides in the nation's best interest? Should national parks and wilderness

areas be sites of preservation or recreation? What are the causes, effects,

implications, and solutions of the mass extinction of species?

- *The Mass Media:* Is the mass media, as Noam Chomsky asserts, being converted

  from a "journalism" to a "propaganda" model: discuss the evidence, the causes,

  the implications, before proposing a means of applying the analysis beyond the

  classroom. Should the "fair and balanced" law (repealed in 1988) be reinstated to

  mitigate the effects of propaganda?

- *Race/Gender discrimination*: What are the causes, effects, implications, and

  solutions regarding gender/race discrimination?

- *Health Care:* Is government health care the best solution?

- *Political Reform:* Are lobbies compatible with democracy? Should negative

  political ads be banned? Should the electoral college be discontinued?

- *Religion:* Should separation of church and state be repealed? Is school prayer a

  violation of separation of church and state? Should Creationism be taught with

  Evolution in the schools?

Unveiling the Problem: A Dialogic Sequence of Liberatory Learning

Though each of these "generative themes" merits critical reflection in the academic

writing workshop, for the purposes of this discussion I will focus on one, which as a category of

inquiry is particularly useful for implementing a Freirean, problem-posing praxis: the

environment. As a "generative theme," the environment is every bit as significant as the themes

of race, class, and gender that have driven inquiry in academia, and in the writing class in particular, for the last fifty years. Indeed, the problem of global warming has reached such

critical proportions that respected authorities characterize it as posing a more immediate threat

than global terrorism or nuclear war. Stephen Hawking, for example, asserts that "global warming

has eclipsed other threats to the planet, such as terrorism" (qtd. in Satter). Kenneth Benedict, Director

of the Bulletin of Atomic Scientists, similarly observes that "the dangers posed by climate

change are nearly as dire as those posed by nuclear weapons . . . ." Further, the environment is a

useful category for implementing Freirean praxis because it has a concrete immediacy to the

student, whose air, water, and food he/she breathes, drinks, and eats on a daily basis. Further, the

environment offers a host of "generate themes" that can be posed to students as problems,

allowing them to self-select the focus of investigation, as follows.

- *Global warming*: Science or science fiction? Is combating global warming in the
  nation's best interest? Does the government have the right to censure the science
  it sponsors? Primary text: *An Inconvenient Truth*, Gore.

- *Chemical contamination* (of the air, water, and food supply). Is such
  contamination as Rachel Carson asserts, the most dangerous problem we face
  aside from the threat of nuclear war? Should the ban on DDT be lifted to combat
  world-wide malaria? Is banning pesticides/herbicides in the nation's best interest?
  Primary text: *Silent Spring*, Carson.

- *Mass Species Extinction*: Where Have all the Froggies Gone? Scientific studies
  warn that one of every four mammals will become extinct in the next century.
  Select a species as a case study, then analyze and assess the causes, effects,
  implications and solutions to the problem, before devising a plan for applying that
  analysis beyond the classroom, as an intervention upon the problem. Examples

might be manatees vs boaters; wolves vs ranchers; wild horses vs ranchers; buffalo vs. ranchers; dolphins, sea turtles, whales vs fishing fleets etc.

- *The Great Garbage Patch:* An oceanic "soup" of trash (much of it from the 260 billion tons of plastic produced each year) twice the size of Texas, that threatens marine species with extinction and poses hazards to shipping. What are the causes, effects, implications, and solutions to this problem?

- *Resource Extraction vs. Habitat Preservation:* Big Oil vs ANWAR; Big Oil vs. The Coastlines; Big Mining vs. The Colorado river; Big Timber vs. The Roadless Wilderness; Big Timber vs. The Spotted Owl. Given the realities of the energy crisis, can we afford to protect environments rich in fossil fuels or other natural resources?

- *The National Parks: Recreation vs. Preservation.* Should snow mobiles and ATV's be banned from national parts and wilderness areas? Primary Text: *Desert Solitaire:* "Industrial Tourism," Abbey;

- *Eco-Activism:* Is extreme activism by groups such as Earth First and Greenpeace justified as a means of protesting environmental degradation? Tree-sitting, tree-spiking, the scuttling of whaling ships, anti-whaling tactics, Monkey-wrenching, fire-bombing SUV dealerships? Primary Text: *The Monkey Wrench Gang,* Abbey

- *The Environment and Eco-Feminism:* Is the environment a site that reinforces traditional gender stereotypes. What are the implications of the female scientist in nature? Analyze and assess, using the careers of Goodall, & Fossey as case studies. Primary text: *Primate Visions*: "Teddy Bear Patriarchy," Haraway.

- *Eco-Ethnicity: A Racial Perspective on the Environment.* What might we learn from the intersection of race and the environment? Compare and contrast Native American and Euro-American views of the environment. Analyze and assess the implications of these differing perspectives for the sustainability of the eco-system? Analyze and assess the influence of Native American perspectives on the modern environmental movement. Primary Text: *Lame Deer: Seeker of Visions:* "Talking to the Owls and the Butterflies;" "The Green Frog Skin;"

- *Ocean Pollution:* The world-wide death of reefs;

- *Freshwater Pollution:* Industrial/Agricultural waste vs The Wetlands; Perchlorate contamination of Lake Mead; Phosphate "kill-offs" in the Hillsborough river;

- *Exotic species vs the Environment:* the Asian eel, the water hyacinth, the Japanese elm beetle etc.;

- *Nuclear Waste:* Should the Cold War's nuclear waste be stored in Yucca mountain? Is the production of nuclear energy in the nation's best interest?

Once the "generative theme" of the investigation is decided upon, a dialogic sequence of activities characterizes the "unveiling" of the problem, as follows:

The Project: Students select the form (genre) that their term-long analysis of the problem will assume, for its public dissemination, as follows:

- Formal research paper/ journal article
- Web-site
- Brochure
- Power-point presentation
- Slide presentation

- Overhead projector presentation

The Free-Write:

- to inaugurate the inquiry, the students begins the process of "coming into voice" on the "generative theme" by simply free-writing in a reading response/field journal for several minutes, in response to the central question for inquiry, recording thoughts, feelings, opinions, at random, as they occur.

- Follow-up: At home, they pick up where they left off, and add-on to this free-write.

- Follow-up: to broaden their awareness of the "various schools of thought" regarding the problem, students free-write from the opposite point of view, assuming the persona of a stake-holder in the particular reality under investigation;

- Follow-Up: in small groups or mentoring pairs, students share their free-writes, either reading them aloud or summarizing their views;

- Follow-up: Time is allotted for informal feed-back, dialogue on the "generative theme;"

- Follow-up: Students then underline their favorite sentence of the free-write;

- Follow-Up: volunteers read aloud their free-writes to the class as a whole, by way of introducing the class to the "generative theme."

The Field Interview(s)

- Students take to the "field" to interview five members of the local community, regarding their views, opinions, feelings with respect to the "generative theme." These are recorded in the field journal. The samplings should reflect a cross-section of community members: with respect to age, gender, race: room-mates, students beyond the class, citizens of the community, university employees etc.

- Follow-up: the results are shared in collaborative groups or mentoring pairs;

- Follow-up: students underline the best "quote" from the five interviews, for possible use in their write-up of the investigation;

- Volunteers share their results with the class.

Contact with the Reality:

- Early in the process, students are encouraged to join an environmental group related to the problem they are "unveiling;"

- Follow-up: they are encouraged to attend meetings, to correspond with its members, to visit its website, to critique its web-site, to study and record the various kinds of writing this group engages in, to make contacts for possible guest-speaker engagements or interview subjects;

- Follow-Up: the student then makes a presentation to the class or peer group, constructing a narrative of their experience with it--of the kinds of actions, writing, communication channels the group engages in, its mission, activities, achievements, funding, defeats etc.

- Follow-Up: at this stage, students begin contacting advocates in the community or within the academic community, or both, reflecting the "various schools of thought" on the problem being unveiled. Possible campus resources might include The Environmental Protection Agency, the Brookings Institute, the Environmental Studies Department, The Biology/Zoology Departments; The School of Agriculture; the Geology Department; The School of Medicine. Government agencies might include the Department of the Interior, Bureau of Land Management, National Park Service, Forest Service. Arrangements are made to either interview these advocates, or invite them to class as guest speakers, to confront the students with the problem, in person. Advocates are encouraged to use slides, hand-outs, power point presentations, whatever "channels of communication" best suit their presentations—not only as a means of heightening awareness in the student audience, but by way of modeling the effective "unveiling" of a problem or perspective on that problem.

The Critical Readings:

- Students commence the "unveiling" process in earnest, locating primary and secondary texts related to the "generative theme" (problem). The search for relevant information should be comprehensive, including library and electronic sources. Primary classroom texts might include *An Inconvenient Truth, Silent Spring, Primate Visions etc.*

- These texts are supplemented with films/ videos from the library's media resource center, as another means of bringing the students face-to-face with the reality of the problem. Films: *The Cove* (annual slaughter of dolphins)*, An Inconvenient Truth, Erin Brockovich, A Civil Action* etc. Videos: Rachel Carson, Ed Abbey, PBS Documentary: *The National Parks:* "John Muir and the Fight for Hetch Hetchy" (Ken Burns) etc.

- Follow-up: in their journals, students devise a "research plan," listing the sources they will search, and the available means of locating those sources;

- The development of "information literacy" is also a dialogic process, involving research in the library and field in collaborative teams (observations, interviews, data collecting etc), as well as interactive presentation (updates) of research in peer groups;

- Follow-Up: students either bring a source to class (article, book), or Xeroxed copy of the title page, to share with peers in groups or mentoring pairs;

- Follow-Up: In journals, students record relevant facts and quotes from the sources (this in an on-going activity);

- Follow-Up: in journals, students choose a quote, and explicate it in writing for its significance, developing its relation to their central thesis, or if part of a counter-argument, refuting, questioning, or challenging it in writing;

- Follow-up: These cumulative "decodings" are an essential part of their written inquiry;

- Follow-Up: in groups or mentoring pairs, students share their quote and "decoding" with peers, who are invited to respond, either appreciatively or constructively. Any worthwhile feedback is then incorporated into the "decoding," as an addendum to it. Questions to further the inquiry, decoding, critique are solicited and recorded in the journal;

- Follow-up: volunteers share aloud one of these textual "decodings" with the class;

- Follow-Up: Once a mass of these textual "decodings" has been accumulated, students begin the work of cutting and pasting them, of arranging them into thematic categories, grouping them into polemic "movements" within the investigation. These broad thematic movements within the argument will become its structural backbone, the categories of inquiry that impart organization, coherence, and climactic arrangement to the whole;

- Follow-Up: Once this arrangement emerges from the mass of "decodings," students record/list in their reading-response/research/writing journals the several categories/subheads that characterize this arrangement, these broad meta-textual movements within the analysis/assessment.

- Follow-Up: in groups or in mentoring pairs, students share these thematic categories of arrangement, being receptive to any useful suggestions or feedback that is offered, regarding the order of the arrangement, or other possible categories of inquiry that have been over-looked;

Analysis into Writing:

- Having grouped their massed decodings into several thematic categories (criteria of analysis/ subheads of development) students choose one of these categories and in their journals write it up into a draft, consisting of one or more paragraphs;

- Follow-up: this draft is then re-read, its decodings cut and pasted for emphasis and climactic arrangement, the wording refined for clarity, upgraded for scholarly tone, transitions incorporated for clarity, emphasis, and fluency;

- Follow-Up: this revised draft is then printed and shared in groups or in mentoring pairs, as a means of both heightening peers' awareness regarding the problem, and of receiving useful feedback regarding problematic areas of the writing (wordiness, awkward/unclear wording, arrangement, lack of concrete development etc);

- Follow-Up: volunteers share aloud with class, their written-up decodings of the problem;

- Follow-Up: this process continues in journals, as each mass of grouped decodings is written up, then re-written for clarity, coherence, and emphasis, then typed and presented to the group, as a part of a "teaching" moment, as preparation for the formal presentation to peers, and for additional input.

- *Follow-Up/ The Mini-Paper:* At this stage, the student types up a 2-3p mini-paper of the "generative theme" that has been partially unveiled with these "decodings," consisting of a draft introduction and one of these "categories" of development, which us turned in to the teacher for a formal grade and response;

- *Follow-Up/ The Conference*: the teacher gives his or her feedback to the writing in a one-on-one conference, pointing out its strengths and offering constructive advice for improving it, in a line-by-line reading, offering facilitative feedback on the deeper-grammar of the polemical unveiling, leaving aside for now concern with the surface-level issues. This conference opens into a broader one-on-one conference regarding the status of the project: its direction, its central focus, the concrete development of it, the supplementary materials of the presentation; contact with real-world advocates, arrangements for guest speakers; and the plan for applying the knowledge beyond the classroom;

- Follow-Up; the student takes notes during this conference, so as to be able to effectively incorporate this feedback into the pre-final revision of the whole paper;

- For highly problematic mini-papers, students can be offered the opportunity to substantively revise and resubmit for a better grade or for a grade that averages the two scores;

- Follow-Up: Writing Instruction: Returning these mini-papers to students, present the instructor with a "teaching moment." Examples of problematic writing issues are anonymously culled from the mini-papers, typed into an editing worksheet, and distributed to class for group editing practice. These problematic samples are first introduced with a sample of a successful piece of student writing (anonymously Xeroxed). After modeling the first few examples with the class, students edit the next handful in class. These are then reviewed as a whole class, volunteers offering their "rewrites."

- Follow-up: at home, students edit the remainder of the worksheet examples. This contextual approach to editing papers has more immediate relevancy than a de-contextual approach, which reinforces editing in a grammar handbook. Their own writing becomes

the "handbook" for enhancing their editing skills, which situates editing in the real-world
of their writing;

- Follow-Up: Students resume writing-up the thematic "movements (criteria of analysis)
  of massed decodings, which they similarly type up in 1-2 page drafts, and present in
  groups or mentoring pairs: to further hone their oral presentational skills, as a teaching
  moment on the problem being "unveiled," and as a learning moment to receive any useful
  feedback from the peer group;

- Follow-Up: at this stage, guided instruction is provided on the proper conventions for
  integrating cited sources into their text, as well as the various rhetorical strategies for
  blending another's words into their own;

- Follow-Up: in their journals, students practice integrating a quote into their own words,
  with proper source attribution;

- Follow-up: in groups and mentoring pairs, students share their quoted samples, copies of
  which are given to the group for editing. This editing feedback is given to the student-
  writer, who makes notes, in order to incorporate it into the final draft;

- Follow-Up: At this stage, guided instruction is given on strategies associated with
  effective introductory, body, and concluding paragraphs, as well as title and work cited
  pages, by way of transforming the revised drafts into a pre-final edit. Instruction is
  therefore provided on strategies for crafting an effective opening to the paper (question,
  quote, definition of key term etc), for forcefully and succinctly stating a thesis; for
  previewing the arrangement of the "unveiling." Instruction is provided on the effective
  use of transitions for clarity and emphasis, and for heightening the effect of body
  paragraphs with figurative language, parallel constructions, upgraded diction, and

climactic arrangement. Finally, the student is introduced to strategies for crafting an

effective conclusion, that heighten the effect with figuration, an apt quote, an effective

clincher sentence, and/or a sense of climactic assessment—in which the implications of

the problem and its proposed solutions are fully explicated.

- Follow-Up: In journals, students are given a chance to practice each of these rhetorical
  strategies., which they share in groups or mentoring pairs;

- Follow-up: These rhetorical strategies are then incorporated into the pre-final edit, after
  which the paper is typed, and brought to class, to be shared in groups or mentoring pairs.
  At this point, the feedback focuses not only on any lingering issues at the level of the
  paper's deeper grammar (wordiness, awkward/unclear wording/ arrangement/ concrete
  development etc), but at the surface level of usage, diction, and mechanics (spelling,
  fragments/run-ons, subject-verb agreement, punctuation etc).

- Volunteers share aloud samples with the class;

The Eco-Colloquium: Analysis into Application

As a springboard into the application of the student's knowledge beyond the classroom,

the student makes a formal presentation of the project to his or her peers. This functions like a

"dress rehearsal" for the dissemination/application of the project in the real world of the

immediate community. Using the "didactic materials" that have been prepared, which

collectively comprise the "best channels of communication" (text, slides, photographs, graphs,

charts, video, film, power-point, overhead projector, recorded interviews etc), the student

"unveils" the problem to the class in its didactic immediacy, delivering a presentational version

of the analysis/assessment, and previewing the plan for applying it beyond the classroom. This is a teaching moment for the presenter, and a learning moment for his or her peers, which

commences the intervention phase of the project, which heightens awareness of peers regarding

the problem as a prelude to heightening public awareness, as a first intervention upon the

problem. The presentation is followed by a question and answer period, which holds the

presenter accountable for the analysis, assessment, and application phases of the project.

This colloquium is held over several class periods, as a capstone experience to the course.

Follow-Up: The presenter incorporates any useful feedback on the content of the project into the

final edit, as well as any useful notes he or she receives on the presentational style (speaking too

fast, too softly, reading vs presenting etc).

Analysis into Application:

During this project presentation, the student previews the plan for applying this

knowledge in the community, which may include a series of activities, as follows;

- A presentation to a dorm, fraternity, sorority, or campus club/organization;

- A presentation at a campus event: Earth Day etc;

- A presentation to the environmental organization the student joined;

- The offer to speak at any of the organization's meetings, events etc. or to publish the
  results of the investigation in any of the organization's literature, newsletters, journals .

- A follow-up meeting with the advocate invited to class who represented an opposite point
  of view regarding the problem: an advocate of the agricultural, chemical, fishing, timber,
  oil, mining, boating, hunting, or construction, or recreational industry, whose advocacy
  perpetuates the problem, who is presented with the final edit of the written project;

- An offer to debate this advocate at a public forum;

- An offer to speak to his or her employees, club members, fellow advocates;

- The formation of a local chapter of advocates on campus or in the community, advertised with fliers, in the school or local press, whose mission is to heighten awareness in the community, working in solidarity with other eco-organizations;

- Meetings with local advocates, leaders of environmental organizations, who act as consultants regarding possible activities, contacts, events;

- Contact of local schools to do classroom presentations;

- A letter to the editor of the campus paper;

- A letter to the editor of the local newspaper;

- A letter to congressman, senator, mayor, governor, state legislators;

- Local radio stations to be contacted, with the offer to speak of the problem on a talk show;

- Libraries and book stores to be contracted, with a similar offer to speak, in a program of civic engagement.

- State legislors conducting hearings into a particular eco-problem to be contacted, with an offer to speak to the respective committee.

This is merely a selective, not a comprehensive list of possible applications of the classroom analysis in the community at large. This community application of the project could be undertaken similar to a marketing campaign. Time could be set aside in class for students working in peer groups to strategize a community campaign of applied learning, to brain-storm about this critical phase of the problem-posing process, when analysis gives way to application. Once a plan has been devised by the group, it could be represented to the class for further development and enhancement. As part of this application process, peers could volunteer to work with the project-leader, thus extending the dialogic apparatus from the classroom into the community. Recruitment of volunteers could become an active component of the application plan, once a series of activities and interventions have been devised.

Most importantly of all, class time should be reserved for this portion of the process. In other words, the Eco-Colloquium should be convened not in the final week of the course, but at least two weeks prior to the end. In those two weeks, students could be released from class time, to enact their applications in the community, with a requirement to conduct a follow-up presentation to the class on the results—even if this assumes the form of a group discussion/follow-up. Before engaging the community, students would prioritize their applications, in the order to be enacted, with a requirement that they carry out one or more of the applications.

To further maximize the effect of this critical phase of the intervention, it could be *integrated into the course from the beginning*, as a work in progress, with students applying their knowledge as they accumulate it: beginning with the simpler, more do-able applications (writing letters, contacting eco-groups, editors, legislators, forming informal peer discussion groups in dorms, fraternities etc. Possibly, this on-going application of knowledge would then culminate in a formal presentation of the project beyond the classroom to a select, aforementioned audience. Thus, classroom inquiry is extended into the community, not merely as a climactic capstone experience, but throughout the process—in order to maximize the affect of the analysis, of the knowledge generated: to give it the broadest possible dissemination.

The Teacher Models the "Unveiling" of an Eco-Problem (Generate Theme):

As a co-investigator of a problematic reality, the teacher is searching throughout for effective means of enabling student inquiry. One of these is modeling the "decoding" of a primary text, which "unveils" the problem, whether it is *Silent Spring, An Inconvenient Truth, Primate Visions,* or some other text . In this presentation, the teacher models, as well, the student's formal presentation, preparing the "didactic materials" that constitute the "best channels of communication" (writing, slides, video, film, power-point, overhead, photos, hand-outs etc.). Thus, not only is a problem "unveiled' through a primary text, but the text itself is decoded for its meaning-making strategies, for the tactics of its polemics: for its use of logic, counter-arguments, quotes, facts, figuration, charts, graphs, font size, and color schemes; for its appeals to ethos, pathos, and logos; for its strengths and weaknesses; assumptions, omissions, and contradictions. Following, is an example of this teacherly component of the co-investigation, in which an eco-problem is unveiled by a text (*Silent Spring*), and the polemical strategies of the text are "unveiled" by the analysis brought to bear upon it.

The "Generative Theme" to be Unveiled: Chemical contamination of the environment.

Primary Text: *Silent Spring:* "The Obligation to Endure, p5-13, Rachel Carson

Introduction: *The Why & the Wherefore*

Let's begin with a simple question. Why read, study, and write about Rachel Carson's *Silent Spring*? A number of reasons spring to mind, any one of which is sufficient to justify critical inquiry into this text. Critics have justifiably identified *Silent Spring* as one of the most significant and influential texts of the 20th century, not only comparing it to Darwin's *The Origin of Species*, but citing it as the origin of the modern Environmental Movement, for "planting the seeds of a new activism that has grown into one of the great popular forces of all time" (xviii). In his *Introduction,*

Al Gore describes *Silent Spring* as a "brilliantly written argument that changed the course of history" (xv), noting that "in 1992, a panel of distinguished Americans selected *Silent Spring* as the most influential book of the last fifty years" (xxv) . As Gore notes, "the Environmental Protection Agency was established in 1970, in large part because of the concerns and the consciousness that Rachel Carson had raised" (xx). The book led to the direct banning of DDT in America.

Over time, its influence continues to grow. Reading *Silent Spring* would be justified if for no other reason than the direct influence it exerted on Gore's own landmark environmental work. *An Inconvenient Truth*, which similarly sounds an urgent warning about a global environmental crisis, "plants the seeds of a [re]newed activism" that has similarly grown into a popular force worldwide, while garnering similar recognition for its critical influence on environmental policy (Academy Award, Nobel Prize).

Yet, if none of these things were true, *Silent Spring* would yet be eminently worthy of critical inquiry in the first-year writing workshop (and particularly in a course on writing the thesis-driven, research oriented paper) as a compelling model of argumentative discourse. *Silent Spring* is one of those rarest of all texts that merits and rewards critical inquiry by virtue of its singular blend of literary merit, scientific discourse, and polemical strategies. Its contents deeply inform the focus of multiple disciplines: literature, biology, chemistry, sociology, medicine, political policy, environmental studies, and agricultural studies, to name but a few. To the extent it informs these diverse disciplines*, Silent Spring* is a compelling and useful model of argumentation in the first-year writing workshop, not only introducing students to the best practices of argumentative writing, but to the knowledges, issues, and writing-practice specific to a range of disciplines. If you would learn how to write an effective, thesis-driven, research-oriented, persuasive paper, I cannot think of a more compelling model to emulate.

Unveiling the Problem: A Dialogic (Writing-to-Learn) Sequence:

The focus of this critical inquiry into an "Obligation to Endure" will be to identify

Carson's thesis and document the diverse ways in which she develops that thesis, as an example

of best-practices to apply to your own writing—which in this case, will take the form of a brief

(3-5p) analysis/assessment of Carson's argument in "Obligation to Endure."

I. Free Write: In your reading response/writing journals, free-write for 5-10 minutes on one of

the following prompts:

1) Write about your experience with household chemicals, and/or pesticides/herbicides,

including your knowledge, feelings, opinions about them.

2) "The obligation to endure gives us the right to know" (Jean Rostand 13)

- Why would Carson end her chapter with this quote? Why does she use it for the

title of the chapter?

- What is the connection between "enduring" and "knowledge," between the ability

to endure and knowing?

- What conditions might have prompted her to cite this quote, to give it such

emphasis? What problem, if any, might she be calling the reader's attention to?

- What do you think she hopes to achieve by drawing our attention to this quote?

Follow-Up: Share your free-write with a nearby classmate, or in small groups.

Follow-up: Share it aloud with the class as a whole.

Follow-up: Ad on to your free write at home, addressing any of the prompts not addressed in

your initial response.

Follow-Up: Share your expanded response with partner, group, or class at the next session.

II. Thesis & Evidence

Question for Inquiry: What is Carson's thesis in this chapter? What claim does she make about the activities of humans? What does she contend is the "central problem of our age," in addition to the possibility of extinction raised by the nuclear arms race? (8).

Activity/ Individual: Underline the sentence on p. 8 in which her thesis is most succinctly and forcefully stated?

Thesis Review: To be effective, a thesis must have two qualities:

- Succinctness
- Forcefulness

Follow-up: circle the most forceful words in Carson's thesis.

Follow-up: Group: Share in group. As a group, reach a consensus on which sentence is her thesis? Choose a recorder to record the various sentences discussed, as well as the one chosen? Choose a reporter to share with the class as a whole.

Follow-up: Make a journal entry in which you copy this thesis, word for word?

III. Thesis Development/Evidence:

Activity/ Group:

In groups, make lists of the various categories of evidence Carson provides to develop her thesis. Each group is to assign a "recorder" to list the evidence, a "reporter" to report it to the class, and two facilitators to keep the group on task.

Question for Inquiry: What evidence does Carson provide to develop her thesis that chemical contamination of the environment (along with the threat of nuclear extinction) is the "central problem of our age."

Activity/ Groups: Compile a master list of the categories of evidence (development) discovered by the groups, and assign one category to each group.

Group 1: list at least three scientific facts Carson cites to make her argument:

Group 2: List at least three sources she quotes:

Group 3: Find examples where she appeals to logic, emotion, and ethics (logos, pathos, ethos:

Group 4: What are five things that are dangerous or disturbing about the nature of this pollution:

>   Find quotes to support each of these assertions.

Group 5: Explain how Carson's theory of biologic contamination of the environmental food chain works (biologic magnification, 6)

Group 6: What, according to Carson, is problematic about the use of DDT?

- How does it evidence Darwin's theory—of survival of the fittest through inherited adaptive capacity to the environment?

- List four problematic effects of DDT

- Which of the three appeals is she using here (logic, pathos, ethos)?

Follow-up/ Critical Reading:

- Underline sentences that provide evidence;

- Makes notes in margins, noting different kinds of evidence (facts, quotes, logic).

Questions for Reading/Discussion (record responses in reading journal; number and date the entry):

- What is the "most alarming" proof of her thesis?"

- List two ways these insect species are at odds with humans.

- How does she problematize the legacy of WWII? What are the agricultural uses she cites?

- Where are these chemicals applied? Implications?

- How does she contrast the "pace of nature" and these man-made changes? Which of the three appeals is she using here?

- Why does she believe these chemicals should not be called "insecticides," but "biocides?" Which is the more accurate term given their intended use in WWII? Why might the petro-chemical industry favor one over the other?

IV. Refuting the Counter-Arguments

The Pro Arguments/ Question for Inquiry: What is the central argument used to justify the use of chemical contaminants?

The Con Argument/ Question for Inquiry: How does Carson counter the economic argument? (list four counter-arguments she makes):

Questions for Discussion/ Inquiry:

1. What policy does she advocate regarding these chemical methods of control?

2. What arguments does she use to counter the rationale for using these chemicals?

3. What man-made farming practices created the need for pesticides (explain with sufficient detail)? How did these practices subvert nature's built in checks and balances that control insects?

4. What example does she use to reinforce her case.

5. What lesson might be drawn from this historical farming practice? How is the Dust Bowl environmental crisis related to this one?

6. How does nature control insects with "built in checks and balances,"

How has the importation (witting and unwitting) of invasive species contributed to the problem?

1. How are these species introduced?

2. What examples does she cite?

3. What sources does she cite: Eaton's *The Ecology of Invasions.*

4. What facts does she cite: 200,000 plants introduced

5. What metaphor does she use to compare them to:

6. What is ironic about this?

7. What economic logic does she use to destroy the logic of use?

8. What constitutional argument does she use? 12

Follow Up/Free Writes: Composing the Counter Arguments

1) Which is more important: economic production or public safety? Develop a rationale for each. How is this same debate at the heart of the global warming crisis? At the heart of the Oil vs Alaska National Wildlife Arctic Refuge (ANWAR) debate?

2) How might the crisis have been fueled by our stereotypic fear of insects? What works of art (literature, film) might reinforce our fear of insects? What recent events might have reinforced this fear? What historical examples can you cite where a native species was exterminated because of the fear it generated?

Writing Assignment: Take a side on this debate (pro/con use of chemicals), and write a paragraph in which you briefly describe the counter arguments to your own view, and then some or all of those arguments.

Follow Up: share in group, soliciting feedback

Follow Up: rewrite at home, incorporating useful feedback; type and turn in for instructor feedback.

Follow-Up: Include in final draft of paper.

V. The Action Plan

Activity/ Group: Carson concludes her chapter with a comprehensive critique of the practices that are contributing to the problem of chemical contamination of the environment (12-13).

Make a list of her criticisms (find at least 10).

- What practices of the government does she criticize?

- How is she critical of industry?

- What criticism makes an ethical appeal?

- How is she critical of scientists?

Follow-up: share with peer group; teacher compiles master list on board.

Follow-up/ Free Writes:

1) Should use of pesticides be contingent upon public consent and knowledge?

2) Should "advance investigation" of a chemical's effects be mandatory? Consider the tests RU 484 (abortion pill) was subjected to before release to public?

3) Should industrial practices be held to a higher standard, which include criteria other than economic effects, related to the public good, in which the profit motive is balanced against the public good? What governmental practices have contributed to the problem, where the public good is trumped by economic considerations?

Writing Assignment: Taking Carson's criticisms (12-13) as your springboard, devise an "action plan" that addresses each of them.

Follow-up: Share draft in peer group;

Follow-up: Revise at home, incorporating any useful feedback;

Follow-up: Type up and turn in for instructor feedback;

Follow-up: Incorporate in conclusion of final draft of paper;

VI. Analysis of Literary Merit/Style:

Activity/ Group: Each group is responsible for listing examples of a particular element of Carson's style. Each group assigns a "recorder" to record its findings, a "reporter" to report them to the class; and two facilitators. Teacher lists their findings on board.

Question for Inquiry/Discussion: What are the elements of Carson's writing style that help develop her thesis? Which of the three appeals do these stylistic elements reinforce?

> **Group 1:** How does Carson use *syntax (strong language)* to heighten the effect on the reader? Find examples (at least 7):

> **Group 2:** How does Carson use *irony* to develop her thesis? What is ironic about the crisis? (Find at least 5 examples of irony):

> **Group 3:** How does Carson use *metaphor* to make her meaning clear and heighten the effect upon the reader? (find at least 5 examples):

> **Group 4:** Miscellaneous elements of style: alliteration, parallel constructions (find an example of each). What sounds are being alliterated in these examples? What appeal does this literary device reinforce?

Activity/ Writing Assignment: Write a summary paragraph in which analyze the literary merits of Carson's argument, quoting specific examples of each element.

Follow-up: type and hand in

Follow-up: add to portfolio of writing assignments (counter arguments, action plan etc)

VII. Capstone Activity/ Macro Debate:

Resolved: Pesticides and herbicides should be banned because they pose a dangerous threat to public safety. Which is more important: the economy or public health? What should be done to curb or eliminate the use of these chemicals?

Preparation: Develop your view from your mini-papers on the "counter-arguments" and the "action plan" for resolving the problem.

Instructions: Divide class into two groups, those defending agricultural practices and those advocating ban on chemicals. Teacher acts as moderator. Ground rules:

- Don't interrupt another speaker;

- Make your point quickly, get in and get out; don't go on and on;

- Don't take another's disagreement with your view personally, and refrain from making personal attacks;

VIII. Writing Assignment/ Paper: Problem/Solution or Textual Analysis

Instructions: Write a paper (3-5p, 6-8p) in which you comprehensively analyze and assess Carson's argument that contamination of the environment is the "central problem of our age." In addition to analyzing the diverse elements of her argument, you should assess the effectiveness and implications of her argument, while positing an "actual plan" for resolving this problem.

Format/Requirements:

- 1" margins

- Double spaced

- 12 pt font

- Title page

- Pages numbered (not incl. title page)

- Quote liberally from text

Evaluation Criteria:

In your **introduction,** you should:

- Frame the central question of inquiry;

- Succinctly and forcefully state a thesis that answers (or responds to) this question;

- List the several criteria by which you will develop this thesis.

- Edit for correctness and clarity.

In the **body** of your paper, you should:

- Develop your thesis with as many of the following as relevant: quotes, facts, logic, analysis/refutation of the counter arguments; analysis of text's literary merits;

- Effectively organize the supporting evidence;

- Effectively use transitional words, phrases, sentences for emphasis and clarity;

- Effectively integrate quoted material into your own text;

- Edit for correctness and clarity.

In the **conclusion** of your paper, you should:

- Assess the implications/ influence of Carson's argument;

- Succinctly articulate your action plan for resolving the problem;

- Edit for correctness and clarity.

IX. Capstone Activity: (Re)Presenting the Reality

- Show video-bio: Rachel Carson's *Silent Spring* (Library media resource center)
- Show film: *Erin Brockovich, A Civil Action*
- Guest Advocates: Chemical/ Agricultural Industry, Environmental Studies Professor, Environmental Protection Agency

Conclusion:

What is the value of "unveiling" a problematic reality with analysis, and then applying that analysis to reality to hopefully transform it? To Freire, such real-world application of knowledge is what authenticates it, is what characterizes it as an authentic "logos." Thus, "denunciation [of reality] is impossible without commitment to transform [it]" (76). As one of my graduate students, Oscar Oswald, succinctly observes, "the individual's growth as a writer is not complete until it engages in public discourse . . . . a written work is not really anything important or valid until it makes claims upon reality" (3-4). As another of my graduate students, Cynthia Bailin, astutely observes,

> Freire was vitally concerned with providing people with language to articulate
> their own experience as a means of gaining autonomy. Freire's insistence on
> situating educational activity in the lived experience of participants opens up a
> series of possibilities for the way educators can approach practice . . . [and for]
> generating new ways of naming and acting in the world. (3)

A pedagogy of social change proceeds from the assumption that knowledge, in order to be authentic, must engage the world with the word, in the interest of what is collectively possible, good, and just. Education as "the practice of freedom" commences with the act of empowering students with the right to "name their own world," in which language becomes the medium of a liberatory agency: relative to the world, and to the world of signification.

Chapter 15

Eco-Composition:
A Term Long Inquiry

What specific aspects of contemporary reality warrant, indeed insist upon, investigation as part of a liberatory education in which knowledge generated within the classroom is not an end in itself, but a precondition for its application beyond the classroom, at the point of contact with reality: with the advocates who perpetuate it, with other investigators seeking to transform it, or with the public—whose collective opinion regarding the problem either perpetuates it or fuels the possibilities for altering it, by altering the material conditions that sustain it. To the problematics of race, gender, and class, which continue to insist upon critical inquiry and collective intervention, I would add the problematics of capitalism, the war on terror, the environment, the mass media, health care, and education, as aspects of reality that warrant inquiry and intervention, analysis and application of that analysis, if those realities are to be transformed in the interest of the common good and social justice. Inquiry could focus on these "generative themes" individually or in combination, as part of a problem-posing investigation of reality, in which students self-select the "generative theme" to be investigated, and in which the teacher models inquiry in one of these "generative themes" as part of a term-long, collective investigation (or models aspects of the inquiry into a handful of these "generative themes") with primary and secondary readings to focus and inaugurate the inquiry: to provide a signifying

context and a polemical springboard for the investigation.

More specifically, how might inquiry into each of these problematic aspects of reality be

framed in a central question for investigation, as a point of departure for the dialogic "unveiling"

of the problem? After modeling one or two of these central questions for inquiry, the teacher

could invite students to choose the problem they wish to investigate/unveil, and devise their own

inaugural question to shape the inquiry, to define the "generative theme," as follows:

- *The Economy:* Is "free-market" capitalism compatible with democracy? Is

  "consumerism the only form of citizenship being offered young people?" (Giroux

  xxii). Analyze and assess the recent economic "melt-down" (causes, effects,

  implications, and solutions, then devise a means of applying the analysis beyond

  the classroom. Assess the causes, effects, and implications for democracy of

  consumerism and the commodity fetishism that drives it, then devise an action

  plan for applying the analysis beyond the classroom.

- *The War on Terrorism*: Was the invasion of Iraq justified? Are practices and

  policies associated with war compatible with democracy (warrantless wire-

  tapping, imprisonment without trial, torture, biological warfare, embedded media,

  exposure of CIA operatives etc); What role did signification play in the

  manufacture of consent for the war? Analyze and assess the problem, then devise

  a means of applying the analysis beyond the classroom.

- *The Environment:* Is combating global warming in the nation's best interest?

  Does chemical contamination of our air, water, and food sources pose a problem

  as immediate as the threat of nuclear annihilation? Is banning pesticides/

Photo Credits

Index

Note: Page numbers followed by an italicized *f* refer to illustrations and figures.